About Pearson

Pearson is the world's learning company, with presence across 70 countries worldwide. Our unique insights and world-class expertise comes from a long history of working closely with renowned teachers, authors and thought leaders, as a result of which, we have emerged as the preferred choice for millions of teachers and learners across the world.

We believe learning opens up opportunities, creates fulfilling careers and hence better lives. We hence collaborate with the best of minds to deliver you class-leading products, spread across the Higher Education and Test Preparation spectrum.

Superior learning experience and improved outcomes are at the heart of everything we do. This product is the result of one such effort.

Your feedback plays a critical role in the evolution of our products and you can contact us – reachus@pearson.com. *We look forward to it.*

Microsoft

Microsoft Azure Storage: The Definitive Guide

Avinash Valiramani

ISBN 978-93-615-9233-1

First Impression

Published by Pearson India Education Services Pvt. Ltd, CIN: U72200TN2005PTC057128.

Head Office: 1st Floor, Berger Tower, Plot No. C-001A/2, Sector 16B, Noida - 201 301, Uttar Pradesh, India.
Registered Office: Featherlite, 'The Address' 5th Floor, Survey No 203/10B, 200 Ft MMRD Road, Zamin Pallavaram, Chennai – 600 044.

Digitally printed in India by Trinity Academy for Corporate Training Ltd, New Delhi in the year of 2024.

Pearson's Commitment to Diversity, Equity, and Inclusion

Pearson is dedicated to creating bias-free content that reflects the diversity of all learners. We embrace the many dimensions of diversity, including but not limited to race, ethnicity, gender, socioeconomic status, ability, age, sexual orientation, and religious or political beliefs.

Education is a powerful force for equity and change in our world. It has the potential to deliver opportunities that improve lives and enable economic mobility. As we work with authors to create content for every product and service, we acknowledge our responsibility to demonstrate inclusivity and incorporate diverse scholarship so that everyone can achieve their potential through learning. As the world's leading learning company, we have a duty to help drive change and live up to our purpose to help more people create a better life for themselves and to create a better world.

Our ambition is to purposefully contribute to a world where:

- Everyone has an equitable and lifelong opportunity to succeed through learning.
- Our educational products and services are inclusive and represent the rich diversity of learners.
- Our educational content accurately reflects the histories and experiences of the learners we serve.
- Our educational content prompts deeper discussions with learners and motivates them to expand their own learning (and worldview).

While we work hard to present unbiased content, we want to hear from you about any concerns or needs with this Pearson product so that we can investigate and address them.

- Please contact us with concerns about any potential bias at https://www.pearson.com/report-bias.html.

Contents at a Glance

Contents

Acknowledgments

At the outset, I want to express my deepest gratitude to Loretta Yates for bestowing upon me this tremendous responsibility. Only because of your unwavering trust and belief in my abilities, these books have come to fruition. I am forever grateful for the opportunity you have given me.

To my amazing mom, I am incredibly grateful for your unwavering support throughout the past two years as I wrote these books. Your love and understanding have meant the world to me. Thank you for being my rock.

To Celine, my sincere gratitude for being a constant source of guidance and assistance, whenever I needed you, throughout the journey of these last three books. Celine, thank you for your constant presence and encouragement. It has made this journey all the more meaningful.

To my beloved family, I am forever grateful for your understanding and patience during the countless hours I spent engrossed in writing these books.

To my extended family, thank you for tolerating my absence for over two years as I immersed myself in this writing endeavor. Hope to catch up with you all soon.

A heartfelt thank you goes to Kate Shoup for her exceptional editing and review work throughout all four books in the series. Your keen eye for detail and guidance throughout these books have been immeasurably valuable. Collaborating with you has been an enriching experience, and I am grateful for your exceptional skills as an editor.

I would also like to express my appreciation to Thomas Palathra, Sarah Kearns, and Tracey Croom for their meticulous contributions that brought this book to its completion. This endeavor has been a collective labor of love, and I am elated and grateful for our collaborative efforts.

Lastly, I extend my thanks to the entire Microsoft Press/Pearson team for their support and guidance throughout this project. Your expertise and guidance have been instrumental in shaping this book, and I am grateful for the opportunity to work alongside such a dedicated team.

Thank you all for being a part of this incredible journey. Your contributions and support have made these books a reality, and I am humbled and grateful for each and every one of you.

About the author

Avinash Valiramani is a highly experienced IT Infrastructure and Cloud Architect, specializing in Microsoft Technologies such as Microsoft Azure, Microsoft 365, Windows Server, Active Directory, Microsoft Exchange, SCCM, Intune, and Hyper-V. With over 17 years of expertise, he has worked with large and mid-size enterprises globally, designing their Cloud Architecture, devising migration strategies, and executing complex implementations. Avinash holds multiple certifications in Azure Infrastructure, Azure Artificial Intelligence, Azure Security, and Microsoft 365.

As part of the Microsoft Azure Best Practices series, Avinash is currently publishing four books, including this one, that draw from extensive real-world experiences. These books provide a comprehensive and concise resource for aspiring technologists and professionals alike. In addition to his Microsoft expertise, Avinash is also certified in Amazon AWS, Barracuda, Citrix, VMware, and other IT/Security industry domains, which further complements his skill set.

Avinash's contributions extend beyond writing books. He has authored an Azure Virtual Desktop course for O'Reilly Media and has plans for creating additional courses in the near future. You can stay updated with Avinash's insights and updates by following him on Twitter at @avaliramani. Furthermore, he will be sharing frequent blogs on his websites www.avinashvaliramani.com and www.cloudconsulting.services.

With his wealth of experience, industry certifications, and passion for advancing cloud technologies, Avinash Valiramani is a trusted advisor and sought-after resource in the realm of Microsoft Azure and Microsoft Office365. His expertise and dedication make him an invaluable asset for anyone seeking to leverage the full potential of the cloud.

Introduction to Microsoft Azure Storage

Welcome to *Microsoft Azure Storage: The Definitive Guide*. This book includes in-depth information about the various Azure services that provide storage capabilities and shares best practices based on real-life experiences with these services in different environments.

This book focuses primarily on Azure storage services generally available during 2022, encompassing development work done on these services over the years. A few storage features and functionalities were under preview at the time of this writing and could change before they are widely available; thus, we will cover the most notable ones in subsequent iterations of this book as they go live globally.

Overview

Over the years, Microsoft has introduced services related to the Azure storage stack to address various types of application and infrastructure requirements. Microsoft has released regular updates to these services, introducing additional features and functionality, enhancing each service's support matrix, and making these services easier to deploy and manage with each iteration.

Following is a brief timeline of the announcement of each of these services in public preview or general availability:

- **Azure Blob Storage** February 2010
- **Azure Queue Storage** February 2010
- **Azure Files** September 2015
- **Azure Managed Disks** February 2017
- **Azure Data Box** September 2017
- **Azure Data Share** July 2019

Each service provides customers with different options and features to address their storage requirements. This book dives into each of these services to highlight important considerations in deploying and managing them and to share associated best practices.

Each chapter focuses first on the features provided by a service. The chapter then explores in-depth the concepts behind that service and the components that comprise it so you will understand how that service can deliver value in your Azure deployment. Finally, each chapter focuses on deployment considerations and strategies where necessary, with step-by-step walkthroughs to illustrate deployment and management methods, followed by some best practices.

Cloud service categories

As in earlier books in this series, let's start by first discussing the different types of cloud service categories. Currently, cloud services are broken down into four main categories: infrastructure as a service (IaaS), platform as a service (PaaS), function as a service (FaaS), and software as a service (SaaS). SaaS is not relevant to the content covered in this Microsoft Azure book series; thus, we will focus on better understanding the first three categories:

- **Infrastructure as a service (IaaS)** Using virtual machines (VMs) with storage and networking is generally referred to as infrastructure as a service (IaaS). This is a traditional approach to using cloud services in line with on-premises workloads. Most on-premises environments use virtualization technologies such as Hyper-V to virtualize Windows and Linux workloads. Migrating to IaaS from such an environment is much easier than migrating to PaaS or FaaS. Over time, as an organization's understanding of various other types of cloud services grows, it can migrate to PaaS or FaaS.
- **Platform as a service (PaaS)** One of the biggest benefits of using a cloud service is the capability to offload the management of back-end infrastructure to a service provider. This model is called platform as a service (PaaS). Examples of back-end infrastructure include different layers of the application, such as the compute layer, storage layer, networking layer, security layer, and monitoring layer. Organizations can use PaaS to free up their IT staff to focus on higher-level tasks and core organizational needs instead of on routine infrastructure monitoring, upgrade, and maintenance activities. Azure Storage Service and Azure Data Share are examples of Azure PaaS offerings.

- **Function as a service (FaaS)** Function as a service (FaaS) offerings go one step beyond PaaS to enable organizations to focus only on their application code, leaving the entire back-end infrastructure deployment and management to the cloud service provider. This provides developers with a great way to deploy their code without worrying about the back-end infrastructure deployment, scaling, and management. It also enables the use of microservices architectures for applications. An example of an Azure FaaS offering is Azure Functions. There are no such examples for storage services.

In the Azure storage stack, some services fall under the PaaS category, including the following:

- **Azure Queue Storage** This PaaS service enables you to store large numbers of messages in a queue that can be ingested and processed by various application workloads.
- **Azure File Share** This PaaS service allows you to configure and manage SMB/NFS file shares in the Azure cloud platform and access them from Azure or on-premises environments.

Each cloud-service category has various features and limitations. Limitations might relate to the application, technological know-how, costs for redevelopment, among others. As a result, most organizations use some combination of different types of these cloud services to maximize their cloud investments.

Each service provides a different level of control and ease of management. For example:

- IaaS provides maximum control and flexibility in migration and use.
- FaaS provides maximum automation for workload deployment, management, and use.
- PaaS provides a mix of both at varying levels, depending on the PaaS service used.

Each service also offers varying levels of scalability or redundancy. For example:

- IaaS might require the use of additional services to achieve true geographical redundancy—for example, using Azure Site Recovery services, a PaaS service, to replicate Azure VMs and the underlying Azure managed disks across multiple Azure regions for redundancy and disaster recovery.
- PaaS and FaaS services are generally designed with built-in scalability and load-balancing features—for example, Azure Blob Storage with GRS redundancy level automatically replicates data to another Azure region.

Cost-wise, each service provides varying levels of efficiency. For example:

- FaaS offerings charge for compute based only on the usage hours for compute services, making them extremely cost-effective.
- IaaS offerings charge for compute services regardless of usage once the compute service (for example, a VM) is online.
- PaaS offerings are a mixed bag depending on how the services are configured. Some PaaS products charge for storage resources regardless of usage, while others, if configured correctly, charge based on usage alone. For example:
  - Azure standard file shares are charged based on the storage used to store the data in the primary region and secondary region, if configured for GRS.
  - Azure premium file shares are charged based on the storage allocated to store the data in the primary region and secondary region, if configured for GRS, regardless of the storage used.

Migration factors and strategies

Along with these features and limitations, there are certain migration factors to consider when deciding which category of cloud storage service might be the best solution in an organization's cloud journey. (See Figure I-1.) Of course, organizations can always start with one type of storage service and migrate to another type of storage service over time as their understanding of the cloud matures.

Let's examine the flow chart shown in Figure I-1 in more detail:

- **Lift-and-shift migration strategy** In a lift-and-shift migration, the organization migrates its existing on-premises environment as-is to the cloud, without redeveloping or redesigning the application stack. A lift-and-shift migration strategy generally involves less effort because no code changes are necessary. Application components remain as-is and are migrated in their current state to the cloud. This is a preferred migration approach for organizations in which:
  - A hardware refresh or procurement is planned.
  - Scaling or security limitations require the organization to migrate to the cloud as quickly as possible, with the least amount of disruption.
  - The organization wants to use IaaS mainly to host its application and database workloads.

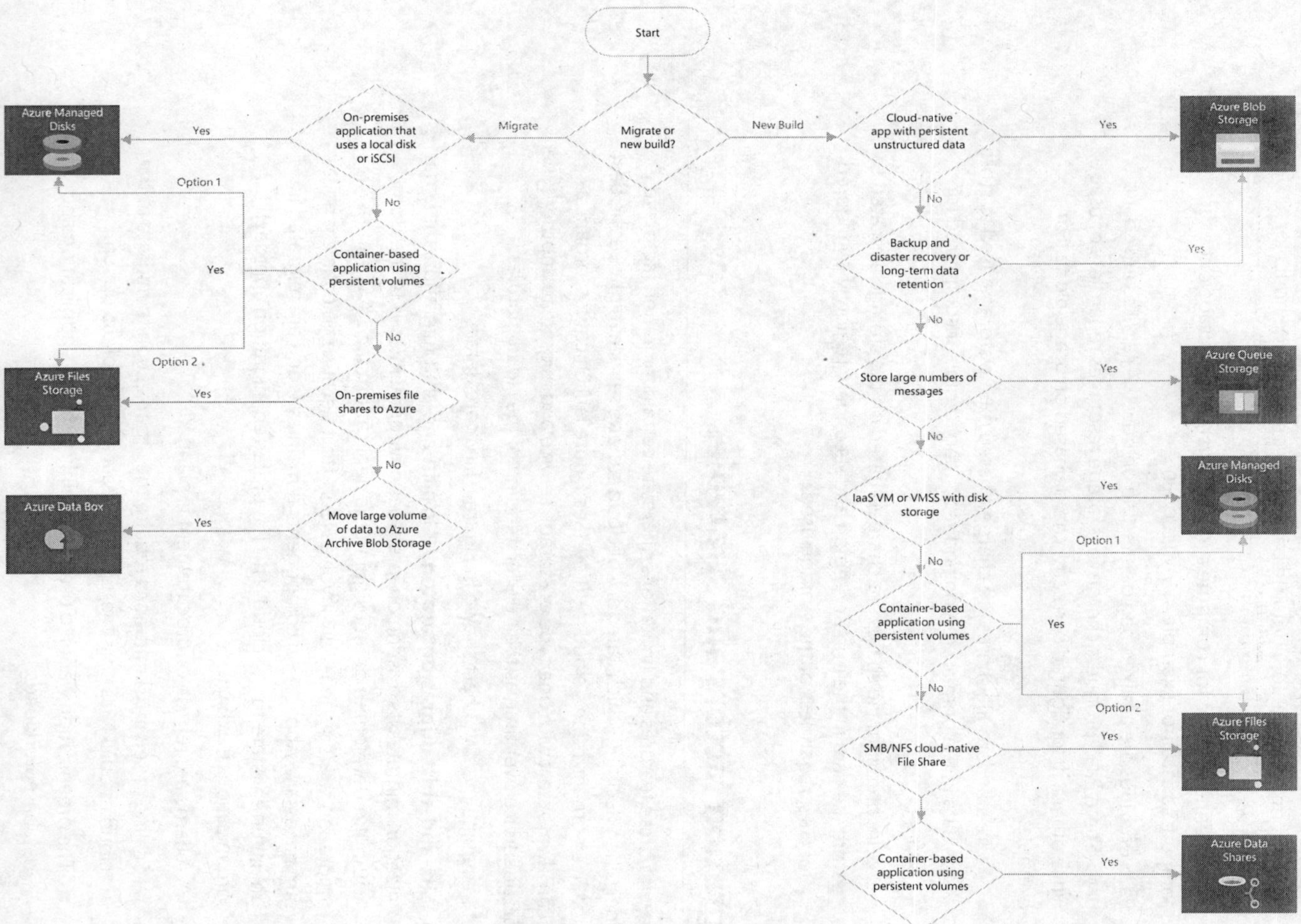

FIGURE I-1 Cloud-migration considerations.

- **Cloud-optimized strategy** With cloud-optimized migrations, the organization redesigns or recodes its application as necessary to use PaaS-based storage services. This enables the organization to use microservice architectures, allowing it to truly benefit from the scalability and cost benefits that a cloud service like Azure provides.

Organizations can use a lift-and-shift migration strategy, a cloud-optimized migration strategy, or a combination of the two. For example, an organization might use the flexibility provided by the Azure Managed Disks service to quickly migrate their existing on-premises VMs to Azure using a lift-and-shift approach to quickly benefit from the scaling and global availability of Azure. Then, over time, the organization could migrate to more cloud-optimized PaaS services, such as the Azure File Shares or Azure Blob Storage service, to meet those same needs.

Who is this book for?

Azure Storage: The Definitive Guide is for anyone interested in Azure infrastructure solutions—IT and cloud administrators, network professionals, security professionals, developers, and engineers. It is designed to be useful for the entire spectrum of Azure users. Whether you have basic experience using Azure or other on-premises or cloud virtualization technologies, or you are an expert, you will still derive value from this book. *Azure Storage: The Definitive Guide* provides introductory, intermediate, and advanced coverage of each widely used storage service.

The book especially targets those who are working in medium to large enterprise organizations; have at least basic experience in administering, deploying, and managing Azure infrastructure or other virtualization technologies such as Microsoft Hyper-V; and want to enhance their understanding of how to build resiliency and redundancy in their on-premises and cloud environments and to leverage the wide range of infrastructure services provided by Microsoft Azure.

How is this book organized?

This book is organized into six chapters:

- Chapter 1: Azure Blob Storage
- Chapter 2: Azure Files
- Chapter 3: Azure Managed Disks
- Chapter 4: Azure Queue Storage

- Chapter 5: Azure Data Box
- Chapter 6: Azure Data Share

Each chapter focuses on a specific Azure storage service, covering its inner workings in depth, with walkthroughs to guide you in building and testing the service and real-world best practices to help you maximize your Azure investments.

The approach adopted for the book is a unique mix of didactic, narrative, and experiential instruction:

- The didactic component covers the core introductions to the services.
- The narrative leverages what you already understand and acts as a bridge to introduce concepts.
- The experiential instruction takes into account real-world experiences and challenges in small and large environments and the factors to consider while designing and implementing workloads. Step-by-step walkthroughs on how to configure each Azure monitoring and management service and its related features and options enable you to take advantage of all the benefits each service has to offer.

System requirements

To get the most out of this book, your system must meet the following requirements:

- **An Azure subscription** Microsoft provides a 30-day USD200 trial subscription that can be used to explore most services covered in this book. Some services, such as dedicated hosts, cannot be created using the trial subscription, however. To test and validate these services, you will need a paid subscription. If you plan to deploy any of these restricted services, you will need to procure a paid subscription.
- **Windows 10/11** This should include the latest updates from Microsoft Update Service.
- **Azure PowerShell** For more information, see *https://docs.microsoft.com/en-us/powershell/azure/install-az-ps.*
- **Azure CLI** For more information, see *https://docs.microsoft.com/en-us/cli/azure/install-azure-cli.*
- **Display monitor** This must be capable of 1024 x 768 resolution.
- **Pointing device** You need a Microsoft mouse or compatible pointing device.

About the companion content

The companion content for this book can be downloaded from one of the following pages:

https://MicrosoftPressStore.com/StorageTDG/downloads

https://github.com/avinashvaliramani/AzureStorageTDG

The companion content includes the following:

- PowerShell code for each walkthrough in the book (where applicable)
- CLI code for each walkthrough in the book (where applicable)

Errata, updates, & book support

We've made every effort to ensure the accuracy of this book and its companion content. You can access updates to this book—in the form of a list of submitted errata and their related corrections—at:

MicrosoftPressStore.com/StorageTDG/errata

If you discover an error that is not already listed, please submit it to us at the same page.

For additional book support and information, please visit *MicrosoftPressStore.com/Support*.

Please note that product support for Microsoft software and hardware is not offered through the previous addresses. For help with Microsoft software or hardware, go to *http://support.microsoft.com*.

Stay in touch

Let's keep the conversation going! We're on Twitter: http://twitter.com/MicrosoftPress.

Chapter 1

Azure Blob Storage

Overview

Microsoft Azure provides an object storage solution called Blob Storage that enables organizations to store large volumes of unstructured data in the cloud. The unstructured data can consist of text data such as log files, XML files, or binary data, such as images, audio, and video files..

The storage allows you to access the unstructured data in many ways, such as the following:

- Applications can connect using REST APIs over HTTP/HTTPS.
- Users and clients can connect and access the blobs using Azure portal, Azure PowerShell, Azure CLI, or Azure Storage client libraries.

Azure Blob Storage supports various programming languages, including .NET, Python, Node.js, PHP, Java, and Ruby. This enables developers to integrate Azure Blob Storage to meet the needs of various applications to extend or replace the existing underlying storage.

Key concepts

This section explains each of the components that make up the Azure Blob Storage service and the various redundancy types supported for blob storage. It also provides a better understanding of how you can connect to and access a blob storage account using blob endpoints, and of how to manage blob storage encryption and data integrity.

Storage components

Azure Blob Storage has three main components:

- **Storage account** Every storage account in Azure has a unique namespace that helps construct the unique base address for every blob stored in that storage account. The unique base address is a combination of the storage account name and the Azure Blob Storage endpoint address.
- **Containers** Containers are like folders in a Windows directory structure, and similar to folders, containers store blobs that are the text and binary data files.

- **Blobs** Blobs are text or binary data, such as audio, video, log, image, csv, and other such file types. They contain the data that you want to store in that storage account. There are three blob types supported by Azure Blob Storage: Block blobs, Append blobs, and Page blobs. We will review these in more detail in the subsequent sections.

Blobs are stored in containers. Storage accounts can hold a number of containers, making it possible to host numerous blobs in a single storage account. (See Figure 1-1.) You also can create multiple storage accounts in a single Azure subscription spread across different Azure regions, depending on your needs.

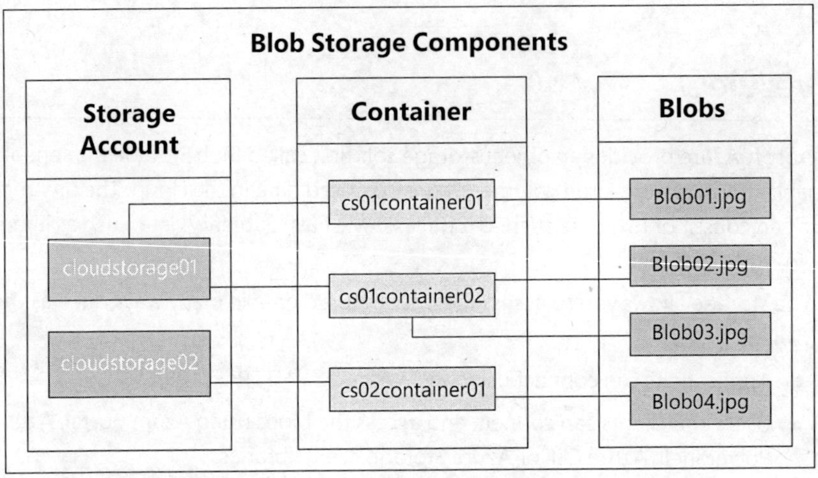

FIGURE 1-1 Account, container, and blob structure.

> ***NOTE*** **Storage containers are like disk volumes, containers are similar to folders, and blobs are the final file content.**

Storage accounts

A storage account is a unique namespace that contains containers and blobs. Every blob stored in a storage account has a unique address, which is a combination of the namespace and the Azure Blob Storage endpoint. For example, for a storage account named *azureblobstorageaccount*, the blob endpoint address would be https://azureblobstorageaccount.blob.core.windows.net. In turn, for a blob stored in this storage account in a container named *blobcontainer*, the URL address would be https:// azureblobstorageaccount.blob.core.windows.net/blobcontainer/blobname.extension.

> ***IMPORTANT*** **Storage account names must be between 3 and 24 characters and can contain numbers and lowercase characters only.**

Data in a storage account is accessible from anywhere in the world over HTTP or HTTPS. Data is stored in a redundant manner and is massively scalable to accommodate your organization's expanding needs. You can create multiple storage accounts in a single Azure subscription to meet your organization's various redundancy, latency, and usage needs.

There are three storage account types that support blobs:

- **Standard general purpose v2** These storage accounts support various storage types, such as blob, files, queue storage, and table storage. This is the most commonly used storage account type for Azure Blob Storage because it provides a good balance of price, speed, redundancy, and reliability to meet general storage requirements.
- **Premium block blobs** These storage accounts support both block and append blob types. They use solid-state disks (SSDs) to provide low latency and high input/output operations per second (IOPS). This makes them ideal for applications that require high IOPS, low latency, or the storage of large volumes of small files. For example:
  - Data analytics and data querying across large datasets
  - Real-time streaming analytics
  - Artificial intelligence (AI)/machine learning (ML) workloads
  - Internet of Things (IoT) data processing and analytics
  - High-volume e-commerce businesses
- **Premium page blobs** These storage accounts support page blobs only. Like premium block blobs storage, they use SSDs for low latency and high IOPS. They are ideal for storing virtual machine hard disks (VHDs) that require high transaction volume or need to support low-latency workloads.

Standard general purpose v2 storage accounts support the following types of storage:

- Local-redundant storage (LRS)
- Zone-redundant storage (ZRS)
- Geo-redundant storage (GRS)
- Read-access geo-redundant storage (RA-GRS)
- Geo-zone-redundant storage (GZRS)
- Read-access geo-zone-redundant storage (RA-GZRS)

In contrast, premium page blobs provide only locally redundant storage (LRS), and premium block blobs provide LRS and ZRS.

Storage costs for premium data storage are higher than for standard general v2 storage. However, transaction costs are lower. If you are storing a large volume of data, but interactions with that data would be limited or would not require fast response times, then a standard general purpose v2 storage account might be the right choice. However, if you need high IOPS and low latency, then the added costs of premium storage could be justified.

Containers

Containers help organize the block, page, or append blobs in a storage account. They provide a structure to the storage account similar to folders. So, you can organize related blobs together in a container or a set of containers.

Each storage account can hold an unlimited number of containers, and each container can hold an unlimited number of blobs, as long as the total size of these assets do not exceed the storage account's overall size limits.

Container names must meet the following requirements:

- Names must be between 3 and 63 characters long.
- Names must start with either a number or a lowercase character.
- Names can contain only numbers, lowercase characters, and dashes (-). No other special characters can be used.
- Names cannot contain two or more consecutive dashes (--).
- The name of every container within a storage account must be unique.

Blobs

Azure Blob Storage accounts support three types of blobs:

- **Block blobs** These contain text and binary data files (referred to as blocks) that can be individually managed. File types include TXT, HTML, XML, JPG, WAV, MP3, MP4, AVI, PNG, and other similar text, image, audio, and video file formats. Each block blob contains multiple blocks indicated by a block ID. A single block blob can contain 50,000 blocks. At the time of this writing, the maximum block blob size is 190.7 tebibytes (TiB), assuming the latest service APIs for put operations are used. Block blobs are optimized to support efficient uploading of large amounts of data with multiple parallel data streams.
- **Append blobs** These are block blobs optimized for append operations. They are ideal for log files. Append blob operations add blocks only to the end of a blob, ensuring no tampering can occur in the log file. Like block blobs, a single append blob can contain 50,000 blocks, but the current maximum append blob size is 195 gibibytes (GiB).
- **Page blobs** These are optimized for random read and write operations. This makes them ideal for use as VMD files or as storage for platform as a service (PaaS) offerings, such as Azure SQL DB. Each page blob is a collection of 512-byte pages that provide the ability to read/write arbitrary ranges of bytes. The current maximum page blob size is 8 TiB. You can create both premium and standard page blobs based on your storage account type. Page blobs provide REST APIs to access and interact with the blobs. The underlying storage is extremely durable, making page blobs ideal for storing index-based and sparse data structures like disks for Azure VMs and Azure SQL DB storage.

Storage tiers

Blob Storage also provides multiple storage tiers, such as Hot, Cool, and Archive tiers. This enables data to be stored and accessed at different costs based on your differing user or application needs. This helps organizations use Azure Blob Storage to address various scenarios such as the following:

- Audio and video streaming
- Storing logs that require to be appended on an ongoing basis
- Preserving data for backup or archival purposes
- Storing and serving static content websites directly to the storage
- Hosting Azure VM disks

Now that we have a brief understanding of the components, structure, and some of the use cases of Azure Blobs, let's dive in to learn in more detail.

Storage redundancy types

Storage redundancy helps ensure that in the event of an outage, your data can be brought online and accessed within the specific period stated in your service level agreement (SLA). Outages can be planned or unplanned. An unplanned outage might occur due to a natural disaster, power outage, fire, cooling, network issues in the Azure datacenter, or storage hardware failures.

As mentioned in the "Storage accounts" section earlier in this chapter, Azure Blob Storage provides various levels of storage redundancy, depending on which storage account type you select for your Azure Blob Storage. These levels of redundancy (from least redundancy to most redundancy) are LRS, ZRS, GRS, RA-GRS, GZRS, and RA-GZRS. We'll talk more about each of these levels in the sections that follow.

As the level of redundancy increases, the availability of your data increases, too—but so does the cost of storage. It is therefore important for you to consider your organization's and application's requirements, with respect to data availability and redundancy, along with the overall budget available for the storage, to select the storage account that's best for your needs.

You can split your data across different storage accounts, providing different levels of redundancy based on the requirements of individual applications or application components. Some storage options also maintain an active read-only copy of your data in a secondary region. Before selecting this storage option, be sure your application is capable of using such read-only storage in the event of an outage. Also ensure that in the event of an outage in the primary region, your application will be available or recoverable in the secondary region by using the storage in that secondary region.

Locally redundant storage (LRS)

LRS is the cheapest redundancy option in Azure Blob Storage. With LRS storage, Azure maintains three replicas of your data in a single datacenter within your primary Azure region. Data is synchronously committed to each replica to ensure there is no data loss in the event of an outage. (See Figure 1-2.)

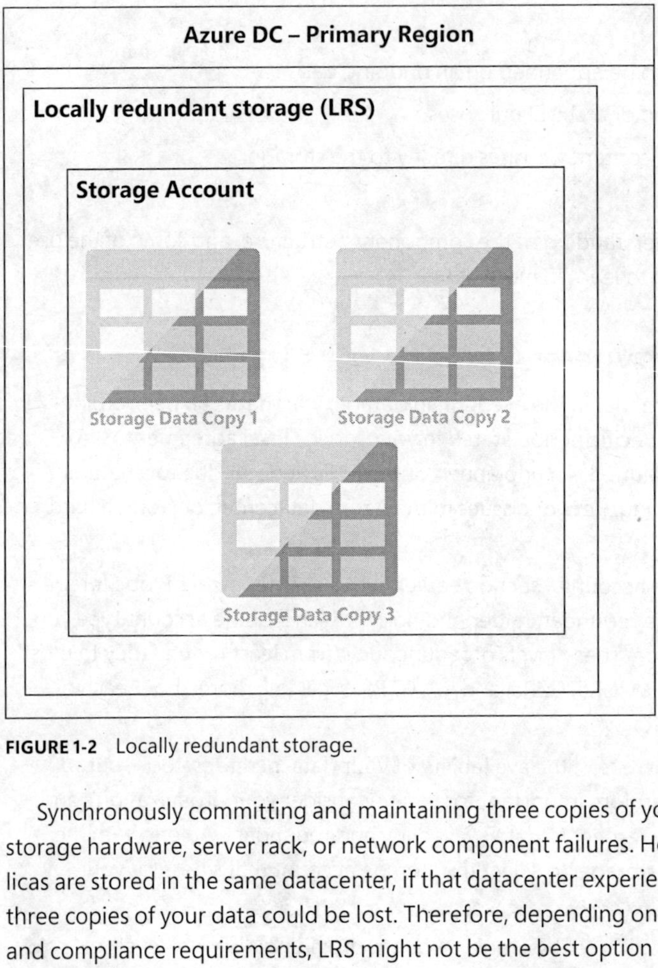

FIGURE 1-2 Locally redundant storage.

Synchronously committing and maintaining three copies of your data protects against local storage hardware, server rack, or network component failures. However, because all three replicas are stored in the same datacenter, if that datacenter experiences some type of disaster, all three copies of your data could be lost. Therefore, depending on your application, redundancy, and compliance requirements, LRS might not be the best option for you.

> ***NOTE*** **The LRS SLA ensures at least 99.999999999% (11 nines) availability over the course of a given year.**

Zone-redundant storage (ZRS)

Like LRS, ZRS synchronously commits and maintains three replicas of your data in your primary Azure region. However, instead of storing each replica in a single datacenter, they are spread across three availability zones. (See Figure 1-3.) An availability zone is an independent datacenter in your Azure primary region with its own power, cooling, and networking components. So, if a disaster occurs in one availability zone, your data will still be accessible (unless the disaster also affects the other availability zones in that region).

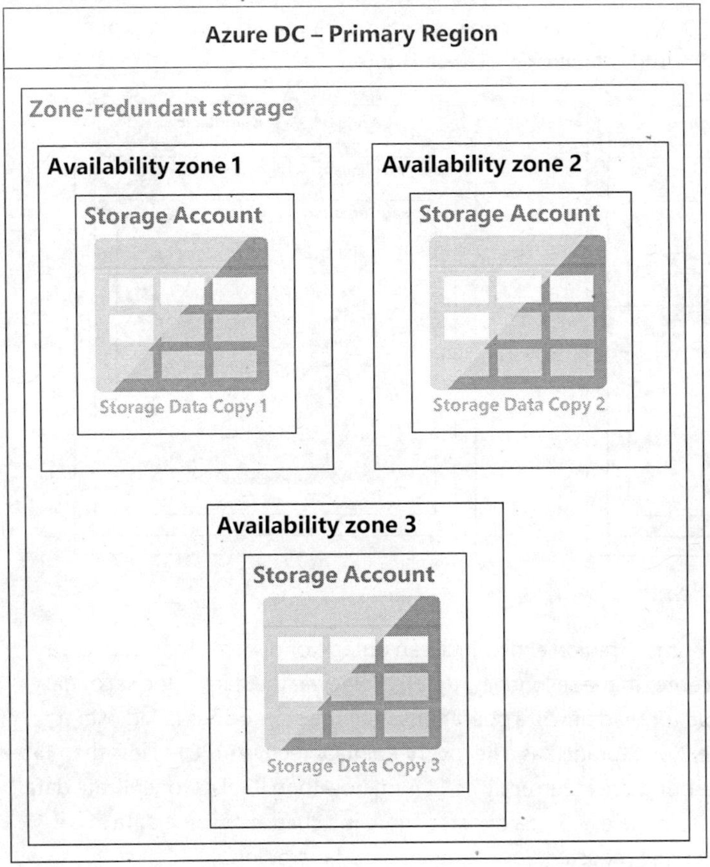

FIGURE 1-3 Zone-redundant storage.

If an outage occurs in one availability zone, ZRS relies on automated network changes on the Microsoft back end to divert DNS endpoints from one zone to another, which could involve a small gap in availability. This could affect your application's performance if it is not configured to retry connections in the event one attempt to connect fails. Still, if your organization has data governance requirements that limit the storage of data within specific geographical regions, then ZRS might not be the most appropriate option for your environment.

> ***NOTE*** **The ZRS SLA ensures at least 99.9999999999% (12 nines) availability over the course of a given year.**

Geo-redundant storage (GRS)

With GRS, Azure synchronously commits and maintains three replicas of your data in your primary Azure region in LRS. Then, three more replicas of your data in a secondary Azure region (selected automatically by Microsoft) are updated to match the three replicas in the primary Azure region, again using LRS. So, you have six copies of your data spread across two geographical regions that are hundreds of miles apart. (See Figure 1-4.)

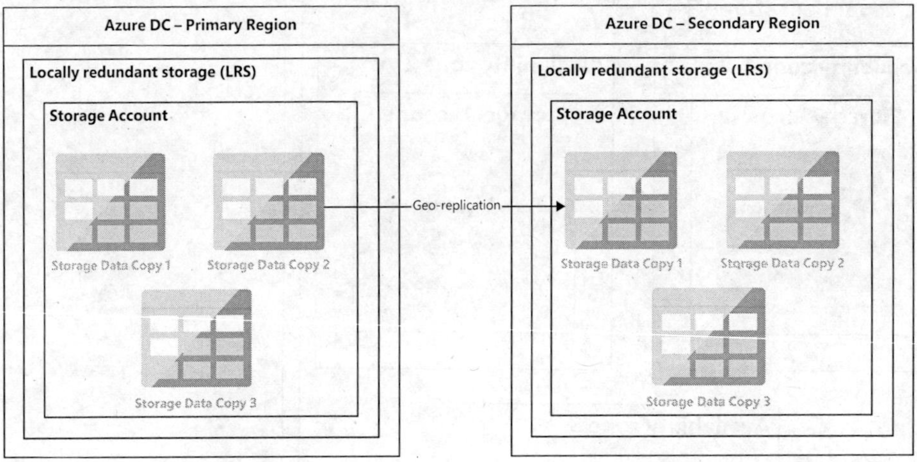

FIGURE 1-4 Geo-redundant storage.

If the datacenter in your primary region experiences an outage or disaster, then your data will be available in the datacenter in the secondary region. However, the data in the secondary region might not be available for read or write operations until the storage has failed over to the secondary region. Azure Blob Storage has a Recovery Point Objective (RPO) of less than 15 minutes for geo-replication, but there is currently no SLA on how long it takes to replicate data to the secondary region. Also, in the event of a disaster, there is a chance of some data loss if not all write operations have been replicated over to the secondary region.

> ***NOTE*** **The GRS SLA ensures at least 99.99999999999999% (16 nines) availability over the course of a given year. It also ensures 99.9% for availability (read and write operations) for the hot tier and 99% for the cool tier. (More on hot tiers and cool tiers later in this chapter.)**

Geo-zone-redundant storage (GZRS)

GZRS is just like GRS, but the three replicas of your data in the primary region use ZRS, while the replicas in the secondary region use LRS. So, there is additional redundancy in the primary region. (See Figure 1-5.) The SLA for GZRS is similar to GRS.

NOTE **The GZRS SLA is the same as the GRS SLA.**

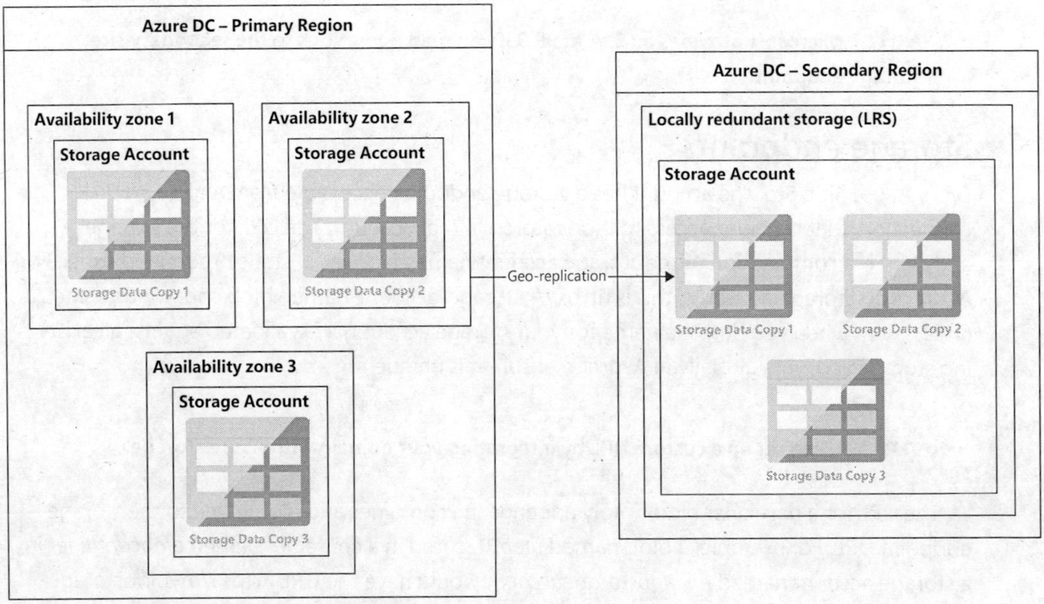

FIGURE 1-5 Geo-zone-redundant storage.

Read-only geo-redundant storage (RA-GRS) and read-only geo-zone-redundant storage (RA-GZRS)

RA-GRS and RA-GZRS function in the same manner as GRS and GZRS, respectively. The only difference is that RA-GRS and RA-GZRS provide the ability to perform read operations on the secondary region in case of an outage in the primary region. (See Figure 1-6.) This allows your application to function partially while the storage is failed over to the secondary site. Also, while Microsoft manages the failover of the geo-redundant storage in the event of a disaster in the primary Azure region, you can perform a manual failover to the secondary region if you are using a standard general purpose v2 storage account.

NOTE **Microsoft provides an SLA of 99.99% on read operations to the secondary site storage endpoint.**

Storage endpoints

Every Azure Blob Storage account has a storage endpoint, accessible from an HTTP/HTTPS connection, that provides access to blobs stored in that account. The URL for the storage endpoint is a combination of the storage account namespace and a static predefined suffix. For Azure Blob Storage accounts, this is https://<storage-account-name>.blob.core.windows.net. (This is why, when you define a name for your storage account, it is validated against all existing storage accounts globally in Azure to ensure it is unique.)

TIP **You can set up a custom URL by integrating your domain with Azure storage.**

The URL for a particular blob simply appends the container and blob name to the storage endpoint URL. For example, a blob named *blob01* stored in a container named *blobcontainer* in a storage account named *myblobstorageaccount* would have the URL https://myblobstorageaccount.blob.core.windows.net/blobcontainer/blob01.

Storage encryption for at-rest data

Azure Blob Storage accounts use AES 256-bit encryption to transparently encrypt and decrypt data. Encryption is applied on the underlying disks, similar to BitLocker encryption on Windows. As a result, the end client does not require access to the key to read or write from the storage account. This ensures that the underlying disks cannot be read when removed from the storage in the Azure storage cluster without access to the encryption key.

Azure Storage encryption is enabled by default on all Azure Blob Storage accounts and cannot be disabled. This applies regardless of the storage redundancy selected and the storage tier selected. This encryption extends even to the object metadata. This is offered at no additional charge.

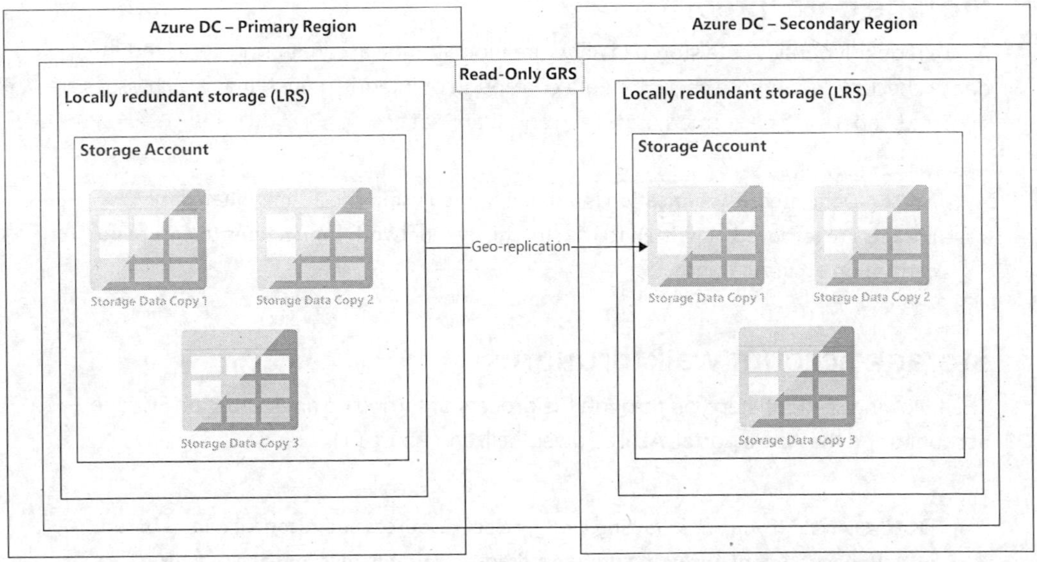

FIGURE 1-6 Read-only geo-redundant storage and read-only geo-zone-redundant storage.

The keys used for encryption can be Microsoft-managed, customer-managed, or customer-provided. Customers can select which type to use based on their organizational requirements for handling data within each storage account. Customer-managed keys must be stored in Azure Key Vault or Azure Key Vault Managed Hardware Security Model (HSM). With customer-provided keys, the client connecting to the blob for a read or write operation can provide the key along with the access request to allow the data to be encrypted and decrypted at that time.

Azure Blob Storage also offers infrastructure encryption, which offers encryption on the infrastructure level and on the storage service level. This uses 256-bit AES encryption. With infrastructure encryption, the encryption keys are different from the ones used for service-level encryption, even if Microsoft is managing them both. This ensures that a breach in one level does not compromise the other level. You cannot use customer-managed keys for infrastructure encryption.

> ***NOTE*** **You can apply different encryption key management strategies within a single Azure subscription.**

Depending on which option you choose, as a best practice, you might need to devise a key-hosting and rotation strategy to ensure keys are rotated on a regular basis but can still be accessed by the blob storage service for read/write operations. If you choose Microsoft-managed encryption keys, then Microsoft ensures those keys are available to the service for operational use and rotates the keys on a regular basis. (You cannot change the frequency at which this occurs.)

Storage data integrity

Azure regularly verifies data stored in an Azure Blob Storage account using cyclic redundancy checks (CRCs). These check for data corruption or integrity issues. If any such issues are detected, repairs are performed using the redundant data copies.

> ***NOTE*** **Data integrity verification is also performed using checksums when data packets are retrieved or written to the storage over network connections to ensure no corruption occurs in transit.**

Storage account walkthrough

The following sections step you through the process of setting up an Azure Blob Storage account using the Azure portal, Azure PowerShell, and Azure CLI.

> ***IMPORTANT*** **If you are following along, select resources and resource names based on your environment, including unique storage account names for each of your deployments.**

> ***IMPORTANT*** **If you are following along, be sure to delete any unwanted resources after you have completed testing to reduce charges levied by Microsoft.**

USING AZURE PORTAL

To set up an Azure Blob Storage account using the Azure portal, follow these steps:

1. Log in to the Azure portal, type **storage** in the search box, and select **storage accounts** from the list that appears. (See Figure 1-7.)
2. On the Storage Accounts page (see Figure 1-8), click the **Create Storage Account** button.

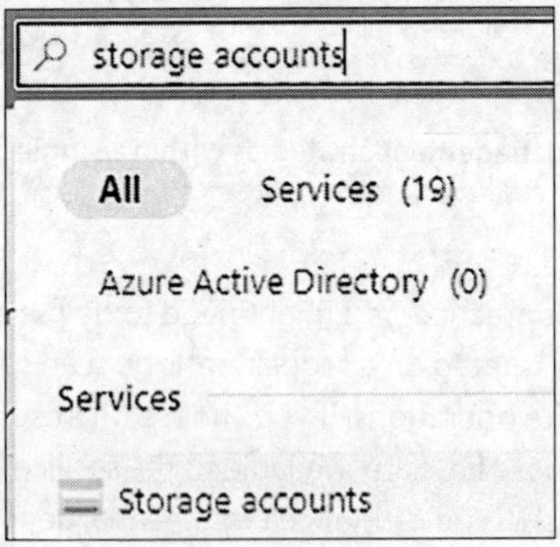

FIGURE 1-7 Search for storage accounts in the Azure portal.

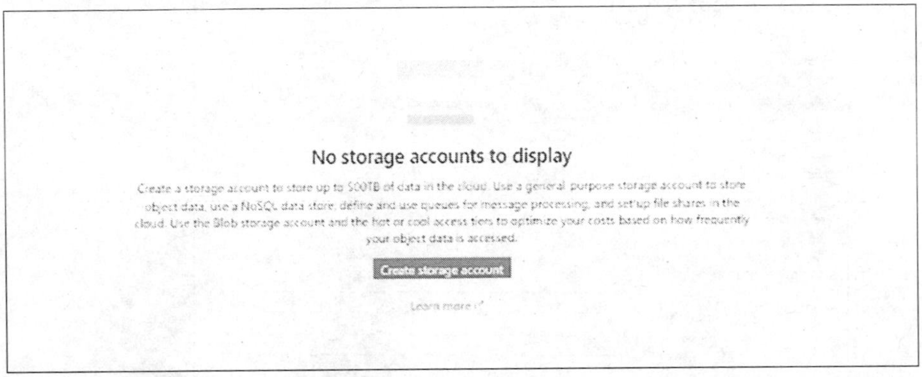

FIGURE 1-8 Create a storage account.

NOTE **If this is not the first storage account you've created using this subscription, you won't see the button shown in Figure 1-8. In that case, click the Create button near the top of the Storage Accounts page.**

3. In the **Basics** tab of the Create a Storage Account wizard (see Figure 1-9), enter the following information and click **Next**:
   - **Subscription** Select the subscription in which you want to create the Azure Blob Storage account.
   - **Resource Group** Select an existing resource group or create a new one in which to create the Azure Blob Storage account.
   - **Storage Name** Enter a unique name for the storage account.
   - **Region** Select the Azure region you want to host the storage account.
   - **Performance** Select the **Standard** or **Premium** option button, depending on your needs.
   - **Redundancy** Select the redundancy type you want to use for the storage.
   - **Make Read Access to Data Available in the Event of Regional Unavailability** Select this check box.

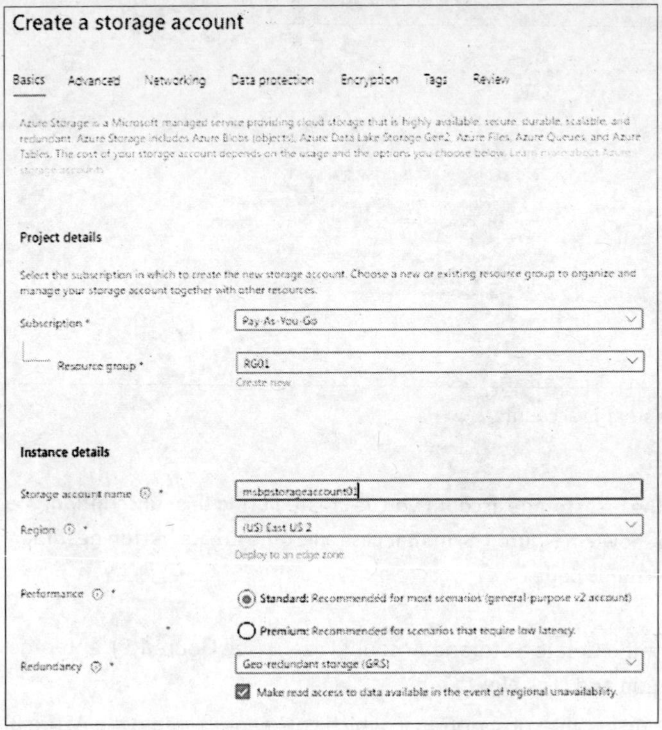

FIGURE 1-9 The Basics tab of the Create a Storage Account wizard.

4. In the **Advanced** tab (see Figure 1-10), select the Default to Azure Active Directory Authorization in the Azure Portal check box, leave the other options set to their default values, and click **Next**.
5. In the **Networking** tab of the Create a Storage Account wizard (see Figure 1-11), for the sake of example, leave the **Network Connectivity** and **Network Routing** options set to their default values (**Enable Public Access from All Networks** and **Microsoft Network Routing**, respectively) and click **Next**.

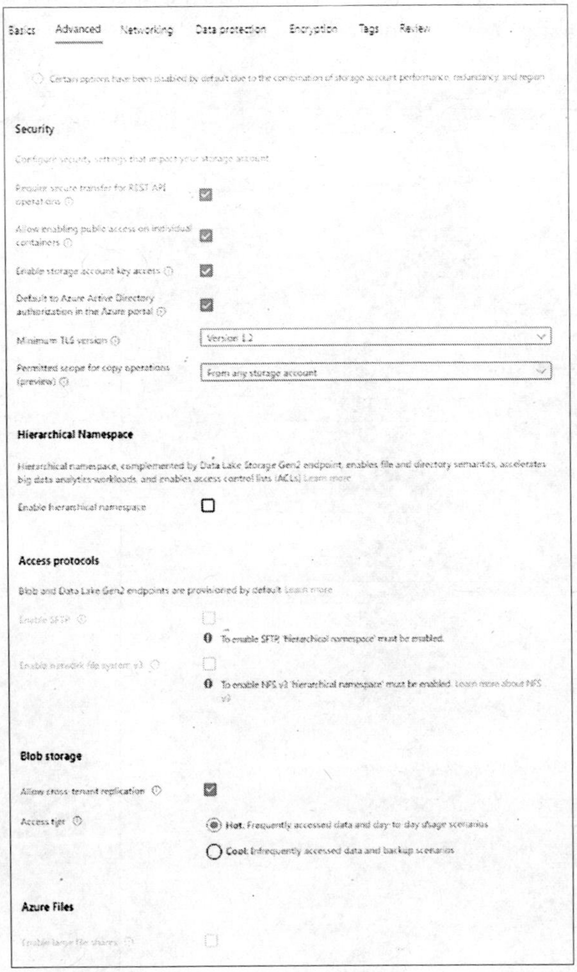

FIGURE 1-10 The Advanced tab of the Create a Storage Account wizard.

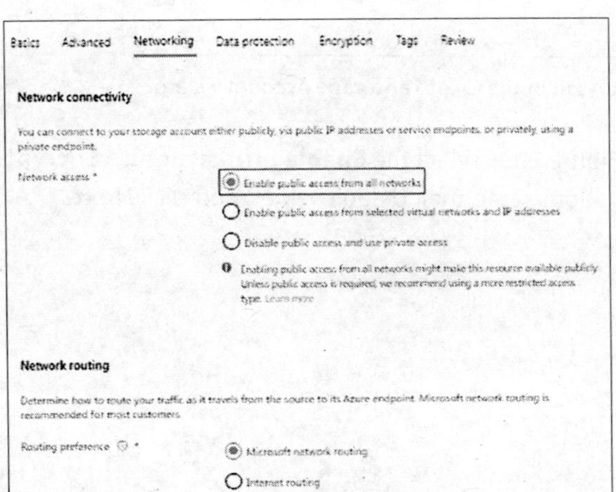

FIGURE 1-11 The Networking tab of the Create a Storage Account wizard.

6. In the **Data Protection** tab (see Figure 1-12), leave the options set to their default values (unless your organization data-protection requirements dictate otherwise) and click **Next**.

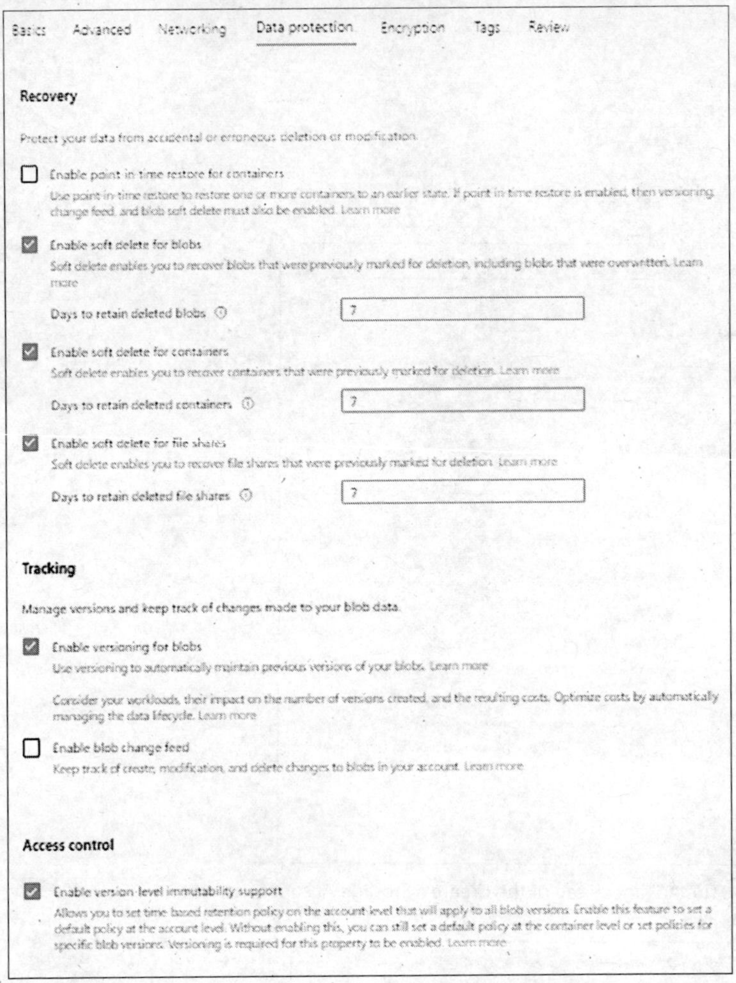

FIGURE 1-12 The Data Protection tab of the Create a Storage Account wizard.

7. In the **Encryption** tab (see Figure 1-13), select the **Enable Infrastructure Encryption** check box, leave the other options set to their default values, and click **Next**:

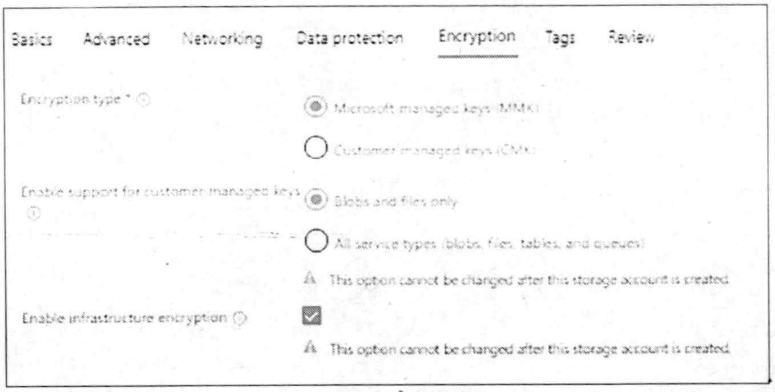

FIGURE 1-13 The Encryption tab of the Create a Storage Account wizard.

8. In the **Tags** tab (see Figure 1-14), enter any tags you want to associate with the Azure Blob Storage account and click **Next**.

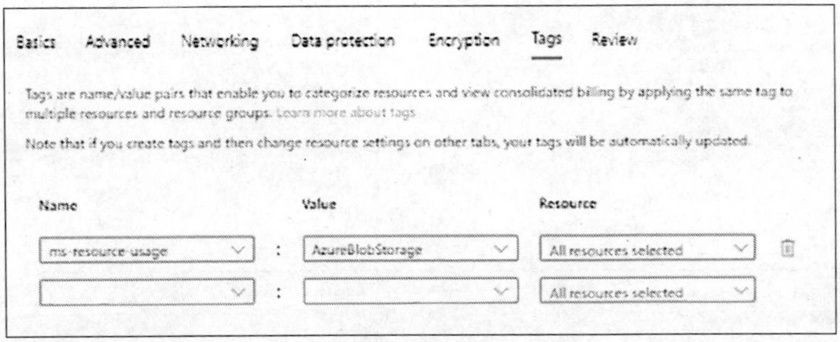

FIGURE 1-14 The Tags tab of the Create a Storage Account wizard.

9. In the **Review** tab (see Figure 1-15), review your settings. Then click **Create** to create the Azure Blob Storage account.
10. After the account is created, click **Go to Resource** to access the new account's page. (See Figure 1-16.)

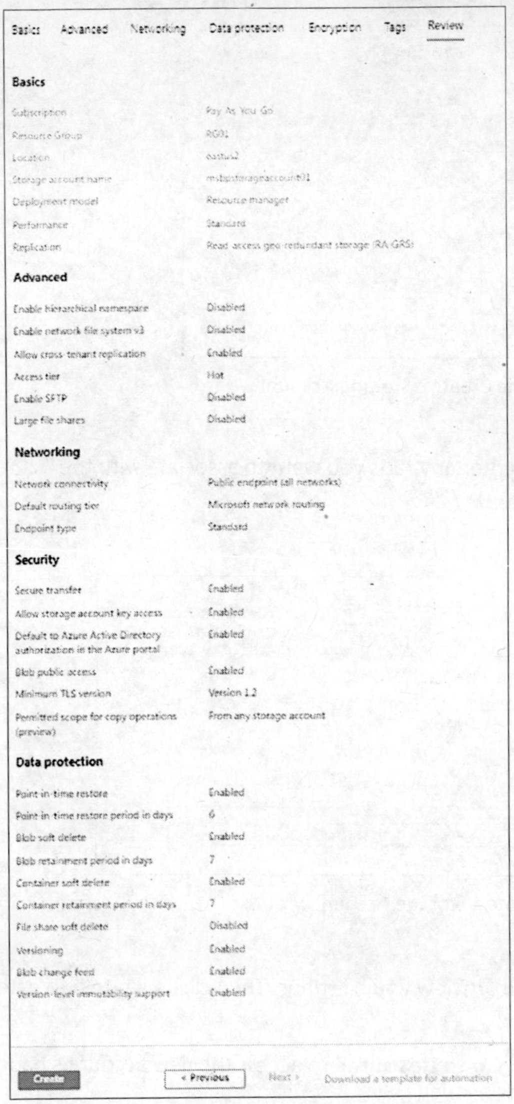

FIGURE 1-15 The Review tab of the Create a Storage Account wizard.

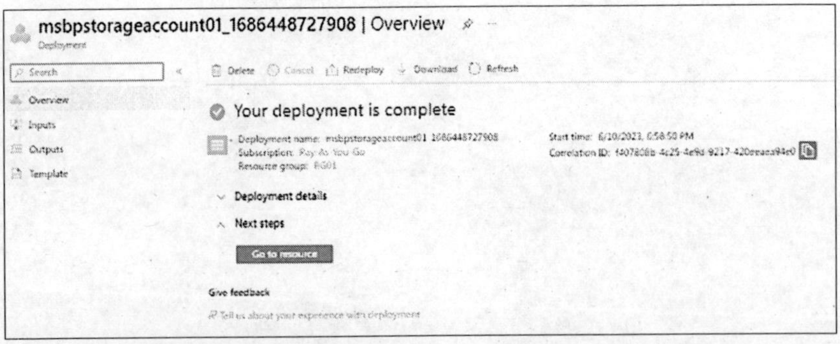

FIGURE 1-16 Storage deployment completion.

Your next step is to create a container inside the new storage account.

11. In the left pane of the Azure Blob Storage account page, click **Containers**. Then click the **Container** button in the pane that opens on the right. (See Figure 1-17.)

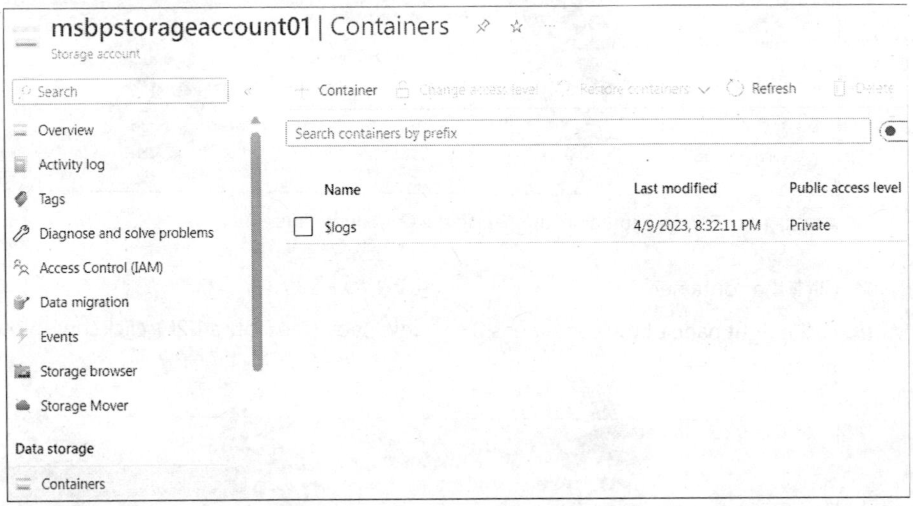

FIGURE 1-17 The Containers page for the new storage account.

12. On the New Container page, enter the following details and click **Create**. (See Figure 1-18.)
    - **Name** Enter a unique name for the container.
    - **Public Access Level** Select **Private**.
    - **Encryption Scope** Leave these options set to their default values.

FIGURE 1-18 Create a new container.

13. The new container appears in the account's Container page. (See Figure 1-19.) Now you're ready to upload a blob (files) to the new container.

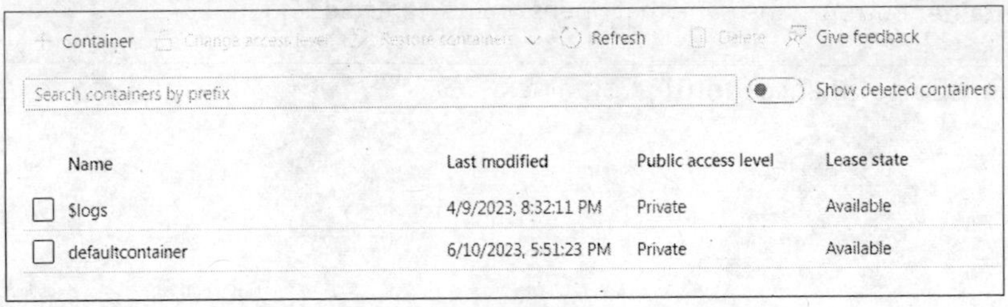

FIGURE 1-19 The new container appears in the Container page.

14. Click the container.
15. In the right pane of the container's **Overview** page (see Figure 1-20), click the Upload button.

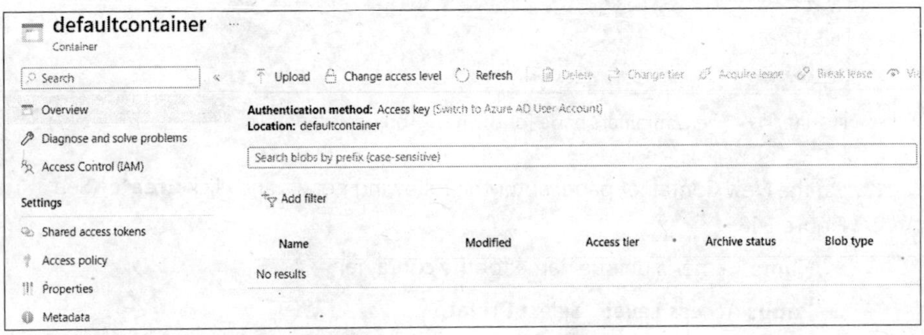

FIGURE 1-20 Start the blob upload.

16. In the **Upload Blob** dialog box (see Figure 1-21), enter the following information (leave the rest of the options set to their default values) and click **Upload**:
    - **Files** Select the files to upload. You can select a single or multiple files.
    - **Overwrite If Files Already Exist** Since this is the first upload, leave this unchecked.
    - **Authentication Type** Select **Account Key**.
17. When the upload is complete, the file(s) you selected will appear in the container's Overview page. (See Figure 1-22.)

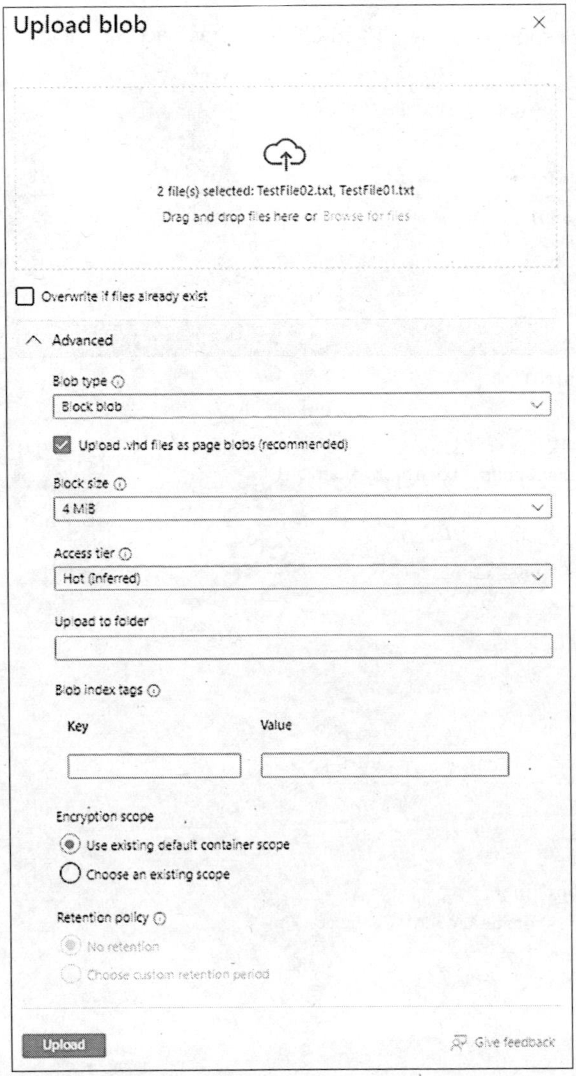

FIGURE 1-21 Upload Blob dialog box.

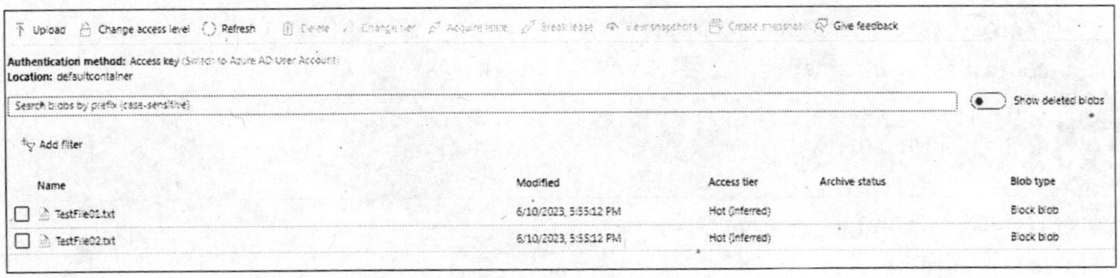

FIGURE 1-22 The files are uploaded to the container.

USING AZURE POWERSHELL

Use the following Azure PowerShell code to create an Azure Blob Storage account and container and add a blob to it:

```
#Define required variables
$resourceGroup = "RG01"
$region = "eastus"
$storageaccname = "mbspblobstorage01"
$container = "container"
$vnet = "vNET01"
$subnet = "default"
$endpointname = "PrivateEndpoint"
$vaultname = "RecoveryServicesVault01"

#Create Azure Blob storage account
New-AzResourceGroup -Name $resourceGroup -Location $region

$storageAccount = New-AzStorageAccount `
    -ResourceGroupName $resourceGroup `
    -Name $storageAccName `
    -Location $region `
    -Kind StorageV2 `
    -AllowBlobPublicAccess $true `
    -SkuName Standard_RAGRS `
    -MinimumTlsVersion TLS1_2

#Create container
New-AzStorageContainer `
                      -Name $Container `
                      -Context $storageAccount.Context `
                      -Permission Blob

#Upload data to  Blob storage
cd "~/CloudDrive/"
Get-Date | Out-File -FilePath "TextFile01.txt" -Force

Set-AzStorageBlobContent `
   -Context $storageAccount.Context `
   -container $container `
   -File "TextFile01.txt" `
   -Blob "TextFile01.txt"

#Verify data in  Blob Storage
Get-AzStorageBlob `
   -Context $storageAccount.Context `
```

```
    -container $container `  |
  Select-Object -Property Name

# Download file from  Blob Storage
Get-AzStorageBlobContent  `
     -Context $storageAccount.Context `
     -container $container `
     -Blob "TextFile01.txt" `
     -Destination ".\TextFile01.txt" `
     -Force
```

USING AZURE CLI

Use the following code to create an Azure Blob Storage account and container and add a blob to it in the Azure CLI:

```
#Define required variables
resourceGroup="RG01"
region="eastus"
storageaccname="mbspblobstorage01"
container="container"
directory="directory"
vnet="vNET01"
subnet="default"
endpointname="PrivateEndpoint"
vaultname="RecoveryServicesVault01"

#Create Azure Blob Storage account
az group create \
     --name $resourceGroup \
     --location $region

az storage account create \
     --name $storageaccname \
     --resource-group $resourceGroup \
     --location $region \
     --kind StorageV2 \
     --sku Standard_ZRS \
     --encryption-services blob \
     --output none \
     --min-tls-version TLS1_2 \
     --allow-blob-public-access true

#Create container
az storage container create \
     --account-name $storageaccname \
```

```
    --name $container

#Upload data to Blob container
cd ~/clouddrive/
date > TextFile01.txt

az storage blob upload \
    --account-name $storageaccname \
    --container-name $container \
    --name TextFile01.txt \
    --file TextFile01.txt

#Verify data in container
az storage blob list \
    --account-name $storageaccname \
    --container-name $container \
    --output table

# Download file from container
az storage blob download \
    --account-name $storageaccname \
    --container-name $container \
    --name TextFile01.txt \
    --file "./TextFile01.txt"
```

Data access authorization

To access data in Azure Blob Storage, the client application you use for the access request must be authorized. Azure supports three main authorization methods:

- Azure Active Directory (Azure AD)
- Shared Key authorization
- Shared access signature (SAS) key

> ***NOTE*** **The next three sections discuss these methods in detail.**

In addition to these methods, Azure supports the following less-secure methods:

- **Anonymous public read access** This method allows anyone to connect to the blob storage to read data without authorization. This is not recommended for use and can be disabled on the storage account level. Disabling this prevents containers within the storage account from being used to share blobs with anonymous access.
- **Storage local users** This approach can be used to authorize access to blob storage only when accessing the storage via Secure File Transfer Protocol (SFTP). Permissions are

defined on the storage container level for the storage local user. You can then provide the credentials to the connecting party, who can use the password or the public SSH key in a public-private key pair to access the storage over SFTP.

Azure Active Directory (Azure AD)

Integrating Azure Blob Storage with Azure AD is the recommended data-authorization approach (as long as your application supports it). It uses built-in Azure role-based access control (RBAC) to perform identity-based authorization and grant access permissions to users, groups, or an application service principal. (These are called *security principals*.) Azure AD also enables you to leverage Azure attribute-based access control (ABAC) to add conditions to Azure role assignments for more granular access to resources in Azure Blob Storage.

When you use this method to authenticate access to an Azure Blob Storage account, the security principal first authenticates against Azure AD. When this occurs, Azure AD generates an OAuth 2.0 token, which the security principal can then use to gain authorization to the Azure Blob Storage service.

> ***NOTE*** **This authorization method is the most secure of all the available options.**

Azure ABAC

If you require fine-grained access to the Azure Blob Storage resources, you can use Azure ABAC to configure conditions for role assignments. With Azure ABAC, you can limit access on a more granular basis and to specific resources within the Azure Blob Storage account. Azure ABAC defines access levels based on attributes associated with security principals, resources, and requests. Conditions can be based on the following attributes:

- Account name
- Blob index tags
- Blob path
- Blob prefix
- Container name
- Encryption scope name
- Is current version
- Is hierarchical namespace enabled
- Snapshot
- Version ID

Resource scope

When planning the RBAC strategy for your environment, it is a good practice to first define the scope of the access that you would like each security principal to have. This helps ensure that access is limited to a specific set of resources in an Azure subscription. The levels at which you can scope access include the following:

- **Azure management group** A management group is a combination of multiple subscriptions. This scope allows access to all storage accounts in all resource groups within all subscriptions in that management group. This is the widest scope for which you can provide access. Microsoft recommends against allowing this scope for client applications that require access only to specific Azure Blob Storage resources.
- **Azure subscription** Access is granted to all resource groups and to all Azure Blob Storage accounts and containers within those resource groups.
- **Azure resource group** Access is granted to all Azure Blob Storage accounts and all storage containers within that resource group.
- **Azure storage account** Access is granted to all Azure Blob Storage containers within that storage account.
- **A single Blob Storage container** Access is granted to a specific container and all objects and metadata in that container. This is the narrowest scope of access and is generally the recommended approach.

Built-in roles for RBAC

Azure provides multiple built-in RBAC roles to authorize access to blob data using Azure AD and OAuth. These include the following:

- **Storage Blob Data Contributor** Grants read/write/delete permissions to the Azure Blob Storage resources.
- **Storage Blob Data Reader** Grants read-only access permissions to the Azure Blob Storage resources.
- **Storage Blob Delegator** Grants access to obtain a user delegation key to then create a SAS URL signed with Azure AD credentials for a container or blob (more on signed URLs in a moment).

NOTE **In addition to using these built-in roles, you can create custom roles with specific permissions based on your needs.**

Shared Key

This authorization approach uses the storage account key to authorize access to the Azure Blob Storage account. The client application signs every request using the storage account key, which provides root access to the entire storage account and all containers and blobs stored within it.

Azure Blob Storage supports the following Shared Key authorization schemes for version 2009-09-19 and later:

- **Shared Key for blob, queue, and file services** This authorization scheme is used to make requests against the blob, queue, and file services. Shared Key authorization in version 2009-09-19 and later supports an augmented signature string for enhanced security. (You must update your service to authorize the use of this augmented signature.)
- **Shared Key Lite** This authorization scheme is used to make requests against the blob, queue, table, and file services. For version 2009-09-19 and later of the blob and queue services, Shared Key Lite authorization supports using a signature string identical to what was supported against Shared Key in previous versions of the blob and queue services. You can therefore use Shared Key Lite to make requests against the blob and queue services without updating your signature string.

Shared Key authorization requires you to store your storage account keys in your application. Any breach or misconfiguration in the application code that results in the key being exposed can result in data exfiltration. It is, therefore, advised to use this method only in testing or staging environments, and to leverage Azure AD or SAS keys (discussed next) for production deployments.

Shared Keys walkthrough

The following section walks you through the process of creating Shared Keys using the Azure portal.

USING AZURE PORTAL

To set up Shared Keys using the Azure portal, follow these steps:

1. In the left pane of the Azure Blob Storage account page, click **Access Keys**.

   The Access Keys page opens, with two keys displayed. (See Figure 1-23.) You can use the keys in the application configuration as needed.
2. To see a key's value, click the **Show** button next to the **Key** box.
3. To see a key's connection string, click the **Show** button next to the **Connection String** box.
4. To set a reminder to rotate the keys on a regular basis, click **Set Rotation Reminder** near the top of the Access Keys page.
5. In the Set a Reminder to Rotate Access Keys dialog box (see Figure 1-24), enter the following information and click **Save**:
   - **Enable Key Rotation Reminders** Select this check box.
   - **Send Reminders** Choose an option from this drop-down list. (I chose **Custom**.)
   - **Remind Me Every** Enter a value and a unit (in this case, **60** and **Days**) to indicate how frequently you want to be reminded to rotate access keys.

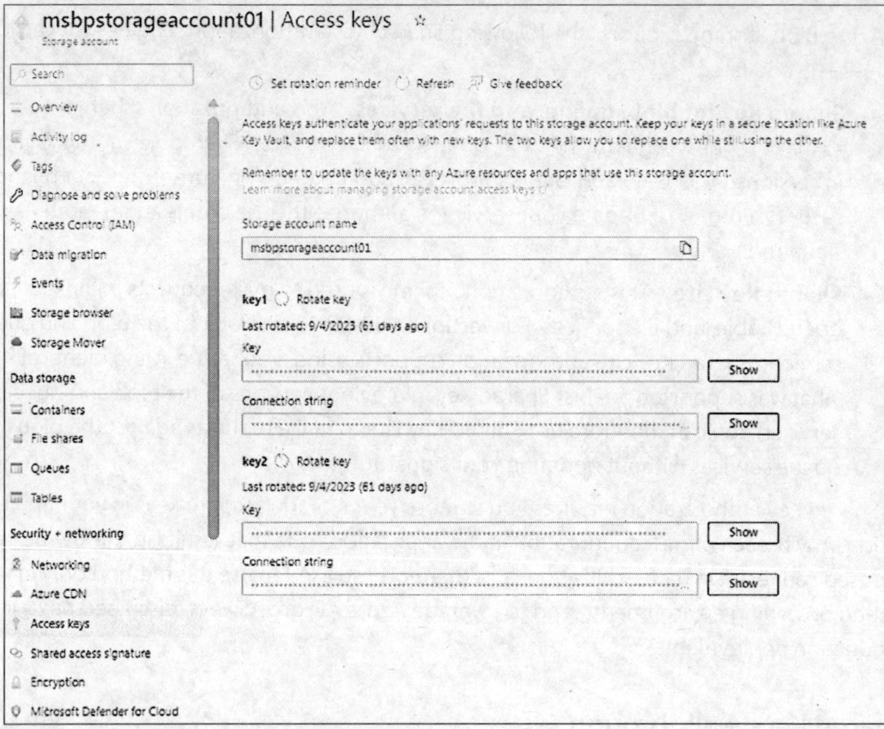

FIGURE 1-23 The Access Keys page for the storage account.

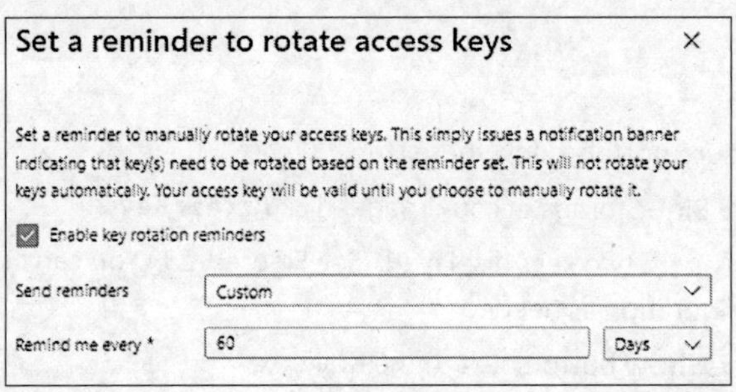

FIGURE 1-24 The Set a Reminder to Rotate Access Keys dialog box.

When you set up a reminder to rotate the access key, Azure does not automatically generate a new access key at that time. The key rotation has to be performed manually.

6. Click Yes to confirm that you want to generate a new access key. (See Figure 1-25.)

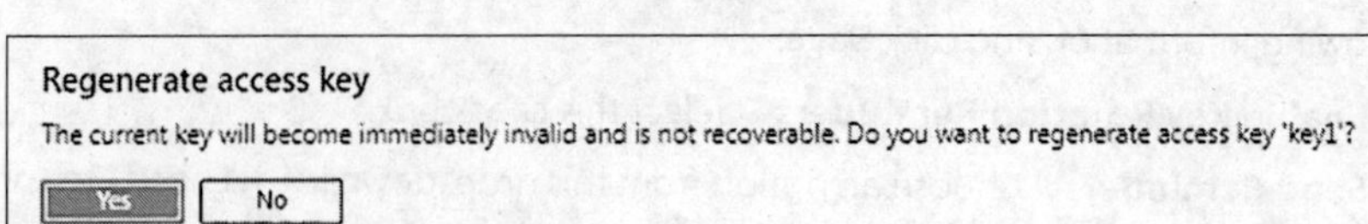

FIGURE 1-25 Generating a new access key.

Shared access signature (SAS)

If you are unable to employ Azure AD for blob authorization, you can provide access using a shared access signature (SAS) for authorization. This involves generating a SAS uniform resource locator (URL) to define access to storage resources based on permission levels, object types (blob, file, queue, or table), allowed IP ranges, and allowed protocols (HTTP or HTTPS), for a period that you specify. Client applications can then use the SAS URL to gain access to the defined storage resources in a time-bound manner without sharing the storage account key or exposing the storage resource to unauthorized security principals.

There are three types of shared access signatures:

- **Account-level SAS** When you create an account-level SAS, it delegates access to resources in one or more storage services. This allows you to provide access to resources in a blob, queue, file, and table at the same time using a single account-level SAS URL. An account-level SAS also allows you to grant access to service-level operations that are currently not supported using a service-level SAS (discussed next). These include write and delete operations for Azure Blob Storage containers.
- **Service-level SAS** With a service-level SAS, access is delegated to a single service and the resources within that service. You can define the level of access to provide, and client application operations will be limited accordingly. With this approach, a SAS token is generated that contains a query string with the permission, protocol, IP ranges, and validity parameters, and is signed using the storage account keys. The URL for a service-level SAS consists of the URL to the resource to which the SAS grants access, followed by the SAS token. A service-level SAS can also reference a stored access policy, which provides an added layer of control over a set of signatures. This includes the ability to modify or revoke access to the resource if necessary.
- **User-delegation SAS** This is a SAS URL signed using Azure AD user credentials. If you must use SAS rather than Azure AD, this is the recommended approach. With user-delegation SAS, you first request a user delegation key and then generate the SAS URL. So, there are two layers of authorization checks: one based on the Azure AD user's RBAC permissions and another on the additional restrictions defined in the SAS URL itself. With this approach, there is no storage key stored in your application code, making it highly secure.

Shared access signature (SAS) walkthrough

The following sections step you through the process of setting up SAS authorization by first creating a shared access token, URL, and a stored access policy using the Azure portal, Azure PowerShell, and Azure CLI.

USING AZURE PORTAL

To set up SAS authorization using the Azure portal, follow these steps:

1. Navigate to the page for the container in your storage account for which you want to set up SAS authorization.

2. In the left pane of the container page, click **Shared Access Token**.

3. On the Shared Access Tokens page (see Figure 1-26), enter the following information, and click the **Generate SAS Token and URL** button:

   - **Signing Method** Select the **Account Key** option button (the default).
   - **Signing Key** Select the storage account key to use.
   - **Stored Access Policy** For now, select **None**. You will create and apply a new stored access policy momentarily.
   - **Permissions** Select a permission level and leave this set to **Read**.
   - **Start** Select the start date, time, and time zone for the SAS token to indicate when the token should become active.
   - **Expiry** Select an expiration date, time, and time zone to indicate when the SAS token should expire.
   - **Allowed IP Addresses** To allow access using the access token via specific IP addresses only, enter those addresses here.
   - **Allowed Protocols** Choose which protocols to allow.

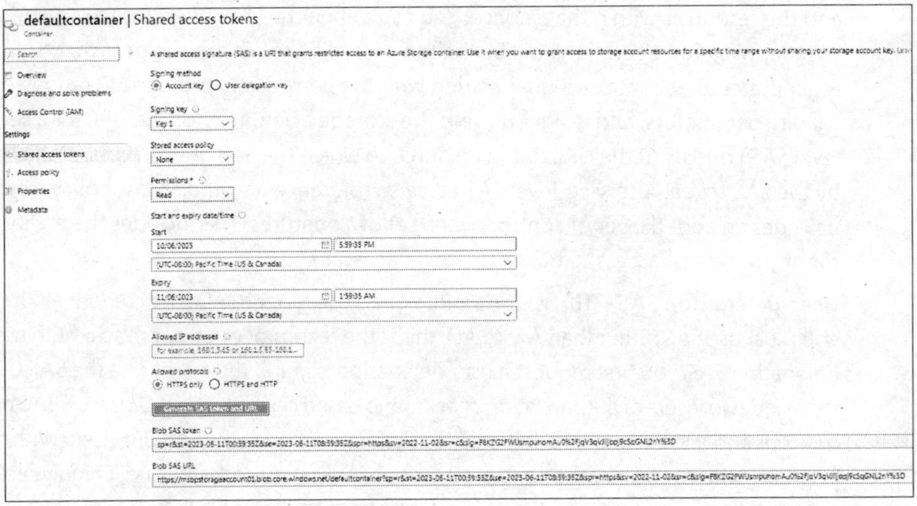

FIGURE 1-26 Generating a SAS token and URL.

You can now select and use the SAS URL to access the storage account and container from your application. Next, you'll add a stored access policy.

4. In the left pane of the container page, click **Access Policy**.

5. On the Access Policy page, under **Stored Access Policies**, click **Add Policy**. (See Figure 1-27.)

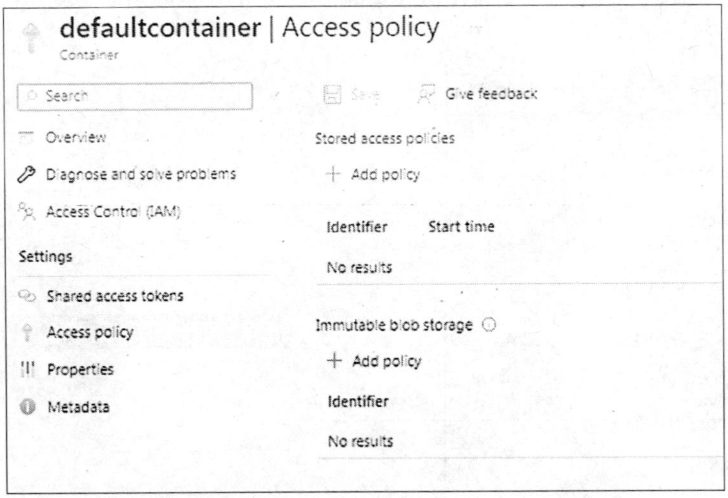

FIGURE 1-27 The container's Access Policy page.

6. In the Add Policy dialog box (see Figure 1-28), enter the following information and click **OK**:
   - **Identifier** Enter a unique name for the storage access policy.
   - **Permissions** Specify which permissions you want to assign.
   - **Start Time** Select a start date, time, and time zone to indicate when the stored access policy should become active.
   - **Expiry Time** Select an expiration date, time, and time zone to indicate when the stored access policy should expire.

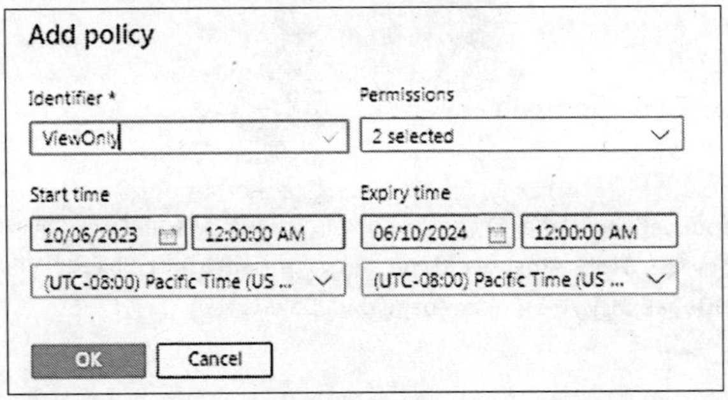

FIGURE 1-28 Add a stored access policy.

7. In the Access Policy page, click the **Save** button above the Stored Access Policy section. (See Figure 1-29.)

FIGURE 1-29 Saving the new stored access policy.

USING AZURE POWERSHELL

```
#Define required variables
$resourceGroup = "RG01"
$region = "eastus"
$storageaccname = "mbspblobstorage01"
$container = "container"
$vaultname = "RecoveryServicesVault01"
$blob = "TextFile01.txt"

#Generate SAS Access URL
Set-AzCurrentStorageAccount -ResourceGroupName $resourcegroup -Name $storageaccname
New-AzStorageAccountSASToken -Service Blob -ResourceType Service,Container,Object -Permis-
sion "racwdlup" -Protocol HTTPSOnly -ExpiryTime (Get-Date).AddDays(5)
```

USING AZURE CLI

```
#Define required variables
resourceGroup="RG01"
region="eastus"
storageaccname="mbspblobstorage01"
container="container"
directory="directory"
#Generate SAS Access URL
```

```
az storage account  generate-sas \
                    --account-name $storageaccname \
                    --account-key 00000000 \
                    --expiry 2024-12-31 \
                    --https-only \
                    --permissions acuw \
                    --resource-types sco \
                    --services b
```

Networking

Azure Blob Storage supports the use of various network routing components, networking protocols, and network security features. You can use these to access and secure each individual storage account in your environment based on the needs of your application workload or end client. You can set these options either when you create the storage account or at a later time as your needs evolve.

Network routing

Azure provides two routing methods for Azure Blob Storage service endpoints. You can select which method you want to use. The options are as follows:

- **Microsoft routing** With Microsoft routing, traffic is routed from your endpoint to the closest Microsoft edge point of presence (POP), at which point it traverses the Microsoft global fiber backbone to the Azure Blob Storage endpoint. (See Figure 1-30.) This generally results in lower latency and better network performance, and this is the default option for most Azure services. This routing type also supports all methods of authentication covered in the previous section.

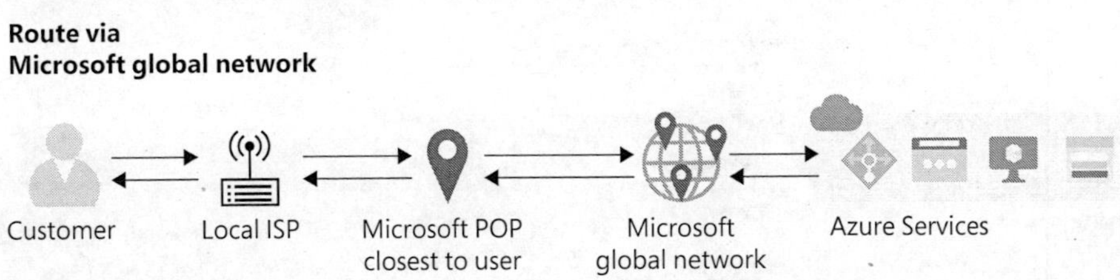

FIGURE 1-30 Microsoft routing.

- **Internet routing** With internet routing, most traffic is routed from the customer over the public internet until it reaches the Microsoft POP that is closest to the Azure Blob Storage endpoint. (See Figure 1-31.) This can result in higher latency and performance issues, depending on your ISP. However, this routing method does help lower networking costs.

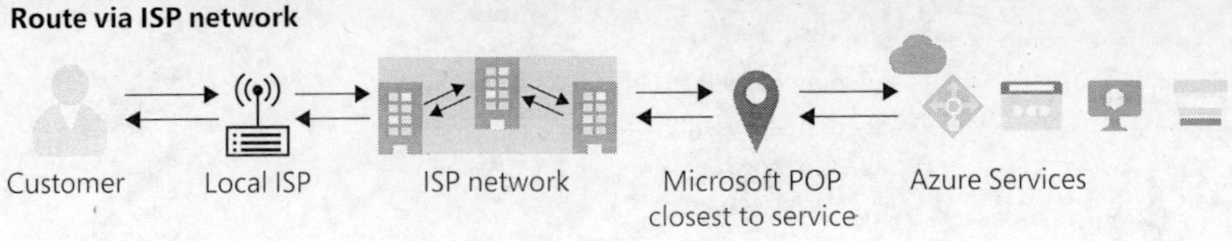

FIGURE 1-31 Internet routing.

Network routing walkthrough

The following sections step you through the process of selecting network routing options using the Azure portal, Azure PowerShell, and Azure CLI.

USING AZURE PORTAL

To select network routing options using the Azure portal (in this example, internet routing), follow these steps:

1. In the left pane of the Azure Blob Storage account page, under **Security + Networking**, click **Networking**.
2. In the **Firewalls and Virtual Networks** tab on the Networking page (see Figure 1-32), under **Network Routing**, enter the following information. Then click the **Save** button near the top of the page:
   - **Routing preference** Select the **Internet Routing** option button.
   - **Publish Route-Specific Endpoints** Select the Internet Routing check box.

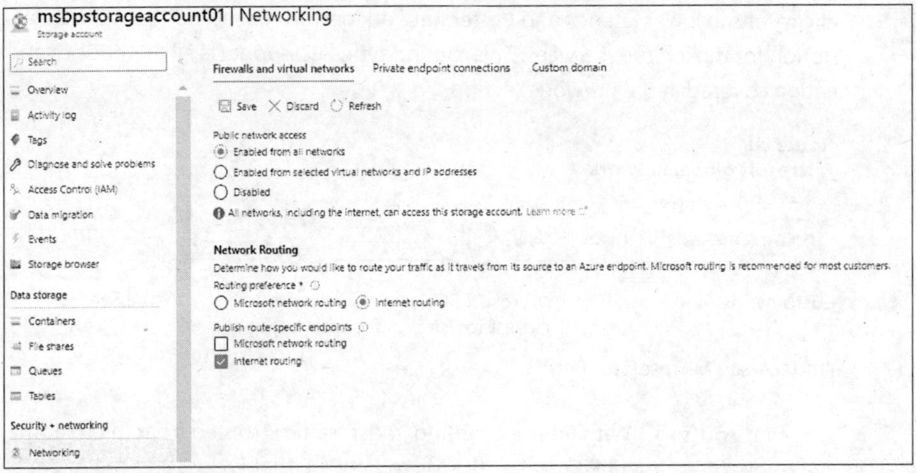

FIGURE 1-32 Setting up internet routing.

USING AZURE POWERSHELL

Use the following Azure PowerShell code to set up network routing:

```
#Define required variables
$resourceGroup = "RG01"
$region = "eastus"
$storageaccname = "mbspblobstorage01"
$container = "container"

#Configure network routing options
Set-AzStorageAccount -ResourceGroupName $resourcegroup `
 -AccountName $storageaccname `
 -RoutingChoice InternetRouting `
 -PublishInternetEndpoint $true
```

USING AZURE CLI

Use the following code to set up network routing from the Azure CLI:

```
#Define required variables
resourceGroup="RG01"
region="eastus"
storageaccname="mbspblobstorage01"
container="container"
directory="directory"
vnet="vNET01"
subnet="default"
endpointname="PrivateEndpoint"
vaultname="RecoveryServicesVault01"
#Configure network routing options
az storage account update \
                        --name $storageaccname \
                        --routing-choice InternetRouting \
                        --publish-internet-endpoints true
```

Network File System (NFS) 3.0 protocol

Azure Blob Storage supports the use of Linux clients hosted in an Azure VM or in an on-premises datacenter to mount Azure Blob Storage containers using the Network File System (NFS) 3.0 protocol.

NFS 3.0 support also enables legacy application workloads, such as high-performance computing (HPC), to run in the cloud. HPC workloads generally require the use of NFS or SMB protocols to access data and enable hierarchical namespaces. This was generally not offered by cloud storage services, causing HPC clients to resist migration to the cloud. Azure Blob Storage introduced the ability to enable hierarchical namespaces in September 2021. This, combined with NFS protocol support, allows these legacy applications to run in the cloud.

SSH File Transfer (SFTP) protocol

Azure Blob Storage has introduced support for SSH File Transfer (SFTP) protocol, to connect to an Azure Blob Storage endpoint using an SFTP endpoint. This allows you to easily and securely share data with others, without requiring a server to host the SFTP service or integrating a third-party SFTP service on top of the Azure Blob Storage.

You can create local user accounts on the storage to provide access over port 22. SFTP does require the storage account to use a hierarchical namespace. This enables you to create a structure of directories and subdirectories, similar to a file system on a Windows or Linux VM. You must define a home directory for each local user. This serves as their default folder when they connect. Then, depending on the container-level permissions you define, they will be able to navigate to the containers and access the data within.

Currently, there is no support for Azure Active Directory (Azure AD), Azure Active Directory Domain Services (Azure AD DS), or on-premises Active Directory with SFTP. The only method to set up access to storage over SFTP is to create local users with either a password or a Secure Shell (SSH) private key to connect and access the data. Passwords are auto-generated by Microsoft. Currently, custom user-provided passwords are not supported. You can enable both password and SSH public-private key options, and users can choose their preferred method to connect.

> ***NOTE*** **SFTP is charged at the rate of USD 0.30 per hour that the service is kept online.**

Storage account firewall and virtual networks

You can configure an Azure storage account to restrict access to the public endpoint using a storage account firewall. The storage account firewall is effectively a network policy on the storage account that restricts access based on your defined access list. Using a storage account firewall, you can restrict access from a public endpoint to specific public IP addresses, specific public IP address ranges, an Azure virtual network, or a private endpoint.

> ***NOTE*** **When you restrict access to one or more virtual networks, the virtual network's service endpoints are used to control access.**

Storage account firewall and virtual networks walkthrough

The following sections step you through the process of setting up a storage account firewall and virtual network restrictions using the Azure portal, Azure PowerShell, and Azure CLI.

> ***IMPORTANT*** **If you are following along, select resources and resource names based on your environment, including unique storage account names for each of your deployments.**

IMPORTANT If you are following along, be sure to delete any unwanted resources after you have completed testing to reduce charges levied by Microsoft.

USING AZURE PORTAL

To configure the storage account firewall using the Azure portal, follow these steps. You'll first learn how to allow access to the storage account only to connections that originate from specific virtual networks and IP addresses. Then you'll learn how to allow access to the storage account only to connections from a specific private endpoint:

1. In the left pane of the Azure Blob Storage account page, under **Security + Networking**, click **Networking**.
2. In the **Firewalls and Virtual Networks** tab on the Networking page (see Figure 1-33), under **Public Network Access**, select the **Enabled from Selected Virtual Networks and IP Addresses** option button.

FIGURE 1-33 Setting up a storage account firewall.

3. Under **Virtual Networks**, click **Add Existing Virtual Network**.

4. In the Add Networks dialog box (see Figure 1-34), enter the following information and click **OK**:

   - **Subscription** Select the subscription that contains the virtual network subnets you want to add.
   - **Virtual Networks** Select the virtual network(s) you want to add.
   - **Subnets** Select the subnet(s) you want to add.

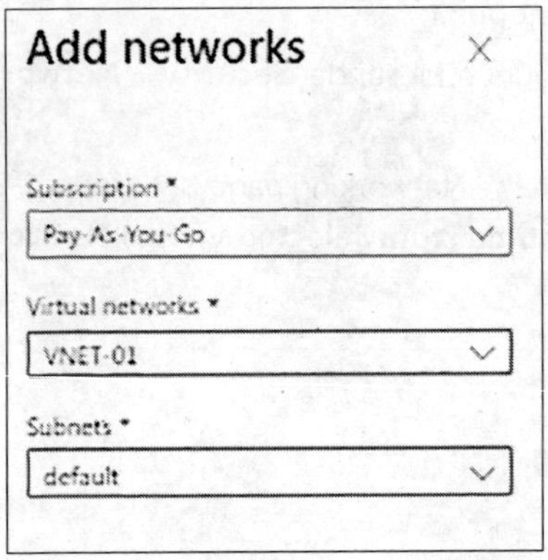

FIGURE 1-34 The Add Networks dialog box.

5. Back in the **Firewalls and Virtual Networks** tab on the Networking page (refer to Figure 1-33), enter the following information. Then click **Save** near the top of the page:

   - **Firewall** Select the **Add Your Client IP address** check box to allow your public IP address access to the storage.
   - **Resource Instances** To allow access by specific resource instances, select the instance type in the **Resource Type** list and the specific instance in the **Instance Name** list. (For this example, leave these blank.)
   - **Exceptions** Select any of the check boxes in this section if you want to allow access to the storage in certain cases. In this example, select **Allow Azure Services on the Trusted Services List to Access This Storage Account**.
   - **Network Routing Preference** Choose **Microsoft Network Routing** or **Internet Routing**. (Refer to the section "Network routing walkthrough" earlier in this chapter for more information.)
   - **Public Route-Specific Endpoints** Optionally, specify whether route-specific endpoints should be published by selecting the **Microsoft Network Routing** and/or **Internet Routing** check box. (For this example, leave these unchecked.)

   After you click Save, you'll see the virtual network you added in the Virtual Networks section. (See Figure 1-35.) You can test access to the storage account from the selected virtual network. (You will have to provision a VM in that network and then connect to the storage from that VM.)

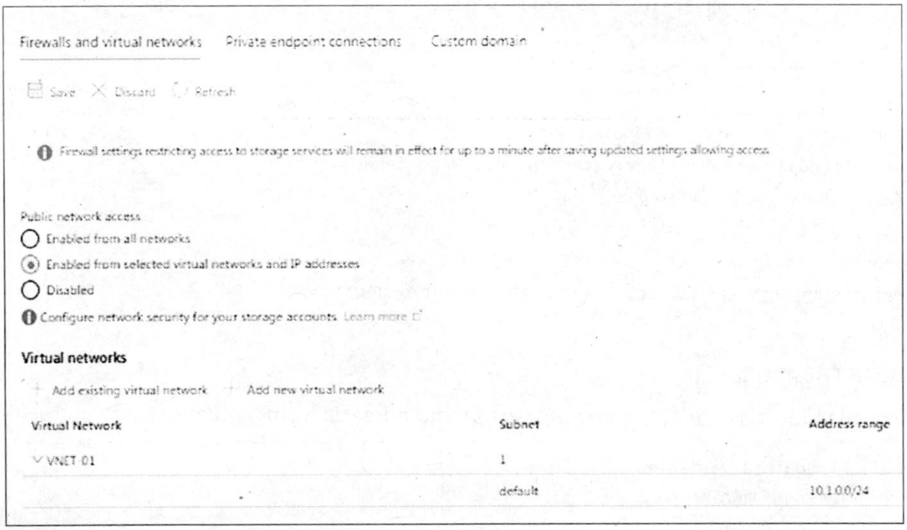

FIGURE 1-35 The virtual network you added appears on the list.

USING AZURE POWERSHELL

Use the following Azure PowerShell code to set up a storage account firewall:

```
#Define required variables
$resourceGroup = "RG01"
$region = "eastus"
$storageaccname = "mbspblobstorage01"
$container = "container"
$vnet = "vNET01"
$subnet = "default"
#Setting up Storage account firewall
#Setup access from Subnet
Update-AzStorageAccountNetworkRuleSet -ResourceGroupName $resourcegroup -Name $storage-
account -DefaultAction Deny
Get-AzVirtualNetwork -ResourceGroupName $resourcegroup -Name $vnet | Set-AzVirtualNet-
workSubnetConfig -Name $subnet -AddressPrefix "10.0.0.0/24" -ServiceEndpoint "Microsoft.
Storage" | Set-AzVirtualNetwork

$subnet = Get-AzVirtualNetwork -ResourceGroupName $resourcegroup -Name $vnet | Get-AzVir-
tualNetworkSubnetConfig -Name $subnet
Add-AzStorageAccountNetworkRule -ResourceGroupName $resourcegroup -Name $storageaccount
-VirtualNetworkResourceId $subnet.Id

#Block Public access
Set-AzStorageAccount -ResourceGroupName $resourceGroup -Name $storageAccount -PublicNet-
workAccess Disabled
```

```
# Create a private link service connection to the storage account.
$privateEndpointConnection = New-AzPrivateLinkServiceConnection `
        -Name "$storageAccount-Connection" `
        -PrivateLinkServiceId $storageAccount.Id `
        -GroupId "blob" `
        -ErrorAction Stop

#Configure the private endpoint
$privateEndpoint = New-AzPrivateEndpoint -Name $endpointname `
-ResourceGroupName $resourcegroup `
-Location $region `
-Subnet $subnet `
-PrivateLinkServiceConnection $privateEndpointConnection
```

USING THE AZURE CLI

Use the following code to set up a storage account firewall from the Azure CLI:

```
#Define required variables
resourceGroup="RG01"
region="eastus"
storageaccname="mbspblobstorage01"
container="container"
directory="directory"
vnet="vNET01"
subnet="default"
endpointname="PrivateEndpoint"
#Setting up Storage account firewall for traffic from specific subnets
#Setup access from Subnet
subnetid=$(az network vnet subnet show \
        --resource-group $resourceGroup \
        --vnet-name $vnet \
        --name $subnet \
        --query "id" | \
    tr -d '"')

az network vnet subnet update \
    --ids $subnetid \
    --service-endpoints Microsoft.Storage \
    --output none

az storage account network-rule add \
                        --resource-group $resourceGroup \
                        --account-name $storageaccname \
                        --vnet-name $vnet \
                        --subnet $subnet
```

```
az storage account update \
      --resource-group $resourceGroup \
      --name $storageaccname \
      --bypass "AzureServices" \
      --default-action "Deny" \
      --output none

#Block Public access
az storage account update \
    --resource-group $resourceGroup \
    --name $storageaccname \
    --bypass "AzureServices" \
    --default-action "Deny" \
    --public-network-access Disabled \
    --output none

# Create a private link service connection to the storage account
storageAccount=$(az storage account show \
       --resource-group $resourceGroup \
       --name $storageaccname \
       --query "id" | \
    tr -d '"')

privateEndpoint=$(az network private-endpoint create \
       --resource-group $resourceGroup \
       --name "$storageaccname-PrivateEndpoint" \
       --location $region \
       --vnet-name $vnet \
       --subnet $subnet \
       --private-connection-resource-id $storageAccount \
       --group-id "file" \
       --connection-name "$storageaccname-Connection" \
       --query "id" | \
    tr -d '"')
```

Networking endpoints

Azure Blob Storage can be accessed over either the public internet or a private connection such as Azure ExpressRoute or VPN. Depending on your organization's security and access requirements, your approach might involve the use of one or both methods.

Public endpoints

By default, Azure Blob Storage assets are accessible over the internet by way of a public endpoint using the SMB protocol. This makes it convenient to access the storage if you have an active internet connection. The public endpoint is in the format https://<storage-account-name>.file.core.windows.net.

Many internet service providers (ISPs) and most organizations block SMB port 445 over the internet. So, to allow access, you will have to either contact your ISP to unblock the port or unblock it on your organization's firewalls. This is the easiest method for accessing the storage. However, some organizations consider this to be insecure because the storage is accessible over a public endpoint. In such scenarios, organizations can use private endpoints, discussed next.

Private endpoints

In brief, private endpoints provide the ability to assign a private or internal IP to the Azure Blob Storage asset and make it accessible over an Azure ExpressRoute, Azure peering, or Azure VPN connection. The private endpoint is in the format https://<privateendpoint-name>.privatelink.file.core.windows.net.

Private endpoints walkthrough

The following sections step you through the process of creating a private endpoint using the Azure portal, Azure PowerShell, and the Azure CLI.

> ***IMPORTANT*** **If you are following along, select resources and resource names based on your environment, including unique resource names for each of your deployments.**

> ***IMPORTANT*** **If you are following along, be sure to delete any unwanted resources after you have completed testing to reduce charges levied by Microsoft.**

USING AZURE PORTAL

To configure the private endpoint using the Azure portal, you must first disallow access to the storage account from the public network. Then you create a private endpoint and allow connections only from that specific private endpoint. Follow these steps:

1. In the **Firewalls and Virtual Networks** tab on the Networking page, under Public Network Access, select the **Disabled** option button. Then click **Save**. (See Figure 1-36.)

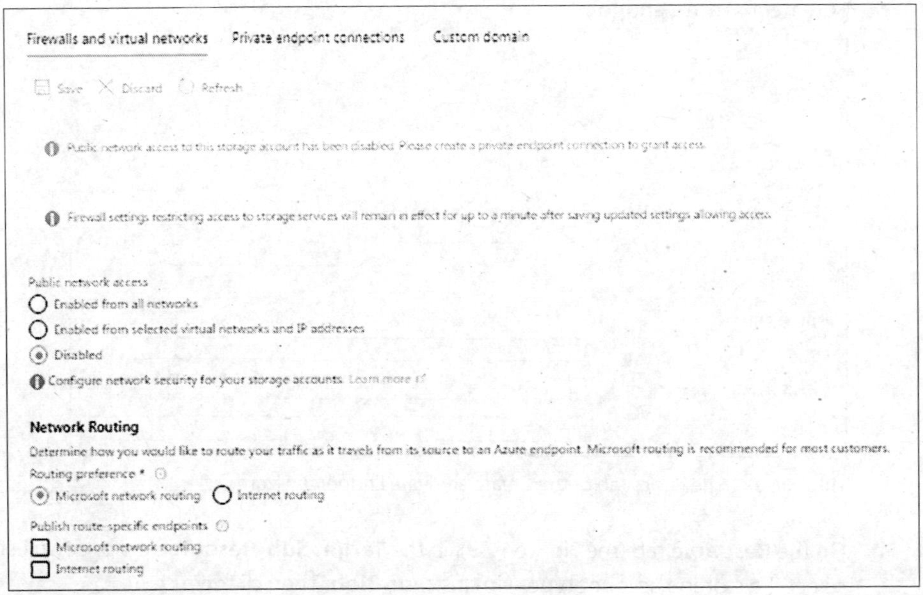

FIGURE 1-36 Disabling public network access.

2. Click the **Private Endpoint Connections** tab. Then click **Private Endpoint** near the top of the page. (See Figure 1-37.)

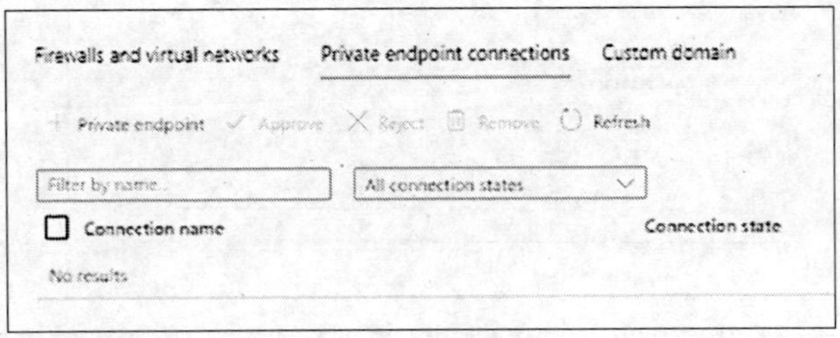

FIGURE 1-37 Setting up a private endpoint.

3. In the **Basics** tab of the Create a Private Endpoint wizard (see Figure 1-38), enter the following information and click **Next**:
   - **Subscription** Select the subscription in which you want to create the private endpoint.
   - **Resource group** Select an existing resource group or create a new one in which to create the private endpoint.
   - **Name** Enter a unique name for the private endpoint.
   - **Network Interface Name** Enter a unique name for the private endpoint network interface.
   - **Region** Select the Azure region where you want to host the private endpoint. This should be the same region as the Azure Blob Storage account.

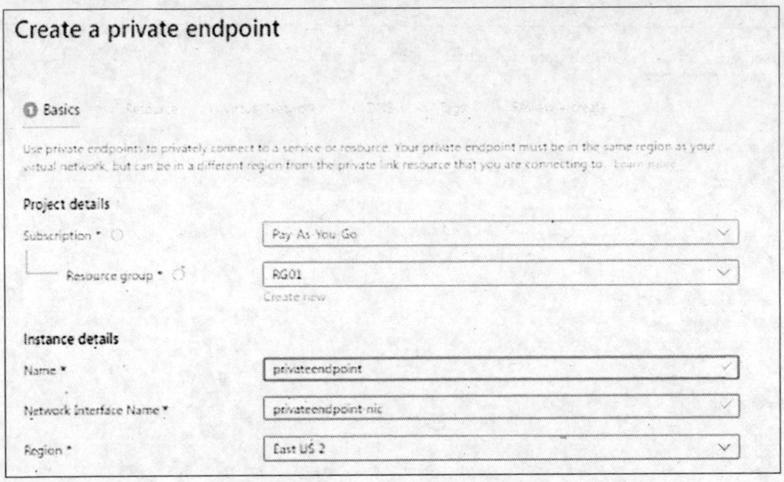

FIGURE 1-38 The Basics tab of the Create a Private Endpoint wizard.

4. On the **Resource** tab (see Figure 1-39), in the **Target Sub-Resource** drop-down list, select the storage account type—in this case, **Blob**. Then click **Next**.

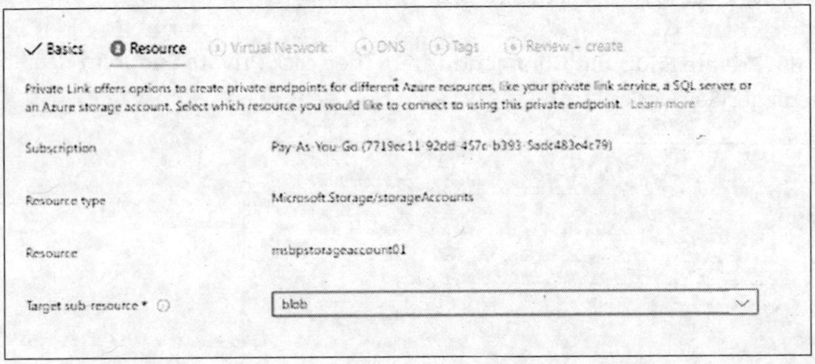

FIGURE 1-39 The Resource tab of the Create a Private Endpoint wizard.

5. On the **Virtual Network** tab (see Figure 1-40), enter the following information and click **Next**:
   - **Virtual Network** Select the virtual network on which you want to create the private endpoint.
   - **Subnet** Select the subnet on which you want to create the private endpoint.
   - **Private IP Configuration** Select the **Dynamically Allocate IP Address** or **Statically Allocate IP Address** option button, depending on your needs.
   - **Name** Enter a unique name for the private endpoint.
   - **Private IP** Enter an IP address for the private endpoint.
   - **Application Security Group** Leave this blank (the default).

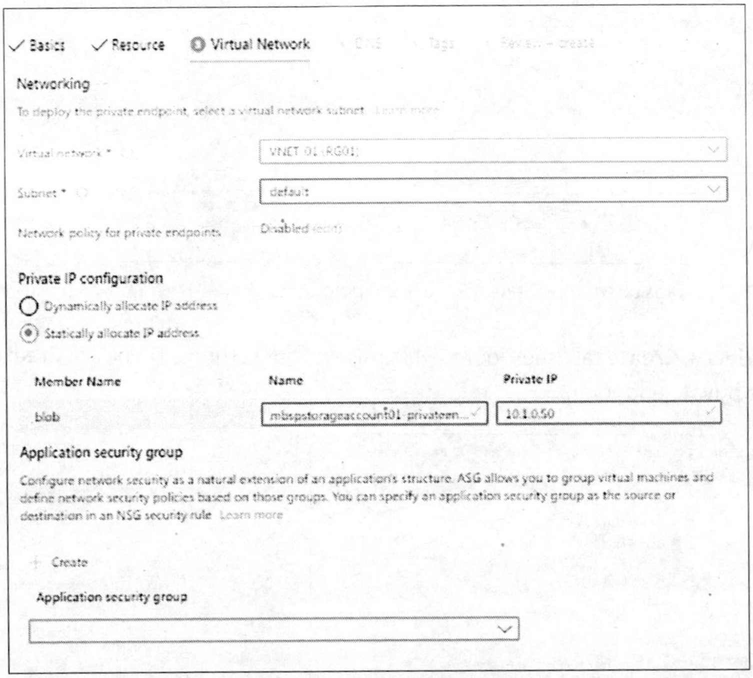

FIGURE 1-40 The Virtual Network tab of the Create a Private Endpoint wizard.

6. On the **DNS** tab (see Figure 1-41), enter the following information and click **Next**:
   - **Integrate with Private DNS Zone** Select the **Yes** option button.
   - **Subscription** Select the subscription to use for the private DNS zone.
   - **Resource Group** Select the resource group to use to create the private DNS zone.

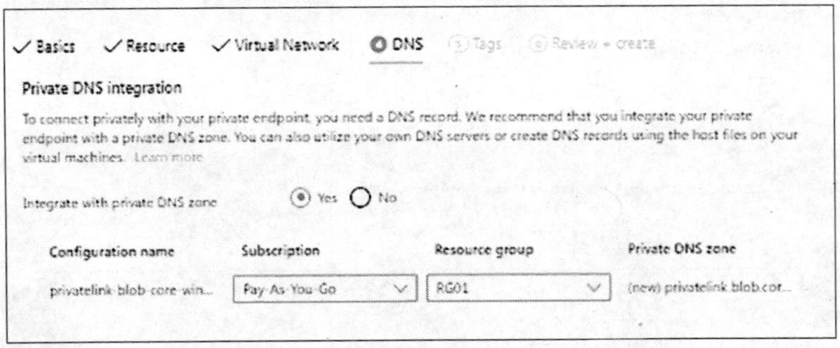

FIGURE 1-41 The DNS tab of the Create a Private Endpoint wizard.

7. In the **Tags** tab (see Figure 1-42), add any tags you want to associate with the private endpoint, and click **Next**.

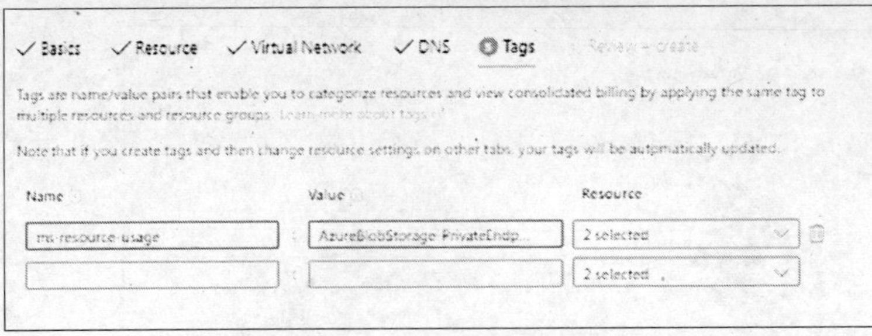

FIGURE 1-42 The Tags tab of the Create a Private Endpoint wizard.

8. In the **Review + Create** tab (see Figure 1-43), review your settings. Then click **Create** to create the private endpoint.

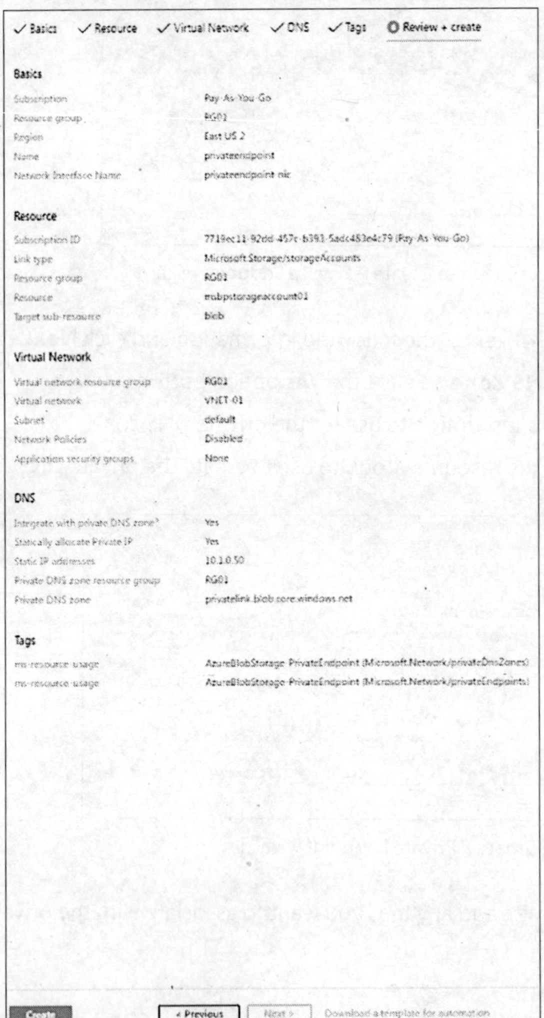

FIGURE 1-43 The Review + Create tab of the Create a Private Endpoint wizard.

9. After the private endpoint is created, click **Go to Resource** to access it. (See Figure 1-44.)

FIGURE 1-44 Accessing the new private endpoint.

The new private endpoint appears in the Networking page's Private Endpoint Connections tab with its Connection State listed as Approved. (See Figure 1-45.)

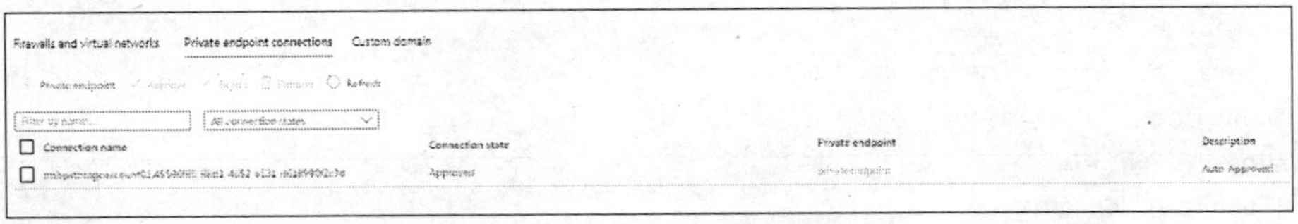

FIGURE 1-45 The new private endpoint appears in the Private Endpoint Connections tab of the Networking page.

10. Click the private endpoint to open its Overview page.
11. On the right side of the pane, click the **Network Interface** link. (See Figure 1-46.)

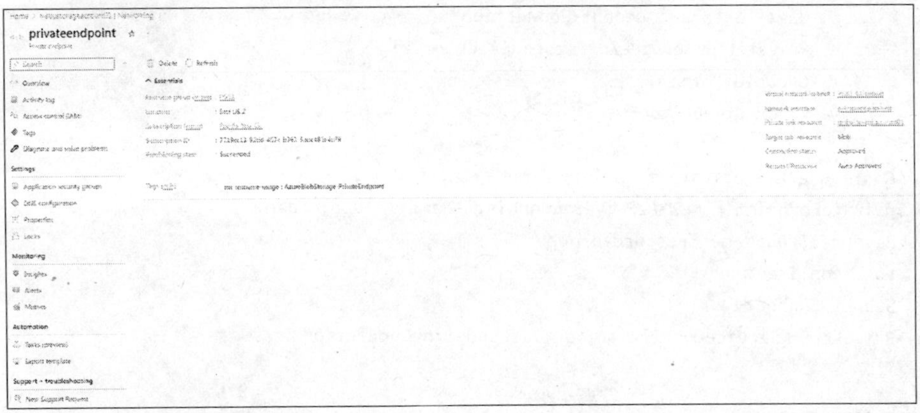

FIGURE 1-46 The private endpoint's Overview page.

The network interface's page (see Figure 1-47) contains the private IP address that you assigned earlier to the network interface. You can now use the private IP address to connect to the storage from a network connected to that subnet.

FIGURE 1-47 The private endpoint's network interface page.

USING AZURE POWERSHELL

Use the following Azure PowerShell code to create a private endpoint:

```
#Define required variables
$resourceGroup = "RG01"
$region = "eastus"
$storageaccname = "mbspblobstorage01"
$container = "container"
$vnet = "vNET01"
$subnet = "default"

#Block Public access
Set-AzStorageAccount -ResourceGroupName $resourceGroup -Name $storageAccount -PublicNet-
workAccess Disabled

# Create a private link service connection to the storage account.
$privateEndpointConnection = New-AzPrivateLinkServiceConnection `
        -Name "$storageAccount-Connection" `
        -PrivateLinkServiceId $storageAccount.Id `
        -GroupId "blob" `
        -ErrorAction Stop

#Configure the private endpoint
$privateEndpoint = New-AzPrivateEndpoint -Name $endpointname `
-ResourceGroupName $resourcegroup `
-Location $region `
-Subnet $subnet `
-PrivateLinkServiceConnection $privateEndpointConnection
```

USING AZURE CLI

Use the following code to create a private endpoint in the Azure CLI:

```
#Define required variables
resourceGroup="RG01"
```

```
region="eastus"
storageaccname="mbspblobstorage01"
container="container"
directory="directory"
vnet="vNET01"
subnet="default"
endpointname="PrivateEndpoint"

#Block Public access
az storage account update \
    --resource-group $resourceGroup \
    --name $storageaccname \
    --bypass "AzureServices" \
    --default-action "Deny" \
    --public-network-access Disabled \
    --output none

# Create a private link service connection to the storage account
storageAccount=$(az storage account show \
        --resource-group $resourceGroup \
        --name $storageaccname \
        --query "id" | \
    tr -d '"')

privateEndpoint=$(az network private-endpoint create \
        --resource-group $resourceGroup \
        --name "$storageaccname-PrivateEndpoint" \
        --location $region \
        --vnet-name $vnet \
        --subnet $subnet \
        --private-connection-resource-id $storageAccount \
        --group-id "file" \
        --connection-name "$storageaccname-Connection" \
        --query "id" | \
    tr -d '"')
```

Storage access tiers

Azure Blob Storage provides three storage tiers to help you structure your data storage to achieve an optimal balance between use and cost. Each tier has different data storage costs, transaction costs, and data access costs. The tiers are as follows:

- **Hot** In this tier, data is available online at all times. This tier is optimal for data that must be frequently accessed and modified. It has the highest data storage costs but the lowest data access costs. It is optimized for high numbers of transactions, making it ideal for active applications, active logs, data processing, and so on. All storage redundancy options support hot tiers, as do block, append, and page blobs.

- **Cool** Data on the cool tier is online at all times but slightly less available than data on the hot tier. However, durability, retrieval latency, and throughput on the cool tier are the same as on the hot tier. This tier is ideal for storing processed data that will be accessed infrequently after processing, short-term backups that must be restored in a timely manner, data stored for disaster recovery purposes, and so on. Data storage costs are lower than with the hot tier, but access costs are higher. Data in the cool tier must be stored for a minimum of 30 days. All storage redundancy options support cool tiers. Block and append blobs support cool tiers, but page blobs do not.
- **Archive** This is an offline tier optimized to store data that is rarely accessed. Compared to the hot and cool tiers, it has the lowest storage costs but the highest data access costs. It is ideal for long-term backups and for preserving data for compliance or historical reference purposes, or other data that does not require immediate access. You must store data in the archive tier for a minimum of 180 days; otherwise, you will be charged early deletion fees. Archive tiers are supported only on storage accounts configured for LRS, GRS, and RA-GRS. There is currently no support for this tier when using ZRS, GZRS, or RA-GZRS. Block and append blobs support archive tiers, but page blobs do not.

Rehydrating archived blobs

To access an archived blob, you must first rehydrate the blob. You cannot perform read or write operations until the blob is rehydrated. Blob rehydration can take up to 15 hours using the standard data rehydration priority option. You can expedite this, but doing so increases the charges significantly. However, the metadata of an archived blob is set for read access at all times. This allows you to list all the blobs in an archive tier and read the blob properties, metadata, and any index tags. Still, you cannot modify any metadata until rehydration has been performed.

NOTE **Archived blobs do not support snapshots at this time. Snapshots are covered in more detail later in this chapter.**

Although these are three distinct access tiers, you can store data in a storage account across these three tiers without any limits for each individual tier. Storage capacity is defined at the storage account level, and the tiers within can be used in any combination, as long as they are within the overall limits available for the storage account.

Early deletion fees

If you remove data from the cool or archive tier before its minimum period has elapsed—30 days for the cool tier and 180 days for the archive tier—you will be charged early deletion fees for the remaining period. For example, if you remove a blob stored in the archive tier after just 30 days, you will be charged an early deletion fee for the remaining 150 days. Early deletion fees are equivalent to the fees you would have paid to store the blob in that tier for the remaining 150 days. You must carefully plan your storage strategy before moving data into these tiers to avoid these charges.

Default access tier configuration

If you upload a blob to a storage account without specifying which tier that blob should use, a tier will be applied to it automatically. By default, the default tier for any new standard general purpose v2 storage accounts is hot. However, you can change this to cool when you create the storage account or at some later point in time.

If you change the default access tier for a storage account after you have already uploaded blobs into that account, the new tier will be applied to those existing blobs. This can result in significant transaction charges. So again, it is important to plan this configuration in advance if you can.

Storage access tier walkthrough

The following sections step you through the process of setting up a default access tier or changing the access tier using the Azure portal, Azure PowerShell, and Azure CLI.

USING AZURE PORTAL

To set up a default blob access tier or change the access tier of an existing blob using the Azure portal, follow these steps:

1. In the left pane of the Azure Blob Storage account page, under **Settings**, click **Configuration**.
2. Near the bottom of the Configuration page, under **Blob Access Tier (Default)**, select the **Cool** or **Hot** option button. (See Figure 1-48.) Then click **Save** near the top of the page.

   The next steps show you how to change an existing blob's access tier.
3. Navigate to the page for the container in which the blob whose tier you want to change is stored.
4. Select the check box next to the name of the blob whose access tier you want to change. Then click **Change Access Tier**. (See Figure 1-49.)

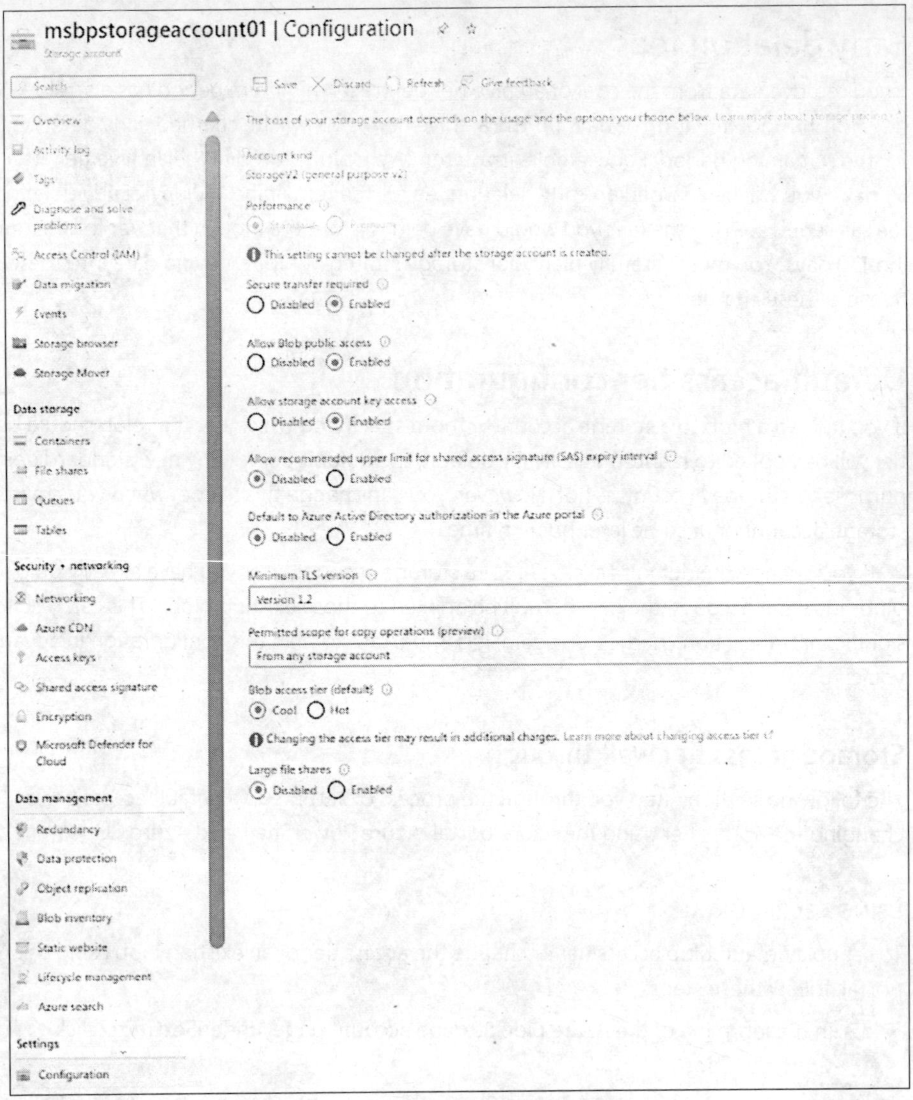

FIGURE 1-48 Setting up the default access tier.

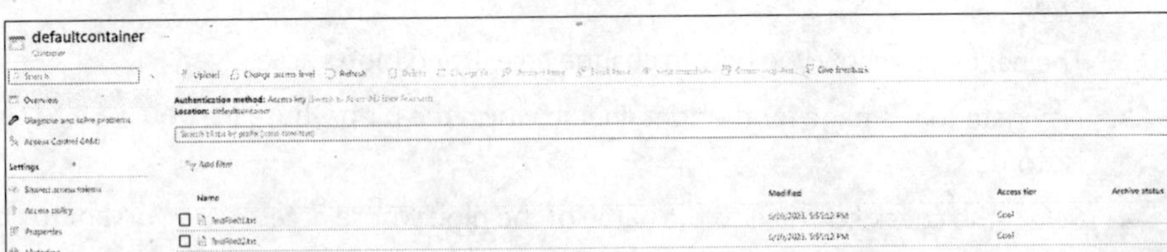

FIGURE 1-49 Changing an individual blob's access tier.

5. In the Change Tier dialog box (see Figure 1-50), click the **Access Tier** drop-down list and choose a different access tier. Then click **Save**.

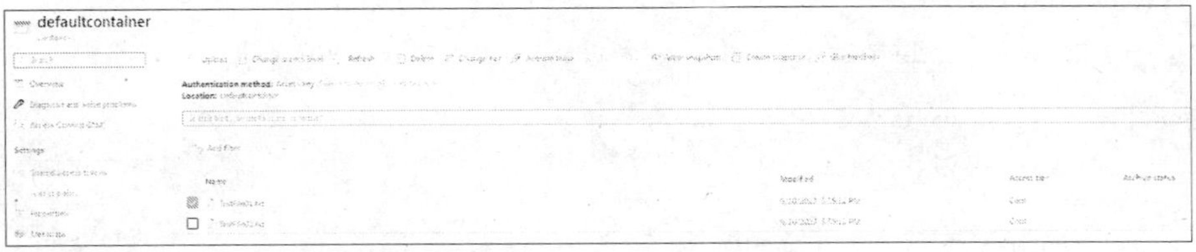

FIGURE 1-50 The Change Tier dialog box.

The blob's entry in the container page reflects the change. (See Figure 1-51.)

FIGURE 1-51 The blob's access tier has been changed.

USING AZURE POWERSHELL

Use the following Azure PowerShell code to assign a storage access tier:

```
#Define required variables
$resourceGroup = "RG01"
$region = "eastus"
$storageaccname = "mbspblobstorage01"
$container = "container"
$blob = "TextFile01.txt"

#Set Default access tier
Set-AzStorageAccount `
-ResourceGroupName $resourcegroup `
                   -Name $storageaccname `
                   -AccessTier Cool
#Change blob access tier
$storagectx = (Get-AzStorageAccount `
      -ResourceGroupName $resourceGroup `
      -Name $ storageaccname).Context

$blobtochange = Get-AzStorageBlob -Container $container -Blob $blob -Context $storagectx
$blobtochange.BlobClient.SetAccessTier("Archive", $null, "Standard")
```

USING AZURE CLI

Use the following code to assign a storage access tier from the Azure CLI:

```
#Define required variables
resourceGroup="RG01"
region="eastus"
storageaccname="mbspblobstorage01"
container="container"
directory="directory"

#Set Default access tier
az storage account update \
    --resource-group $resourceGroup \
    --name $storageaccname \
    --access-tier Cool

#Change blob access tier
az storage blob set-tier \
    --account-name $storageaccname \
    --container-name $container \
    --name TextFile01.txt \
    --tier Archive
```

Blob lifecycle management

Azure Blob Storage introduced blob lifecycle management, or the ability to define rule-based policies to move data between different access tiers based on certain conditions. Conditions can include the time of last modification, time of last access, and date of creation. Once your defined conditions are met, you can set up the storage account to do one of the following:

- Move the blob to the cool tier.
- Move the blob to the archive tier.
- Delete the blob.
- Move the blob to the cool tier, but move it back to the hot tier if it is accessed.

With these policies, you can automatically store data for long-term retention based on your organization's compliance requirements across the different tiers, and to remove data that the organization no longer needs.

You can also define these policies using filters to identify data based on the first few characters of a blob name, a specific blob container, or a combination of the two. You can also define whether to target block blobs, append blobs, or both, and whether to include blob snapshots and versions in the targets or limit the rule to just the base blob.

NOTE With append blobs, you can delete only the blob, snapshots, and version based on a timeframe you select.

When moving a blob between the cool and archive tiers, keep these points in mind:

- In a storage account whose default tier is cool, any blob that inherits this tier when it is uploaded will be automatically moved to the archive tier according to the lifecycle management policy, and it will not be subjected to any early deletion charge.
- A blob whose access tier has been explicitly set to cool (either upon upload or at some later time) will be subject to early deletion charges if it is moved to the archive tier according to the lifecycle management policy before its minimum period has elapsed.

NOTE Lifecycle management policies do not apply to $logs or $web containers.

Blob lifecycle management walkthrough

The following sections step you through the process of setting up blob lifecycle management policies using the Azure portal and Azure PowerShell.

USING AZURE PORTAL

To set up a blob lifecycle management policy using the Azure portal, follow these steps:

1. In the left pane of the Azure Blob Storage account page, under **Data Management**, click **Lifecycle Management**.
2. In the Lifecycle Management page, click **Add a Rule**. (See Figure 1-52.)

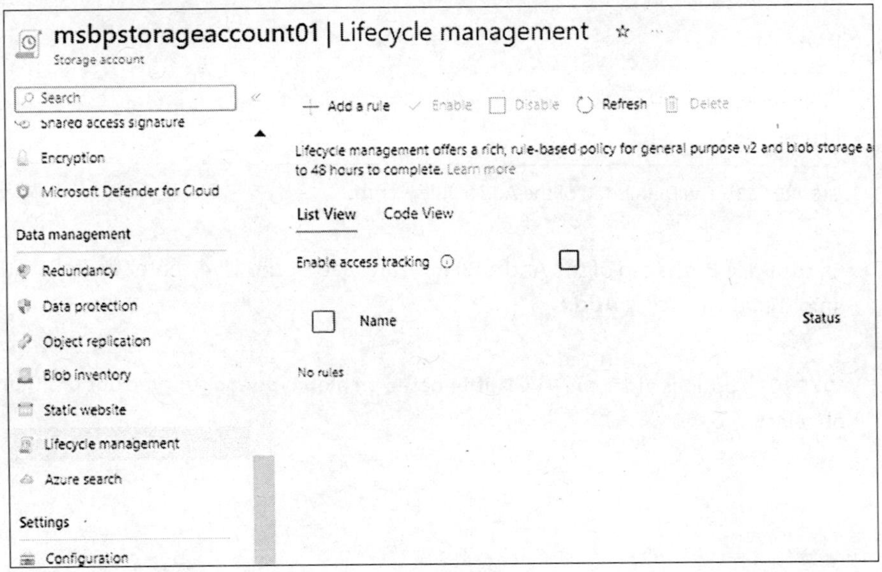

FIGURE 1-52 Setting up blob data lifecycle management.

3. In the **Details** tab of the Add a Rule wizard (see Figure 1-53), enter the following information and click **Next**:
   - **Rule Name** Enter a unique name for the lifecycle management policy.
   - **Rule Scope** Specify whether the new policy applies to all blobs in this storage account or to a subset of blobs based on criteria you select. For the sake of example, select **Apply Rule to All Blobs in Your Storage Account**.
   - **Blob Type** Specify the blob types to which the policy should apply. In this case, select **Block Blobs**.
   - **Blob Subtype** Specify the blob subtypes to which the policy should apply. In this example, choose **Base Blobs**.

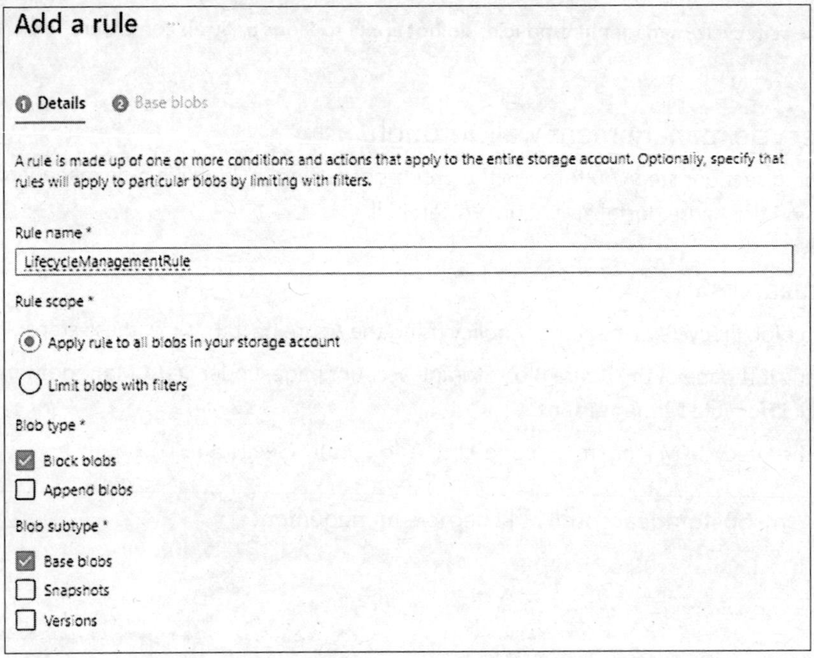

FIGURE 1-53 The Details tab of the Add a Rule wizard.

4. In the **Base Blobs** tab of the Add a Rule wizard (see Figure 1-54), enter the following information and click **Add**:

> ***NOTE*** **The options in this view will differ based on blob type and subtype options that you select.**

- **Base Blobs Were** Select the **Last Modified** or **Created** option button.
- **More Than (Days Ago)** Enter the number of days after which you want the policy to apply.
- **Then** Select the action to perform when the criteria have been met.

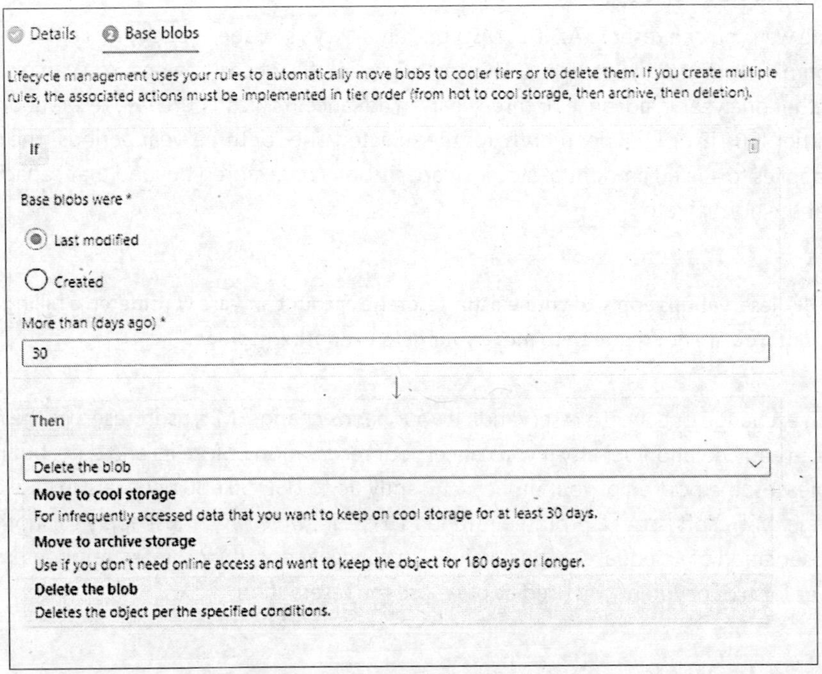

FIGURE 1-54 The Base Blobs tab of the Add a Rule wizard.

USING AZURE POWERSHELL

Use the following Azure PowerShell code to set up a blob lifecycle management policy:

```
#Define required variables
$resourceGroup = "RG01"
$storageaccname = "mbspblobstorage01"

# Create a new action object.
$lcaction = Add-AzStorageAccountManagementPolicyAction -InputObject $lcaction `
    -BaseBlobAction TierToArchive `
    -daysAfterModificationGreaterThan 90

# Create a new rule object.
$lifecyclerule1 = New-AzStorageAccountManagementPolicyRule -Name sample-rule `
    -Action $lcaction
```

```
# Create the policy.
Set-AzStorageAccountManagementPolicy -ResourceGroupName $resourcegroup `
    -StorageAccountName $storageaccname `
    -Rule $lifecyclerule1
```

Storage reservations

In the same way you can reserve Azure VMs, you can reserve storage capacity at a discounted rate to optimize your storage accounts. This can bring significant cost savings. You can reserve storage either one year in advance or three years in advance. You can purchase reservations in units of either 100 TiB or 1 PiB per month, for the selected one- or three-year periods. The reservation applies to a fixed amount of storage capacity; any data stored beyond that capacity is charged at the normal rate.

> ***NOTE*** **Reservations apply to your existing storage account and are considered a billing discount. You are not required to move your data to another storage.**

You can exchange or cancel a reservation if your needs change. Microsoft reserves the right to charge an early deletion penalty if you cancel your reservation before its end date, but it will refund at least some portion of your money (currently up to USD 50,000 per year). In case of an exchange, Microsoft issues a prorated refund as a credit, which you must apply to another storage reservation of an equal or higher value. For cancellations, the prorated refund is issued in whatever form of payment you used to purchase the reservation.

Static website hosting

You can leverage Azure Blob Storage to host a static content website that contains HTML, CSS, JavaScript, and image files, without additional web server infrastructure. When you enable the static website hosting feature on an Azure Blob Storage account, Azure creates a $web container in the storage account to host all the web server content. You can then use tools such as Visual Studio, the Azure portal, Azure PowerShell, or Azure CLI to upload your web content files to the $web container and render your site.

Although this is a great way to start hosting a static website, there are limitations to this approach. You cannot configure host headers for your website, and neither authentication nor authorization is supported. Keep this in mind before you use this feature.

> ***NOTE*** **Static website hosting support could be affected if you enable other features such as Network File System (NFS) 3.0 protocol, Data Lake Storage Gen2, or the SSH File Transfer Protocol (SFTP) on the storage account.**

Data protection

In addition to the storage account redundancy options covered earlier in this chapter to help you to maintain or recover access to an Azure Blob Storage account in case of a local, regional, or geographical outage, Microsoft provides other features to help you quickly recover individual containers or blobs. These features include soft delete for containers and blobs and blob versioning. Other related tools and techniques include the blob change feed, point-in-time restores, integration with Azure Backup, and blob snapshots. These features can help you quickly identify, react to, and recover from malicious or accidental deletion or corruption of data. It is critical that you understand and use each of these features in your environment, as they offer an extremely cost-effective method of data protection.

Soft delete for containers and blobs

Soft delete protects your containers and blobs by allowing you to recover them quickly if they are accidentally or maliciously deleted. It works by maintaining the deleted data in the system for the period of time that you specify. This retention period can range from 1 to 365 days. You can define this period for containers and blobs independently of each other to align with your overall data recovery strategy. Within the retention period, you can recover containers and blobs using the Azure portal, Azure PowerShell, Azure CLI, or REST APIs. After the retention period elapses, the data is permanently deleted and cannot be restored unless it has been stored on a separate backup.

When you restore a container, all blobs, snapshots, and versions associated with that container are also restored. However, you cannot restore individual blobs if the parent container was not deleted, too. To be able to restore individual blobs, blob snapshots, or versions when the parent container hasn't been deleted, you must also configure soft delete. You can also soft delete just a blob snapshot without deleting the base blob.

> ***NOTE*** **The soft delete feature does not incur additional charges. However, the data storage charges for soft-deleted containers, blobs, blob snapshots, and versions are the same as for your active data.**

Blob versioning

You can enable blob versioning to automatically maintain previous versions of a blob. With blob versioning, a new version of the blob is created each time a write operation occurs on the blob. Each version is maintained with a version ID, which identifies the point-in-time state of that blob.

When blob versioning is enabled, you can access earlier versions of a blob to recover your data if it is modified or deleted. You can read and delete a specific version of the blob by providing the version ID associated with that version. However, blob versions cannot be modified. They are unique. The value of each version is based on the timestamp that the change occurred.

Blob change feed

The blob change feed was brought into preview by Microsoft in November 2019 and became generally available in September 2020. This feature tracks blob changes in a guaranteed, ordered, and durable manner.

> **NOTE** **Before the release of the blob change feed, you could use storage events and Storage Analytics logging to obtain a feed of blob changes, but these changes were not ordered, making it difficult to trace the sequence of events to identify the change you wanted to track.**

The blob change feed details every change taking place on the blob or metadata in that storage account in order. The feed is written to the storage account under a special $blob-changefeed container and ensures that the data is durable, immutable, and read-only. This makes it reliable for compliance and auditing purposes. (See Figure 1-55.)

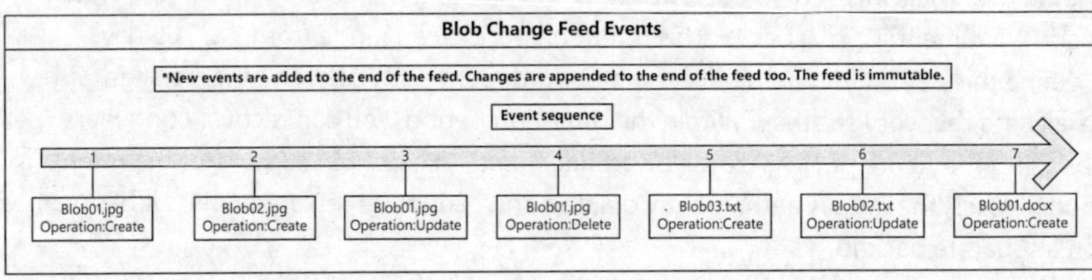

FIGURE 1-55 Blob change feed events.

You can read the blob change feed as a stream or in batch mode. To do this, you develop client applications to use the blob change feed processor library provided with the change feed processor SDK. In this way, you can build low-cost, scalable solutions to process and manage change events.

Logs from the blob change feed are retained for a retention period that you define, so you can maintain them as long as necessary. The logs are charged at standard Azure Blob Storage rates. Because all the logs are maintained in the storage container, you can consume the logs in a synchronous or asynchronous manner, in single or multiple parallel streams from different applications. This enables you to integrate the logs with monitoring as well as compliance and analytical applications at the same time. You can monitor the logs for specific events that trigger automated actions or workflows.

> **NOTE** **This feature is supported by both standard general purpose v2 and premium block Azure Blob Storage accounts.**

Point-in-time restore

Point-in-time restore allows you to recover block blob data going back to a specific date in the event of the accidental or malicious deletion or corruption of data due to application error or other means. In other words, you can restore all data in a container to a specific point-in-time before the deletion or corruption event. You can use this feature even in testing scenarios, where the impact of certain application changes must be tested on the storage to correct issues caused during testing.

At this time, point-in-time restore is supported only on standard general purpose v2 storage accounts. In addition, you cannot use point-in-time restore for data in the archive tier; only data in hot and cool tiers can be recovered in this way.

When you set up point-in-time restore, you configure a retention period measured in days. For point-in-time restore to work, blob soft delete, blob versioning, and the blob change feed must also be enabled and configured with a retention period that is higher than the point-in-time restore threshold. After you have configured all these features, any blobs existing within their defined scope are subject to these restoration features. You cannot restore blobs to a point-in-time prior to the configuration of these features.

When performing a restore, you have one of two choices:

- Define no specific ranges of containers or blob names, in which case everything will be restored.
- Specify lexicographical ranges of container and blob names to target for the restoration. You can define up to 10 such ranges in a single restore operation. You can perform multiple restore operations one at a time.

> ***NOTE*** **A restore operation, once triggered, cannot be canceled. However, you can undo a restore after it is complete by running a second restore to the point-in-time immediately before you ran the first one to reverse the changes.**

When you initiate a point-in-time restore, not all data is necessarily restored. Based on restoration criteria that you select, only data that has changed since the point-in-time selected for the restore operation will be restored. This analysis is performed by the restoration operation. In addition, any blob that fails the restoration operation will result in the entire restoration operation failing.

All read and write operations are temporarily paused for any storage container that is within the scope of the restore operation. Once the restoration operation completes or fails, read and write operations automatically resume.

Data protection walkthrough

The following sections step you through the process of setting up data protection options using the Azure portal, Azure PowerShell, and Azure CLI.

USING AZURE PORTAL

To set up data protection options using the Azure portal, follow these steps:

1. In the left pane of the Azure Blob Storage account page, under **Data Management**, click **Data Protection**.
2. On the Data Protection page (see Figure 1-56), enter the following information and click **Save**:
   - **Enable Point-in-Time Restore for Containers** Select this check box.
   - **Maximum Restore Point (Days Ago)** Enter the number of days to retain point-in-time restore snapshots.
   - **Enable Soft Delete for Blobs** Select this check box.
   - **Keep Deleted Blobs for (in Days)** Enter the number of days to retain deleted blobs.
   - **Enable Soft Delete for Containers** Select this check box.
   - **Keep Deleted Containers for (in Days)** Enter the number of days to retain deleted containers.
   - **Enable Blob Change Feed** Leave this set at **Keep All Logs** (the default).

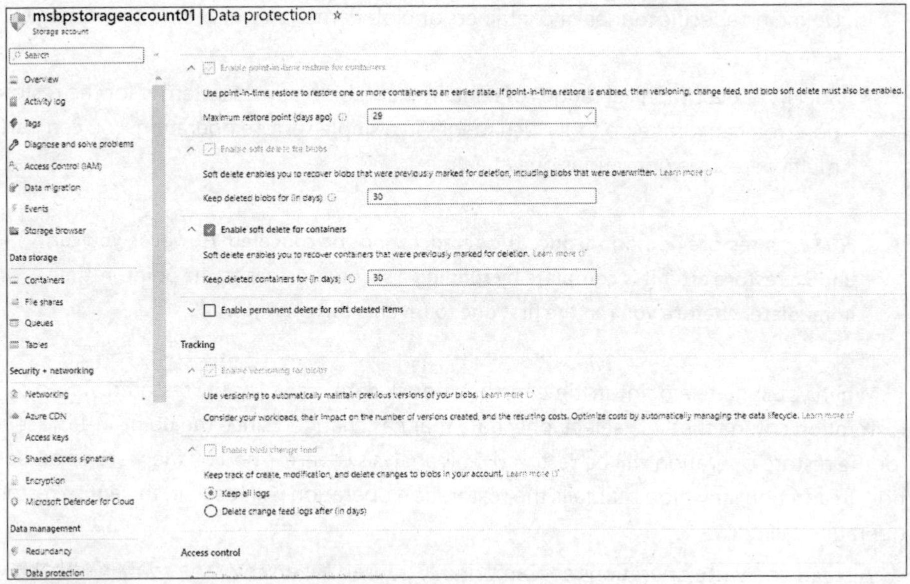

FIGURE 1-56 Data protection configuration options.

3. In the left pane of the Azure Blob Storage account page, under **Data Storage**, click **Containers**.

   The Containers page now contains an entry for a $blobchangefeed container. (See Figure 1-57.) This container contains the logs for the blob change feed.

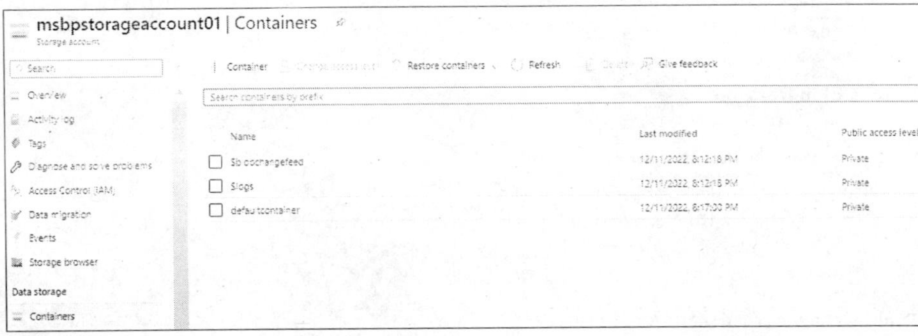

FIGURE 1-57 Notice the $blobchangefeed container.

4. To view blob versions, click a blob in the Containers page.

   The blob's page opens. If versions of this blob have been saved, you will see them here. (See Figure 1-58.) You can select a version to download, restore, or delete.

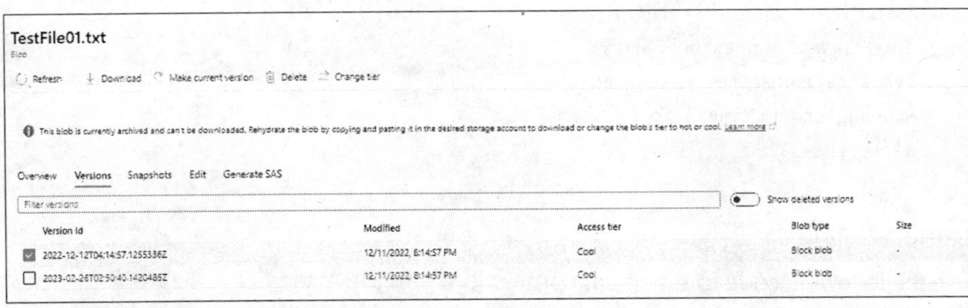

FIGURE 1-58 Blob versions.

USING AZURE POWERSHELL

Use the following Azure PowerShell code to set up data protection options:

```
#Define required variables
$resourceGroup = "RG01"
$region = "eastus"
$storageaccname = "mbspblobstorage01"
$container = "container"

#Enable soft delete for containers
Enable-AzStorageContainerDeleteRetentionPolicy `
    -ResourceGroupName $resourcegroup `
    -StorageAccountName $storageaccname `
    -RetentionDays 30

#Enable soft delete for blobs
Enable-AzStorageBlobDeleteRetentionPolicy `
    -ResourceGroupName $resourcegroup `
```

```
    -StorageAccountName $storageaccname `
    -RetentionDays 30

#Enable blob versioning
Update-AzStorageBlobServiceProperty `
    -ResourceGroupName $resourcegroup `
    -StorageAccountName $storageaccname `
    -IsVersioningEnabled $true


#Enable change feed and versioning.
Update-AzStorageBlobServiceProperty `
    -ResourceGroupName $resourcegroup `
    -StorageAccountName $storageaccname `
    -EnableChangeFeed $true `
    -IsVersioningEnabled $true

#Enable point-in-time restore
Enable-AzStorageBlobRestorePolicy `
    -ResourceGroupName $resourcegroup `
    -StorageAccountName $storageaccname `
    -RestoreDays 29
```

USING AZURE CLI

Use the following code to set up data protection from the Azure CLI:

```
#Define required variables
resourceGroup="RG01"
region="eastus"
storageaccname="mbspblobstorage01"
container="container"
directory="directory"
vnet="vNET01"
subnet="default"
endpointname="PrivateEndpoint"
vaultname="RecoveryServicesVault01"
#Enable soft delete for containers
az storage account blob-service-properties update \
    --account-name $storageaccname \
    --resource-group $resourceGroup \
    --enable-container-delete-retention true \
    --container-delete-retention-days 30

#Enable soft delete for blobs
az storage account blob-service-properties update \
    --account-name $storageaccname \
```

```
    --resource-group $resourceGroup \
    --enable-delete-retention true \
    --delete-retention-days 30

#Enable blob versioning
az storage account blob-service-properties update \
    --resource-group $resourceGroup \
    --account-name $storageaccname \
    --enable-versioning true

#Enable point-in-time restore
az storage account blob-service-properties update \
    --resource-group $resourceGroup \
    --account-name $storageaccname \
    --enable-change-feed true \
    --enable-restore-policy true \
    --restore-days 29
```

Azure Backup integration

You can use the cloud-native Azure Backup service to perform short-term and long-term backups of your Azure storage containers. You can define custom retention policies for different containers based on the requirements of each container. The Azure Backup service allows for seamless backup integration. You can create backup retention policies that control how long the backups are retained. Azure Backup integration also provides backup monitoring, alerting, and reporting capabilities, making it easier for administrators to manage all blob storage backups in one single location.

The primary backup method available for production use at this time is continuous backup, which performs backups as changes are made. All backups are stored in the source storage account and do not require transfer to a backup vault. Because the backups are continuous, there is no need to define a backup schedule.

Continuous backup uses a feature called operational backup. Operational backup provides point-in-time restore capability by leveraging soft delete, change feed, and versioning features to store data based on a retention policy that you define. In addition, a lock is placed on the storage account to prevent the account's accidental or unauthorized deletion. All these features are automatically configured when you set up this feature.

> ***NOTE*** **The maximum backup retention period is 360 days, 51 weeks, or 11 months.**

This backup can protect blobs only—not containers themselves. If you delete an entire container, the backup will not be able to restore that container. It is therefore recommended that you set up soft delete for containers you want to protect in addition to this operational backup.

When performing data restores, you can restore all the block blobs, individual blobs, or a subset of blobs (using a prefix) to the source storage account. Microsoft centralizes backup management through the Backup Center. There, you can manage backups and restores for all storage accounts from a single location.

Azure Backup integration walkthrough

The following sections step you through the process of integrating Azure Backup with an Azure Blob Storage account using the Azure portal, Azure PowerShell, and Azure CLI.

> ***IMPORTANT*** **If you are following along, select resources and resource names based on your environment, including a unique backup vault name for each of your deployments.**

> ***IMPORTANT*** **If you are following along, be sure to delete any unwanted resources after you have completed testing to reduce charges levied by Microsoft.**

USING AZURE PORTAL

To set up Azure Blob Storage to use Azure Backup using the Azure portal, follow these steps:

1. In the left pane of the Azure Blob Storage account page, under **Data Management**, click **Data Protection**.
2. Near the top of the Data Protection page (see Figure 1-59), under **Recovery**, select the **Enable Operational Backup with Azure Backup** check box.

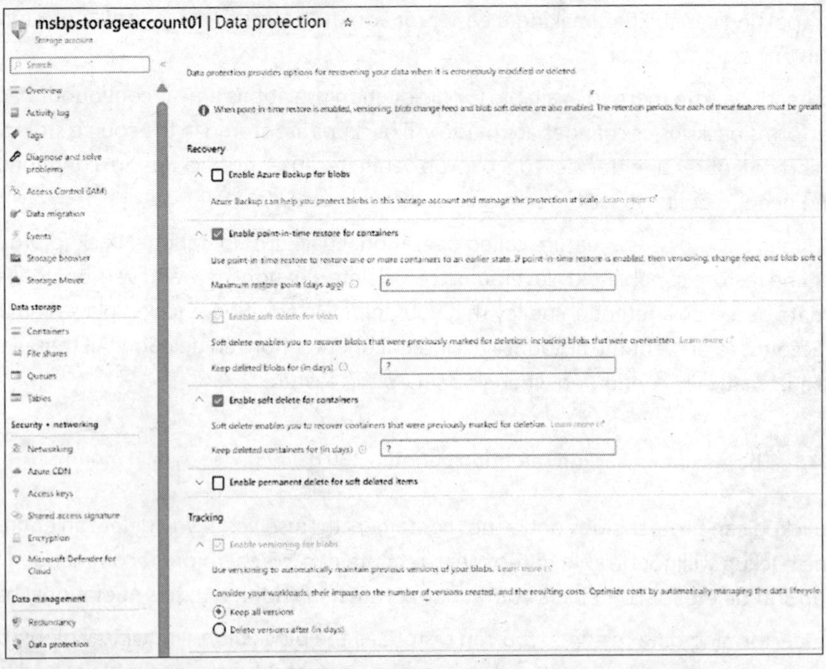

FIGURE 1-59 Integrating Azure Backup with your Azure Blob Storage account.

3. Click the **Backup Vault** drop-down list and select an existing backup vault—or, as in this example, the **Add New** link under the Backup Vault box. (See Figure 1-60.)

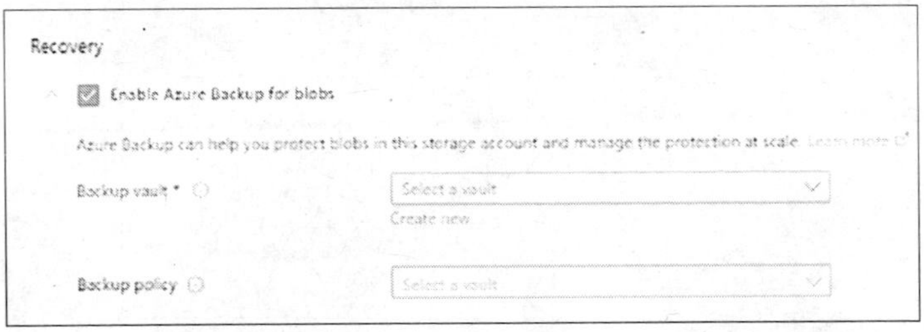

FIGURE 1-60 Enable operational backup with Azure Backup.

4. In the Create a New Backup Vault dialog box (see Figure 1-61), enter the following information and click **Create**:
   - **Vault Name** Enter a unique name for the backup vault.
   - **Resource Group** Select an existing resource group or create a new one in which to create the backup vault.
   - **Backup Storage Redundancy** Select the redundancy level of backup storage. (Note that you cannot change the redundancy level after you create a backup, so choose carefully.)

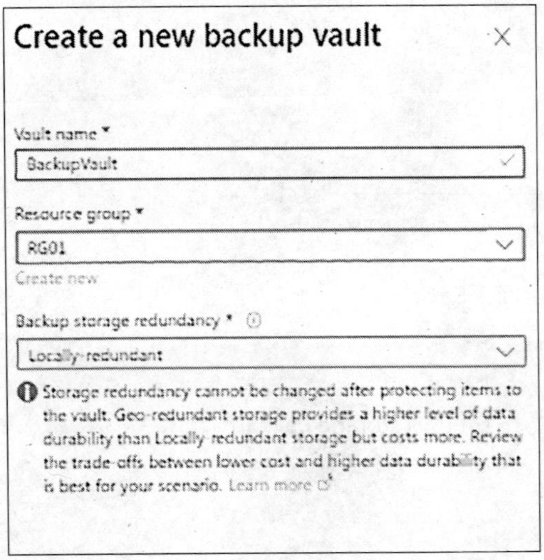

FIGURE 1-61 Creating a new backup vault.

5. Back on the Data Protection page, click the **Backup Policy** drop-down list and select an existing backup policy. Or, as in this example, click the **Add New** link under the Backup Policy box. (See Figure 1-62.)

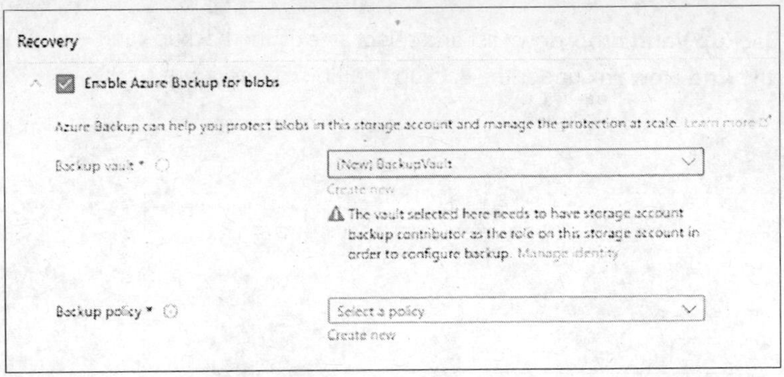

FIGURE 1-62 Creating a new backup policy.

6. In the Create a New Backup Policy dialog box (see Figure 1-63), enter the following information and click **Create**:
   - **Policy Name** Enter a unique name for the backup policy.
   - **Retention (in Days)** Indicate how long backups should be retained.

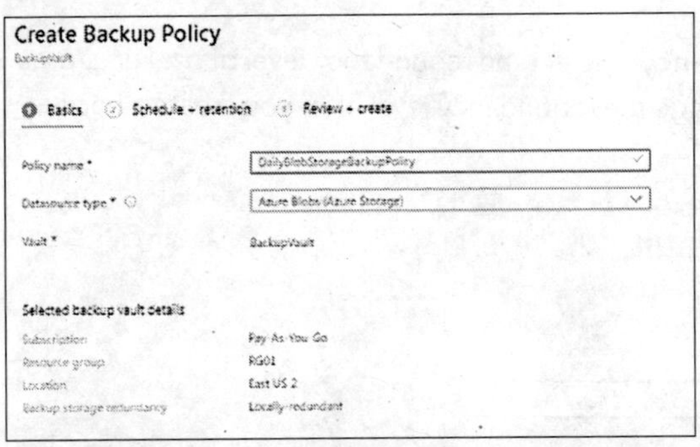

FIGURE 1-63 The Create a New Backup Policy dialog box.

7. Back on the Data Protection page, click **Save**.

USING AZURE POWERSHELL

Use the following Azure PowerShell code to set up a storage backup:

```
#Define required variables
$resourceGroup = "RG01"
$region = "eastus"
$storageaccname = "mbspblobstorage01"
$container = "container"
$vnet = "vNET01"
$subnet = "default"
$endpointname = "PrivateEndpoint"
$vaultname = "RecoveryServicesVault01"
#Setting up Azure Backup Integration
#Creating Backup Vault
```

```
$bkpvaultstorage = New-AzDataProtectionBackupVaultStorageSettingObject -Type GeoRedundant
-DataStoreType VaultStore
New-AzDataProtectionBackupVault -ResourceGroupName $resourcegroup -vaultName $vaultname
-Location $region -storagesetting $bkpvaultstorage

#Create Backup policy
$policyDefinition = Get-AzDataProtectionPolicyTemplate -DatasourceType AzureBlob
$BkpPolicy=New-AzDataProtectionBackupPolicy `
                    -ResourceGroupName $resourcegroup `
                    -VaultName $vaultname `
                    -Name "DefaultBlobBackupPolicy" `
                    -Policy $policyDefinition

#Enable Backup
$bkp = Initialize-AzDataProtectionBackupInstance -DatasourceType AzureBlob -DatasourceLo-
cation $region -PolicyId $BkpPolicy[0].Id -DatasourceId $storageaccount.Id
New-AzDataProtectionBackupInstance -ResourceGroupName $resourcegroup -VaultName $Vault-
Name -BackupInstance $bkp
```

USING AZURE CLI

Use the following code to set up a storage backup from the Azure CLI:

```
#Define required variables
resourceGroup="RG01"
region="eastus"
storageaccname="mbspblobstorage01"
container="container"
directory="directory"
vnet="vNET01"
subnet="default"
endpointname="PrivateEndpoint"
vaultname="RecoveryServicesVault01"

#Setting up Azure Backup Integration
#Create Backup vault
az backup vault create -resource-group $resourceGroup \
    --name $vaultname \
    --location $region

#Set the storage redundancy and cross region restore config
az backup vault backup-properties set -name $vaultname  \
    --resource-group $resourceGroup \
    --backup-storage-redundancy "GeoRedundant" \
    --cross-region-restore-flag "True"
#Create Backup Policy
az dataprotection backup-policy get-default-policy-template -datasource-type AzureBlob
```

```
{
  "datasourceTypes": [
    "Microsoft.Storage/storageAccounts/blobServices"
  ],
  "name": "DefaultBlobPolicy",
  "objectType": "BackupPolicy",
  "policyRules": [
    {
      "isDefault": true,
      "lifecycles": [
        {
          "deleteAfter": {
            "duration": "P30D",
            "objectType": "AbsoluteDeleteOption"
          },
          "sourceDataStore": {
            "dataStoreType": "OperationalStore",
            "objectType": "DataStoreInfoBase"
          }
        }
      ],
      "name": "Default",
      "objectType": "AzureRetentionRule"
    }
  ]
}

#Create Backup json - Replace all the resource groups and resource values in the command
before proceeding
az dataprotection backup-instance initialize -datasource-type AzureBlob  -location
$region -policy-id "/subscriptions/xxxxxxxx-xxxx-xxxx-xxxx-xxxxxxxxxxxx/resourceGroups/
RG-01/providers/Microsoft.DataProtection/backupVaults/BackupVault01/backupPolicies/Default-
BlobBackupPolicy" -datasource-id "/subscriptions/xxxxxxxx-xxxx-xxxx-xxxx/resourcegroups/
RG-01/providers/Microsoft.Storage/storageAccounts/mbspblobstorage01" > backup_instance.
json
#Enable Backup
az dataprotection backup-instance create -resource-group $resourceGroup -vault-name
$vaultname -backup-instance backup_instance.json
```

Blob snapshots

A blob snapshot is a point-in-time read-only copy of a blob that you create and store in the hot or cool tier. The snapshot is identical to the base blob, except it is a point-in-time copy, allowing you to access that version of the blob. A snapshot copies all the system properties and metadata from the base blob (unless explicitly configured otherwise). You can have any number of snapshots of a blob, and each snapshot will persist until you either delete the snapshot or delete the base blob itself.

The URL for a snapshot is the same as the base blob, except the snapshot date and time value are appended to the end of the URL. For example, if the URL for a base blob is http://blockblobstorageaccount.blob.windows.net/blobcontainer/blob01, a snapshot for that blob taken on January 3, 2022, at 11 p.m. would have a URL similar to http://blockblobstorageaccount.blob.windows.net/blobcontainer/blob01?snapshot=2022-03-01T23:00:00.938291Z.

You can store snapshots on different storage tiers from base blobs. This can help reduce the cost of the snapshots. If you do not specify the storage tier to use, the snapshot is stored in the same tier as the base blob, and you will be charged for it at the same rate as for the base blob after the base blob changes and no longer matches the snapshot. If you store the snapshot in a different access tier, then you are charged for the entire blob based on the access tier rates. You should take this into account when planning your storage protection strategy.

NOTE **Snapshots of blobs in the archive tier are not supported at this time.**

Blob snapshots walkthrough

The following sections step you through the process of creating and managing blob snapshots using the Azure portal, Azure PowerShell, and Azure CLI.

USING AZURE PORTAL

To create and manage blob snapshots using the Azure portal, follow these steps:

1. Locate the page for the container for the blob for which you want to create a snapshot, select the check box for that blob and click **Create Snapshot**. (See Figure 1-64.)

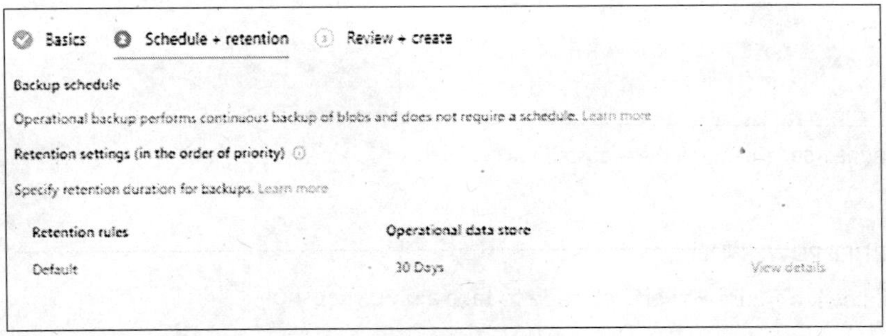

FIGURE 1-64 Create a blob snapshot.

2. To view the snapshot (and any other snapshots associated with the same blob), select the file and click **View Snapshots** (refer to Figure 1-64).

   The snapshot is listed in the Snapshots tab. (See Figure 1-65.)

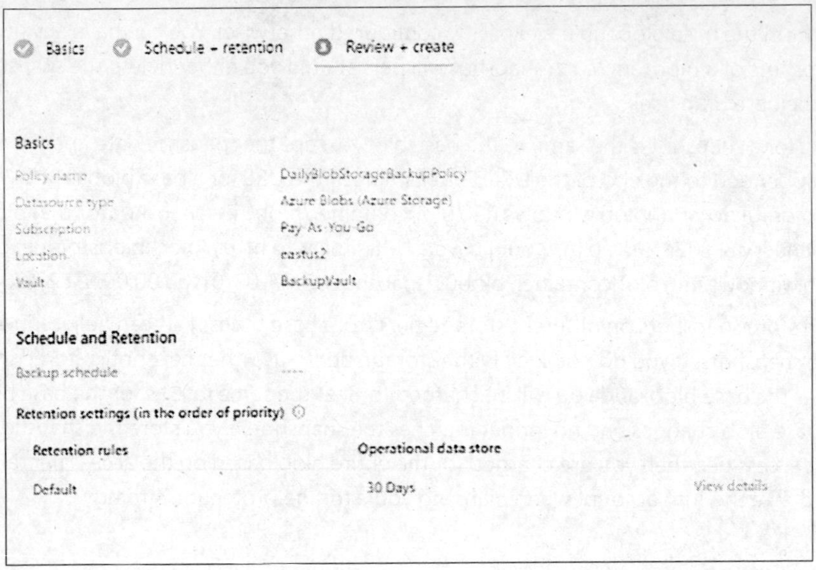

FIGURE 1-65 View snapshots.

3. Optionally, to change the snapshot's access tier, select the snapshot in the **Snapshots** tab and click **Change Tier**. Then open the **Access Tier** drop-down list in the Change Tier dialog box to choose a different tier and click **Save**. (See Figure 1-66.)

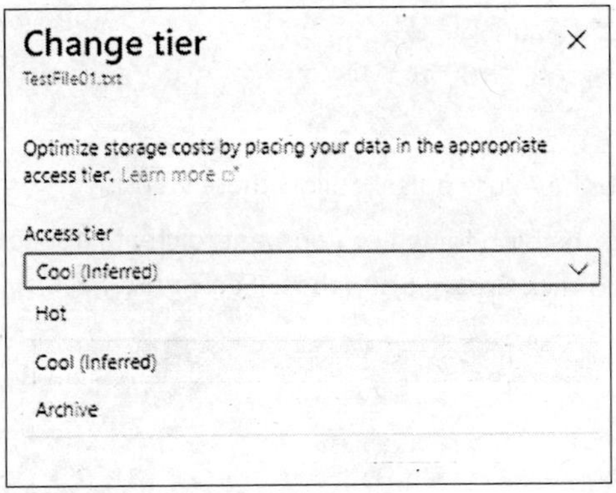

FIGURE 1-66 Changing the snapshot's access tier.

USING AZURE POWERSHELL

Use the following Azure PowerShell code to take a blob snapshot:

```
#Define required variables
$resourceGroup = "RG01"
$region = "eastus"
$storageaccname = "mbspblobstorage01"
```

```
$container = "container"
$vaultname = "RecoveryServicesVault01"
$blob = "TextFile01.txt"

#Generate Blob snapshot
$blob = Get-AzStorageBlob -Container $container -Blob $blob -Context $storageaccount.
context
$blob.BlobClient.CreateSnapshot()
```

USING AZURE CLI

Use the following code to take a blob snapshot from the Azure CLI:

```
#Define required variables
resourceGroup="RG01"
region="eastus"
storageaccname="mbspblobstorage01"
container="container"
directory="directory"
#Generate Blob snapshot
az storage blob snapshot \
    --container-name $container \
    --name TextFile01.txt \
    --account-name $storageAccount
```

Disaster recovery

Disaster recovery is a critical component of any application architecture. The higher the criticality of the application, the more redundancy is required to ensure minimal to no downtime or data loss.

While setting up the data redundancy for the storage account and taking regular backups does ensure that you are able to recover from an outage, you must take into account other application components in your disaster recovery planning, too. This includes components such as the web application firewall or application gateway, web applications or application servers, connected API services, and so on. This ensures that in a disaster scenario, once the blob storage is online, all other related components can also be recovered and can read the storage with minimal interruption and data loss.

We've covered earlier how storage redundancy options such as GRS, GZRS, RA-GRS, and RA-GZRS can replicate your data asynchronously to a secondary Azure region.

One caveat to note: If the primary region becomes unavailable, you can set up your applications to automatically switch to the secondary region to perform read operations in case you are using either RA-GRS or RA-GZRS storage accounts. This will ensure that the application is online in some form while a full storage failover is performed, either by you or by Microsoft.

Once the storage has failed over completely, write operations to the storage account in the secondary region are also allowed, and your application can then start to commit changes to the storage as earlier. In case of GRS or GZRS storage, the read and write operations can only be performed once the storage has been failed over to the secondary region.

You saw earlier that the primary blob storage endpoint points to *https://<storage-account-name>.blob.core.windows.net/<container-name>*. Similarly, the secondary storage endpoint would be reachable at *https://<storage-account-name>-secondary.blob.core.windows.net/<container-name>*. (The *-secondary* suffix is appended automatically by the secondary endpoint.) You can use this endpoint to connect to the secondary storage. The storage account access keys would remain the same in both the primary and secondary endpoints.

Storage account failover

There are two ways you can fail over a storage account to the secondary region:

- **Microsoft-managed failover** In the event of a region-wide outage, Microsoft performs a full region failover to the secondary region. In such cases, you need not perform manual failover operations on your storage accounts. You would only have to ensure that when the DNS entries for the storage are updated, your applications are ready to resume normal operations.
- **Customer-managed failover** In addition, you are able to perform a manual failover on your own, in case of an outage. When an outage occurs, Microsoft will initially actively work toward restoring the data and operations in the primary region, if possible. If they are unable to do so, they will declare that region as unrecoverable and initiate the failover to the secondary region. In case you are unable to wait until such time, you can perform a manual failover from your storage account properties to bring your storage account online and make it accessible to your applications.
- In either scenario, DNS entries must be updated automatically or manually before write operations to the storage can begin. Also take into account any private endpoints you may have created in the primary region; you need to make sure the same endpoints are set up in the secondary region, too.

Last Sync Time

Data synchronized using GRS is often behind data in the primary region. The data sync is asynchronous to avoid affecting write operations and storage performance in the primary region. This allows write operations to be committed on the primary storage without waiting for the same operations to be written and acknowledged by the secondary storage. However, at the time of a disaster, some data written and committed to the primary storage might not yet have been committed to the secondary storage—in which case, that data would be lost.

You can determine whether this has happened by checking the Last Sync Time property for your storage account. This value is a GMT date/time value that you can query using Azure PowerShell, Azure CLI, or one of the Azure Storage client libraries. Any write operations performed after this Last Sync Time property value are most likely missing in the secondary region and might not be available for read operations. Incorporating this into your application logic can allow you to plan in advance how to handle such contingencies.

Last Sync Time walkthrough

The following sections step you through the process of checking the Last Sync Time on a storage account using Azure PowerShell and Azure CLI.

USING AZURE POWERSHELL

Use the following Azure PowerShell code to retrieve the Last Sync Time on a storage account:

#Define variables

```
$rg = "RG01"
$storageaccname = "mbspblobstorage01"

#Retrieve the last sync time
$LastSyncTime = $(Get-AzStorageAccount -ResourceGroupName $rg `
    -Name $storageaccname `
    -IncludeGeoReplicationStats).GeoReplicationStats.LastSyncTime
```

USING THE AZURE CLI

Use the following Azure CLI code to retrieve the Last Sync Time on a storage account:

#Define required variables

```
rg="RG01"
storageaccname="mbspblobstorage01"

#Retrieve the last sync time
$LastSyncTime=$(az storage account show \
    --name $storageaccname \
    --resource-group $rg \
    --expand geoReplicationStats \
    --query geoReplicationStats.lastSyncTime \
    --output tsv)
```

Best practices

Following are some general best practices regarding setting up and using Azure Blob Storage accounts:

- **Protect your access keys** Storage account access keys provide root access to the storage account, bypassing any permissions or authorization restrictions you have put in place. It is therefore of utmost importance that you limit the use of and protect access to the storage account access keys. Instead, use Azure Active Directory (Azure AD) to authorize access requests to the Azure Blob Storage account. You can use Azure Key Vault to automate the rotation of the access keys or manually rotate the keys if you suspect a compromise has taken place.

- **Plan your redundancy strategy** Plan your storage redundancy strategy in advance so you select the correct storage redundancy options when creating the Azure Blob Storage account. If you decide to change the redundancy level at a later stage, you may have to migrate all data from one storage account to another, which can result in extensive transaction costs (depending on the amount of data you have stored).
- **Document recovery procedures and review regularly** Once you have your redundancy strategy in place, document any recovery procedures, such as manual storage failover for geo-redundant storage, and review them regularly with your team. You may have to include the failover of other related components as well, along with the storage endpoint, to ensure that all interconnected components are online in case of a disaster. Regular reviews will help ensure that any changes to the Azure Blob Storage capabilities or feature set are incorporated in your design and you can optimize the recovery further if possible.
- **Limit mixing of storage account types** When using general purpose v2 storage accounts, you can deploy a mix of blob, file, table, and queue storage in the same account. However, it is highly recommended to only deploy Azure Blob Storage containers together in the same storage account. This ensures that you can consider performance requirements related to Azure Blob Storage independently of any other file services. In a mixed storage account, it can get difficult to manage performance issues, as different storage account types using different protocols access the storage from a varied set of clients and share the same limits associated with the storage account.
- **Enable soft delete on all important containers** Soft delete is a great feature to help you quickly recover your containers in the event of accidental or malicious deletion. As far as possible, enable soft delete on all your containers, and set up a retention period longer than the minimum time it will take your team to respond and to perform a restore, if necessary.
- **Enable soft delete on blobs** Enabling soft delete for blobs allows you to easily restore blobs in case of accidental or malicious deletion. Select the time range for data retention based on your organization's compliance, auditory, and data restoration RPO requirements to ensure you are able to restore blobs as quickly as possible.
- **Enable blob versioning to maintain previous versions** Enabling blob versioning for all critical containers makes it easy to restore blobs in the event of unwanted modifications, data corruption, or malware attacks, without having to restore backups.
- **Use private endpoints for storage access** Private endpoints enable you to access the Azure Blob Storage endpoint over a secure internal network connection via VPN or ExpressRoute. This allows you to control which network subnets are allowed to access

the endpoint and limit access as necessary. This also allows you to closely monitor the connections to the blob endpoint over your internal firewall and detect any anomalies. It is highly recommended to use private endpoints if your environment and application access requirements allow for it.

- **Limit use of public endpoints** While public endpoints can be secured with encryption in transit and firewall restrictions, it is highly recommended to turn them off unless allowing them is absolutely necessary. Instead, use private endpoints, as they are much more secure. Private endpoints allow you to control access more granularly from your internal networks to the internal storage endpoint.
- **Setup storage firewall restrictions** Unless you completely disable the public endpoint, be sure you set up storage firewall restrictions to allow access over the public endpoint only from administrative or known IP addresses. This will help limit the exposure of that public endpoint and prevent malicious actors from attacking and accessing the storage.
- **Force secure transfers only** While Azure Blob Storage supports connections over both HTTP and HTTPS, it is highly recommended to force secure transfer only, so that all connections are secured. You can configure this setting using the Azure portal, Azure PowerShell, Azure CLI, and REST APIs. If you set up the storage using the Azure portal, this setting is enabled by default. If you use any other methods, you must enable this setting manually.
- **Integrate with Azure Monitor** Azure Monitor can closely monitor storage capacity and performance metrics to provide you with a comprehensive view of the storage IOPS and space utilization. This can help you in planning any changes to address capacity or IOPS issues before they affect your clients. You can build custom dashboards to monitor the metrics that are most important to your organization and share them with all administrators to ensure a consistent view across the monitoring environment. You can also set up alerting to highlight anomalous performance behavior to be able to respond to such events in a more time-effective manner.
- **Ensure regular backups using Azure Backup** Azure Backup has a built-in integration with Azure Blob Storage to provide a seamless backup experience. You can configure backup policies to define how long to store operational backup data. You can configure different backup jobs with different backup policies based on your Azure Blob Storage requirements. Make sure you set up backups in line with your organization's data recovery and retention requirements.

Chapter 2

Azure Files

Overview

Microsoft introduced the Azure Files service in September 2015. It provides support for the Server Message Block (SMB) protocol and a whole host of features to enable organizations to migrate from on-premises file storage hosted on Windows Servers to the Azure Cloud. Over the years, several features have been added to Azure Files, including the following:

- Support for Network File System (NFS) protocol for access using Linux and MacOS clients
- Storage encryption for secure data hosting
- Integration with Azure Backup for seamless backups and restores
- Low latency data access through caching features of Azure File Sync with on-premises file servers using SMB and various other features

Organizations leverage Azure Files to address various use cases, such as the following:

- Common file storage between on-premises and cloud-hosted applications and servers for data exchange and sharing.
- Replacement of on-premises server-based file shares with serverless file shares that provide built-in high availability (HA) and disaster recovery (DR).
- Migration of legacy applications relying on file storage services to the cloud.
- Creation of modern applications that use REST APIs to access Azure Files as storage for application containerization or data access and exchange.
- Replacement of User Profile Disks (UPDs) in Windows Virtual Desktop with FSLogix profile containers hosted on Azure Files.
- Low latency file storage for users through Azure File Sync.

Key features

Some key features and benefits of Azure Files are as follows:

- **Microsoft-managed service** Azure Files is a fully managed service provided by Microsoft. The end user does not manage the back-end hardware infrastructure or any underlying operating system (OS). This significantly reduces the workload of the IT management team in managing the hardware.

- **High-availability and disaster recovery** Azure Files provides built-in high availability (HA) and disaster recovery (DR) features. This relieves the IT department of the overhead involved with building and managing these capabilities to increase the redundancy and reliability of the file storage services.
- **Support for different storage disk types** Azure Files supports the creation of standard or premium file shares, based on your scalability and performance needs. Storage accounts for standard file shares can scale up to 5 petabytes (PB), while storage accounts for premium file shares can scale up to 100 terabytes (TB). Similarly, the maximum input/output operations per second (IOPS) supported by storage accounts for standard file shares is 20,000 IOPS and 100,000 IOPS for premium file shares.
- **Cost-effective storage** Azure Files is extremely cost-effective compared to traditional file shares, especially when you consider overall costs, such as for hardware, networking infrastructure, backup infrastructure, OS licensing, and infrastructure upkeep and management.
- **Scalability** Azure Files supports easy scaling of storage capacity over time. You can provision storage based on your current requirements, and scale it with just a few clicks as your requirements increase. This eliminates the need to procure and provision large amounts of storage capacity in advance in both primary and secondary locations.
- **Support for SMB and NFS protocols** Azure Files supports both SMB and NFS protocols, making it accessible using Windows, Linux, and MacOS clients.
- **Support for Azure portal and Azure Storage Explorer** You can manage Azure Files using the Azure portal, which provides a GUI-based experience. You can also manage Azure Files using Azure Storage Explorer, which enables you to easily build, manage, and upload/download content from the file storage.
- **Support for PowerShell and Azure CLI** Azure Files supports the use of Azure PowerShell and Azure CLI commands to build and manage the shares and to automate activities.
- **Support for application integration using REST APIs** Azure Files supports application integration using file system I/O APIs and existing application code to read and write from the file storage. You can also use Azure Storage REST APIs and Azure Storage Client Libraries for application integrations.
- **Integration with Active Directory Domain Services and Azure Active Directory Domain Services** Azure Files supports using both Active Directory Domain Services (AD DS) and Azure Active Directory Domain Services (AAD DS) for seamless identity authentication. This can help organizations leverage their existing authentication and authorization models to provide access to their users.

- **Data encryption at rest and in transit** Azure Files supports data encryption in transit by default over both SMB and NFS protocols. In addition, Azure Files supports data encryption at rest using either Microsoft-managed or customer-managed encryption keys.
- **Access over private and public networks** You can access Azure Files storage over private networks using Azure private endpoints over a VPN or ExpressRoute. This ensures that all communication between your clients and the storage service is over a private network only. You can also access the file storage over a public network if required.
- **Sync with on-premises SMB file servers for local latency** You can integrate Azure Files with on-premises file servers that support the SMB protocol using the Azure File Sync service. This provides low-latency storage closer to your end clients, while also offering redundancy and cloud-based recoverability in the case of a loss of network or hardware in your on-premises environment.

Key concepts

Now that you have an initial understanding of Azure Files, let's dive deeper into the different deployment models, features, and management concepts to get you ready to deploy your first file storage.

Deployment models

Azure Files can be deployed in one of two ways:

- **On serverless cloud-hosted storage** In this model, you can mount the Azure Files storage using SMB or NFS protocols or directly access the storage using REST APIs or file system I/O APIs. This eliminates the overhead associated with the ongoing maintenance and management of on-premises file servers, including OS patching, hardware replacement, and workload protection. It also simplifies the file storage redundancy options, as you can easily set up geo-redundant storage.
- **Cached in on-premises storage using Azure File Sync** In this model, you synchronize your on-premises file share to Azure Files using Azure File Sync to enhance redundancy and resiliency. This allows you to maintain your on-premises file storage, which is presumably closer to your end users, to support lower latency. It also maintains a redundant copy of the data in the cloud, providing resiliency in case of a disaster in the on-premises environment.

Storage accounts

As discussed in Chapter 1, storage accounts form the backbone of Azure's storage service options. Storage accounts are a pool of storage disks that constitute the top-level object under which different storage account types, such as blobs, files, queues, and tables, can be created.

Two types of storage accounts support file shares, as follows:

- **General purpose v2 storage accounts** This type of account supports the deployment of file shares along with storage options such as blob containers, tables, and queues. General purpose storage accounts use standard HDD disks for back-end storage. They are suitable for high volumes of storage that are not sensitive to latency. General purpose v2 storage accounts support only the SMB protocol for data access.
- **FileStorage storage accounts** These are storage accounts backed up by premium solid-state SSD disks, providing high IOPS. FileStorage storage accounts support both the SMB and NFS protocols.

> ***NOTE*** **You cannot set up any other type of storage—for example, blob, queue, or table storage—inside a FileStorage storage account.**

Depending on your Azure subscription, you might still be able to create general purpose v1 and classic storage accounts. Both also support file storage. However, Microsoft does not recommend using either option to create new Azure Files storage accounts. Most new features of Azure Files are not available in these two storage account types. If you have an existing storage account on either storage type, it is highly recommended to migrate to either of the other two storage options as soon as possible.

Storage accounts walkthrough

The following sections step you through the process of creating an Azure Files storage account using the Azure portal, Azure PowerShell, and the Azure CLI.

> ***IMPORTANT*** **If you are following along, select resources and resource names based on your environment, including a unique file share name for each of your deployments.**

> ***IMPORTANT*** **If you are following along, be sure to delete any unwanted resources after you have completed testing to reduce charges levied by Microsoft.**

> ***PREREQUISITES*** **If you are following along and want to use the Azure AD DS authentication method, you must set up an instance of Azure AD DS and join a Windows 10/11 client to the Azure AD DS service to access the file storage in a seamless manner, as necessary throughout this chapter.**

USING AZURE PORTAL

To create an Azure Files storage account using the Azure portal, follow these steps:

1. Log in to the Azure portal, type **storage** in the search box, and select the **Storage Accounts** option from the list that appears. (See Figure 2-1.)

FIGURE 2-1 Searching for storage services in the Azure portal.

2. On the Storage Account page, click the Create Storage Account button. (See Figure 2-2.)

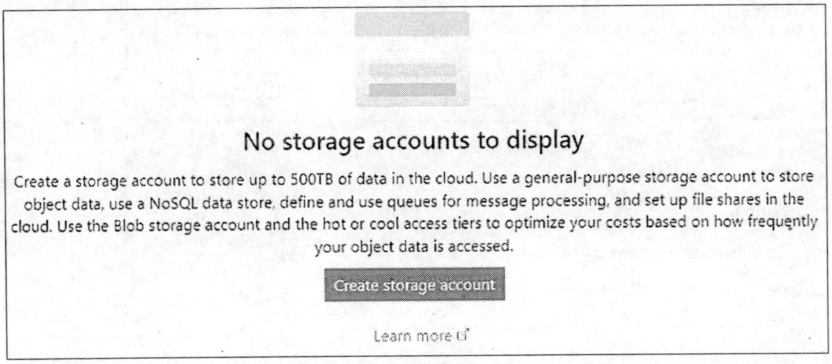

FIGURE 2-2 Creating a storage account.

> ***NOTE*** **If this is not the first storage account you've created using this subscription, you won't see the button shown in Figure 2-2. In that case, click the Create button near the top of the Storage Accounts page.**

3. In the **Basics** tab of the Create a Storage Account wizard (see Figure 2-3), enter the following information and click **Next**:
   - **Subscription** Select the subscription in which you want to create the Azure Files storage account.
   - **Resource Group** Select an existing resource group or create a new one in which to create the Azure Files storage account.

- **Storage Name** Enter a unique name for the storage account.
- **Region** Select the Azure region where you want to host the storage account.
- **Performance** Select a performance type—in this case, choose **Premium**.
- **Premium Account Type** Choose **File Shares**.
- **Redundancy** Select a redundancy type for the file share—in this example, **Locally-Redundant Storage (LRS)**.

> ***NOTE*** **Chapter 1 discussed redundancy types. Redundancy types are also discussed in more detail later in this chapter.**

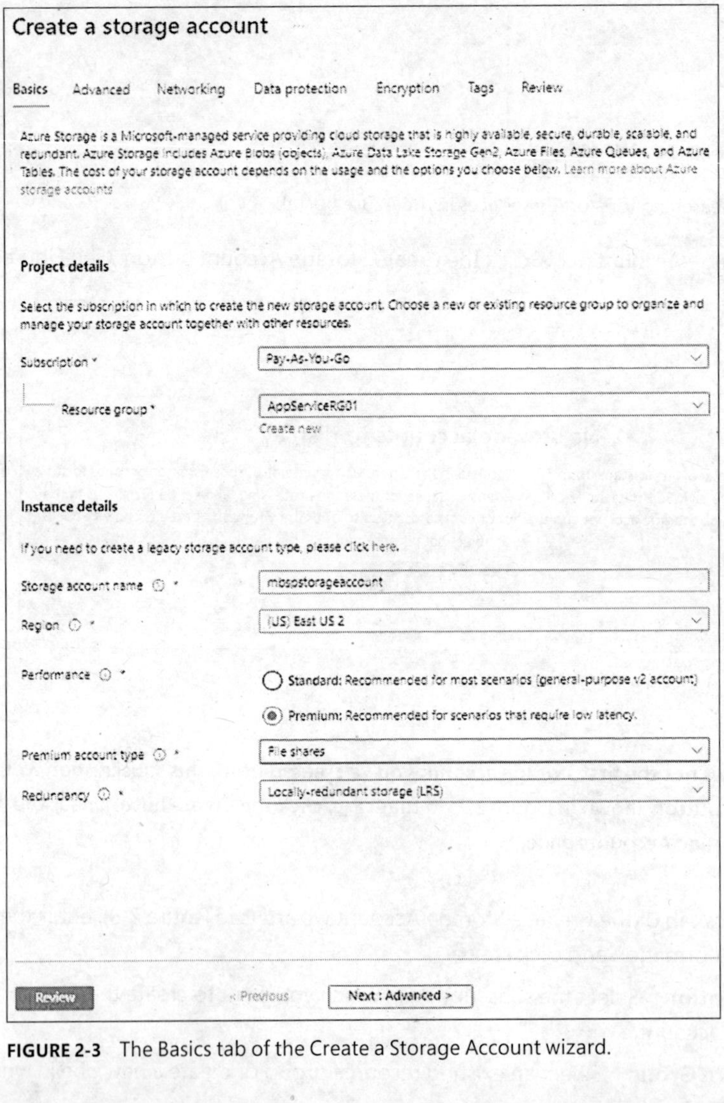

FIGURE 2-3 The Basics tab of the Create a Storage Account wizard.

4. In the **Advanced** tab of the Create a Storage Account wizard (see Figure 2-4), select the **Default to Azure Active Directory Authorization in the Azure Portal** check box but leave all the options set to their default value. Then click **Next**.

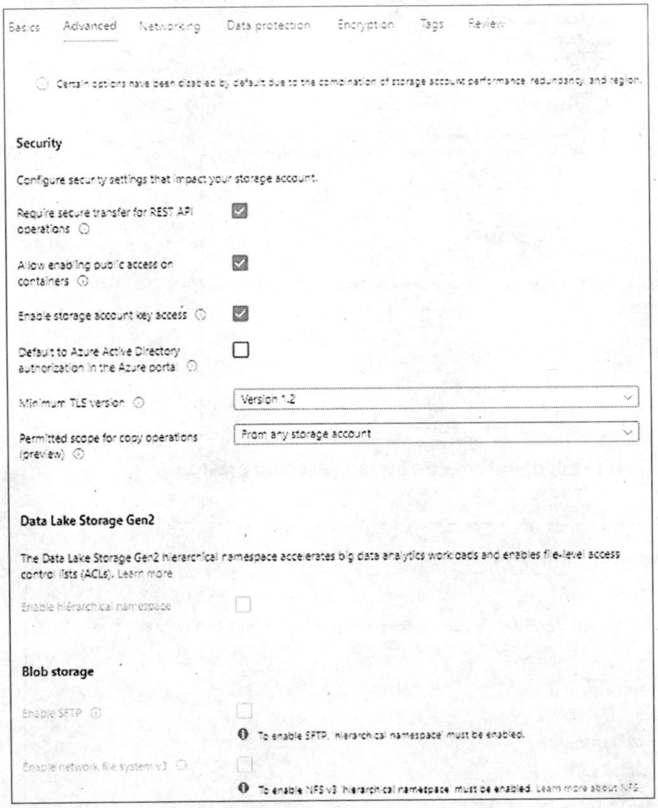

FIGURE 2-4 The Advanced tab of the Create a Storage Account wizard.

5. In the **Networking** tab of the Create a Storage Account wizard (see Figure 2-5), leave the **Network Connectivity** and **Network Routing** options set to their default values (**Enable Public Access from All Networks** and **Microsoft Network Routing**, respectively) and click **Next**.

NOTE We talk more about network routing options later in this chapter.

6. In the **Data Protection** tab of the Create a Storage Account wizard (see Figure 2-6), leave the **Enable Soft Delete for File Shares** check box checked and type **14** in the Days to Retain Deleted File Shares box. Then click **Next**.

NOTE We talk more about using soft delete for file shares later in this chapter.

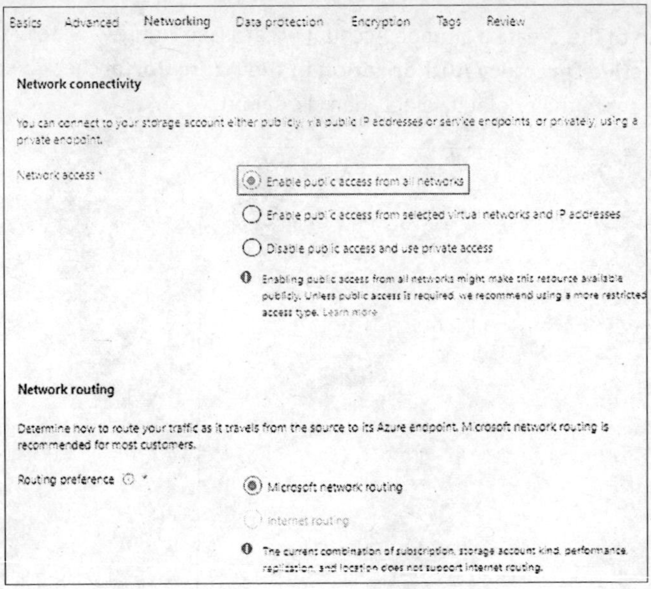

FIGURE 2-5 The Networking tab of the Create a Storage Account wizard.

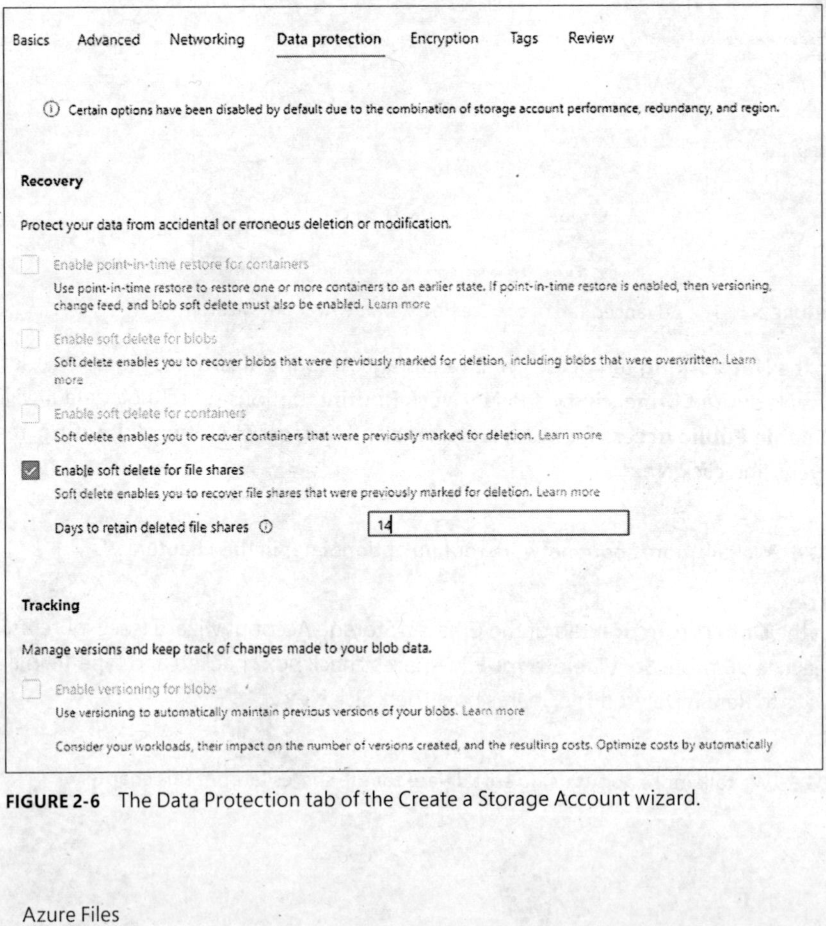

FIGURE 2-6 The Data Protection tab of the Create a Storage Account wizard.

7. In the **Encryption** tab of the Create a Storage Account wizard (see Figure 2-7), select the **Enable Infrastructure Encryption** check box, leave the other options set to their default values, and click **Next**.

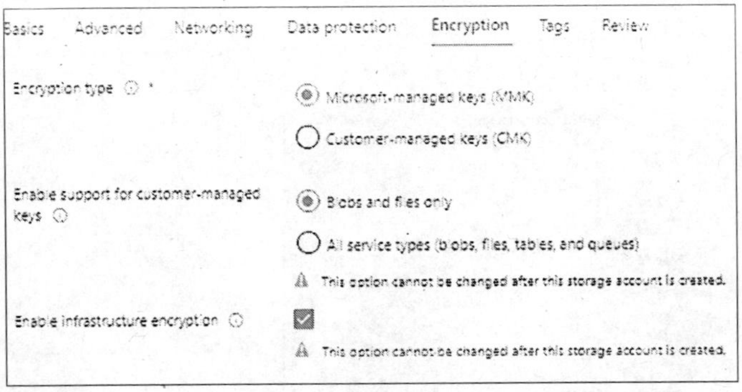

FIGURE 2-7 The Encryption tab of the Create a Storage Account wizard.

8. In the **Tags** tab (see Figure 2-8), enter a name and value for any tags you want to associate with the storage account, and click **Next**.

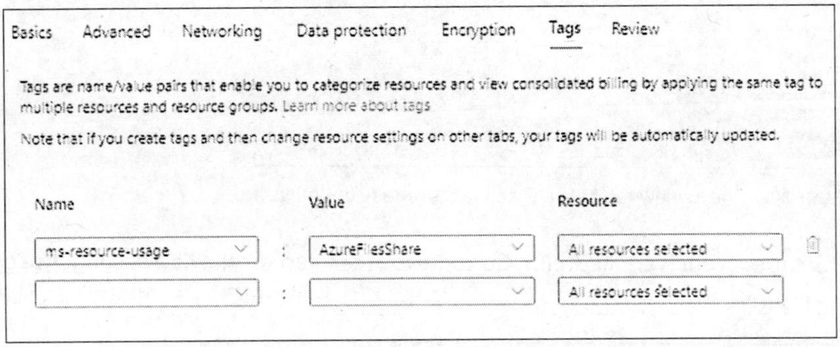

FIGURE 2-8 The Tags tab of the Create a Storage Account wizard.

9. In the **Review + Create** tab of the Create a Storage Account wizard (see Figure 2-9), review your settings, and click **Create** to create the Azure Files storage account.

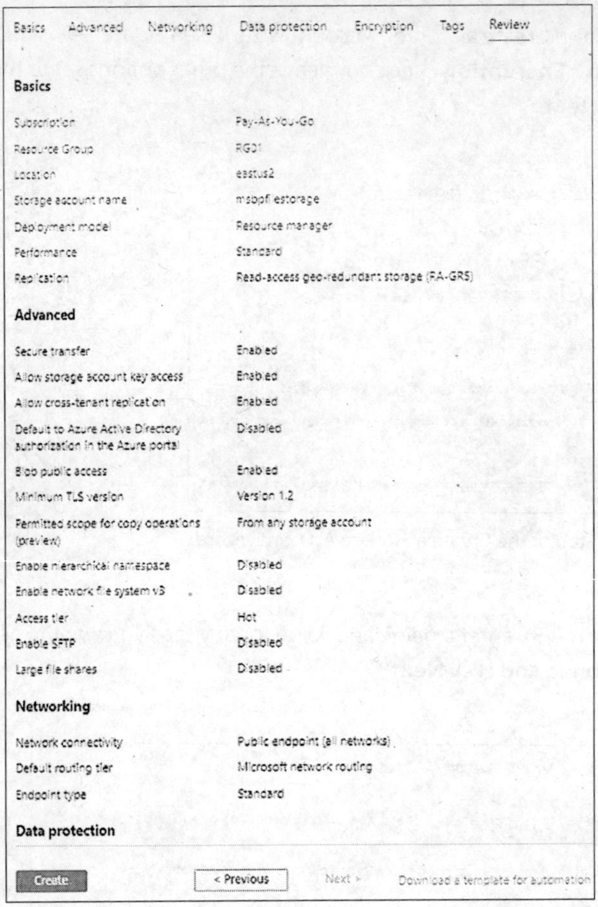

FIGURE 2-9 The Review tab of the Create a Storage Account wizard.

10. After the account is created, click **Go to Resource** to access the new account's page. (See Figure 2-10.)

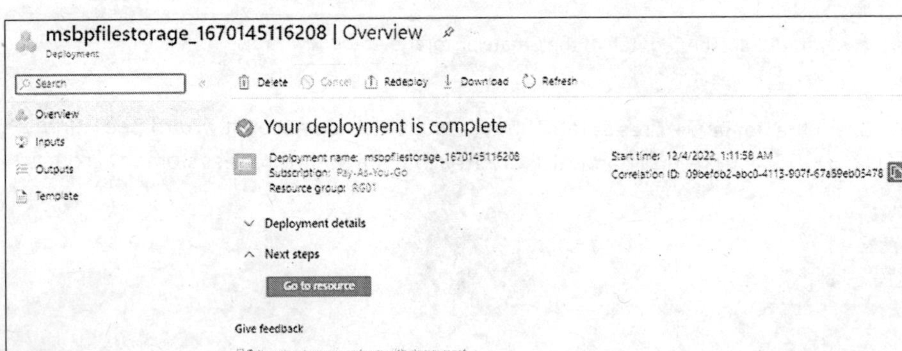

FIGURE 2-10 Storage deployment completion.

USING AZURE POWERSHELL

Use the following Azure PowerShell code to create an Azure Files storage account:

```
#Define required variables
$resourceGroup = "RG01"
$region = "eastus"
$storageaccname = "mbspfilesharestorage02"
$share = "fileshare"
$directory = "directory"
$vnet = "vNET01"
$subnet = "default"
$endpointname = "PrivateEndpoint"
$vaultname = "RecoveryServicesVault01"

#Create Azure File Share storage account
New-AzResourceGroup -Name $resourceGroup -Location $region

$storageAccount = New-AzStorageAccount `
    -ResourceGroupName $resourceGroup `
    -Name $storageAccName `
    -Location $region `
    -Kind FileStorage `
    -AllowBlobPublicAccess $true `
    -SkuName Premium_LRS `
    -MinimumTlsVersion TLS1_2

# Set up Soft Delete Configuration
Update-AzStorageFileServiceProperty `
    -ResourceGroupName $resourcegroup `
    -StorageAccountName $storageaccount `
    -EnableShareDeleteRetentionPolicy $true `
    -ShareRetentionDays 14
```

USING AZURE CLI

Use the following code to create an Azure Files storage account in the Azure CLI:

```
#Define required variables
resourceGroup="RG01"
region="eastus"
storageaccname="mbspfilesharestorage01"
share="fileshare"
directory="directory"
vnet="vNET01"
subnet="default"
endpointname="PrivateEndpoint"
```

```
vaultname="RecoveryServicesVault01"

#Create Azure File Share storage account
az group create \
    --name $resourceGroup \
    --location $region
az storage account create \
    --resource-group $resourceGroup \
    --name $storageaccname \
    --location $region
    --kind FileStorage \
    --sku Premium_LRS \
    --output none \
    --min-tls-version TLS1_2 \
    --allow-blob-public-access true

# Set up Soft Delete Configuration
az storage account file-service-properties update \
    --resource-group $resourceGroup \
    --account-name $storageaccname \
    --enable-delete-retention true \
    --delete-retention-days 14
```

File shares

A file share is a shared location that can be used to store data for collaboration purposes or by application or services to perform read and write operations via the SMB or NFS protocols. As mentioned, Azure Files supports the creation of standard or premium file shares, based on your scalability and performance needs.

You can create an unlimited number of file shares in a storage account as long as the overall storage account size limits are maintained. While file shares on standard GPv2 storage accounts do not have a minimum size requirement, file shares hosted on premium storage have a minimum size of 100 GB per share.

The maximum size of a single file share supported on both standard GPv2 and premium accounts is 100 TiB. However, the standard on GPv2 is 5 TiB. Support for 100 TB on GPv2 is available only if you enable the large file share feature.

File shares walkthrough

The following sections step you through the process of creating a file share, uploading data to that file share, connecting to the file share, and changing the size and performance characteristics of file share using the Azure portal, Azure PowerShell, and the Azure CLI.

IMPORTANT If you are following along, select resources and resource names based on your environment, including a unique file share name for each of your deployments.

IMPORTANT If you are following along, be sure to delete any unwanted resources after you have completed testing to reduce charges levied by Microsoft.

USING AZURE PORTAL

To create a file share, create a directory within that file share, upload data to that file share, connect to the file share, and change the size and performance characteristics of the file share using the Azure portal, follow these steps:

1. In the left pane of the Azure Files storage account page, under **Data Storage**, click **File Shares**.
2. On the File Shares page, click **File Share**. (See Figure 2-11.)

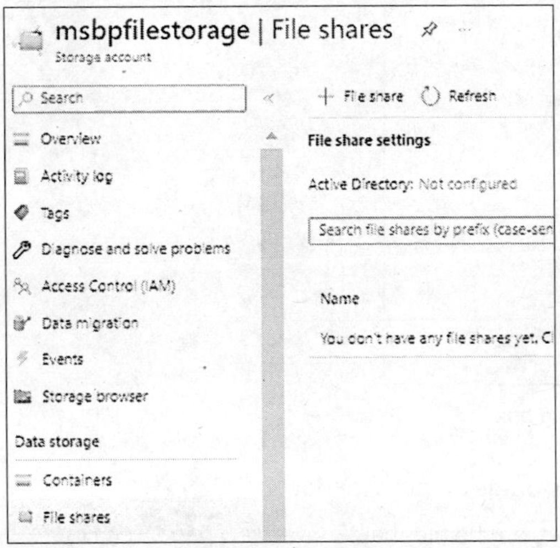

FIGURE 2-11 Creating a file share.

3. In the New File Share dialog box (see Figure 2-12), enter the following information and click **Create**:
   - **Name** Enter a name for the file share that is unique within this storage account. The share name must contain at least three characters.
   - **Provisioned Capacity** Select the file share's starting capacity.
   - **Protocol** In this example, select the SMB option button.

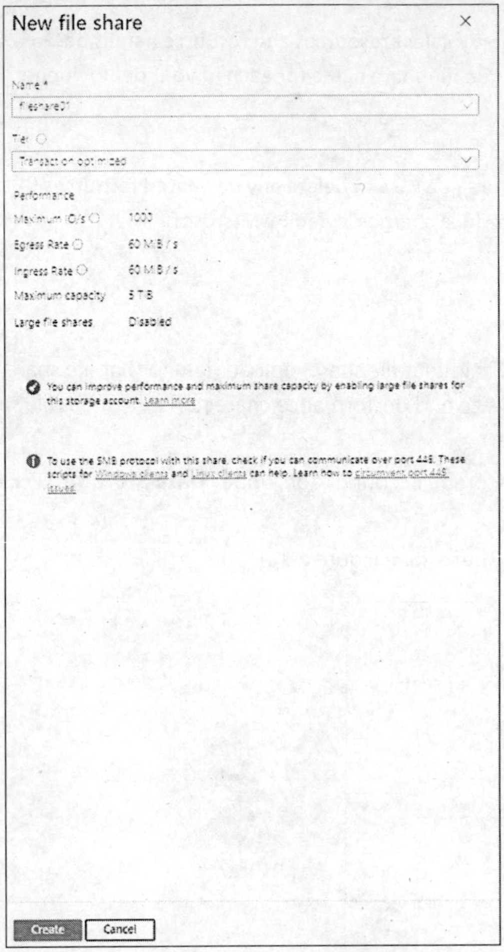

FIGURE 2-12 The New File Share dialog box.

The new file share appears in the storage account window.

4. Click the file share to select it. Then, on the file share's Overview page (see Figure 2-13), click **Add Directory**.

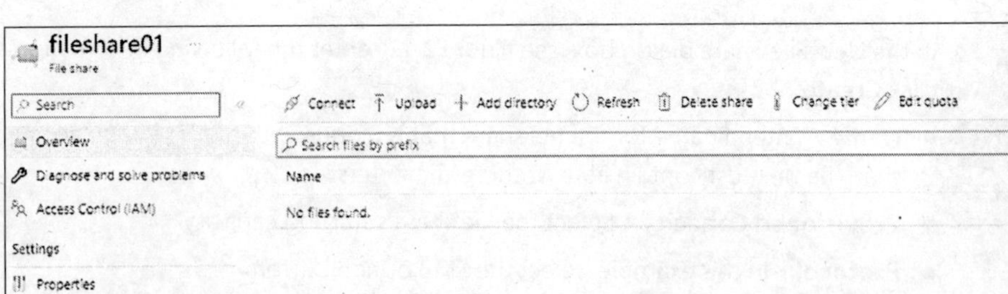

FIGURE 2-13 Creating a new directory.

5. In the New Directory dialog box (see Figure 2-14), enter a name that is unique within this file share, and click **OK**.

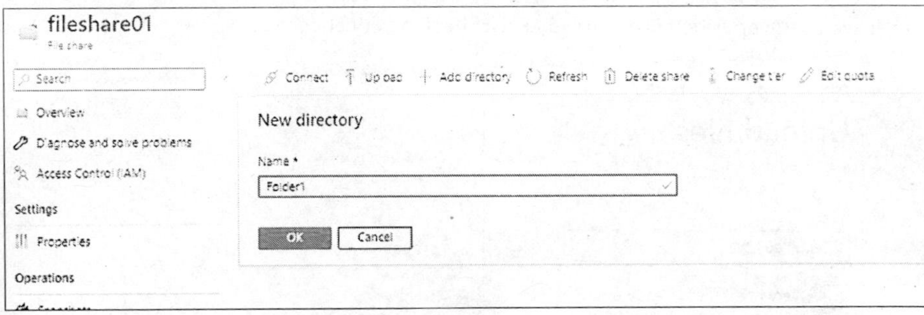

FIGURE 2-14 Enter a unique name for the new directory.

The directory appears on the file share's Overview page. (See Figure 2-15.)

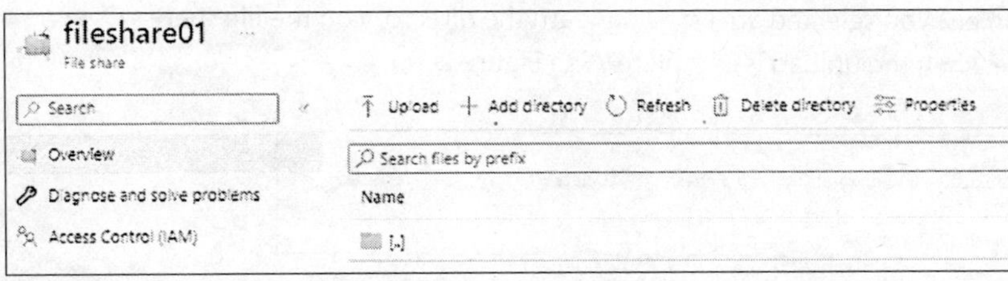

FIGURE 2-15 The new directory appears.

6. On the file share's Overview page (refer to Figure 2-13), click **Add Directory** to create a new directory in the file share.
7. Click **Upload**.

8. In the Upload Files dialog box (see Figure 2-16), click the **Browse** button to locate and select the file(s) you want to upload to the new directory. Then click **Upload**.

NOTE Because this is the first time you're uploading files to this file share, you can leave the Overwrite If Files Already Exist check box unchecked.

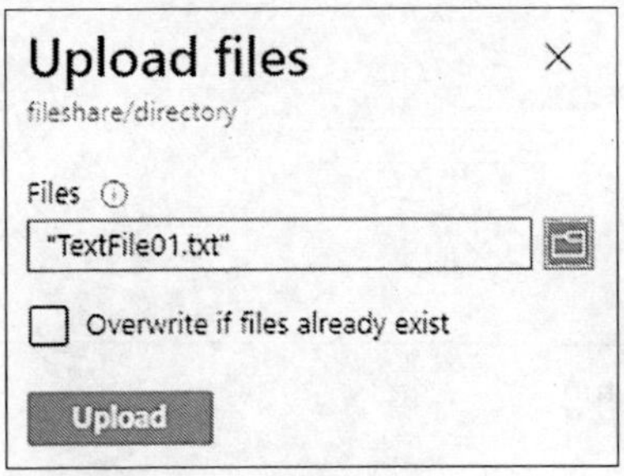

FIGURE 2-16 Uploading files to file share directory.

9. The file(s) you selected are listed beneath the directory on the file share's Overview page when the upload is complete. (See Figure 2-17.)

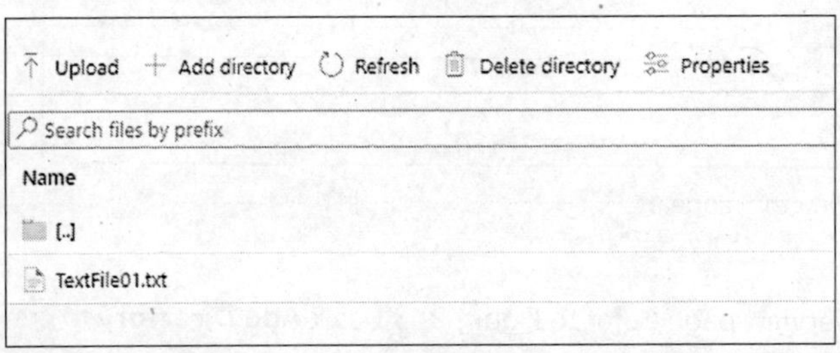

FIGURE 2-17 Upload completed.

Now you're ready to access the file share using a Windows, Linux, or MacOS client. In this example, we'll set up a Windows client.

10. On the file share's Overview page, click **Connect**.
11. In the Connect dialog box (see Figure 2-18), perform the following actions. Then click **Done**.
    - **Drive Letter** Select a drive letter to use for the file share mapping.
    - **Authentication Method** For this example, select the **Storage Account Key** option button, because we haven't yet configured Active Directory.
    - **Show Script** Click this button to reveal the script for the mapping. Then copy the script shown. You'll use this script to map the file share drive to a Windows client.
12. To map the drive to a Windows client, log into the client, open its PowerShell window, paste the script you just copied, and run the script. (See Figure 2-19.)

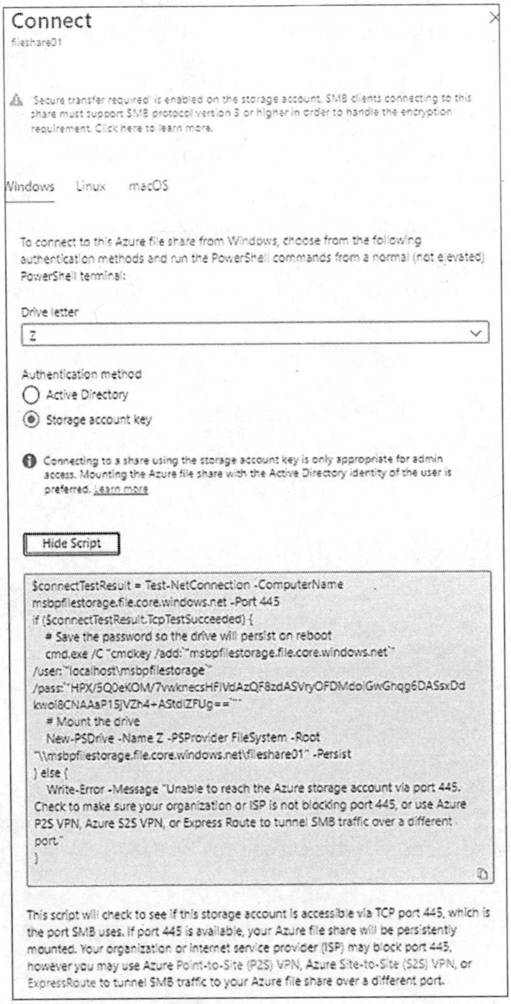

FIGURE 2-18 Connecting to the file share.

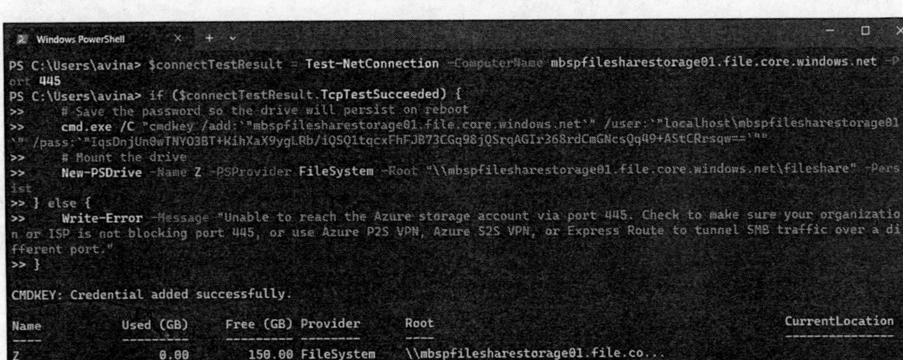

FIGURE 2-19 Running a script to map the file share on a Windows client.

13. On the Windows client, use Windows Explorer to browse to the file share. You should be able to access it as you would any other storage, and to add, delete, and manage files and directories within the share.

    Next, you'll change the size and performance of the file share.

14. On the file share's Overview page (refer to Figure 2-13), click **Change Size and Performance**.
15. In the Size and Performance dialog box (see Figure 2-20), enter a new value in the **Provisioned Capacity** box and click **Save**.

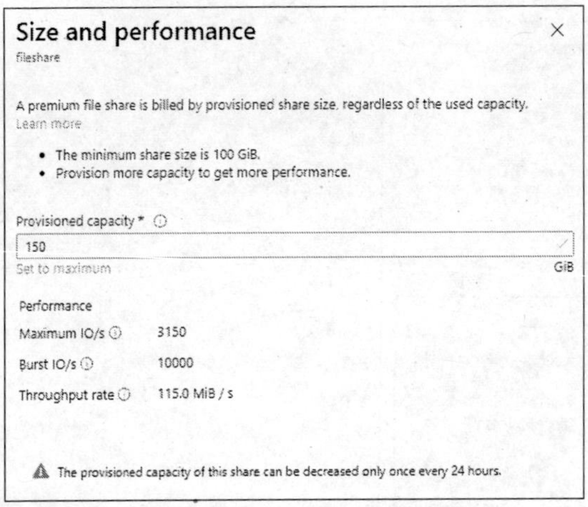

FIGURE 2-20 Changing the file share size.

16. The file share is resized within a few seconds—in this case, from 100 GB to 150 GB. (See Figure 2-21.)

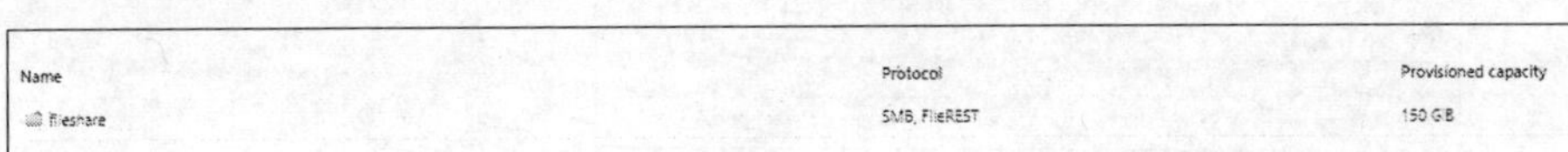

FIGURE 2-21 The file share size has changed.

> ***NOTE*** **You can increase the storage size many times, but you can reduce the size only once every 24 hours.**

USING AZURE POWERSHELL

Use the following Azure PowerShell code to create a file share, create a directory within that file share, upload data to that file share, connect to the file share, and change the size and performance characteristics of the file share:

```
#Define required variables
$resourceGroup = "RG01"
```

```
$region = "eastus"
$storageaccname = "mbspfilesharestorage02"
$share = "fileshare"
$directory = "directory"
$vnet = "vNET01"
$subnet = "default"
$endpointname = "PrivateEndpoint"


#Create file share
New-AzRmStorageShare `
    -StorageAccount $storageAccount `
    -Name $share `
    -EnabledProtocol SMB `
    -QuotaGiB 100

New-AzStorageDirectory `
   -Context $storageAccount.Context `
   -ShareName $share `
   -Path $directory

#Upload data to File Share
cd "~/CloudDrive/"
Get-Date | Out-File -FilePath "TextFile01.txt" -Force

Set-AzStorageFileContent `
   -Context $storageAccount.Context `
   -ShareName $share `
   -Source "TextFile01.txt" `
   -Path "Directory\TextFile01.txt"

#Verify data in File Share
Get-AzStorageFile `
    -Context $storageAccount.Context `
    -ShareName $share `
    -Path "Directory\" | Get-AzStorageFile

# Download file from File Share
Get-AzStorageFileContent `
    -Context $storageAccount.Context `
    -ShareName $share `
    -Path "Directory\TextFile01.txt" `
    -Destination "TextFile01.txt" `
    -Force
#Enable SMB Multichannel
```

```
Update-AzStorageFileServiceProperty `
-ResourceGroupName $resourceGroup `
-AccountName $storageAccName `
-EnableSmbMultichannel $true

# Changing Size and Performance
Update-AzRmStorageShare `
    -ResourceGroupName $resourceGroup `
    -StorageAccountName $storageAccount `
    -Name $share `
    -QuotaGiB 150
```

USING AZURE CLI

Use the following code to create a file share, create a directory within that file share, upload data to that file share, connect to the file share, and change the size and performance characteristics of the file share in the Azure CLI:

```
#Define required variables
resourceGroup="RG01"
region="eastus"
storageaccname="mbspfilesharestorage01"
share="fileshare"
directory="directory"
vnet="vNET01"
subnet="default"
endpointname="PrivateEndpoint"
vaultname="RecoveryServicesVault01"


#Create file share
az storage share-rm create \
    --resource-group $resourceGroup \
    --storage-account $storageaccname \
    --name $share \
    --quota 100 \
    --enabled-protocols SMB \
    --output none

az storage directory create \
                        --name $directory \
                        --share-name $share \
                        --account-name $storageaccname

#Upload data to File Share
cd ~/clouddrive/
```

```
date > TextFile01.txt

az storage file upload \
    --account-name $storageaccname \
    --share-name $share \
    --source "TextFile01.txt" \
    --path $directory/TextFile01.txt

#Verify data in File Share
az storage file list \
    --account-name $storageaccname \
    --share-name $share \
    --path "$directory" \
    --output table

# Download file from File Share
az storage file download \
    --account-name $storageaccname \
    --share-name $share \
    --path "$directory/TextFile01.txt" \
    --dest "./TextFile01.txt" \
    --output none

# Changing Size and Performance
az storage share-rm update \
    --resource-group $resourceGroup \
    --storage-account $storageaccname \
    --name $share \
    --quota 150
```

Storage tiers for file shares

To accommodate the needs of different organizations, such as workload types, performance requirements, and storage price, Microsoft offers four tiers for the Azure Files service:

- Premium
- Transaction-optimized
- Hot
- Cool

Each of these offers varying levels of performance, costs, and billing models. Let's examine each in more detail to help you in your storage tier selection:

Premium file shares

Premium file shares provide the highest level of performance and lowest latency among all the storage tiers offered by the Azure Files service. They use Solid-State Drives (SSDs) in the back end and are great for IO-intensive workloads such as databases and high-traffic web services. Premium file shares support both SMB and NFS protocols, making them accessible over Windows, Mac, and UNIX operating systems to meet varying client bases of an organization.

Premium file shares are deployed on the FileStorage account type and work on the provisioned billing model, which means that the storage is billed based on the amount of storage and required IOPS defined at the time of provisioning the storage. You can scale up the provisioned storage at any time to get more capacity or IOPS, and the changes would take effect within a few minutes. You can also scale down the storage once every 24 hours to reduce the capacity or the IOPS provisioned for the storage. Although you can scale down below your current storage usage, you will still be billed based on your actual usage in this scenario while keeping your storage IOPS at the threshold specified for the storage capacity.

Transaction-optimized file shares

Transaction-optimized file shares are ideal for workloads that perform a large volume of transactions but do not require the low latency offered by Premium file shares. They are a good mix of performance and price, making them ideal for organizations that would like a better performance than those offered by Hot file shares while not incurring the higher costs of Premium file shares. Transaction-optimized file shares are hosted on standard storage hardware backed by hard-disk drives (HDDs).

Transaction-optimized file shares are deployed in a General Purpose v2 (GPv2) storage account type and charged in a pay-as-you-go model. They are optimized to charge the lowest transaction prices but have higher data at-rest storage prices when compared to Hot and Cool file shares.

Hot file shares

Like Transaction-optimized file shares, Hot file shares use standard storage hardware backed by hard-disk drives (HDDs) in the back end, making them ideal for general-purpose file share scenarios such as a replacement for an on-premises file server, where the transaction volume is not high.

Hot file shares are deployed in a General Purpose v2 (GPv2) storage account type and charged in a pay-as-you-go model. They have lower data at-rest prices but higher transaction prices when compared to Transaction-optimized file shares.

Cool file shares

Cool file shares are the most cost-efficient of all four storage tiers when comparing data at-rest prices. In comparison, they are the highest of all four storage tiers when comparing transaction fees. They are ideal for online archiving or backup scenarios where data is stored for a long period of time with minimal data access transactions.

Cool file shares are also deployed in a General Purpose v2 (GPv2) storage account type and charged in a pay-as-you-go model.

NOTE Standard file shares, used by Transaction-optimized, Hot, and Cool storage tiers, support enabling large file shares with 100 TiB capacity. However, this has certain limitations, such as a lack of support for GRS, ZGRS, and RA-GRS redundancy types.

Networking considerations

When designing and deploying an Azure Files file share service, you must take multiple networking considerations into account. These range from selecting the network protocol, the type of access endpoint, networking routing options, and whether to use encryption-in-transit. Each of these considerations can affect the security, latency, and performance of the file share service.

Network protocols

Azure Files supports two file system protocols for mounting file shares: Server Message Block (SMB) and Network File System (NFS). Both protocols are industry-standard file system protocols used in different operating environments, enabling organizations to choose the protocol that meets their needs. Azure Files also provides a REST API (called FileREST API) to access data hosted in Azure file shares.

NOTE **Although you can use the same storage account to host SMB and NFS file shares, a single file share can only support the SMB or NFS protocol at any given time.**

Server Message Block (SMB)

SMB, also known as Common Internet File System (CIFS) protocol, is an industry-standard network file sharing protocol used extensively in Microsoft Windows server and client operating systems. It is supported by MacOS and various Linux distributions as well.

NOTE **Check the latest information from Microsoft in their Azure Files guidance online to ensure you are up-to-date on the supported operating systems.**

SMB file shares support most Azure Files features, including the following:

- Accessibility over the public internet using SMB 3.*x*
- Support for on-premises caching using Azure File Sync
- User-based identity authorization using AD domain join and access control lists (ACLs)
- Integrated backups with Azure Backup

- Support for Azure private endpoints
- Protection from accidental deletion using the soft-delete feature
- Support for SMB Multichannel on premium file shares to increase network throughput
- Support for integrated snapshots using Volume Shadow Copy Service (VSS)

Support for these features makes SMB file shares ideal for replacing or complementing on-premises file servers and for serving as back-end storage for Windows-based applications and databases. The following sections dive further into each of these features.

Network File System (NFS)

NFS is an industry-standard network distributed file system protocol used predominantly in Unix-based operating systems. While it is also supported by Microsoft Windows–based operating systems and MacOS, there are feature limitations when compared to SMB-based file shares.

NFS file shares are characterized as follows:

- Supported only on premium file shares that use solid-state drives (SSDs)
- Not supported for use by Windows clients
- Used primarily for UNIX clients
- Fully POSIX-compliant file system
- Supports both hard links and symbolic links
- Does not support Kerberos authentication (AD domain join authentication scenarios require Kerberos authentication support)
- Does not support encryption-in-transit, requiring the use of private endpoints for access over internal networks or restricted public endpoints
- Does not support delegation or callbacks

FileREST API

Azure Files also provides a REST API to access data hosted in Azure file shares, called FireREST. The FireREST API works over HTTPS endpoints, ensuring all communication is secure. It is ideal for the development of new applications or for existing application redevelopment projects that leverage new APIs instead of the native file system APIs used by the SMB and NFS protocols. The main way to use this API is to use the Azure SDKs to write code in any popular programming language, such as Python, Java, C#, JavaScript, or Go.

The primary benefits of using the FileREST API include the following:

- It supports all Azure Files features.
- It is used by the Azure portal, Azure PowerShell, and the Azure CLI.
- It provides more efficient data transfer between Azure Files storage than the SMB and NFS protocols.

Networking endpoints

Azure Files supports access over SMB or NFS to the file share service. You can access the storage over either the public internet or a private connection such as Azure ExpressRoute or VPN. Depending on your organization's security and access requirements, your approach might involve the use of one or both methods.

Public endpoints

By default, Azure Files file shares are accessible over the internet by way of a public endpoint using the SMB protocol. This makes it convenient to access the storage if you have an active internet connection. The public endpoint is in the format https://<storage-account-name>.file.core.windows.net.

However, many internet service providers (ISPs) and most organizations block SMB port 445 over the internet. So, to allow access, you will have to either contact your ISP to unblock the port or unblock it on your organization's firewalls. This is the easiest method for accessing the storage. However, some organizations consider this to be insecure because the storage is accessible over a public endpoint. In such scenarios, organizations can use private endpoints, discussed next.

Private endpoints

In brief, private endpoints provide the ability to assign a private or internal IP to the Azure Files share and make it accessible over an Azure ExpressRoute, Azure peering, or Azure VPN connection. The private endpoint is in the format https://<privateendpoint-name>.privatelink.file.core.windows.net.

> **NOTE** To use a private endpoint, you must set up your internal DNS to resolve the DNS name of the storage account using the private IP address assigned to the file share.

> **NOTE** Another book in this series, ***Microsoft Azure Networking: The Definitive Guide,*** devotes an entire chapter (Chapter 9) to covering private endpoints in detail.

Private endpoints walkthrough

The following sections step you through the process of creating a private endpoint using the Azure portal, Azure PowerShell, and the Azure CLI.

> **IMPORTANT** If you are following along, select resources and resource names based on your environment, including unique resource names for each of your deployments.

IMPORTANT If you are following along, be sure to delete any unwanted resources after you have completed testing to reduce charges levied by Microsoft.

USING AZURE PORTAL

To create a private endpoint using the Azure portal, follow these steps:

1. In the left pane of the Azure Files storage account page, under **Security + Networking**, click **Networking**.
2. In the **Firewalls and Virtual Networks** tab on the Networking page (see Figure 2-22), under **Public Network Access**, select the **Disabled** option button. Then click **Save**.

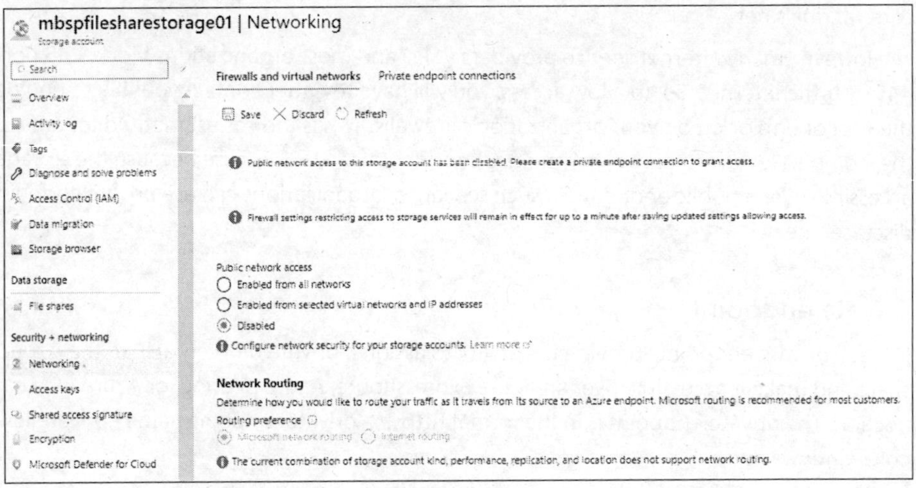

FIGURE 2-22 Disabling public network access.

3. Click the **Private Endpoint Connections** tab. Then click **Private Endpoint** near the top of the page. (See Figure 2-23.)
4. In the **Basics** tab of the Create a Private Endpoint wizard (see Figure 2-24), enter the following information and click **Next**:
   - **Subscription** Select the subscription in which you want to create the private endpoint.
   - **Resource group** Select an existing resource group or create a new one in which to create the private endpoint.
   - **Name** Enter a unique name for the private endpoint.
   - **Network Interface Name** Enter a unique name for the private endpoint network interface.
   - **Region** Select the Azure region where you want to host the private endpoint. This should be the same region as the file share.

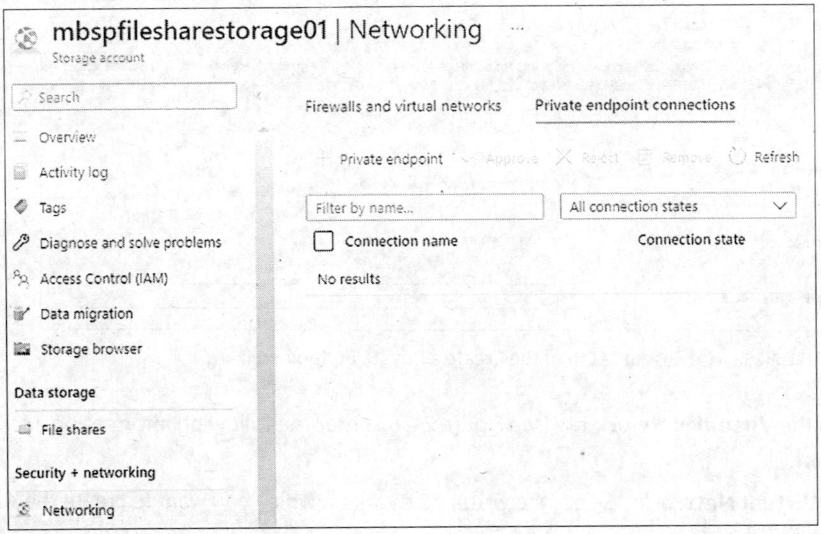

FIGURE 2-23 Setting up a private endpoint.

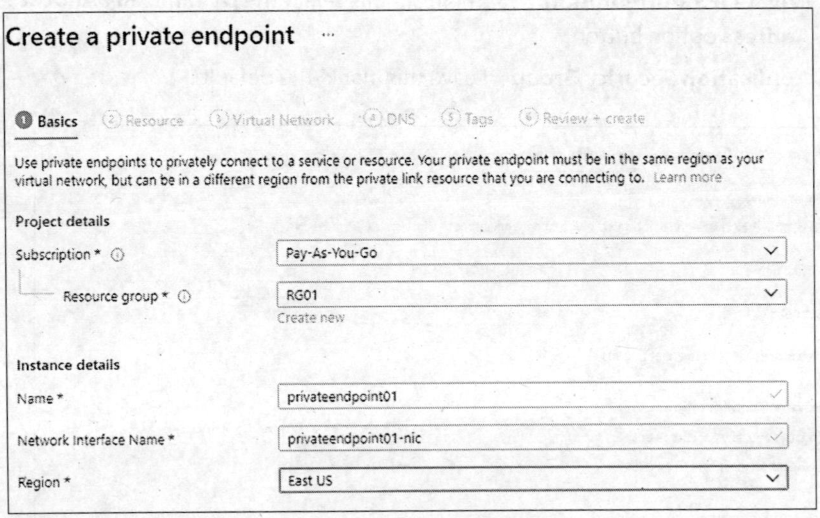

FIGURE 2-24 The Basics tab of the Create a Private Endpoint wizard.

5. On the **Resource** tab (see Figure 2-25), in the **Target Sub-Resource** box, select the storage account type—in this case, **File**. Then click **Next**.

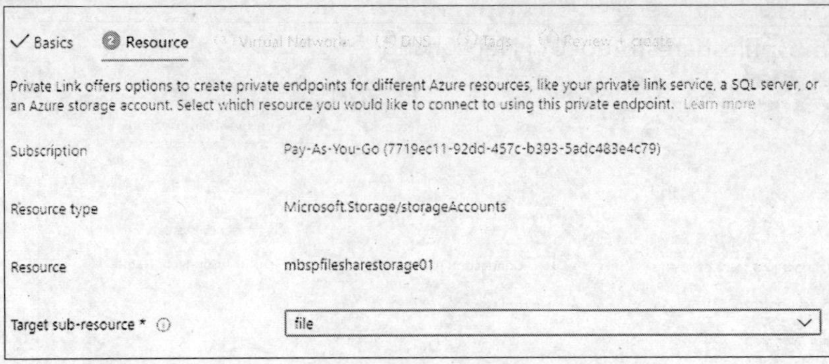

FIGURE 2-25 The Resource tab of the Create a Private Endpoint wizard.

6. On the **Virtual Network** tab (see Figure 2-26), enter the following information and click **Next**:
   - **Virtual Network** Select the virtual network on which you want to create the private endpoint.
   - **Subnet** Select the subnet on which you want to create the private endpoint.
   - **Private IP Configuration** For this example, select the **Dynamically Allocate IP Address** option button.
   - **Application Security Group** Leave this blank (the default).

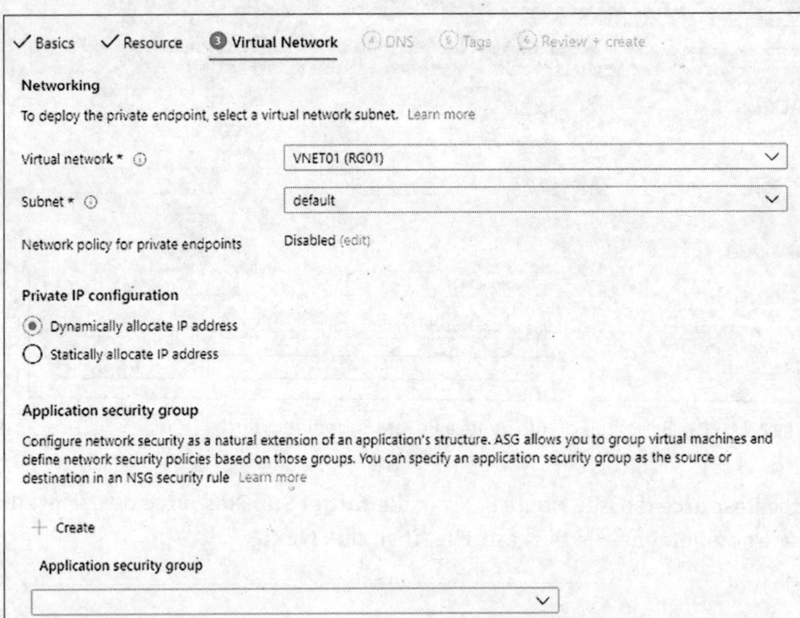

FIGURE 2-26 The Virtual Network tab of the Create a Private Endpoint wizard.

7. On the **DNS** tab (see Figure 2-27), enter the following information and click **Next**:
   - **Integrate with Private DNS Zone** Select the **Yes** option button.
   - **Subscription** Select the subscription to use for the private DNS zone.
   - **Resource Group** Select the resource group to use to create the private DNS zone.

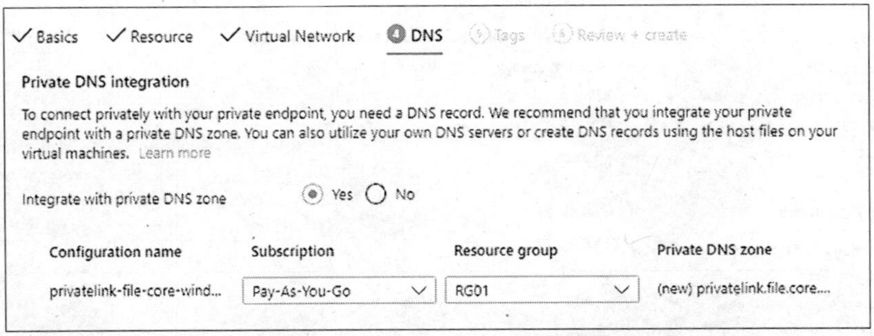

FIGURE 2-27 The DNS tab of the Create a Private Endpoint wizard.

8. In the **Tags** tab (see Figure 2-28), add any tags you want to associate with the private endpoint, and click **Next**.

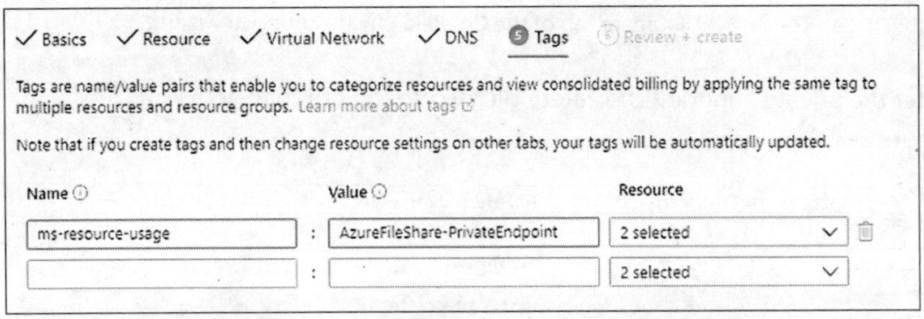

FIGURE 2-28 The Tags tab of the Create a Private Endpoint wizard.

9. In the **Review + Create** tab (see Figure 2-29), review your settings. Then click **Create** to create the private endpoint.

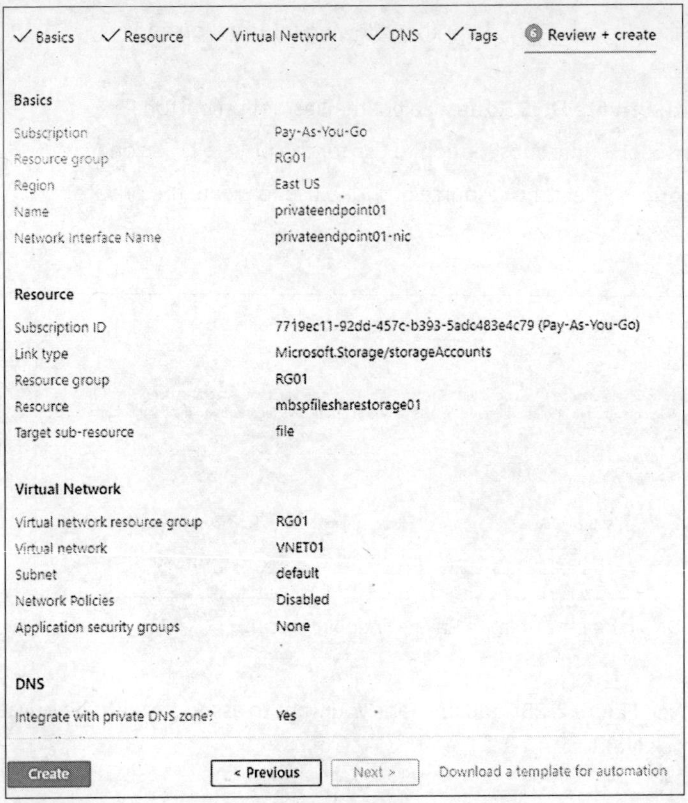

FIGURE 2-29 The Review + Create tab of the Create a Private Endpoint wizard.

10. After the private endpoint is created, click **Go to Resource** to access it. (See Figure 2-30.)

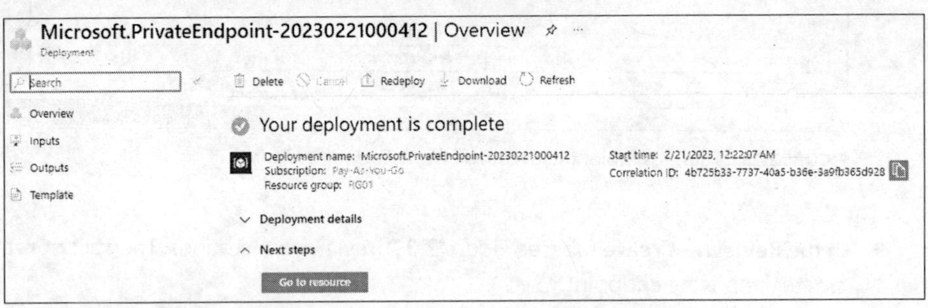

FIGURE 2-30 Create a private endpoint wizard: Completion.

USING AZURE POWERSHELL

Use the following Azure PowerShell code to create a private endpoint:

```
#Define required variables
$resourceGroup = "RG01"
```

```
$region = "eastus"
$storageaccname = "mbspfilesharestorage02"
$share = "fileshare"
$directory = "directory"
$vnet = "vNET01"
$subnet = "default"
$endpointname = "PrivateEndpoint"


#Block Public access
Set-AzStorageAccount -ResourceGroupName $resourceGroup -Name $storageAccount -PublicNet-
workAccess Disabled

# Create a private link service connection to the storage account.
$privateEndpointConnection = New-AzPrivateLinkServiceConnection `
        -Name "$storageAccount-Connection" `
        -PrivateLinkServiceId $storageAccount.Id `
        -GroupId "file" `
        -ErrorAction Stop

#Configure the private endpoint
$privateEndpoint = New-AzPrivateEndpoint -Name $endpointname `
-ResourceGroupName $resourcegroup `
-Location $region `
-Subnet $subnet `
-PrivateLinkServiceConnection $privateEndpointConnection
```

USING AZURE CLI

Use the following code to create a private endpoint in the Azure CLI:

```
#Define required variables
resourceGroup="RG01"
region="eastus"
storageaccname="mbspfilesharestorage01"
share="fileshare"
directory="directory"
vnet="vNET01"
subnet="default"
endpointname="PrivateEndpoint"
vaultname="RecoveryServicesVault01"


#Block Public access
az storage account update \
    --resource-group $resourceGroup \
```

```
    --name $storageaccname \
    --bypass "AzureServices" \
    --default-action "Deny" \
    --public-network-access Disabled \
    --output none

# Create a private link service connection to the storage account
storageAccount=$(az storage account show \
        --resource-group $resourceGroup \
        --name $storageaccname \
        --query "id" | \
    tr -d '"')

privateEndpoint=$(az network private-endpoint create \
        --resource-group $resourceGroup \
        --name "$storageaccname-PrivateEndpoint" \
        --location $region \
        --vnet-name $vnet \
        --subnet $subnet \
        --private-connection-resource-id $storageAccount \
        --group-id "file" \
        --connection-name "$storageaccname-Connection" \
        --query "id" | \
    tr -d '"')
```

Network routing

You must specify which routing method the file share should use. Azure provides two options:

- **Microsoft routing** With Microsoft routing, traffic is routed from the end client to the closest Microsoft edge point of presence (POP), at which point it traverses the Microsoft global fiber backbone to the Azure file share service endpoint. (See Figure 2-31.) This generally results in lower latency and better network performance, and is the default option for most Azure services. This routing type also supports all methods of authentication (covered later in this chapter in the section "Identity and access considerations").
- **Internet routing** With internet routing, most traffic is routed from the end client over the public internet until it reaches the Microsoft POP that is closest to your file share service. (See Figure 2-32.) This can result in higher latency and performance issues, depending on your ISP. Internet routing only supports the use of the Azure storage account key for storage access. AD domain join options are not supported. (You will learn more about these later in this chapter in the section, "Identity and access considerations.")

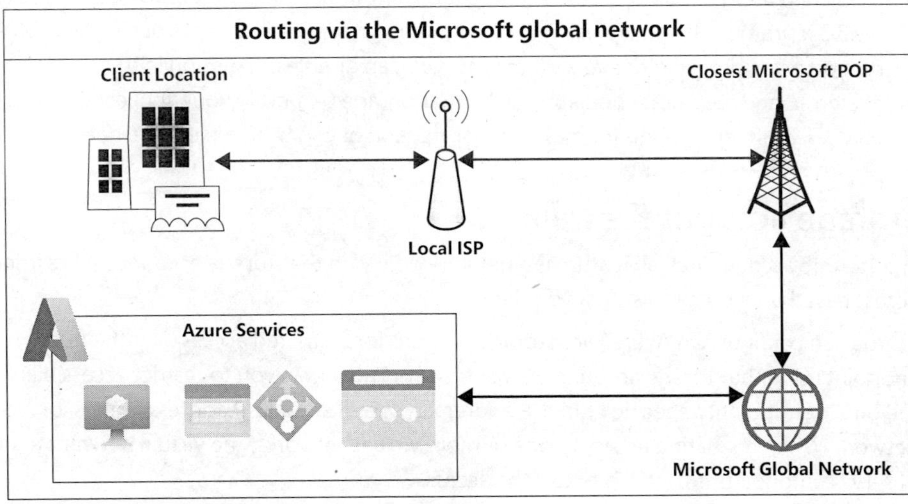

FIGURE 2-31 Routing via the Microsoft global network.

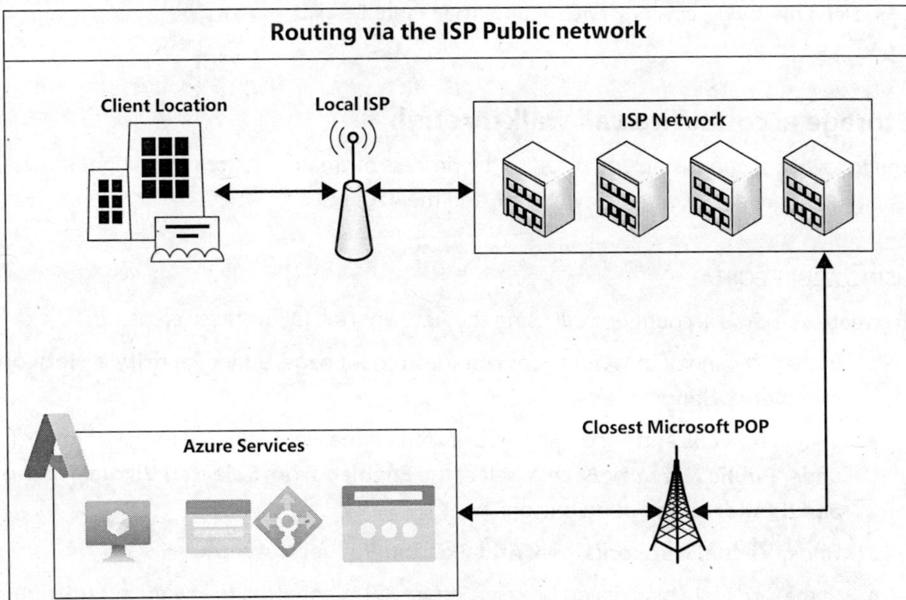

FIGURE 2-32 Routing via internet routing.

Encryption in transit

Encryption in transit refers to the encryption of data while it traverses a network between the Azure file share and the customer endpoint to prevent an attacker from intercepting and reading this data. By default, all Azure storage account types encrypt data in transit if you access them using the SMB protocol or the FileREST API. However, NFS file shares do not support the use of this feature.

Even when using the SMB protocol, encryption in transit is supported only by clients using the SMB 3.*x* protocol. If you are using SMB 3.*x*, but your application does not support SMB encryption or is using an older version of SMB, you can disable encryption in transit. However, the preferred and recommended approach is to upgrade or modify your application to support SMB 3.*x* with encryption for maximum protection of your Azure file share data.

Storage account firewall

The storage account firewall feature is a network policy on the storage account that restricts access based on an access list that you define.

You can configure an Azure Files storage account for restricted access over the public endpoint using the storage account firewall feature. This allows you to restrict accessibility to the public endpoint to specific public IP addresses, specific public IP address ranges, or a virtual network. When restricting access to one or more virtual networks, the virtual network feature of service endpoints is used to control the access.

> ***NOTE*** Chapter 1 of another book in this series, *Microsoft Azure Networking: The Definitive Guide*, covers service endpoints in more detail.

Storage account firewall walkthrough

The following sections step you through the process of creating a storage account firewall using the Azure portal, Azure PowerShell, and the Azure CLI.

USING AZURE PORTAL

To create a storage account firewall using the Azure portal, follow these steps:

1. In the left pane of the Azure Files storage account page, under **Security + Networking**, click **Networking**.
2. In the **Firewalls and Virtual Networks** tab on the Networking page (see Figure 2-33), under **Public Network Access**, select the **Enabled from Selected Virtual Networks and IP Addresses** option button.
3. Under **Virtual Networks**, click **Add Existing Virtual Network**.
4. In the Add Networks dialog box (see Figure 2-34), enter the following information and click **OK**:
   - **Subscription** Select the subscription that contains the virtual network subnets you want to add.
   - **Virtual Networks** Select the virtual network(s) you want to add.
   - **Subnets** Select the subnet(s) you want to add.

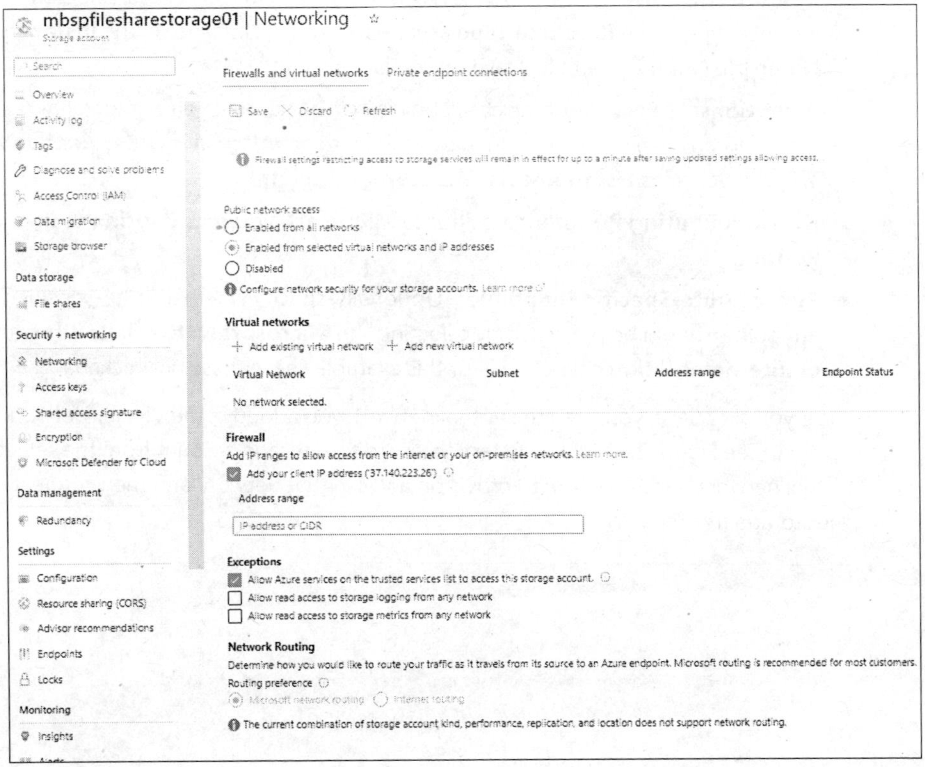

FIGURE 2-33 Setting up a storage account firewall.

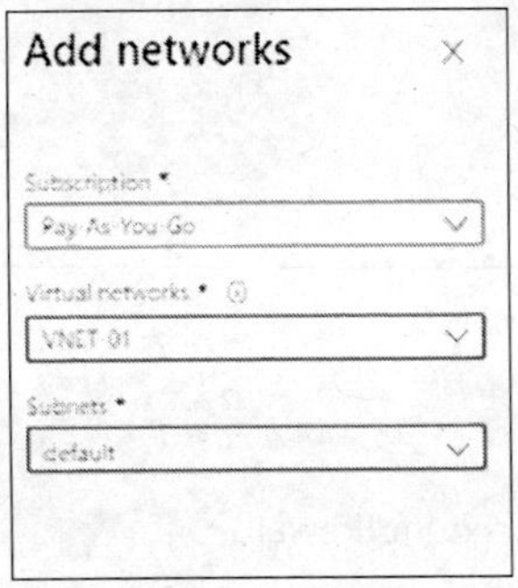

FIGURE 2-34 The Add Networks dialog box.

5. Back in the **Firewalls and Virtual Networks** tab on the Networking page (refer to Figure 2-33), enter the following information. Then click **Save** near the top of the page.
   - **Firewall** Select the **Add Your Client IP Address** check box to allow your public IP address access to the storage.

- **Resource Instances** To allow access by specific resource instances, select the instance type in the **Resource Type** list and the specific instance in the **Instance Name** list. (For this example, leave these blank.)
- **Exceptions** Select any of the check boxes in this section if you want to allow access to the storage in certain cases. In this example, select **Allow Azure Services on the Trusted Services List to Access This Storage Account**.
- **Network Routing Preference** Choose **Microsoft Network Routing** or **Internet Routing**.
- **Public Route-Specific Endpoints** Optionally, specify whether route-specific endpoints should be published by selecting the **Microsoft Network Routing** and/or **Internet Routing** check box. (For this example, leave these unchecked.)

After you click Save, you'll see the virtual network you added in the Virtual Networks section. (See Figure 2-35.) You can test access to the storage account from the selected virtual network. (You will have to provision a VM in that network and then connect to the storage from that VM.)

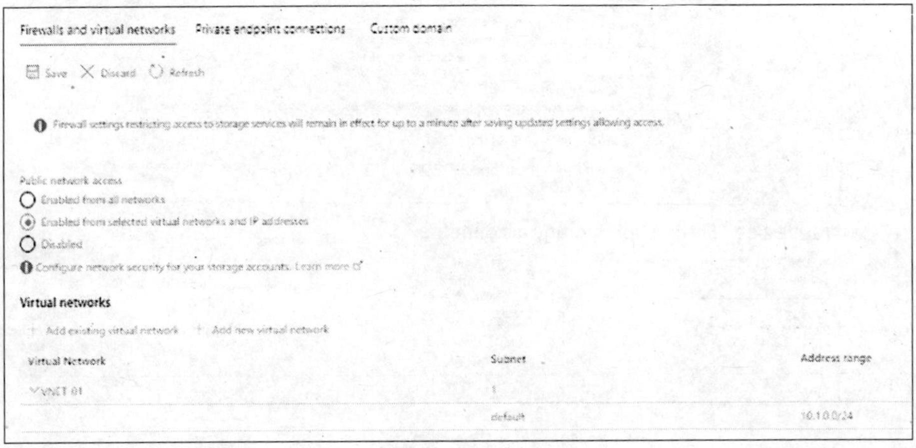

FIGURE 2-35 The virtual network you added appears on the list.

USING AZURE POWERSHELL

Use the following Azure PowerShell code to set up a storage account firewall:

```
#Define required variables
$resourceGroup = "RG01"
$region = "eastus"
$storageaccname = "mbspfilesharestorage02"
$share = "fileshare"
$directory = "directory"
$vnet = "vNET01"
$subnet = "default"
$endpointname = "PrivateEndpoint"
$vaultname = "RecoveryServicesVault01"
```

```
#Setting up Storage account firewall
#Set up access from Subnet
Update-AzStorageAccountNetworkRuleSet -ResourceGroupName $resourcegroup -Name $storage-
account -DefaultAction Deny
Get-AzVirtualNetwork -ResourceGroupName $resourcegroup -Name $vnet | Set-AzVirtualNet-
workSubnetConfig -Name $subnet -AddressPrefix "10.0.0.0/24" -ServiceEndpoint "Microsoft.
Storage" | Set-AzVirtualNetwork

$subnet = Get-AzVirtualNetwork -ResourceGroupName $resourcegroup -Name $vnet | Get-AzVir-
tualNetworkSubnetConfig -Name $subnet
Add-AzStorageAccountNetworkRule -ResourceGroupName $resourcegroup -Name $storageaccount
-VirtualNetworkResourceId $subnet.Id
```

USING AZURE CLI

Use the following code to set up a storage account firewall in the Azure CLI:

```
#Define required variables
resourceGroup="RG01"
region="eastus"
storageaccname="mbspfilesharestorage01"
share="fileshare"
directory="directory"
vnet="vNET01"
subnet="default"
endpointname="PrivateEndpoint"
vaultname="RecoveryServicesVault01"


#Setting up Storage account firewall
#Set up access from Subnet
subnetid=$(az network vnet subnet show \
        --resource-group $resourceGroup \
        --vnet-name $vnet \
        --name $subnet \
        --query "id" | \
    tr -d '"')

az network vnet subnet update \
    --ids $subnetid \
    --service-endpoints Microsoft.Storage \
    --output none

az storage account network-rule add \
                    --resource-group $resourceGroup \
                    --account-name $storageaccname \
```

```
                        --vnet-name $vnet \
                        --subnet $subnet

az storage account update \
      --resource-group $resourceGroup \
      --name $storageaccname \
      --bypass "AzureServices" \
      --default-action "Deny" \
      --output none
```

SMB Multichannel

When using premium file shares with the SMB protocol, SMB 3.*x* clients can benefit from the SMB Multichannel feature. This feature aggregates bandwidth over multiple NICs, allowing SMB 3.*x* clients to connect to the Azure file share using as many as four channels simultaneously. It uses receive side scaling (RSS) on NICs to distribute the IO load across multiple CPUs, thereby providing more throughput and IOPS for every storage client. It also provides network fault tolerance; if one channel fails, the connections over the other channels can continue to function.

SMB Multichannel requires both sides of the connection (including the client-side) to support the feature. SMB Multichannel uses dynamic discovery to determine whether a client supports the multichannel capability, and if necessary, creates additional network connection paths. Currently, Windows and Linux clients that support SMB 3.1.1 support SMB Multichannel.

SMB Multichannel is disabled by default. However, there are no additional charges for using this feature. Hence, in environments with SMB 3.*x* clients connecting to a premium file share, it is highly recommended to turn on this feature.

> ***NOTE*** **Single-threaded application workloads tend to have issues with this feature, so be sure to test this feature with any applications that might access the storage to ensure everything works as expected.**

SMB Multichannel walkthrough

The following section steps you through the process of enabling the SMB Multichannel feature using the Azure portal.

USING AZURE PORTAL

To enable the SMB Multichannel feature, follow these steps:

1. In the left pane of the Azure Files storage account page, under **Data Storage**, click **File Shares**.
2. On the File Shares page, click the **Disabled** link next to the **SMB Multichannel** option along the top. (See Figure 2-36.)

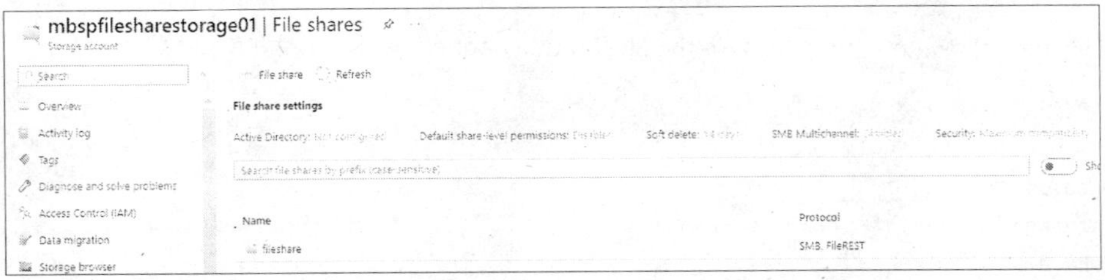

FIGURE 2-36 Setting up SMB Multichannel support.

3. In the SMB Multichannel dialog box (see Figure 2-37), toggle the **SMB Multichannel** option to the on position, and click **Save**.

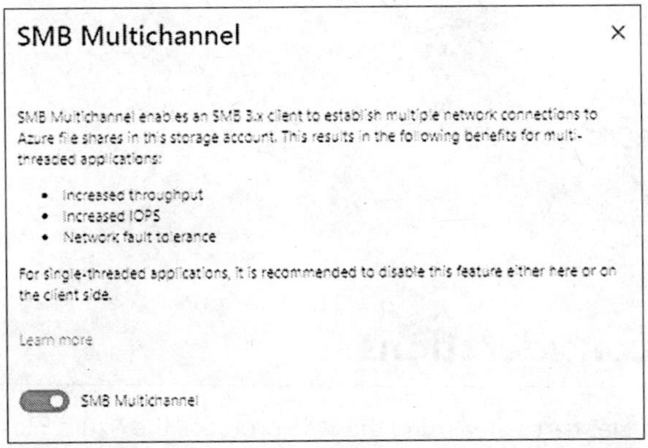

FIGURE 2-37 Enabling the SMB Multichannel option.

USING AZURE POWERSHELL

Use the following Azure PowerShell code to enable the SMB Multichannel feature:

```
#Define required variables
$resourceGroup = "RG01"
$region = "eastus"
$storageaccname = "mbspfilesharestorage02"
$share = "fileshare"
$directory = "directory"
$vnet = "vNET01"
$subnet = "default"
$endpointname = "PrivateEndpoint"
$vaultname = "RecoveryServicesVault01"


#Enable SMB Multichannel
Update-AzStorageFileServiceProperty `
-ResourceGroupName $resourceGroup `
-AccountName $storageAccName `
-EnableSmbMultichannel $true
```

USING AZURE CLI

Use the following code to enable the SMB Multichannel feature in the Azure CLI:

```
#Define required variables
resourceGroup="RG01"
region="eastus"
storageaccname="mbspfilesharestorage01"
share="fileshare"
directory="directory"
vnet="vNET01"
subnet="default"
endpointname="PrivateEndpoint"
vaultname="RecoveryServicesVault01"


#Enable SMB Multichannel
az storage account file-service-properties update \
    --enable-smb-multichannel \
    --storage-account $storageaccname  \
    --resource-group $resourceGroup
```

Identity and access considerations

To allow access to data stored on a file share when using the SMB protocol, the Azure Files service supports three primary authentication methods to confirm the user's identity and to validate their permission to access the data in that file share. The methods are as follows:

> ***NOTE*** **NFS does not support the use of on-premises Active Directory or Azure Active Directory Domain Services providers.**

- **On-premises Active Directory Domain Services (on-premises AD DS)** You can integrate an Azure Files file share with your on-premises AD DS services, similar to other Windows clients or servers. Users can then access the storage using their existing AD DS credentials. You can use AD DS–based groups to set up NTFS permissions for the share to validate the authorization level to the share data. This authentication provider uses the Kerberos authentication protocol. You can integrate with a domain controller hosted in Azure or in your on-premises or other cloud environments as long as there is connectivity to the domain controller over a private network for the Kerberos communication to occur. Figure 2-38 shows the authentication flow for on-premises AD DS.
- **Azure Active Directory Domain Services (Azure AD DS)** As with on-premises AD DS, you can integrate Azure Files with Azure AD DS, which is a Microsoft-managed domain controller hosted in Azure. Azure AD DS also uses the Kerberos authentication protocol. Azure AD DS allows customers to set up their user accounts similar to

on-premises AD DS for authentication and authorization. Figure 2-39 shows the authentication flow for Azure AD DS.

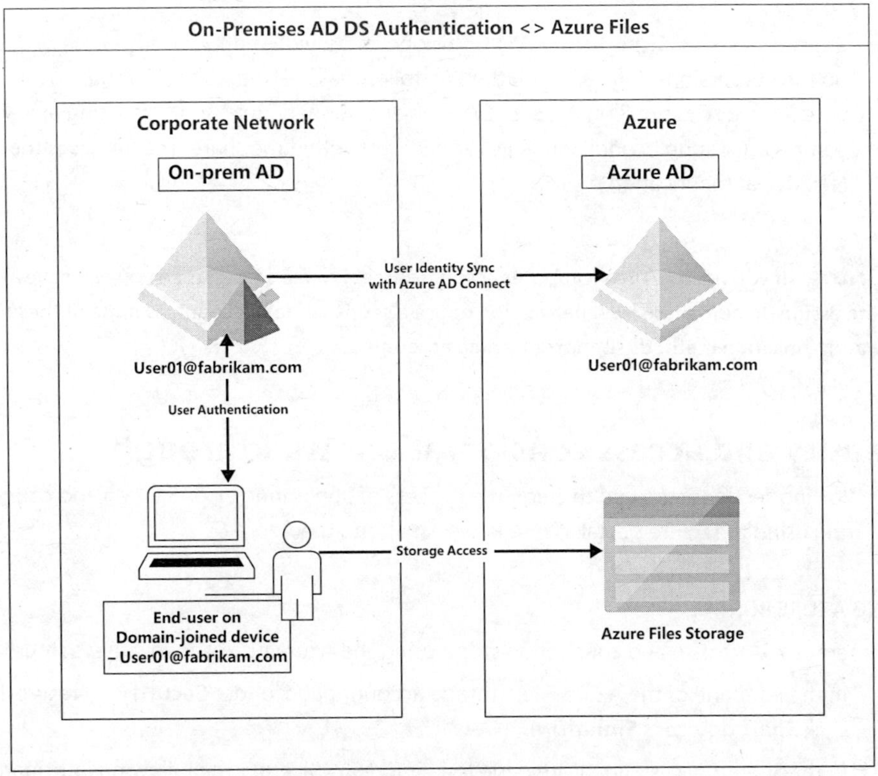

FIGURE 2-38 On-premises AD DS authentication flow.

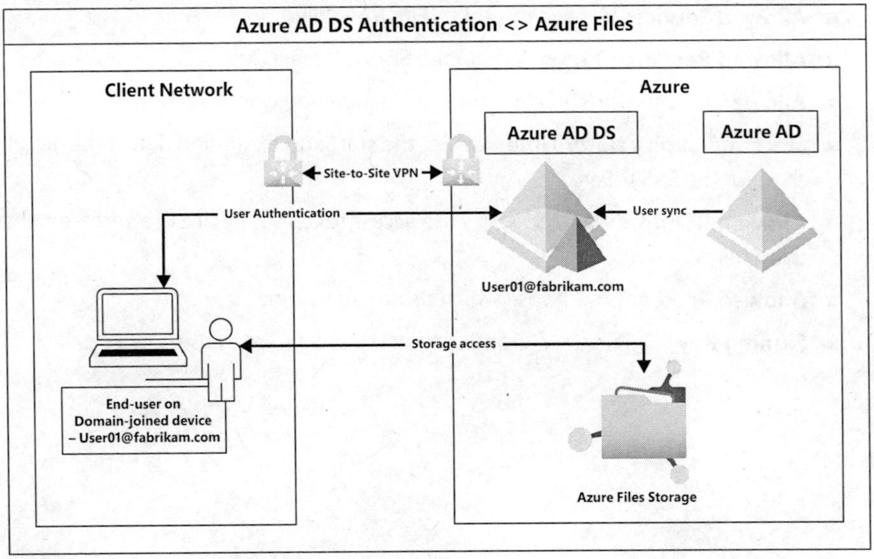

FIGURE 2-39 Azure AD DS authentication flow.

NOTE Neither on-premises AD DS nor Azure AD DS support Azure AD–joined devices or Azure AD–registered devices.

- **Shared Account Signature (SAS)** This option provides administrative access, based on the permissions defined when the SAS token was created, to the file share over SMB via a Shared Account Signature (SAS) token and connection string, bypassing any access control lists set up on individual files and folders within the share. The SAS uses the NTLMv2 authentication protocol over SMB.

NOTE If you need to give computer accounts access to file shares, then you will have to assign default-share level permission or use a service logon account, as none of these authentication methods support machine accounts.

Identity and access considerations walkthrough

The following sections step you through the process of generating an SAS token and connection string using the Azure portal, Azure PowerShell, and the Azure CLI.

USING AZURE PORTAL

To generate a SAS token and connection string using the Azure portal, follow these steps:

1. In the left pane of the Azure Files storage account page, under **Security + Networking**, click **Shared Access Signature**.
2. In the Shared Access Signature page (see Figure 2-40), enter the following information. Then click the **Generate SAS and Connection String** button.
   - **Allowed Services** Leave this set to **File** (the default).
   - **Allowed Resource Types** Select the **Service** check box.
   - **Allowed Permissions** Select the permissions you want to assign.
   - **Start and Expiry Date/Time** Select the start and expiration date, time, and time zone for the SAS token.
   - **Allowed IP Addresses** To apply the access token to specific IP addresses, enter them here.
   - **Allowed Protocols** Choose which protocols to allow.
   - **Signing Key** Select the storage account key you want to use.

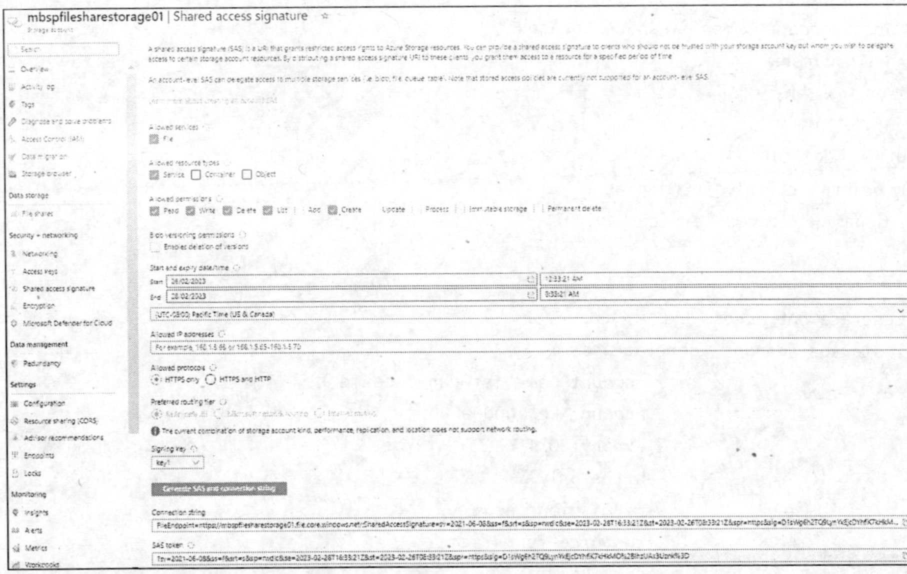

FIGURE 2-40 Generating a SAS token and connection string.

USING AZURE POWERSHELL

Use the following Azure PowerShell code to generate a SAS token and connection string:

```
#Define required variables
$resourceGroup = "RG01"
$region = "eastus"
$storageaccname = "mbspfilesharestorage02"
$share = "fileshare"
$directory = "directory"
$vnet = "vNET01"
$subnet = "default"
$endpointname = "PrivateEndpoint"
$vaultname = "RecoveryServicesVault01"


#Generate SAS Access URL
Set-AzCurrentStorageAccount -ResourceGroupName $resourcegroup -Name $storageaccname
New-AzStorageAccountSASToken -Service File -ResourceType Service,Container,Object -Permis-
sion "racwdlup" -Protocol HTTPSOnly -ExpiryTime (Get-Date).AddDays(5)
```

USING AZURE CLI

Use the following code to generate a SAS token and connection string in the Azure CLI:

```
#Define required variables
resourceGroup="RG01"
```

```
region="eastus"
storageaccname="mbspfilesharestorage01"
share="fileshare"
directory="directory"
vnet="vNET01"
subnet="default"
endpointname="PrivateEndpoint"
vaultname="RecoveryServicesVault01"


#Generate SAS Access URL
az storage account  generate-sas \
                        --account-name $storageaccname \
                        --account-key 00000000 \
                        --expiry 2024-12-31 \
                        --https-only \
                        --permissions acuw \
                        --resource-types sco \
                        --services f
```

Data redundancy

As organizations move their critical information to the cloud, they must consider how to enhance data redundancy to make it easy to recover data in a timely manner while minimizing business impact in the event of an outage.

Azure Files provides various degrees of redundancy to account for local, zonal, and geographical failures, so organizations can choose their level of redundancy based on their requirements. You specify the level of data redundancy when you create your Azure Files storage account, but you can migrate your account to a different level of redundancy later if the need arises. (The migration process differs depending on the storage account type and current redundancy options.)

Chapter 1 discussed the various data redundancy options for Azure Blob Storage. Most of the same redundancy options apply for Azure Files. To review, they are the following:

- **Locally redundant storage (LRS)** With LRS storage, Azure maintains three replicas of your data in a single datacenter within your primary Azure region. This protects against local storage hardware, server rack, or network component failures. However, because all three replicas are stored in the same datacenter, if that datacenter experiences some type of disaster, all three copies of your data could be lost.
- **Zone-redundant storage (ZRS)** Like LRS, ZRS synchronously commits and maintains three replicas of your data in your primary Azure region. However, instead of storing each replica in a single datacenter, they are spread across three availability zones. An availability zone is an independent datacenter in your primary Azure region with its own

power, cooling, and networking components. So, if a disaster occurs in one availability zone, your data will still be accessible (unless the disaster also affects the other availability zones within that Azure region).

- **Geo-redundant storage (GRS)** With GRS, Azure synchronously commits and maintains three replicas of your data in your primary Azure region in LRS. Then, three more replicas of your data in a secondary Azure region (selected automatically by Microsoft) are updated to match the three replicas in the primary Azure region, again using LRS. So, you have six copies of your data spread across two geographical regions that are hundreds of miles apart. If the datacenter in your primary region experiences an outage or disaster, then your data will be available in the datacenter in the secondary region. (This assumes all updates to secondary region were complete before the outage in the primary occurred region. If not, there could be some amount of data loss based on the replication lag.)
- **Geo-zone-redundant storage (GZRS)** GZRS is just like GRS, but the three replicas of your data in the primary region use ZRS, while the replicas in the secondary region use LRS. So, there is additional redundancy in the primary region.

> ***NOTE*** **Chapter 1 covers these redundancy options in more detail, including diagrams.**

As discussed, you can provision Azure Files in different storage accounts. Currently, each type of storage account supports all or a subset of these data-redundancy options, as follows:

- General-purpose v2 storage accounts support all four redundancy options (LRS, ZRS, GRS, and GZRS).
- Premium file shares currently support only LRS and ZRS, although this might change in the future. Review updated Microsoft guidance at the time of your storage build.
- Standard file shares that support a maximum of 5 tebibytes (TiB) can use all four redundancy options (LRS, ZRS, GRS, and GZRS).
- Standard file shares that support more than 5 TiB use only LRS and ZRS, although this might change in the future. Review updated Microsoft guidance at the time of your storage build.

Data protection

The following sections discuss various features provided by Microsoft to protect the data in your Azure Files storage, including encryption for at-rest data, soft delete, Azure Backup integration, the ability to restore shares or files, share snapshots, and Microsoft Defender for Storage integration.

Encryption for at-rest data

Azure Files accounts use the same encryption scheme as Azure Blob Storage accounts, covered in Chapter 1. Encryption is applied on the underlying disks, similar to BitLocker encryption on Windows. This ensures that the client does not require access to the key to read or write from the file share. It ensures that the underlying disks cannot be read when removed from the storage in the Azure storage cluster without access to the encryption key.

The keys used for encryption can be Microsoft-managed or customer-managed. Customers can select which type to use based on their organizational requirements for handling data within each file share. You can select different encryption key management strategies in a single Azure subscription.

Azure Files also offers infrastructure encryption, which supports encryption on the infrastructure level and on the storage service level. This uses 256-bit AES encryption and ensures the encryption keys are different from the ones used for the service-level encryption, even if Microsoft is managing them both. This ensures that a breach in one level does not compromise the other level. You cannot use customer-managed keys for infrastructure encryption.

Depending on which type of key you choose, as a best practice, you might need to develop a key-hosting and rotation to ensure keys are rotated on a regular basis but can still be accessed by the file share service for read/write operations. If you choose Microsoft-managed encryption keys, then Microsoft ensures those keys are available to the service for operational use and rotates the keys on a regular basis.

Soft delete

Azure Files introduced a feature called soft delete to enable customers to easily recover any file shares that might have been deleted accidentally. You define how long the file share should be held in a soft-deleted state before the Azure Files service deletes the file share data permanently. Depending on your environment and the criticality of the file shares, it is highly recommended that you enable this feature and you set a retention period that is long enough to allow for such a recovery to be performed.

> ***NOTE*** **You set up soft delete earlier in this chapter when you created the Azure Files account, in the "Storage accounts walkthrough" section.**

Share snapshots

A share snapshot is a point-in-time read-only replica of your file share. Because snapshots are incremental, each snapshot contains only the changes since the last snapshot.

Share snapshots provide protection against various scenarios, such as the following:

- Data corruption due to malware or application overwrites
- Malicious or accidental data deletion

- Data deletion due to application misconfiguration
- Accidental data overwrite by end users

Each file share supports a maximum of 200 snapshots, with a maximum retention period of 10 years. There are no limits on the amount of space each snapshot can consume, as long as the total space occupied by the share and its snapshots is within the limits supported by the storage account.

Snapshots are stored within the file share itself, so if the file share is deleted, all associated snapshots are also deleted, making a recovery impossible. You will therefore want to use either the soft delete feature to ensure you can recover from any accidental deletion events or Azure Backup to store backup data in a separate service and storage.

When you delete an old snapshot, only files unique to that snapshot will be deleted. This ensures that any subsequent snapshots that rely on the source snapshot can still rely on that snapshot for data recovery. When attempting to delete a file share, you will first be required to delete all associated share snapshots.

You can trigger snapshots using the Azure portal, Azure PowerShell, Azure CLI, REST APIs, and Azure Backup. While snapshots can be taken only on the file share level, data recovery is supported on the individual item level using SMB or REST APIs. Entire file share recovery can also be performed using SMB, REST APIs, Azure portal, Azure PowerShell, or Azure CLI.

You can mount a snapshot to a Windows-based client to view the contents of a snapshot for individual item recovery. This facility is currently not available for Linux clients. However, check Microsoft's updated guidance to verify whether this is still the case when you plan your solution.

Share snapshots walkthrough

The following sections step you through the process of creating and restoring from a share snapshot using the Azure portal and Azure PowerShell.

> ***IMPORTANT*** **If you are following along, select resources and resource names based on your environment for each of your deployments.**

> ***IMPORTANT*** **If you are following along, be sure to delete any unwanted resources after you have completed testing to reduce charges levied by Microsoft.**

USING AZURE PORTAL

To create and restore from a share snapshot using the Azure portal, follow these steps:

1. In the left pane of the page for the file share for which you want to create a snapshot, under **Operations**, click **Snapshots**.
2. On the Snapshots page (see Figure 2-41), click **Add Snapshot**.

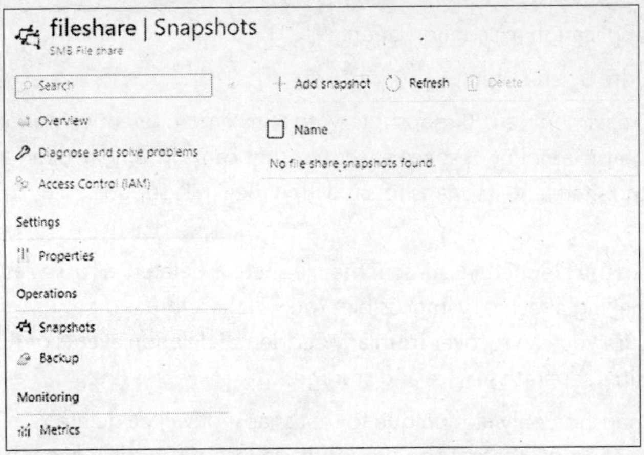

FIGURE 2-41 Creating a file share snapshot.

3. In the Add Snapshot dialog box (see Figure 2-42), enter a name for the snapshot that is unique within the file share and click **OK**.

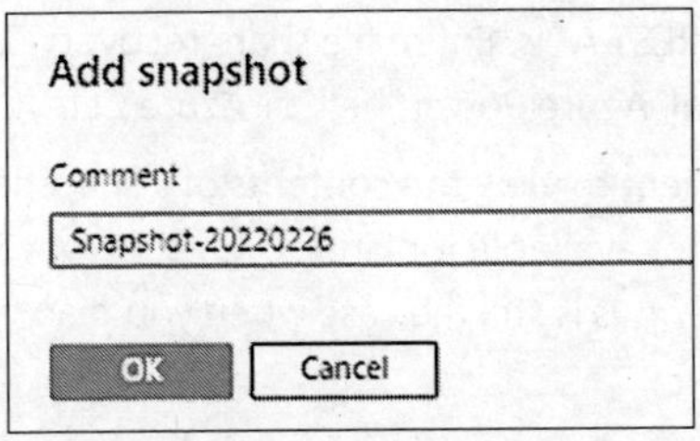

FIGURE 2-42 Adding a snapshot.

After you create a snapshot, you can download it for review or use it to perform a restore.

4. To access the snapshot, open the file share's Snapshots page. Then click the entry for the snapshot to open it. (See Figure 2-43.)

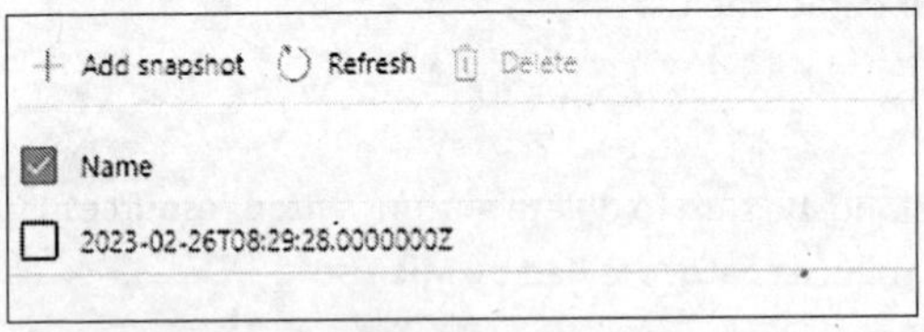

FIGURE 2-43 Selecting a snapshot.

5. Locate the file in the snapshot that you want to download or restore from. Then click the right side of the file entry and choose **Download** or **Restore** from the menu that appears. (See Figure 2-44.)

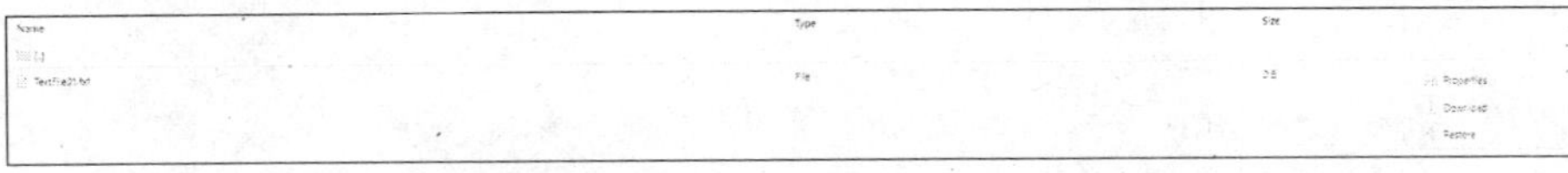

FIGURE 2-44 Restoring from or downloading a snapshot.

USING AZURE POWERSHELL

Use the following Azure PowerShell code to create a share snapshot:

```
#Define required variables
$resourceGroup = "RG01"
$region = "eastus"
$storageaccname = "mbspfilesharestorage02"
$share = "fileshare"
$directory = "directory"
$vnet = "vNET01"
$subnet = "default"
$endpointname = "PrivateEndpoint"
$vaultname = "RecoveryServicesVault01"


#Create and manage snapshots
New-AzRmStorageShare -ResourceGroupName $resourcegroup -StorageAccountName $storage-
accname -Name $share -Snapshot
```

Azure Backup integration

You can use the cloud-native Azure backup service to perform short-term and long-term backups of your Azure file shares. You can define custom retention policies using retention periods of days, weeks, months, years, or a combination of these, for different file shares. The Azure Backup service allows for seamless backup integration. You can create backup schedules and retention policies without deploying any additional infrastructure. Azure Backup also provides backup monitoring, alerting, and reporting capabilities, making it easier for administrators to manage all file share backups in one single location. Figure 2-45 shows how Azure Backup integrates with Azure Files.

Azure Backup creates an incremental snapshot of the file storage each time a backup is triggered. If needed, you can perform an instant data restore from any of these snapshots. The snapshot is leased by the backup service. It is also locked. This prevents the snapshot's deletion except by the backup service itself, based on the defined retention schedule. This lock also prevents any accidental deletion of the file share itself until all the associated backup snapshots are deleted and the lock is removed. Once the retention period for a snapshot expires, Azure Backup releases the lease on the snapshot and deletes it.

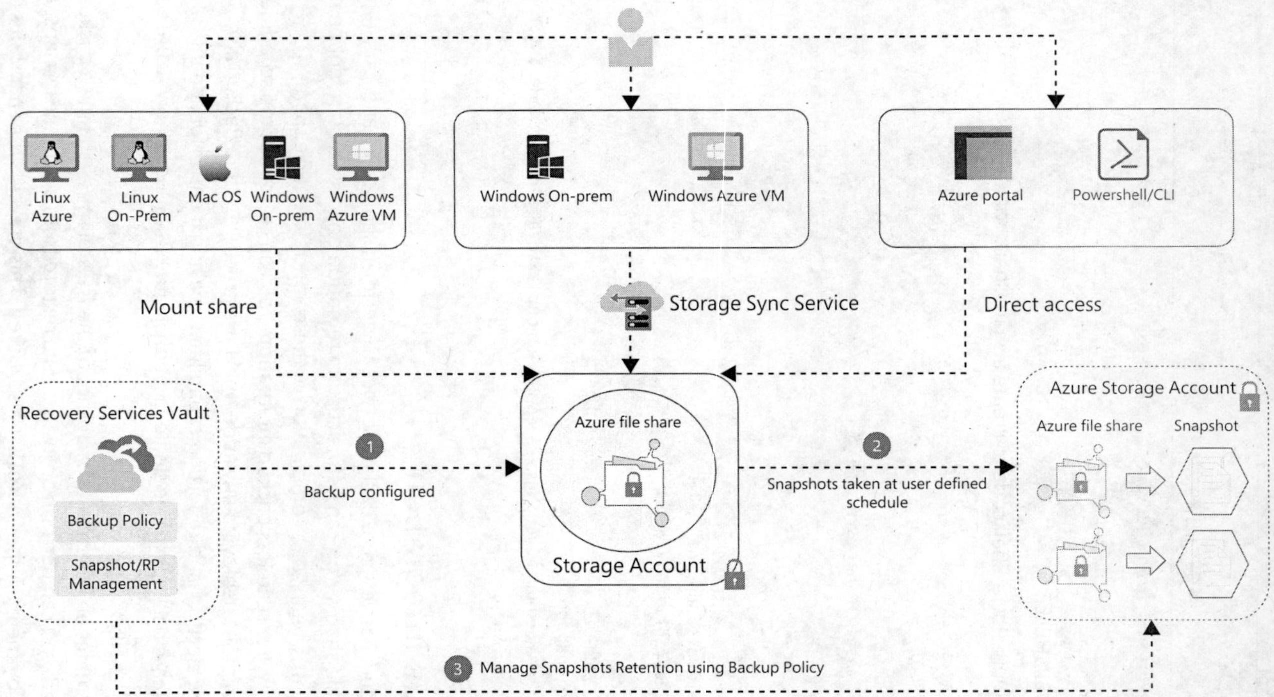

FIGURE 2-45 Azure Backup integration with Azure Files.

NOTE Azure Backup makes the entire backup and recovery process extremely easy to manage, as the entire workflow—taking the snapshot, data transfer, storage transfer, and recovery—is orchestrated by the service and requires little intervention from customers.

Along with share-level recovery, Azure Backup also supports item-level recovery. This makes it possible to restore individual files and folders to the original or an alternate location if needed. Administrators might recover files or folders in an alternate location to compare them before overwriting the original files.

Using Azure Backup does incur a cost based on the amount of snapshot storage consumed and the total size of the protected file shares in a storage account. For an estimate, see Microsoft's Azure Calculator online.

Azure Backup integration walkthrough

The following sections step you through the process of integrating Azure Backup with an Azure Files file share using the Azure portal, Azure PowerShell, and Azure CLI.

IMPORTANT If you are following along, select resources and resource names based on your environment, including a unique backup vault name for each of your deployments.

IMPORTANT If you are following along, be sure to delete any unwanted resources after you have completed testing to reduce charges levied by Microsoft.

USING AZURE PORTAL

To integrate Azure Backup with an Azure Files file share and restore from a backup using the Azure portal, follow these steps:

1. In the left pane of the page for the file share for which you want to set up a backup, under **Operations**, click **Backup**.
2. On the Backup page (see Figure 2-46), next to **Recovery Services Vault**, you can select an existing backup or create a new one. In this case, select the **Create New** option button to create a new one.

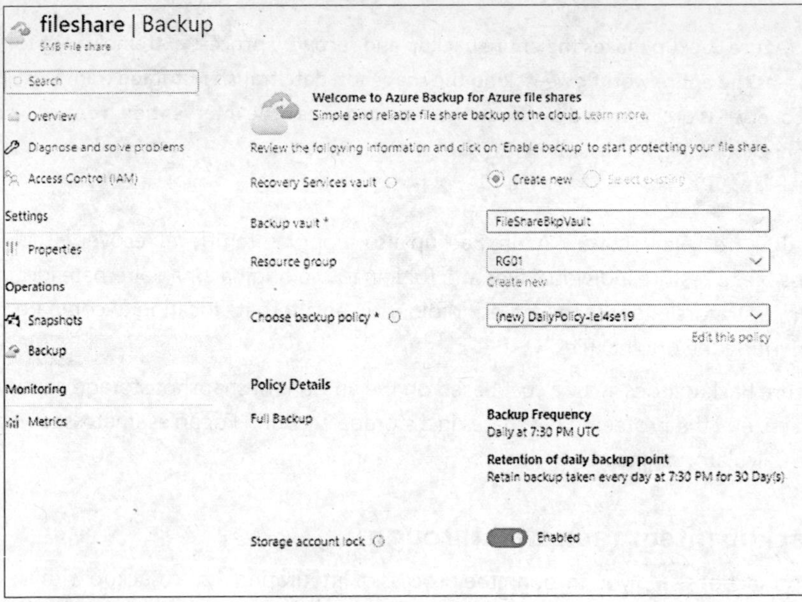

FIGURE 2-46 Integrating Azure Backup with a file share.

3. In the **Backup Vault** box, type a unique name for the new backup vault.
4. Open the **Resource Group** drop-down list and select an existing resource group in which to create the new backup vault. Alternatively, click the **Create New** link and follow the prompts to create a new resource group.
5. Click the **Edit This Policy** link under the **Choose Backup Policy** drop-down list.
6. In the Create Policy dialog box (see Figure 2-47), enter the following information and click **Create**:
   - **Policy Name** Enter a unique descriptive name for the backup policy.
   - **Backup Schedule** Select the backup frequency, time, and time zone.
   - **Retention Range** Specify the retention range for daily, weekly, monthly, and yearly backups.

   The new policy appears in the file share's Backup page. (See Figure 2-48.)

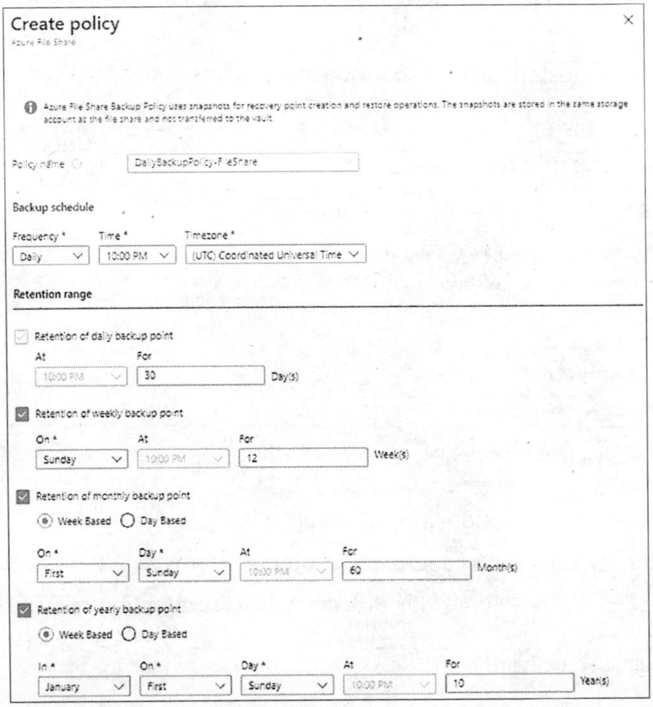

FIGURE 2-47 Creating the file share backup policy.

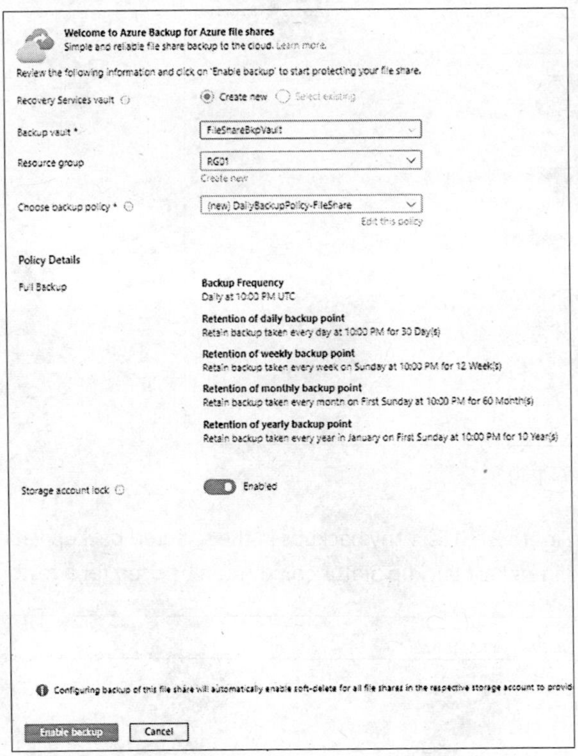

FIGURE 2-48 Use new backup policy.

7. Leave the **Storage Account Lock** option toggled to the **Enabled** position. Then click **Enable Backup**.
8. After the backup vault is created, click **Go to Resource** to access its page. (See Figure 2-49.)

FIGURE 2-49 Backup configuration is complete.

The next steps show you how to restore from a backup.

9. In the left pane of the backup vault's page, under **Protected Items**, click **Backup Items**.
10. On the Backup Items page (see Figure 2-50), click the **Azure Storage (Azure Files)** link.

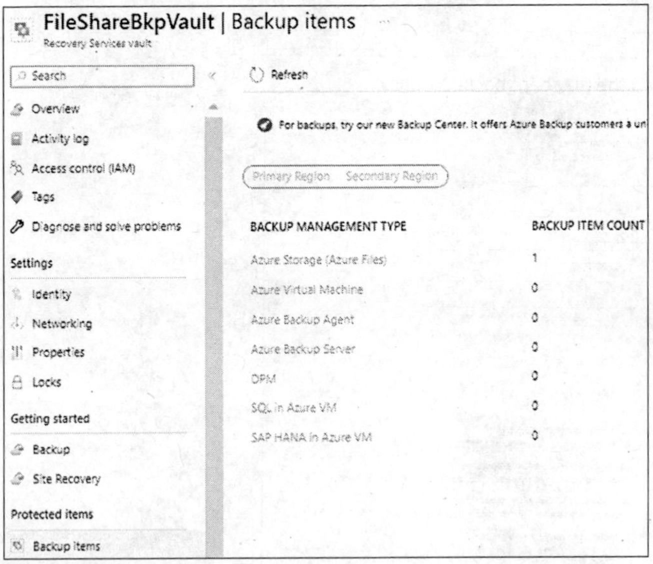

FIGURE 2-50 The Backup Items page.

11. The page that opens (see Figure 2-51) lists any backups in the selected backup vault. Any backup with Success listed in its Last Backup Status column can be used for a restore.

FIGURE 2-51 Manage backup.

12. Click the backup's **View Details** link.

13. In the page that opens (see Figure 2-52), do one of the following:

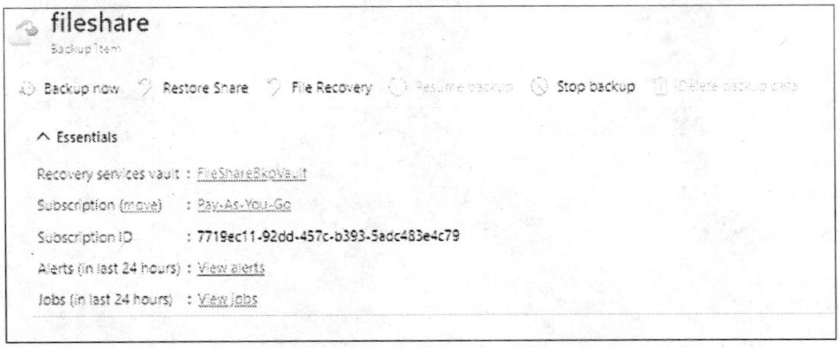

FIGURE 2-52 Backup management options.

- To restore the entire file share, click **Restore Share**. Then, in the Restore dialog box (see Figure 2-53), open the **Restore Point** drop-down list and choose a restore point; choose the **Original Location** or **Alternate Location** option button; and open the **In Case of Conflicts** drop-down list and choose an option for handling file conflicts. Then click **Restore**.

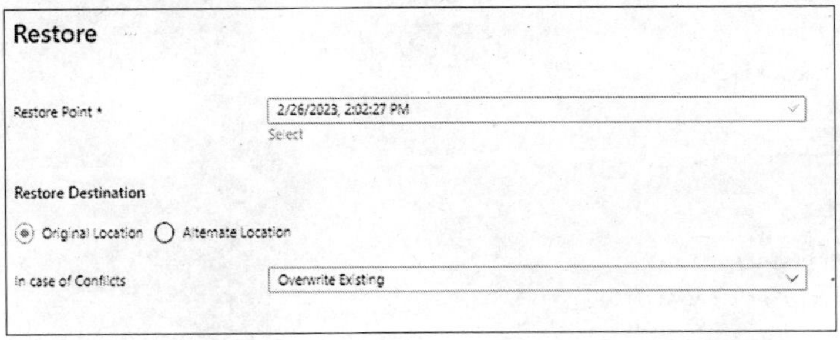

FIGURE 2-53 Restoring an entire file share.

- To restore individual files, click **File Recovery.** Then, in the Restore dialog box (see Figure 2-54), select the restore point and restore destination and click **Add File** to locate and select the file(s) you want to restore. Then click **Restore**.

14. After the restore operation is complete, browse to the restore location to verify your data has been restored successfully.

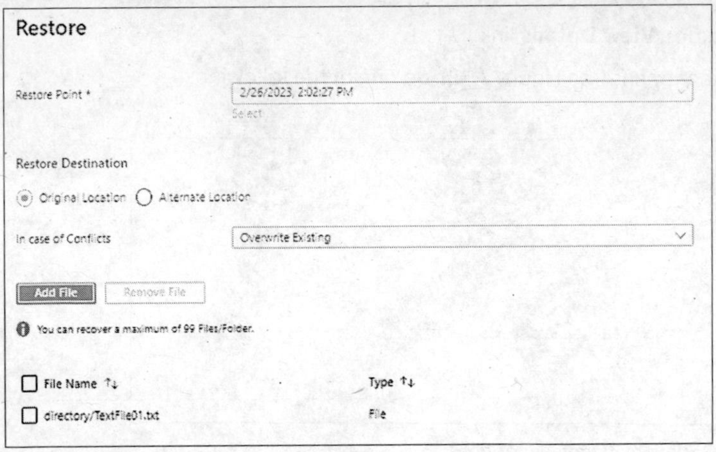

FIGURE 2-54 Restoring files in a file share..

USING AZURE POWERSHELL

Use the following Azure PowerShell code to integrate Azure Backup with a file share and restore from a backup:

```
#Define required variables
$resourceGroup = "RG01"
$region = "eastus"
$storageaccname = "mbspfilesharestorage02"
$share = "fileshare"
$directory = "directory"
$vnet = "vNET01"
$subnet = "default"
$endpointname = "PrivateEndpoint"
$vaultname = "RecoveryServicesVault01"


#Setting up Azure Backup Integration
New-AzRecoveryServicesVault -ResourceGroupName $resourcegroup -Name $vaultname -Location
$region


#Set the storage redundancy and cross region restore config
Get-AzRecoveryServicesVault -Name $vaultname | Set-AzRecoveryServicesVaultContext
Get-AzRecoveryServicesVault -Name $vaultname | Set-AzRecoveryServicesBackupProperty
-BackupStorageRedundancy GeoRedundant -EnableCrossRegionRestore


#Create Backup policy
$SchedulePolicy = Get-AzRecoveryServicesBackupSchedulePolicyObject -WorkloadType
"AzureStorage"
```

```
$Date = Get-Date
$SchedulePolicy.ScheduleRunTimes.Add($Date.ToUniversalTime())
$Retention = Get-AzRecoveryServicesBackupRetentionPolicyObject -WorkloadType
"AzureStorage"
$Retention.DailySchedule.DurationCountInDays = 30
$bkppolicy = New-AzRecoveryServicesBackupProtectionPolicy -Name CustomBackupPolicy01
-RetentionPolicy $Retention -SchedulePolicy $SchedulePolicy -VaultId $vaultname.ID -Work-
loadType AzureStorage

#Enable Azure Files Backup
Enable-AzRecoveryServicesBackupProtection -StorageAccountName $storageaccname -Name
$storageaccname-dailybackup -Policy $bkppolicy

#Trigger Backup Now
$bkpContainer = Get-AzRecoveryServicesBackupContainer -FriendlyName $StorageAcctname
-ContainerType AzureStorage
$BkpItem = Get-AzRecoveryServicesBackupItem -Container $bkpContainer -WorkloadType "Azur-
eFiles" -FriendlyName StorageAcctname-ManualBkp
$job =  Backup-AzRecoveryServicesBackupItem -Item $BkpItem

#Restore share or files
$startDate = (Get-Date).AddDays(-7)
$endDate = Get-Date
$recovery = Get-AzRecoveryServicesBackupRecoveryPoint -Item $BkpItem -VaultId $vaultname.
ID -StartDate $startdate.ToUniversalTime() -EndDate $enddate.ToUniversalTime()
$recovery[0] | fl
Restore-AzRecoveryServicesBackupItem -RecoveryPoint $recovery[0] -TargetStorageAccount-
Name $StorageAccname -TargetFileShareName $share -TargetFolder $directory -ResolveConflict
Overwrite
```

USING AZURE CLI

Use the following code to integrate Azure Backup with a file share and restore from a backup in the Azure CLI:

```
#Define required variables
resourceGroup="RG01"
region="eastus"
storageaccname="mbspfilesharestorage01"
share="fileshare"
directory="directory"
vnet="vNET01"
subnet="default"
endpointname="PrivateEndpoint"
vaultname="RecoveryServicesVault01"
```

```
#Setting up Azure Backup Integration
az backup vault create --resource-group $resourceGroup \
    --name $vaultname \
    --location $region

#Set the storage redundancy and cross region restore config
az backup vault backup-properties set --name $vaultname  \
    --resource-group $resourceGroup \
    --backup-storage-redundancy "GeoRedundant" \
    --cross-region-restore-flag "True"

#Create Backup policy

#Enable Azure Files Backup
az backup protection enable-for-azurefileshare --vault-name $vaultname --resource-group
$resourceGroup --policy-name DefaultFileShareBackupPolicy --storage-account $storage-
accname --azure-file-share $share  --output table

#Trigger Backup Now
az backup protection backup-now --vault-name $vaultname --resource-group $resourceGroup
--container-name $storageaccname --item-name $share --retain-until 20-01-2024 --output
table

#Restore share or files
#Generate list of all recovery points
az backup recoverypoint list --vault-name $vaultname \
                        --resource-group $resourceGroup \
                        --container-name $storageaccname \
                        --backup-management-type azurestorage \
                        --item-name $share \
                        --workload-type azurefileshare \
                        --out table

#Replace rp-name below the name of one of the recovery points generated with the above
command
az backup restore restore-azurefileshare \
                        --vault-name $vaultname \
                        --resource-group $resourceGroup \
                        --rp-name 9019188188828211   \
                        --container-name $storageaccname \
                        --item-name $share \
                    --restore-mode originallocation \
                    --resolve-conflict overwrite \
                    --out table
```

Best practices

Following are some general best practices regarding setting up and using Azure File Shares:

- **Plan redundancy strategy** You must plan your storage redundancy strategy in advance to ensure you select the correct storage redundancy options when you create the file share. If you want to switch to a different redundancy level later, you will have to migrate from one storage account type to another.
- **Document recovery procedures and review them regularly** Once you have your redundancy strategy in place, document any recovery procedures, such as manual storage failover for geo-redundant storage, and review them regularly with your team. You might also need to include the failover of other related components, along with the file share endpoint, to ensure that all interconnected components are online in the event of a disaster. Regular reviews will help ensure that any changes to the file share capabilities or feature sets are incorporated into your design, and so you can optimize the recovery further if possible.
- **Deploy Azure Files file shares with other Azure file shares only** When using general purpose v2 storage accounts, you can deploy a mix of a blob, file, table, and queue storage in the same storage account. But with Azure Files, it is highly recommended to deploy only file shares together in the same storage account. This ensures you can take into account performance requirements related to file shares when planning the storage account mapping. In a mixed storage account, it can become difficult to manage performance issues as different storage account types using different protocols will be accessing the storage from a varied set of clients and sharing the same limits associated with the storage account.
- **Host a single file share in a storage account as much as possible** It is highly recommended to host a single file share in a storage account. This ensures all the storage IOPS limits will be available to the single file share. However, if you are running into issues—due to an organizational issue or Azure restrictions—then plan the file share hosting to ensure that the most active file shares are not placed together in the same storage account.
- **Enable soft delete on all file shares** Soft delete is a great feature to help you quickly recover your file share in the event of accidental or malicious deletion. If possible, enable soft delete on all your file shares and set up a retention period longer than the minimum time it will take your team to respond and to perform a restore, if necessary.
- **Use private endpoints for storage access** Private endpoints enable you to access file share resources over a secure internal network connection over VPN or ExpressRoute. This allows you to control which network subnets are permitted to access the endpoint and to limit access as necessary. It also allows you to closely monitor the connections to the file share endpoint over your internal firewall and detect any anomalies. It is highly recommended to use private endpoints if your environment and application access requirements allow for it.

- **Limit use of public endpoints** It is highly recommended that you use private endpoints to access file shares instead of public endpoints. Although you can secure public endpoints with encryption in transit and firewall restrictions, it is preferable to use private endpoints unless using public endpoints is absolutely necessary. Private endpoints allow you to control access more granularly from your internal networks to the storage as necessary.
- **Set up storage firewall restrictions** Unless you completely disable public endpoints, set up storage firewall restrictions to allow access over public endpoints only from administrative or known IP addresses. This will limit the exposure of that endpoint and prevent malicious actors from attacking and accessing the storage.
- **Disable unwanted protocols** Disable all unwanted protocol versions to limit access to the storage over older protocols such as SMB 1.1 and SMB 2.*x*. This will force all client connections to work over SMB 3.*x* protocols, ensuring that data encryption in transit, SMB Multichannel, and other advanced features are enabled for all connections.
- **Enable Active Directory or Azure AD DS authentication over SMB** It is highly recommended that you integrate the file share with Active Directory or Azure AD DS to manage client authentication and authorization. This will allow you to use existing user accounts to provision access to the file share and manage permission levels in line with your on-premises setup. If you are migrating your on-premises file share to Azure, performing this integration before the migration will help ensure that you are able to copy over the existing permissions to the file share automatically using tools such as robocopy.
- **Force secure transfers only** Although Azure Files supports connections over both HTTP and HTTPS, it is highly recommended to force secure transfer only so that all connections are secured. You can configure this setting using the Azure portal, Azure PowerShell, Azure CLI, and REST APIs. If you set up the storage using the Azure portal, this setting is enabled by default. If you used any of the other methods, you must enable this setting manually.
- **Integrate with Azure Monitor** Azure Monitor can closely monitor storage capacity and performance metrics to provide you with a comprehensive view of the storage IOPS and space utilization. This can help you in planning any file share changes to address capacity or IOPS issues before they affect your clients. You can build custom dashboards to monitor the metrics that are most important for your organization and share them with all administrators to ensure a consistent view across the monitoring environment. You can also set up alerting to highlight any anomalous performance behavior so you can respond to such events in a timelier manner.
- **Ensure regular backups using Azure Backup** Azure Files includes built-in integration with Azure Backup to provide a seamless backup experience. Be sure to set up backups for all your file shares according to your organization's data recovery and retention requirements. Backups are stored in an Azure storage using LRS or GRS, depending on your redundancy requirements. Take this into account when planning for the overall redundancy of the file share environment.

Chapter 3

Azure Managed Disks

Overview

In February 2017, Microsoft announced the general availability for the Azure Managed Disks service, starting with the Standard and Premium disk types. Managed disks enable Azure customers to reduce overhead associated with managing and scaling storages account while creating or managing virtual machine (VM) disks. Microsoft also introduced numerous features that made managed disks a compelling solution for every Azure-hosted infrastructure as a service (IaaS) environment and for customers considering migrating to the cloud. Over time, the list of features and benefits associated with the Azure Managed Disks service has grown, and it has become the default disk solution for most organizations that use Azure for their VMs.

Each Azure managed disk is a fully managed block-level storage volume designed for the highest level of redundancy and availability. Azure currently offers different types of managed disks, including Ultra Disks, Premium SSD Disks, Standard SSD Disks, and Standard HDD disks. Each disk type provides varying levels of performance and scalability.

Key features

Some key features and benefits of using managed disks in your Azure environment include the following:

- **High availability, resiliency, and redundancy** Microsoft provides 99.999% availability for VM workloads that use managed disks. Managed disks are designed to maintain multiple replicas—three to be exact, spread across an Azure region. This makes managed disks extremely resilient, and ensures that your workload can continue to process even if there are issues with one or two replicas. Microsoft provides an industry leading 0% annualized failure rate.
- **High scalability** Microsoft currently supports the deployment of 50,000 managed disks per region per subscription, allowing large enterprises to deploy thousands of VMs in a single subscription.
- **Support for large Virtual Machine Scale Sets (VMSS)** You can use managed disks with VMSS. The scalability of managed disks makes it possible to deploy large VMSS consisting of up to 1,000 nodes.

- **Support for availability sets** Azure Managed Disks provides native integration with availability sets. Disks for VMs that are part of an availability set are spread across multiple fault domains with the selected Azure region and isolated from each other.
- **Support for availability zones** You can deploy managed disks across availability zones to improve redundancy. Availability zones provide additional redundancy over availability sets because the power and networking in each availability zone is independent of the others.
- **Support for existing virtual hard disks (VHDs)** You can easily upload existing VHDs up to 32 terabytes (TB) in size to Azure for use as managed disks. This process makes it extremely easy for organizations to migrate their existing workloads to Azure.
- **Role-based access control (RBAC)** Azure Managed Disks supports permission management using Azure RBAC, making it possible to granularly assign permissions to managed disks to administrators based on their roles and responsibilities.
- **Native integration with Azure Backup** You can use Azure Backup to back up managed disks from within the Azure Managed Disks service. You can schedule backups during off-peak hours and retain backups based on your organizational policies. You restore backups from the Azure Backup service.
- **Disk encryption** Managed disks are encrypted by default. They support multiple types of encryption, including Microsoft-managed encryption keys, customer-managed encryption keys, and double encryption with both types of keys. In addition, managed disks support Azure Disk Encryption, which allows you to encrypt the disk inside the VM using BitLocker for Windows or DM-Crypt for Linux VMs.
- **Easy migration for unmanaged disks** You can easily migrate unmanaged disks stored in Azure Storage accounts to managed disks. This increases the resiliency and redundancy of your IaaS VMs and provides significantly higher availability for your workloads.
- **Support for shared disks for clustered applications** You can set up managed disks as shared disks. This allows you to attach them to multiple VMs to host or migrate clustered applications to Azure.
- **Disk bursting for better performance** Managed disks allow you to increase the IOPS available for use for Premium and Standard SSD disks with on-demand or credit-based bursting models. Each model provides different capabilities to maximize the performance of your workloads when needed.
- **Private Link Support** You can use Private Link to import or export managed disks to or from Azure. This enables organizations to securely transfer disk data over a completely private connection.

Key concepts

Now that you have an initial understanding of the Azure Managed Disks service, let's spend some time going through all the different components and features in detail.

Disk roles

In Azure, disks play three primary roles:

- **Operating system (OS) disk** An OS disk is created by default for every VM you create in Azure. This disk contains the OS running on the VM as well as the boot volume. The OS disk supports partitioning with a master boot record (MBR) and GUID partition table (GPT) depending on the OS requirement. By default, most operating systems use partitioning with MBR, which limits the OS disk capacity to 2 TB. However, you can increase this to 4 TB by converting the disk from MBR to GPT.
- **Temporary disk** Microsoft provides a temporary disk as a non-persistent disk for specific VM models in Azure. When selecting the VM size in Azure, you can see the size of the temporary disk provided with that VM type. Any data you store on the temporary disk should be data that you are willing to lose, such as page files, swap files, or temporary logs. Each time a VM undergoes a forced restart, maintenance, or a redeployment, data on the temporary disk is erased. The VM can retain data stored on these disks only during standard reboot operations. Temporary disks are not encrypted by default, although you can enable encryption if needed. These disks are mapped as D: in Windows VMs and /dev/sdb in Linux-based VMs.
- **Data disk** Data disks are optional, and you can use them based on your workload requirements—for example, separating database installation files from data and log files, which can be stored on their own or individual data disks. As mentioned, OS disks have a maximum capacity of 4 TB, so any data-storage requirements that exceed that would require you to use data disks. The maximum disk capacity for a single data disk is currently 32,767 gigabytes (GB) for Standard HDD, Standard SSD, and Premium SSD disks. However, Ultra disks can be scaled up to 65,536 GB. The number and type of data disks that you can use with a VM depends on the size and type of the VM. Be sure to consider this when selecting the size for your VM.

> ***NOTE*** **Every VM has an OS disk. Whether a VM has a temporary disk depends on the VM model. Data disks are optional based on your workload requirements.**

Disk types

Azure offers four types of disks:

- Standard HDD disks
- Standard SSD disks
- Premium SSD disks
- Ultra disks

Standard HDD disks

Standard HDD disks are suitable for workloads that are less critical and are not latency sensitive and for dev/test environments. These disks provide write latencies of less than 10 milliseconds (ms) and read latencies of less than 20 ms. Their performance varies depending on numerous factors, including IO size and workload pattern. Standard HDD disks are the least expensive (per gigabyte) disk option in Azure.

Standard SSD disks

Standard SSD disks are a great alternative for customers that want better performance, scalability, availability, and reliability than is possible with Standard HDD disks. Standard SSD disks are a great choice for low-intensity workloads that require consistent performance, such as web servers, low-usage business applications, and low IOPS applications. Standard SSD disks of 512 GB or more support credit-based bursting, making them ideal for applications that require a burst of performance only on rare occasions. All Azure VMs support Standard SSD disks.

Premium SSD disks

Premium SSD disks offer the second highest level of disk performance, with single-digit millisecond latencies, targeted IOPS, and defined throughput 99.9% of the time. They are suitable for high-intensity workloads, such as production applications and databases.

Premium SSD disks come in different sizes, and the level of IOPS support differs depending on the size of the Premium SSD disk. For example, P1 4 GB to P4 32 GB disks provide 120 IOPS, P10 128 GB disks provide 500 IOPS, while P80 32 TB disks provide 20,000 IOPS. Disk throughput and burst performance also increase as the capacity of the Premium SSD disks go up.

A few more features of Premium SSD disks are as follows:

- Premium SSD disks support one-year reservations to help you save on costs. You can set reservations for disks 1 TB and larger.
- Premium SSD disks support on-demand and credit-based bursting models. Bursting enables the Premium SSD to increase its performance in the short term to meet workload requirements.
- Only specific Azure VM types support Premium SSD disks. When you select a VM type, Azure shows you which types of disks that VM type supports. Because Microsoft adds and removes VM SKUs on an ongoing basis, I have not listed the VM types here, because they may change by the time you read this.

Ultra disks

Ultra disks currently provide the highest level of performance in terms of IOPS and disk throughput, with sub-millisecond latency 99.99% of the time. This makes Ultra disks suitable for critical high-performance workloads such as SAP HANA, mission-critical databases, and transaction-heavy applications.

By default, each Ultra disk can be scaled up to 32 TB. However, you can contact Azure support to request an increase of up to 64 TB. In terms of IOPS, each Ultra disk supports a minimum of 300 IOPS per gibibyte (GiB) and currently maxes out at 160,000 IOPS per disk.

Ultra disks allow you to adjust IOPS and throughput performance during runtime. You are permitted four adjustments every 24 hours. Each adjustment can take up to one hour to take effect and requires sufficient performance bandwidth capacity to prevent failures.

At present, Ultra disks have numerous limitations. These include lack of support for the following:

- Availability sets
- Azure Dedicated Host
- Disk snapshots
- Azure Backup
- Azure Site Recovery
- Disk exports
- VM image creation

In addition, Ultra disks cannot be used as OS disks. They can only be set up as data disks. For high-performance workloads that call for the use of an Ultra disk, you will want to set up the OS disk as a Premium SSD disk and leverage Ultra disks for all your workload data.

> **TIP** Review the latest guidance available from Microsoft when planning your deployment, as these limitations may have changed by that time.

Managed disk creation walkthrough

The following sections step you through the process of creating a managed disk using the Azure portal, Azure PowerShell, and the Azure CLI.

> **IMPORTANT** If you are following along, select resources and resource names based on your environment.

> **IMPORTANT** If you are following along, be sure to delete any unwanted resources after you have completed testing to reduce charges levied by Microsoft.

USING AZURE PORTAL

To create a managed disk using the Azure portal, follow these steps:

1. Log in to the Azure portal, type **disks** in the search box, and select the **Disks** option in the list that appears. (See Figure 3-1.)

   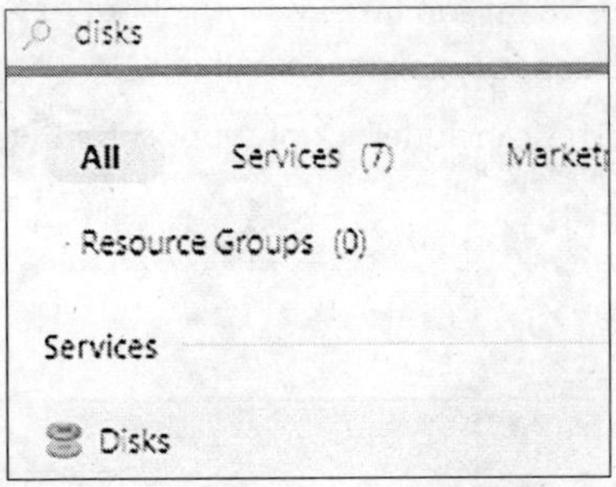

   FIGURE 3-1 Searching for the Disks service in the Azure portal.

2. On the Disks page (see Figure 3-2), click **Create**.

   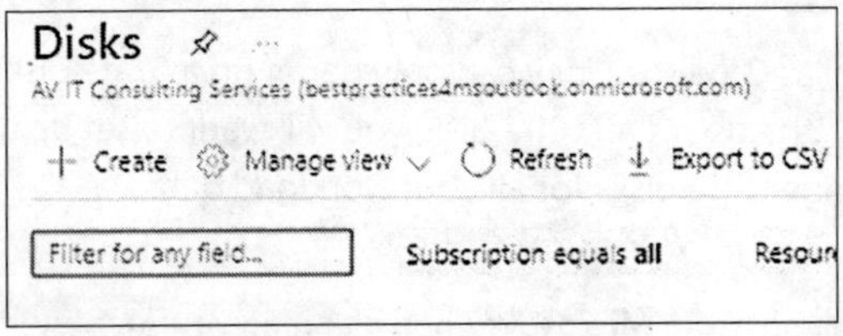

   FIGURE 3-2 Creating a new disk.

3. In the **Basics** tab of the Create a Managed Disk wizard (see Figure 3-3), enter the following information:
   - **Subscription** Select the subscription in which you want to create the new managed disk.
   - **Resource Group** Select an existing resource group in which to create the new managed disk or create a new one.
   - **Disk Name** Enter a unique name for the managed disk.
   - **Region** Select the Azure region where you want to host the managed disk.
   - **Availability Zone** Select the availability zone you want to use or leave this option set to **None** (the default).
   - **Source Type** If the disk will be created from source data, such as a snapshot, storage blob, another disk, etc., select the source type.
4. To create a disk that is a different redundancy level, type, size, or performance tier from the default (1,024 GiB Premium SSD LRS), click the **Change Size** link in the **Size** section of the wizard's **Basics** tab.
5. In the Select a Disk Size dialog box, open the **Disk SKU** drop-down list and choose a disk type/redundancy level pairing. (See Figure 3-4.)

NOTE For more on redundancy levels for managed disks, see the section "Disk redundancy" later in this chapter.

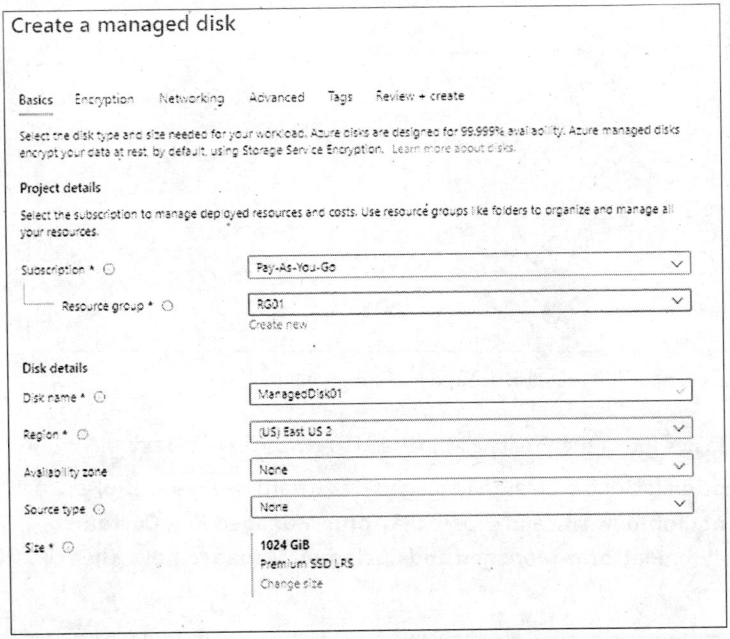

FIGURE 3-3 The Basics tab of the Create a Managed Disk wizard.

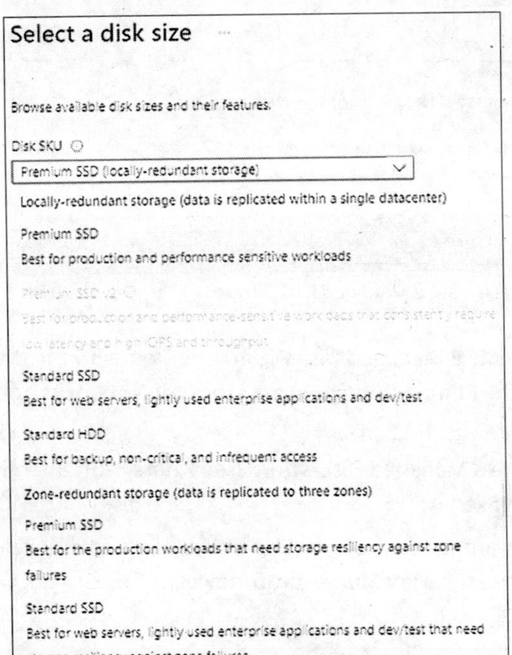

FIGURE 3-4 Choose a disk type and redundancy level.

6. Click a size option in the list to select it. Alternatively, use the **Custom Disk Size (GiB)** and **Performance Tier** drop-down lists to choose a custom size/tier pairing. Then click **OK**. (See Figure 3-5.)

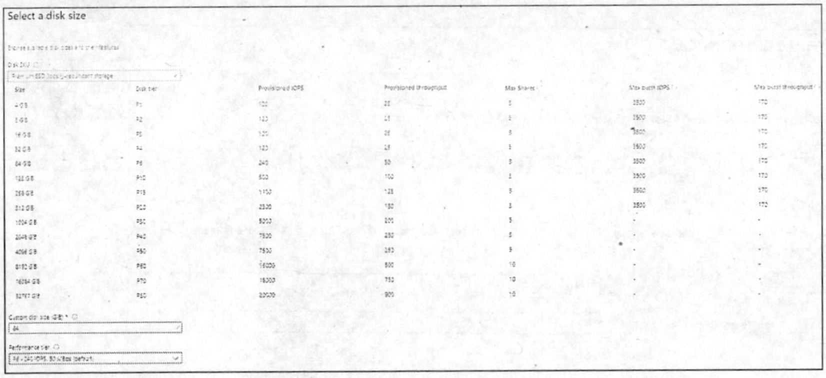

FIGURE 3-5 Selecting a different disk size and performance tier.

7. Back in the **Basics** tab of the Create a Managed Disk wizard, click **Next**.
8. In the **Encryption** tab of the Create a Managed Disk wizard (see Figure 3-6), open the **Key Management** drop-down list and choose **Platform-Managed Key**, **Customer-Managed Key**, or **Platform-Managed and Customer-Managed Keys**. Then click **Next**.

NOTE **To use customer-managed keys, you must first generate and store the keys in the Azure Key Vault service.**

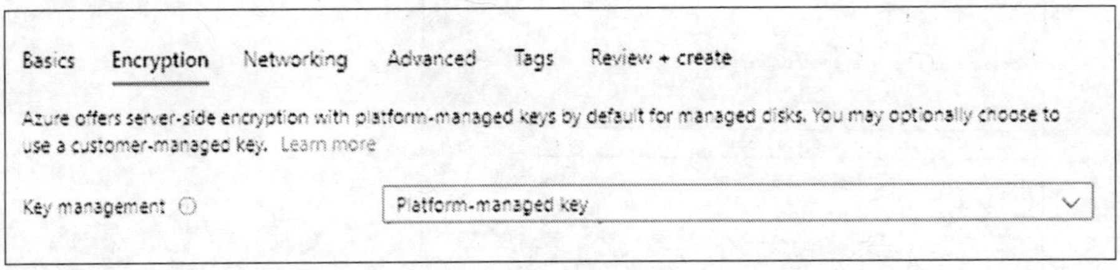

FIGURE 3-6 The Encryption tab of the Create a Managed Disk wizard.

9. In the **Networking** tab of the Create a Managed Disk wizard (see Figure 3-7), in the **Network Access** section, leave the **Enable Public Access from All Networks** option button selected and click **Next**.
10. In the **Advanced** tab of the Create a Managed Disk wizard (see Figure 3-8), enter the following information and click **Next**:
    - **Enable Shared Disk** If you want to use this managed disk as a shared disk, select the **Yes** Option button. Then use the **Max Shares** drop-down list to specify how many VMs will share the disk.

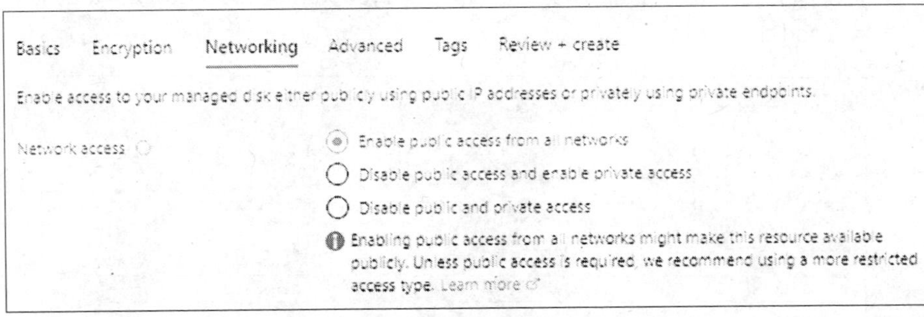

FIGURE 3-7 The Networking tab of the Create a Managed Disk wizard.

NOTE **For more on shared disks, see the section "Shared disks" later in this chapter.**

- **On-Demand Bursting** If you want this managed disk to be capable of on-demand bursting, select the **Enable On-Demand Bursting** check box.

NOTE **The Enable On-Demand Bursting check box is available only if your managed disk is 512 GB or more. This option is covered in more detail later in this chapter.**

- **Enable Data Access Authentication Mode** Optionally, select this check box to enable data access authentication. When you enable data access authentication, you can limit who can download the disk to admins who are authorized using Azure AD and authenticated using an approved account.

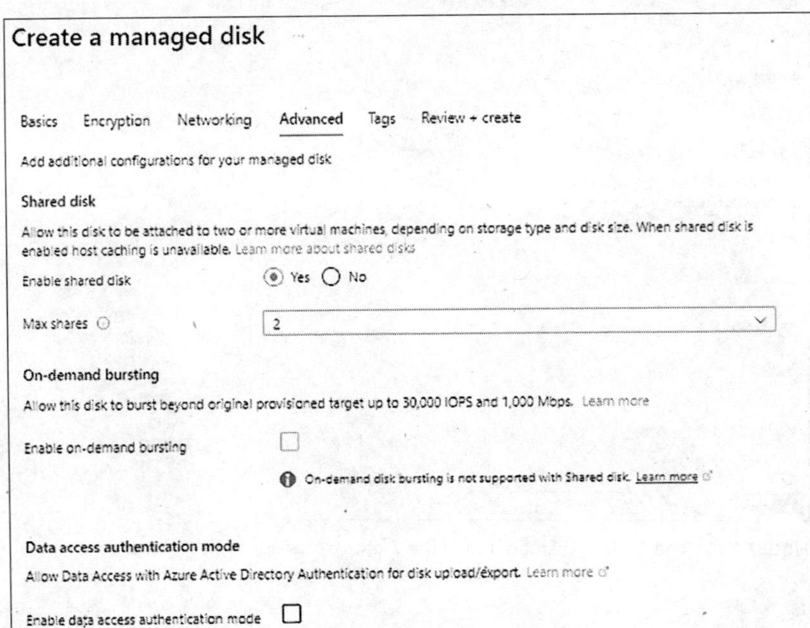

FIGURE 3-8 The Advanced tab of the Create a Managed Disk wizard.

11. In the **Tags** tab (see Figure 3-9), enter any tags you want to associate with the managed disk and click **Next**.

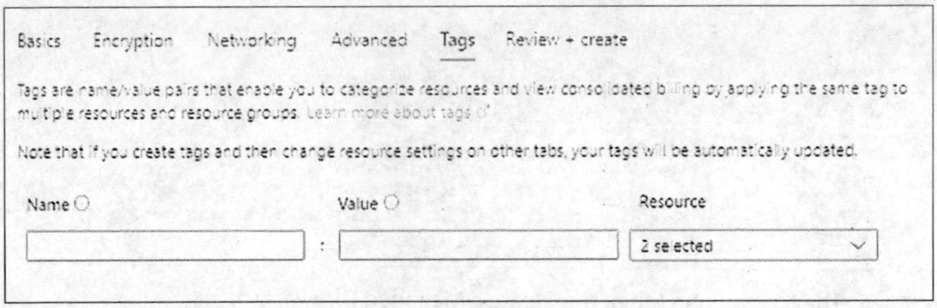

FIGURE 3-9 The Tags tab of the Create a Managed Disk wizard.

12. In the **Review + Create** tab (see Figure 3-10), review your settings, and click **Create** to create the managed disk.

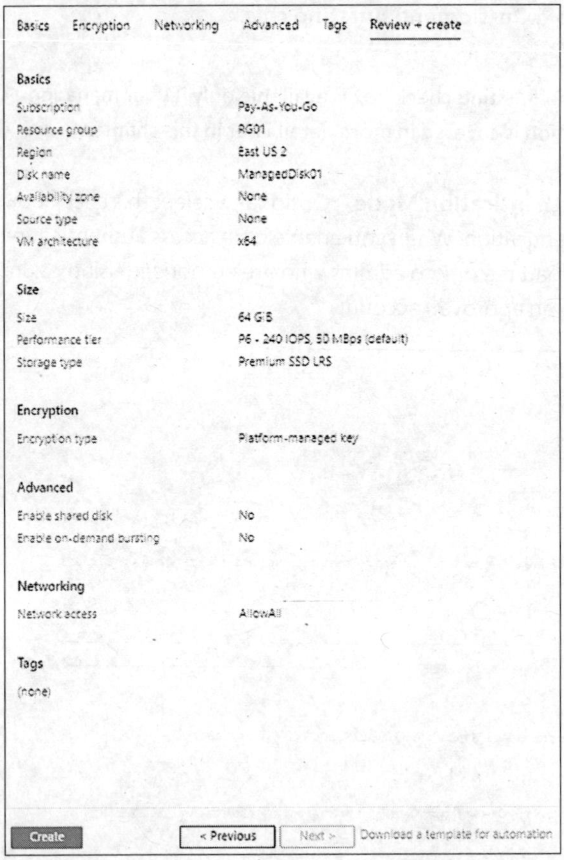

FIGURE 3-10 The Review + Create tab of the Create a Managed Disk wizard.

13. After the managed disk is created, click **Go to Resource** to access its page. (See Figure 3-11.)

FIGURE 3-11 Managed disk deployment completion.

USING AZURE POWERSHELL

Use the following Azure PowerShell code to create a managed disk:

```
#Define variables
$resourceGroup = "RG01"
$location = "EastUS2"
$vm = "SourceVM"
$MgdDiskName = "ManagedDisk01"

#Create a disk config object - Change the disk redundancy as needed
$MgdDiskConfig = New-AzDiskConfig `
    -Location $location `
    -CreateOption Empty `
    -DiskSizeGB 64 `
    -EncryptionType EncryptionAtRestWithPlatformKey `
    -PublicNetworkAccess true `
    -Architecture X64 `
    -SkuName Standard_LRS/Premium_LRS/StandardSSD_LRS/UltraSSD_LRS/Premium_ZRS/
StandardSSD_ZRS

#Create Data Disk
$MgdDisk = New-AzDisk `
    -ResourceGroupName $resourceGroup `
    -DiskName $MgdDiskName `
    -Disk $mgddiskConfig

#Verify disk
Get-AzDisk `
    -ResourceGroupName $resourceGroup `
```

```
    -DiskName $MgdDiskName

#Optional - Attach disk to VM
$Azvm = Get-AzVM `
    -ResourceGroupName $resourceGroup `
    -Name $vm

$Azvm = Add-AzVMDataDisk `
    -VM $vm `
    -Name $MgdDiskName `
    -CreateOption Attach `
    -ManagedDiskId $MgdDisk.Id `
    -Lun 1

Update-AzVM `
    -ResourceGroupName $resourceGroup `
    -VM $Azvm
```

USING AZURE CLI

Use the following code to create a managed disk in the Azure CLI:

```
#Define variables
resourceGroup="RG01"
location="EastUS2"
vm="SourceVM"
MgdDiskName="ManagedDisk01"

#Create managed disk - Change the disk redundancy as needed
az disk create \
                    --resource-group $resourceGroup \
                    --name $MgdDiskName \
                    --size-gb 64 \
      --architecture x64 \
      --encryption-type EncryptionAtRestWithPlatformKey \
      --location $location \
      --public-network-access Enabled \
      --sku Premium_LRS/PremiumV2_LRS/Premium_ZRS/StandardSSD_LRS/StandardSSD_ZRS/
Standard_LRS/UltraSSD_LRS

#Verify disk
mgddisk=$(az disk show \
                    --name $MgdDiskName \
                    --resource-group $resourceGroup)

#Optional - Attach disk to VM
az vm disk attach \
```

```
                    --disks $mgddisk \
    --name $MgdDiskName \
    --resource-group $resourceGroup \
                    --vm-name $vm
```

Private Link integration

Private Link provides secure connectivity to Azure PaaS services and Azure hosted services from your networks over a private endpoint. A private endpoint is a network interface connected to the Azure PaaS service or Azure hosted service, such as Managed Disks, that is attached to an Azure virtual network. With Private Link and private endpoints, you can safely and securely transfer managed disk files between regions using a private connection on the Microsoft backbone network instead of the public internet. You can also import VHD files from an on-premises environment directly to an empty managed disk in Azure over a private connection. Time-restricted Shared Access Signature (SAS) URLs can provide access to the unused managed disks and snapshots for transfer.

> **NOTE** Another book in this series, *Microsoft Azure Networking: The Definitive Guide*, covers Private Link in detail in Chapter 10.

Private Link integration walkthrough

The following sections step you through the process of creating a private endpoint and integrating Private Link with the managed disk using the Azure portal and the Azure CLI.

> **IMPORTANT** If you are following along, select resources and resource names based on your environment.

> **IMPORTANT** If you are following along, be sure to delete any unwanted resources after you have completed testing to reduce charges levied by Microsoft.

USING AZURE PORTAL

To create a private endpoint and integrate Private Link with a managed disk using the Azure portal, follow these steps:

1. Log in to the Azure portal, type **disk accesses** in the search box, and select the **Disk Access** option from the list that appears. (See Figure 3-12.)

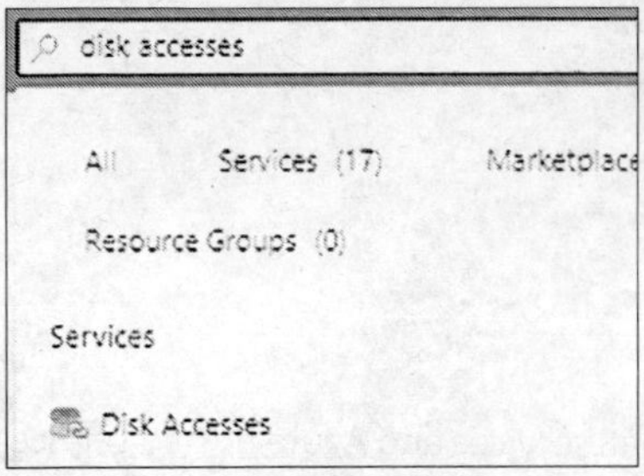

FIGURE 3-12 Searching for disk accesses in the Azure portal.

2. On the Disk Access page, click **Create Disk Access**. (See Figure 3-13.)

FIGURE 3-13 Create disk access.

3. In the **Basics** tab of the Create a Disk Access wizard (see Figure 3-14), enter the following information:
   - **Subscription** Select the subscription in which you want to create the disk access resource.
   - **Resource Group** Select an existing resource group in which to create the disk access resource or create a new one.
   - **Name** Enter a unique name for the disk access resource.
   - **Region** Select the Azure region where you want to host the disk access resource.

   Before you continue with the Create a Disk Access wizard, you need to create the private endpoint. You'll do that next.
4. At the bottom of the **Basics** tab, click **Add**.
5. In the Create a Private Endpoint dialog box (see Figure 3-15), enter the following information and click **OK**:
   - **Subscription** Select the subscription you want to use to create the private endpoint.

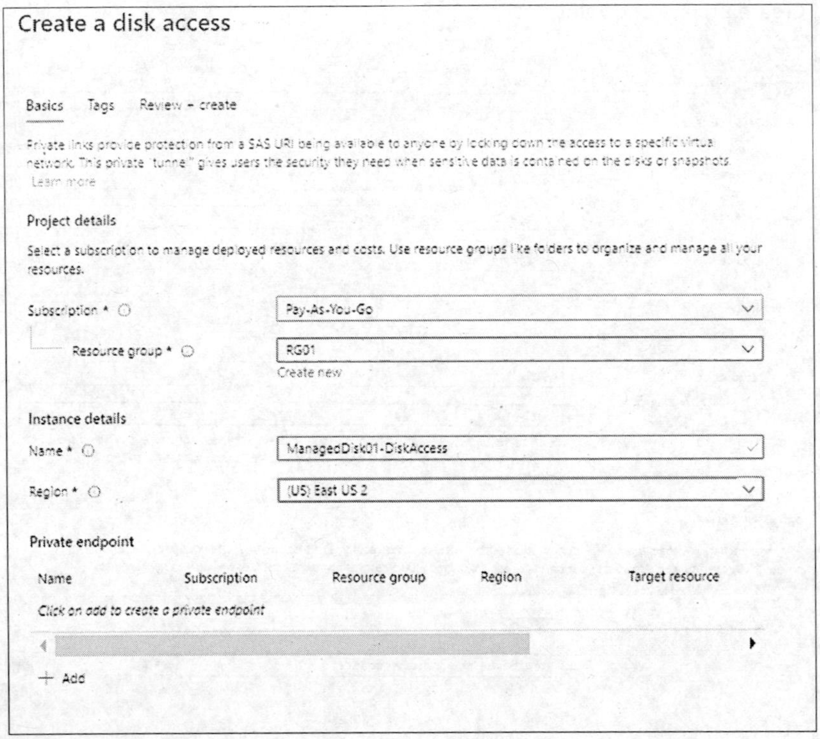

FIGURE 3-14 The Basics tab of the Create a Disk Access wizard.

- **Resource Group** Select an existing resource group in which to create the private endpoint or create a new one.
- **Location** Select the Azure region where you want to host the private endpoint.
- **Name** Enter a unique name for the private endpoint.
- **Target Resource** Select **Disks**.
- **Virtual Network** Select the virtual network on which to create the private endpoint.
- **Subnet** Select the subnet on which to create the private endpoint.
- **Integrate with Private DNS Zone** Select **Yes** to integrate with a private DNS zone or select **No** if you plan to create a DNS record in your own DNS servers or on the host files of the workloads VMs. In this case, select **Yes**.
- **Private DNS Zone** Select the private DNS zone with which you want to integrate the private endpoint. In this case, leave it set to the default, **privatelink.blob.core.windows.net**.

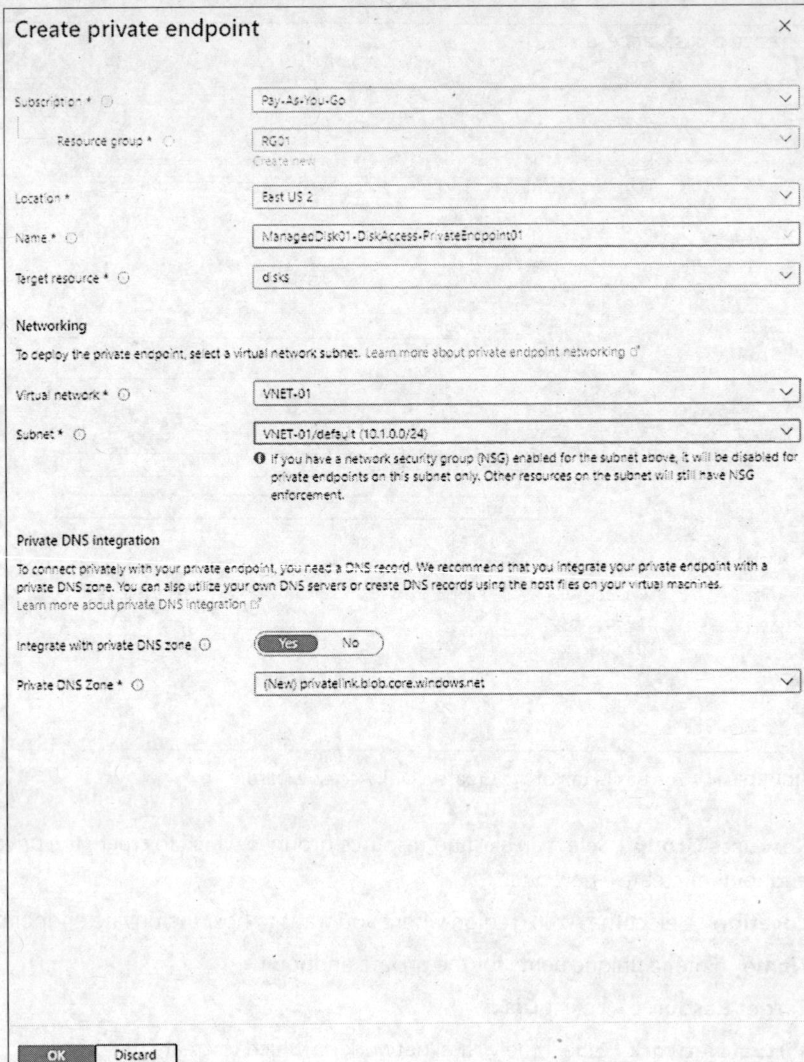

FIGURE 3-15 The Create Private Endpoint dialog box.

6. Click the **Tags** tab (see Figure 3-16), enter any tags you want to associate with the private endpoint, and click **Next**.
7. In the **Review + Create** tab (see Figure 3-17), review your settings and click **Create** to create the private endpoint.

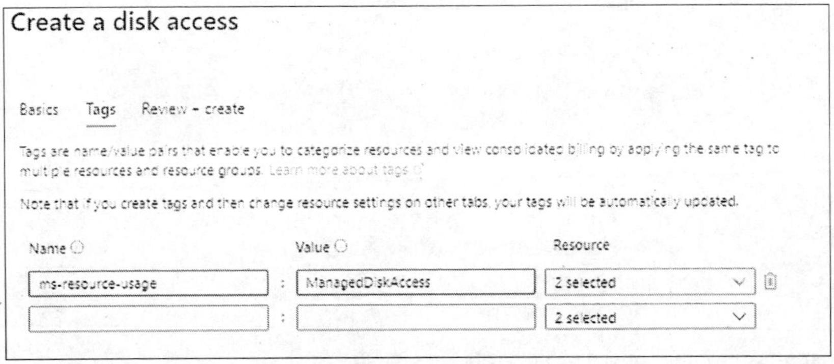

FIGURE 3-16 The Tags tab of the Create a Disk Access wizard.

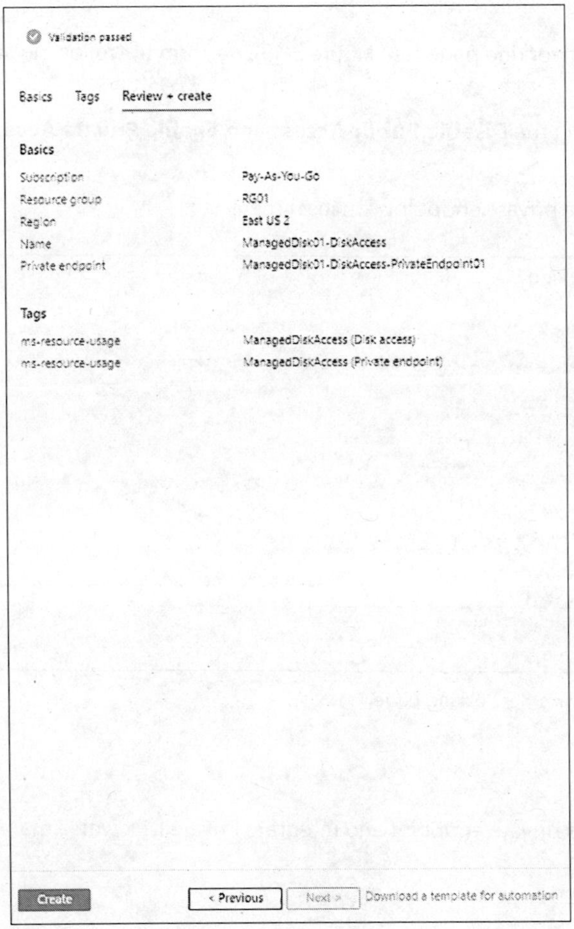

FIGURE 3-17 The Review + Create tab of the Create a Disk Access wizard.

8. After the private endpoint is created, click **Go to Resource** to access its page. (See Figure 3-18.)

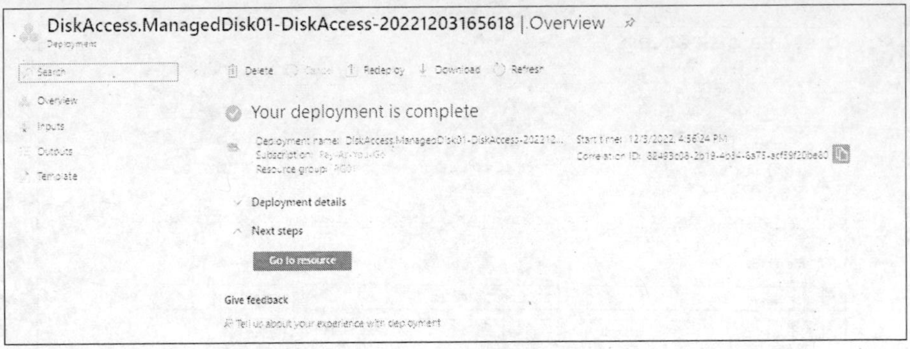

FIGURE 3-18 Private endpoint deployment completion.

9. In the left pane of the page for the managed disk you created earlier, under **Settings**, click **Networking**.
10. On the managed disk's Networking page (see Figure 3-19), perform the following steps and click **Save**:
    - **Network Access** Select the **Disable Public Access and Enable Private Access** option button.
    - **Disk Access** Select the private endpoint you just created.

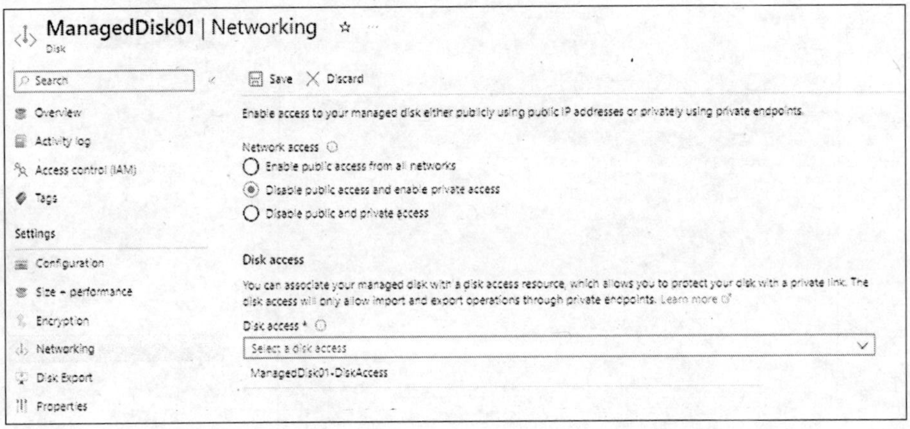

FIGURE 3-19 The managed disk's Networking page.

USING AZURE CLI

Use the following code to create a private endpoint and integrate Private Link with a managed disk in the Azure CLI:

```
#Define variables
resourceGroup="RG01"
```

```
location="EastUS2"
vm="SourceVM"
MgdDiskName="ManagedDisk01"
diskAccess="ManagedDisk01-DiskAccess"
vnet="VNET-01"
subnet="default"
privateEndPoint="ManagedDisk01-DiskAccess-PrivateEndpoint01"
#Create disk access
az disk-access create \
                    --name $diskAccess \
                    --resource-group $resourceGroup \
                    --location $location

diskAccessId=$(az disk-access show \
                    --name $diskAccess \
                    --resource-group $resourceGroup \
                    --query [id] -o tsv)

#Create private endpoint
az network private-endpoint create
    --resource-group $resourceGroup \
    --name $privateEndPoint \
    --vnet-name $vnet  \
    --subnet $subnet \
    --private-connection-resource-id $diskAccessId \
    --group-ids disks \
    --connection-name $privateEndPoint

#Create Private DNS zone config
az network private-dns zone create \
    --resource-group $resourceGroup \
    --name "privatelink.blob.core.windows.net"

az network private-dns link vnet create \
    --resource-group $resourceGroup \
    --zone-name "privatelink.blob.core.windows.net" \
    --name $privateEndPoint-DNSLink \
    --virtual-network $vnet \
    --registration-enabled false

az network private-endpoint dns-zone-group create \
    --resource-group $resourceGroup \
    --endpoint-name $privateEndPoint \
    --name $privateEndPoint-ZoneGroup \
```

```
    --private-dns-zone "privatelink.blob.core.windows.net" \
    --zone-name disks

#Update managed disk with Private Link config
diskAccessId=$(az resource show \
    --name $diskAccess \
    --resource-group $resourceGroup \
    --namespace Microsoft.Compute \
    --resource-type diskAccesses \
    --query [id] -o tsv)

az disk update \
    --name $diskName \
    --resource-group $resourceGroup \
    --network-access-policy AllowPrivate \
    --disk-access $diskAccessId
```

Encryption

Managed disks support two types of disk encryption:

- **Server-Side Encryption (SSE)** SSE manages encryption on the storage layer and is handled by the Azure Storage service. It provides encryption-at-rest and during write operations to the underlying storage, thereby ensuring that disks stored in Azure are not readable in the event of data theft. SSE is enabled by default for all managed disks, snapshots, and images across all Azure regions. SSE supports two types of key management: Azure platform-managed keys or customer-managed keys. You can choose which type of key management you want to use for each managed disk you create.
- **Azure Disk Encryption (ADE)** ADE refers to encryption within the system. It applies to the OS and data disks in an Azure IaaS VM. ADE encryption is performed using BitLocker technology in Windows and DM-Crypt technology in Linux. In both scenarios, the keys are integrated and stored in Azure Key Vault to make it easier for you to manage them.

Managed disk snapshots

Snapshots provide an easy way to back up a point-in-time copy of your managed disk for restore or cloning operations. Snapshots are read-only, crash-consistent copies of the disk. You can use them to create new managed disks without affecting the source managed disk in any way. Snapshots are, by default, stored as standard managed disks, but you can change this during the snapshot creation process.

IMPORTANT While snapshots serve as a great way to create a copy of a managed disk, they are not a replacement for regular backups, and you should not use them as such.

The first time you take a snapshot of a managed disk, it will be a full snapshot. Subsequent snapshots, however, can be incremental. An incremental snapshot captures all changes to the managed disk since the last snapshot of the disk. This reduces your storage footprint. If you need to restore from a single incremental snapshot, Azure automatically identifies all the incremental and full snapshots preceding the current one to reconstruct the entire disk. This makes incremental snapshots extremely cost-effective, making them the preferred option for regular snapshot management.

NOTE If the zone in which the incremental snapshot is created provides ZRS redundancy capabilities, then the incremental snapshot will automatically be saved with ZRS, too, unless specified otherwise.

NOTE If you are using full snapshots on premium storage to scale up VM deployments, we recommend you use custom images on standard storage in the Shared Image Gallery. This will help you achieve a more massive scale with a lower cost. For more on this, see Chapter 2, "Virtual Machine Scale Sets," in *Microsoft Azure Compute: The Definitive Guide*.

Incremental snapshots can also be useful for disaster recovery between Azure regions—that is, you can identify changes between two snapshots of the same disk, and then transfer only the differential changes to the secondary region instead of the entire snapshot. Then, when you restore/rebuild in the secondary region, you can use the snapshot of the base blob of the managed disk in combination with these differential changes. (See Figure 3-20.) This strategy can reduce time, costs, and network requirements for disaster recovery for managed disks.

NOTE Microsoft provides sample .NET code online to help you test this capability if you are interested in exploring it.

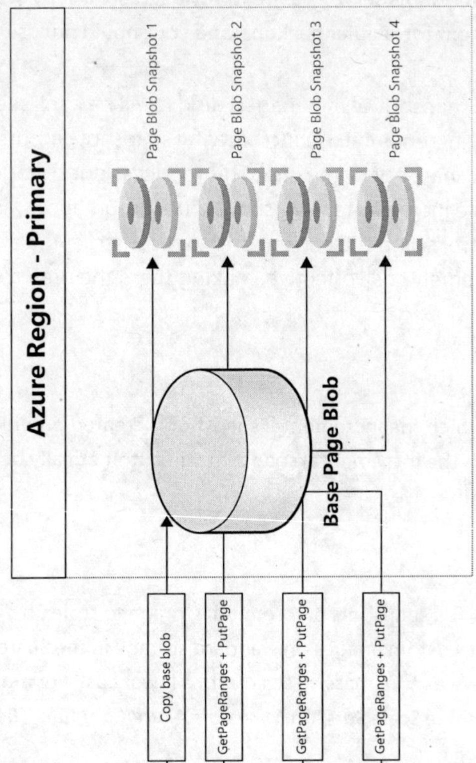

FIGURE 3-20 Incremental snapshots.

Incremental snapshots are a great feature, but they do have some limitations that exist at the time of this writing. By the time you read this, these limitations may have been addressed. Be sure to review Microsoft's latest guidance before finalizing your snapshot management strategy. Some key limitations at present include the following:

- Unlike full snapshots, incremental snapshots always use Standard HDD disks, regardless of the disk type used for the full snapshot.
- A single managed disk supports a maximum of 500 incremental snapshots.
- Each managed disk limits you to creating seven incremental snapshots, with a wait time of 5 minutes between each snapshot.
- The managed disk and snapshots must all be part of the same subscription.
- If you want to move a managed disk to another subscription, you will not be able to do so if the disk has incremental snapshots. You will need to keep this in mind when planning any such migrations.
- Differentials do not work for disks larger than 4 TB.

Managed disk snapshots walkthrough

The following sections step you through the process of creating a snapshot of a managed disk using the Azure portal, Azure PowerShell, and the Azure CLI.

> ***IMPORTANT*** **If you are following along, select resources and resource names based on your environment.**

> ***IMPORTANT*** **If you are following along, be sure to delete any unwanted resources after you have completed testing to reduce charges levied by Microsoft.**

USING AZURE PORTAL

To create a managed disk snapshot using the Azure portal, follow these steps:

1. In the Overview page for the managed disk you created earlier, click **Create Snapshot**. (See Figure 3-21.)

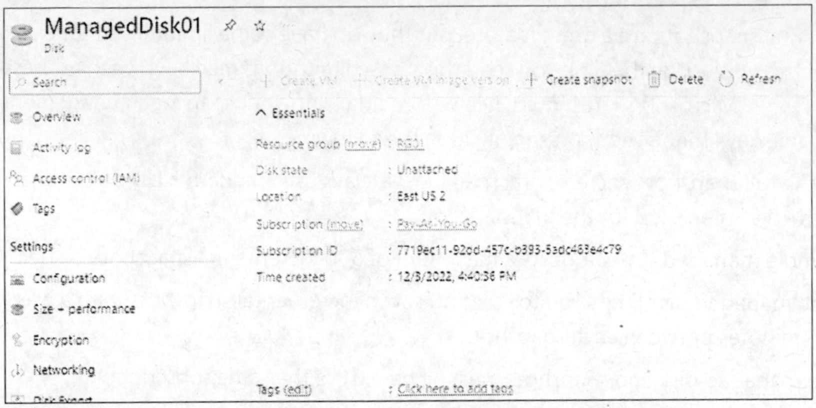

FIGURE 3-21 The Overview page for ManagedDisk01.

2. In the **Basics** tab of the Create Snapshot wizard (see Figure 3-22), enter the following information and click **Next**:
   - **Subscription** Select the subscription in which you want to create the snapshot.
   - **Resource Group** Select an existing resource group in which to create the snapshot or create a new one.
   - **Name** Enter a unique name for the snapshot.
   - **Snapshot Type** Leave this set to the default value of **Full**.

> ***NOTE*** Figure 3-22 shows a Full button and an Incremental button. Your screen might not reflect that because this is the first time you're creating a snapshot of this managed disk. The next time you create a snapshot, you'll want to choose the Incremental button.

   - **Storage Type** Select **Standard HDD**, **Standard SSD**, or **Premium SSD**, depending on your needs. (Remember, this is for the full snapshot; incremental snapshots always use Standard HDD disks.)

3. In the **Encryption** tab of the Create Snapshot wizard (see Figure 3-23), open the Key Management drop-down list and choose **Platform-Managed Key**, **Customer-Managed Key**, or **Platform-Managed and Customer-Managed Keys**. Then click **Next**.

> ***NOTE*** To use customer-managed keys, you must first generate and store the keys in the Azure Key Vault service.

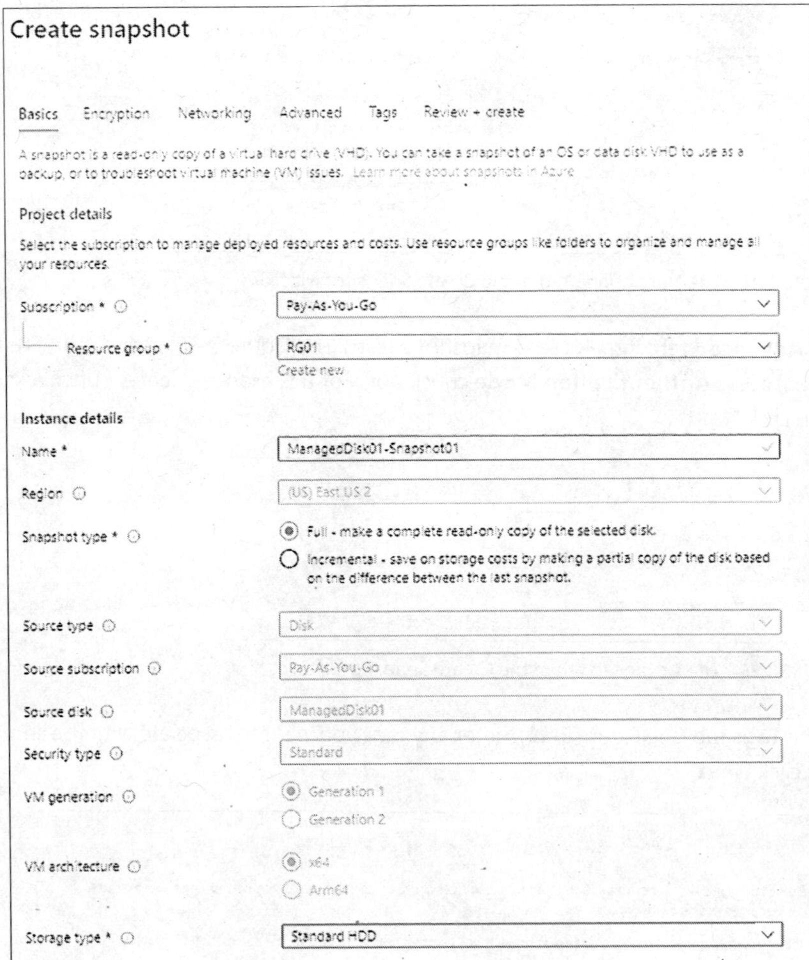

FIGURE 3-22 The Basics tab of the Create Snapshot wizard.

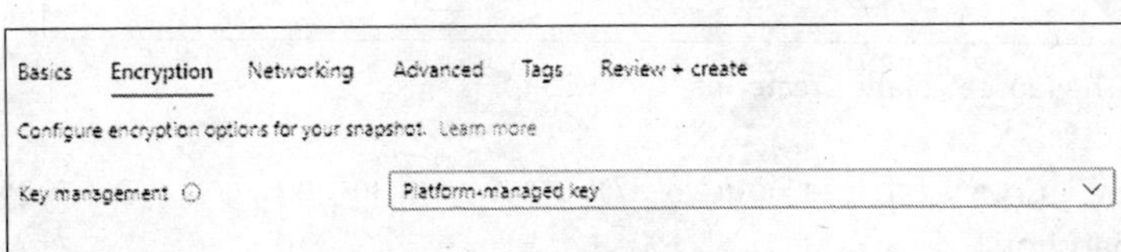

FIGURE 3-23 The Encryption tab of the Create Snapshot wizard.

4. In the **Networking** tab of the Create Snapshot wizard (see Figure 3-24), in the **Network Access** section, select the **Enable Public Access from All Networks** option button.

FIGURE 3-24 The Networking tab of the Create Snapshot wizard.

5. The **Advanced** tab of the Create Snapshot wizard (see Figure 3-25) includes an **Enable Data Access Authentication Mode** check box. For this example, leave it unchecked. Then click **Next**.

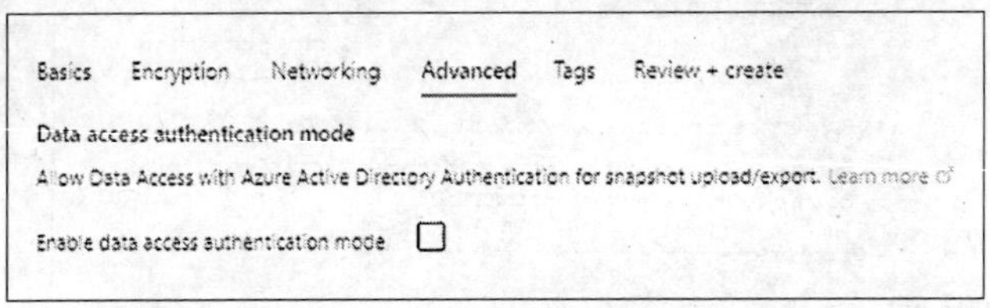

FIGURE 3-25 The Advanced tab of the Create Snapshot wizard.

6. In the **Tags** tab (see Figure 3-26), enter any tags you want to associate with the snapshot and click **Next**.

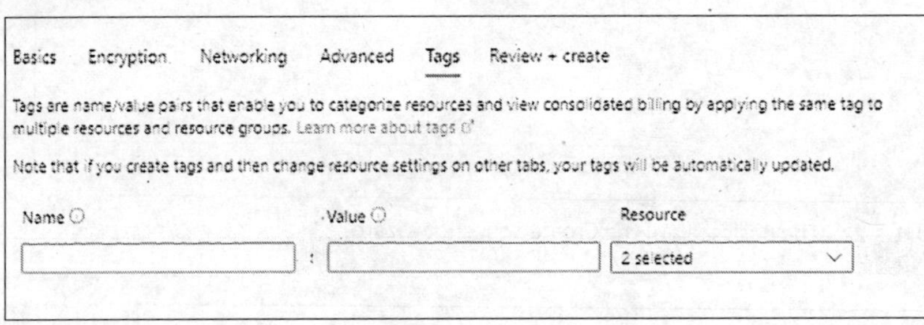

FIGURE 3-26 The Tags tab of the Create Snapshot wizard.

7. In the **Review + Create** tab (see Figure 3-27), review your settings, and click **Create** to create the snapshot.

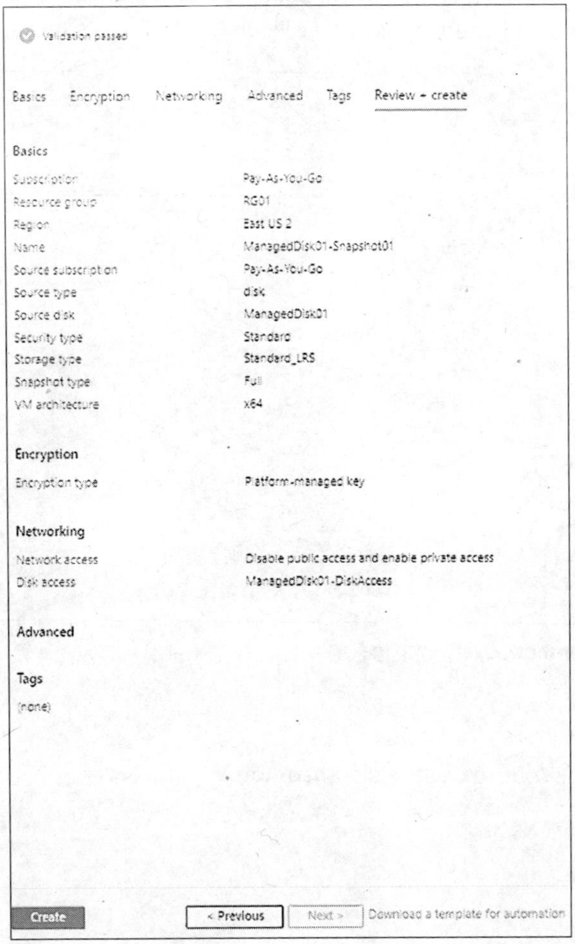

FIGURE 3-27 The Review + Create tab of the Create Snapshot wizard.

8. After the snapshot is created, click **Go to Resource** to access its page. (See Figure 3-28.)

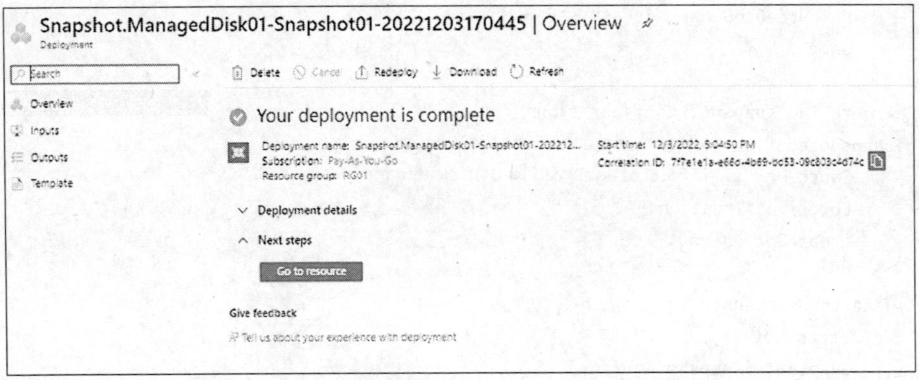

FIGURE 3-28 Snapshot deployment completion.

The snapshot's Overview page displays the properties of the snapshot, as well as Create Disk, Copy Snapshot, Delete, and Refresh options. (See Figure 3-29.)

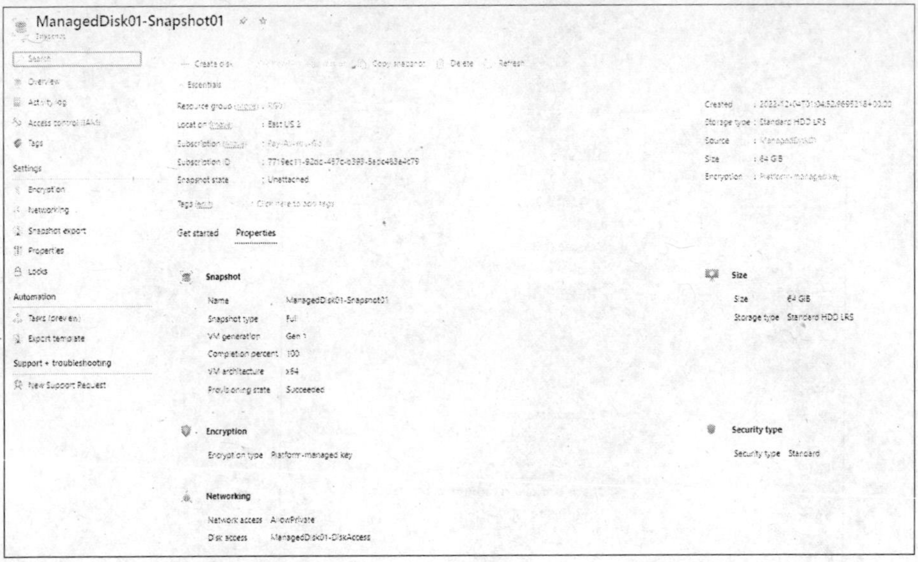

FIGURE 3-29 The new disk snapshot's Overview page.

USING AZURE POWERSHELL

Use the following Azure PowerShell code to create a disk snapshot:

```
#Define variables
$resourceGroup = "RG01"
$location = "EastUS2"
$vm = "SourceVM"
$snapshotName = "SourceVM-Snapshot-20230228"

#get the VM
$vminfo = Get-AzVM `
    -ResourceGroupName $resourceGroup `
    -Name $vm

#Create the snapshot configuration
$snapshotconfig =  New-AzSnapshotConfig `
    -SourceUri $vminfo.StorageProfile.OsDisk.ManagedDisk.Id `
    -Location $location `
    -CreateOption copy

#Take the snapshot.
New-AzSnapshot `
    -Snapshot $snapshotconfig `
```

```
    -SnapshotName $snapshotName `
    -ResourceGroupName $resourceGroup

#Verify snapshot
Get-AzSnapshot `
    -ResourceGroupName $resourceGroup
```

USING AZURE CLI

Use the following code to create a disk snapshot in the Azure CLI:

```
#Define variables
resourceGroup="RG01"
location="EastUS2"
vm="SourceVM"
snapshotName="SourceVM-Snapshot-20230228"

#get the VM
DiskInfo=$(az vm show \
   --resource-group $resourceGroup \
   --name $vm \
   --query "storageProfile.osDisk.managedDisk.id" \
   -o tsv)

#Take the snapshot.
az snapshot create \
   --resource-group $resourceGroup \
                     --source "$DiskInfo" \
                     --name $snapshotName

#Verify snapshot
az snapshot list \
   --resource-group $resourceGroup \
   -o table
```

Managed images

Managed images enable you to create hundreds of copies of customized VMs in Azure without having to create multiple copies of the underlying disks associated with each VM or manage any storage accounts to host them. You can easily create managed images out of managed disks; the resulting managed image will contain the configuration of the source VM, including all the managed disks associated with that source VM. This helps you to scale your VM resources using features like VMSS or Azure Virtual Desktop Session Host Pools, where capacity is added as load increases.

The primary difference between managed disks and managed images is that an image is built from a generalized VM and includes all the associated disks, whereas a snapshot is specific to a single disk and is a point-in-time copy of that disk. Generalizing a VM removes machine and user-specific information from the VM. So, for a VM that has multiple disks using disk spanning, a snapshot currently does not support a coordinated restore of all the disks and, therefore, might not be the right solution.

Managed images walkthrough

The following sections step you through the process of creating a managed image using the Azure portal, Azure PowerShell, and the Azure CLI.

> ***IMPORTANT*** **If you are following along, select resources and resource names based on your environment.**

> ***IMPORTANT*** **If you are following along, be sure to delete any unwanted resources after you have completed testing to reduce charges levied by Microsoft.**

> ***PREREQUISITE*** **If you are following along, you must create a VM to use to create the managed image. Be sure to stop that VM before starting the following procedure, however. The wizard will generalize this VM and make it unusable after the image is captured. (Optionally, you back up the VM and restore it after the process is complete.)**

USING AZURE PORTAL

To create a managed image using the Azure portal, follow these steps:

1. On the Overview page of the VM for which you want to create an image, click **Capture**. (See Figure 3-30.)

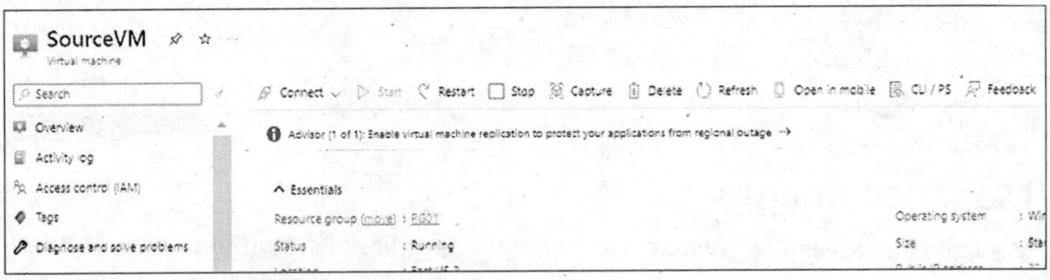

FIGURE 3-30 The Overview page for the VM.

2. In the **Basics** tab of the Create an Image wizard (see Figure 3-31), enter the following information and click **Next**:
   - **Resource Group** Select an existing resource group in which to create the new managed image or create a new one.
   - **Share Image to Azure Compute Gallery** For this walkthrough, select the **No, Capture Only a Managed Image** option button.

- **Automatically Delete this Virtual Machine After Creating the Image** Leave this checkbox unchecked (the default).
- **Zone Resiliency** Select this check box if you want to create a zone redundant image.
- **Name** Enter a unique name for the managed image.

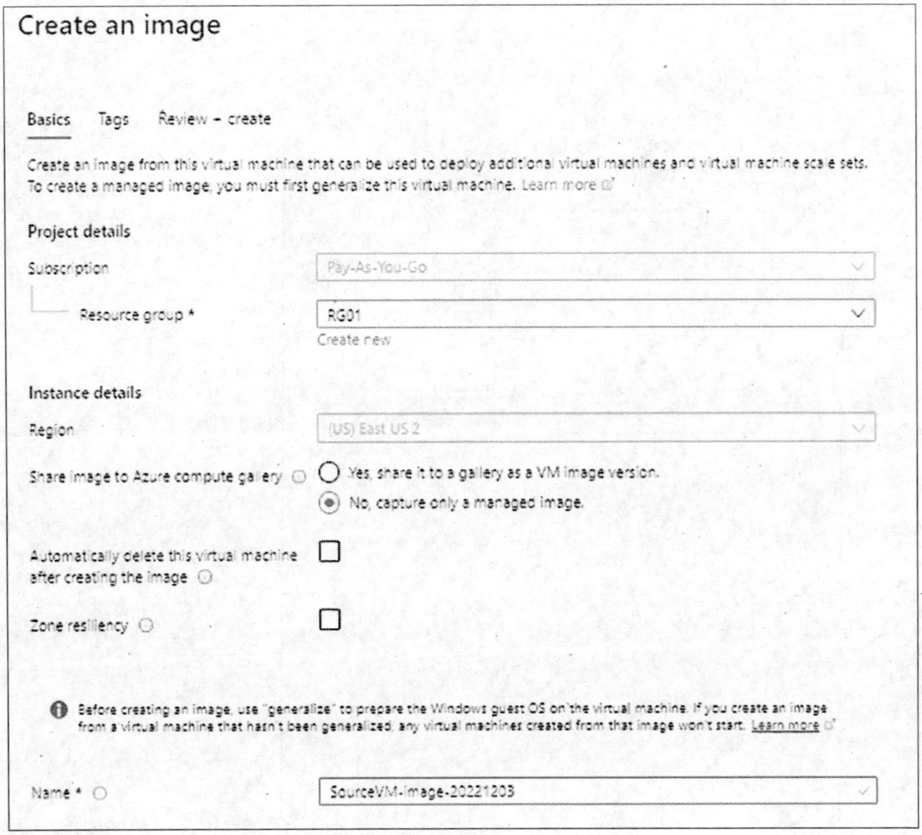

FIGURE 3-31 The Basics tab of the Create an Image wizard.

3. In the **Tags** tab (see Figure 3-32), enter any tags you want to associate with the managed image and click **Next**.

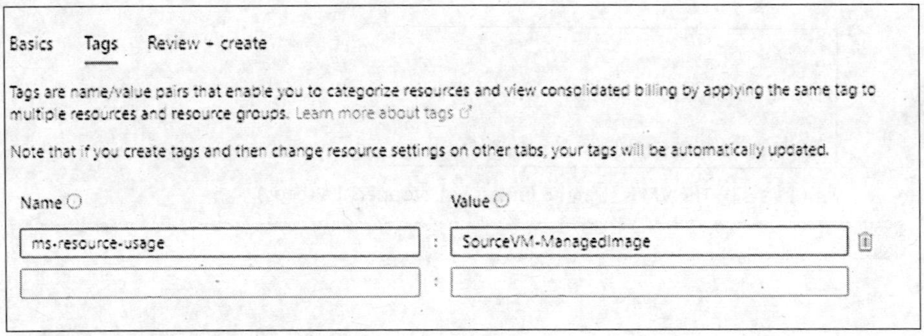

FIGURE 3-32 The Tags tab of the Create an Image wizard.

4. In the **Review + Create** tab (see Figure 3-33), review your settings, and click **Create** to create the managed image.

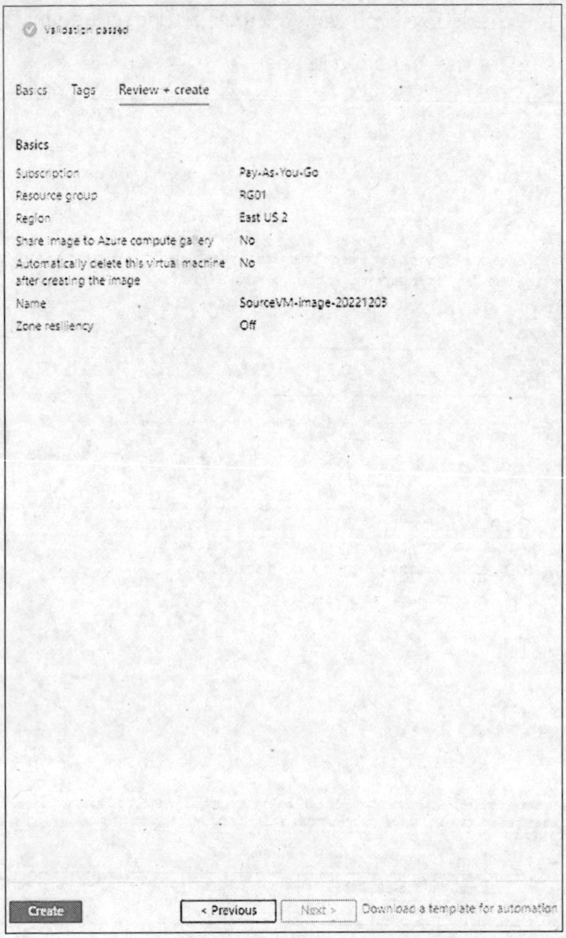

FIGURE 3-33 The Review + Create tab of the Create an Image wizard.

The source VM will be stopped automatically if you haven't turned it off already. (See Figure 3-34.) Azure will then generalize the VM and create the image.

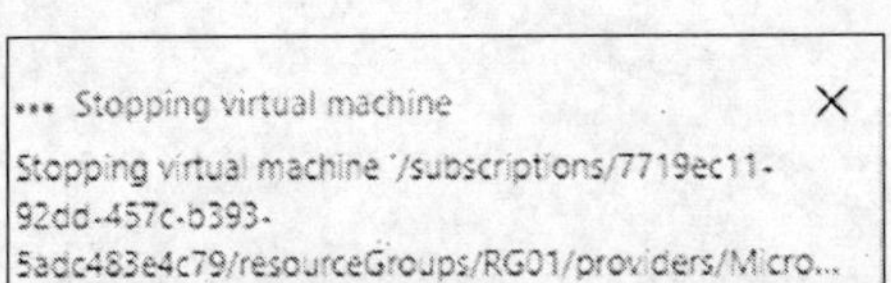

FIGURE 3-34 The VM is stopped (unless you stopped it already).

5. After the managed image is created, click **Go to Resource** to access its page. (See Figure 3-35.)

FIGURE 3-35 Managed image deployment completion.

The managed image's Overview page displays the properties of the managed image as well as Create VM, Clone to a VM Image, Delete, and Refresh options. (See Figure 3-36.)

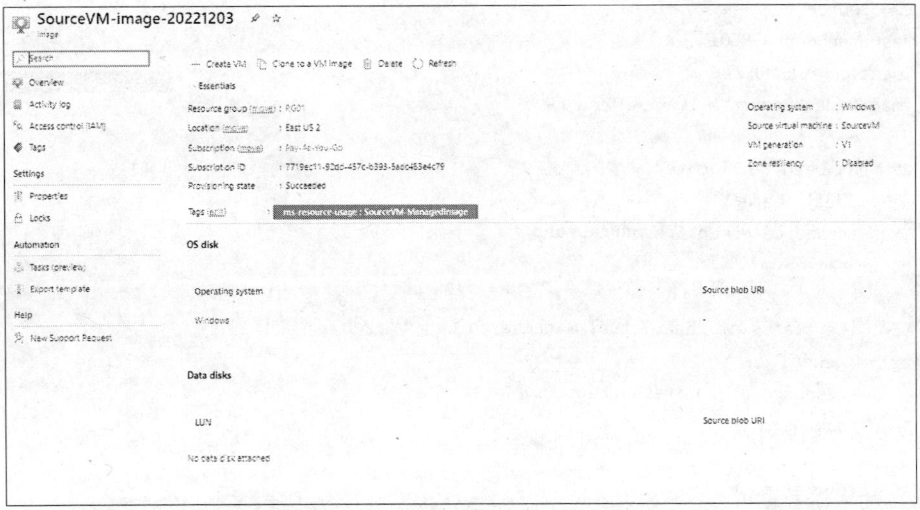

FIGURE 3-36 The new managed image's Overview page.

USING AZURE POWERSHELL

Use the following Azure PowerShell code to create a managed image:

```
#Define variables
$vm = "SourceVM"
$resourcegroup = RG01
$location = "EastUS2"
$imageName = "SourceVM-Image-20221203"
```

```
#VM has been deallocated
Stop-AzVM -ResourceGroupName $resourcegroup -Name $vm -Force

#Set the status of the virtual machine to Generalized.
Set-AzVm -ResourceGroupName $resourcegroup -Name $vm -Generalized

#Create the image configuration.
$vminfo = Get-AzVM -Name $vm -ResourceGroupName $resourcegroup
$vmimage = New-AzImageConfig -Location $location -SourceVirtualMachineId $vminfo.Id

#Create the image.
New-AzImage -Image $vmimage -ImageName $imageName -ResourceGroupName $resourcegroup
```

USING AZURE CLI

Use the following code to create a managed image in the Azure CLI:

```
#Define variables
vm="SourceVM"
resourcegroup=$RG01
location="EastUS2"
imageName="SourceVM-Image-20221203"

#VM has been deallocated
az vm deallocate \
    --resource-group $resourcegroup \
    --name $vm

#Set the status of the virtual machine to Generalized.
az vm generalize \
    --resource-group $resourcegroup \
    --name $vm

#Create the image.
az image create \
    --resource-group $resourcegroup \
--location $location \
--zone-resilient false \
 --name $imageName --source $vm
```

Performance tiering

When you create a managed disk, Azure automatically assigns a default performance target for that disk. This is based on predefined targets associated with the disk provisioned for the managed disk. This determines the IOPS and throughput available for that managed disk. This default performance target is not the maximum performance available for that managed disk, however. You can change the performance tier for a managed disk, without having to change the size of the disk. This can be beneficial in scenarios when you are running workloads that require high IOPS but do not require a lot of space for data storage.

You should use performance tiering in combination with disk bursting (discussed later in this chapter) to determine the ideal performance targets for your managed disks. If you observe your managed disks consistently requiring burst capacity to handle workload traffic, it is highly recommended that you compare any additional costs you are incurring to the costs of permanently changing the performance tier for that managed disk.

> ***NOTE*** **Performance tiering changes can be performed without downtime.**

Using performance tiering does have some limitations. These include the following:

- Performance tiering is supported only for Premium SSD managed disks.
- Currently, P60 and higher performance tiers can be used only by 4 TB or larger disks.
- Shared disks cannot use performance tiering.
- On managed disks created before June 2020, the performance tier can only be changed to the baseline tier for the managed disk size.

Write Accelerator

Premium SSD managed disks connected to M-Series Azure VMs can leverage a feature called Write Accelerator to improve I/O latency for write operations. Write Accelerator is ideal for high-volume log file updates that need to persist to disk. A database solution's transaction logs or redo log disks can benefit from using Write Accelerator as long as the workload is running on M-series VMs.

Performance tiering walkthrough

The following sections step you through the process of updating the performance tier of an existing managed disk using the Azure portal, Azure PowerShell, and the Azure CLI.

> ***IMPORTANT*** **If you are following along, select resources and resource names based on your environment.**

IMPORTANT If you are following along, be sure to delete any unwanted resources after you have completed testing to reduce charges levied by Microsoft.

USING AZURE PORTAL

To update the performance tier for an existing managed disk using the Azure portal, follow these steps:

1. Log in to the Azure portal, type **disks** in the search box, and select the **Disks** option in the list that appears. (See Figure 3-37.)

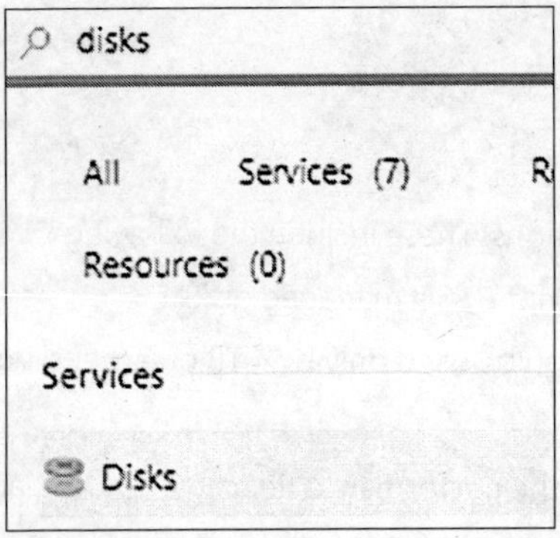

FIGURE 3-37 Searching for the Disks service in the Azure portal.

2. On the Disks page (see Figure 3-38), select the check box for the managed disk whose performance tier you want to update.

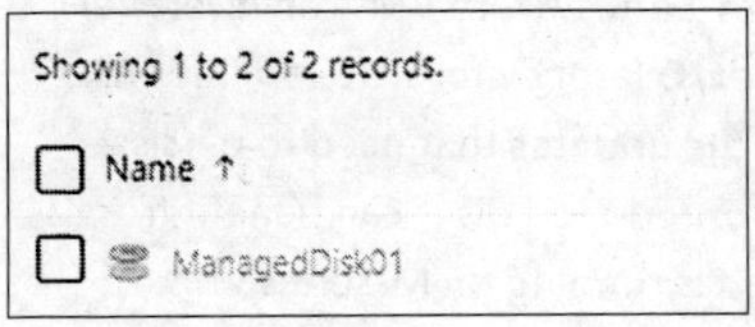

FIGURE 3-38 Select the managed disk whose performance tier you want to update.

3. In the left pane of the page for the managed disk you selected, under **Settings**, select **Size + Performance**.
4. On the managed disk's Size + Performance page, click the **Performance Tier** drop-down list and choose **P40 – 7500 IOPS, 250 Mbps** option (see Figure 3-39). Then click **Save**.

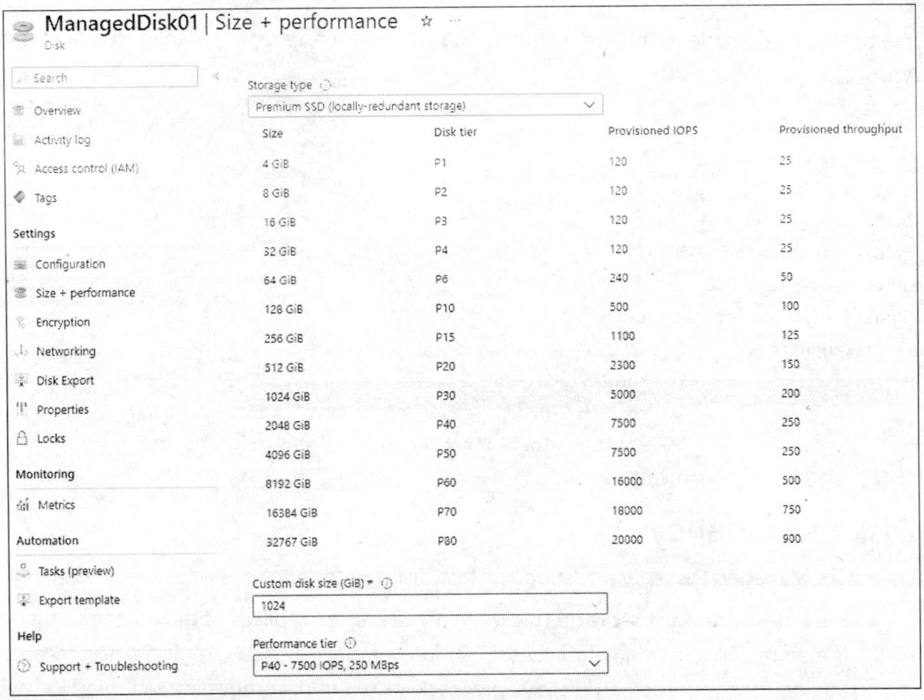

FIGURE 3-39 Changing a managed disk's performance tier.

5. The change will take place immediately, without downtime.

USING AZURE POWERSHELL

Use the following Azure PowerShell code to update the performance tier for an existing managed disk:

```
#Define variables
$resourceGroup = "RG01"
$location = "EastUS2"
$MgdDiskName = "ManagedDisk01"
$performanceTier='P40'
#Update disk performance tier
$newmgddiskconfig = New-AzDiskUpdateConfig -Tier $performanceTier
Update-AzDisk \
                    -ResourceGroupName $resourceGroup \
                    -DiskName $MgdDiskName \
                    -DiskUpdate $newmgddiskconfig
```

USING AZURE CLI

Use the following code to update the performance tier for an existing managed disk in the Azure CLI:

```
#Define variables
resourcegroup="RG01"
location="EastUS2"
vm="SourceVM"
mgddiskname="ManagedDisk01"
performancetier="P40"
#Update disk performance tier
az disk update \
                        --name $mgddiskname \
                        --resource-group $resourcegroup \
                        --set tier=$performancetier
```

Disk redundancy

The Azure Managed Disks service supports two disk-redundancy options:

- **Locally-redundant storage (LRS)** With LRS, three replicas of the managed disk is maintained in a single datacenter within your primary Azure region. This protects against local storage hardware, server rack, or network component failures. However, because all three replicas of the managed disk are stored in the same datacenter, if that datacenter experiences some type of disaster, all data stored on those managed disks could be lost. LRS disks have an SLA of at least 99.999999999% (11 nines) of durability over a given year.
- **Zone-redundant storage (ZRS)** Like an LRS managed disk, a ZRS managed disk synchronously commits and maintains three replicas in your primary Azure region. However, instead of being in a single datacenter, the replicas are spread across three availability zones. An availability zone is an independent datacenter in your Azure primary region with its own power, cooling, and networking components. So, if a disaster occurs in one availability zone, replicas of your managed disk will still be accessible (unless the disaster also affects the other availability zones). You can also share ZRS managed disks between VMs for clustering databases or distributed applications, such as SQL Failover Clustering and Remote Desktop Services User Profile Disks. At present, only Standard SSD disks and Premium SSD disks support ZRS. ZRS disks have an SLA of at least 99.9999999999% (12 nines) of durability over a given year.

Although ZRS managed disks provide higher redundancy, their write latency is higher than LRS managed disks, because their write operations are performed across multiple availability zones rather than within the same datacenter. Apart from that, ZRS managed disks are identical to LRS managed disks.

You can set the disk redundancy option for a managed disk in two different ways:

- **Using the Create a Managed Disk wizard** As described earlier in this chapter, you can set a managed disk's redundancy level at the time of creation. To do so, you click the

Change Size link the Size section of the wizard's Basics tab. Then, in the Select a Disk Size dialog box, you use the Disk SKU drop-down list to choose a disk type/redundancy level pairing.

- **Using the Create Virtual Machine wizard** You can set a managed disk's redundancy level when you create a virtual machine that will use that disk. You do so in the wizard's Disks tab by setting the OS Disk Type option. (See Figure 3-40.)

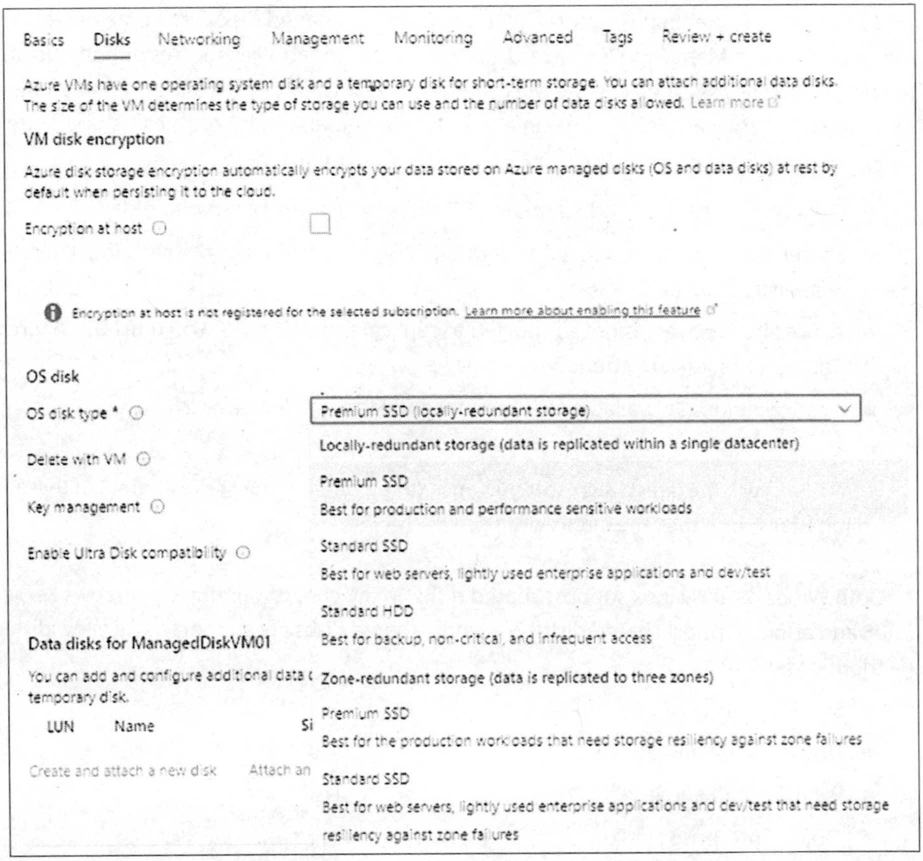

FIGURE 3-40 The Disks tab of the Create a Virtual Machine wizard.

Shared disks

You can use certain types of Azure managed disks as shared disks. These allow you to attach the same disk to multiple VMs simultaneously. In this way, you can deploy or migrate databases or applications that require clustering capabilities.

Clustered applications use SCSI Persistent Reservations (SCSI PR) to reserve the active node in the cluster. This node determines which VM will perform read and write operations to the shared disk. SCSI PR is an industry standard, and applications designed to run on storage area network (SAN) storage are built to this standard. This makes it possible to migrate clustered applications to Azure or to deploy them in Azure and migrate the required code or databases later.

NOTE Shared disks require the use of cluster management tools such as Windows Server Failover Cluster to handle node communication, configuration management, and write locking.

As described earlier in this chapter, you can share a managed disk at the time of creation using the Create a Managed Disk wizard. (In the Advanced tab, click the Yes option button next to Enable Shared Disk. Then use the Max Shares drop-down list to specify how many VMs will share the disk.) You can also change an existing managed disk so it becomes a shared disk.

Shared disks have numerous limitations, including the following:

- Only Ultra, Premium, and Standard SSD disks can be used as shared disks.
- Shared disks do not support Azure Disk Encryption (ADE). They only support Server-Side encryption (SSE).
- Azure Site Recovery is not supported to replicate shared disks. You must use Azure Disk Backup to build any redundancy plans.
- Host caching isn't available for Premium and Standard SSDs.

NOTE Check the latest Microsoft guidance to see whether they have addressed these limitations since the time of this writing.

Both Windows and Linux support shared disks. In the case of Windows, Windows Server 2008 and above support shared disks. For Linux, shared disks are supported by a few different distributions:

- SUSE SLE HA 15 SP1 and above
- Ubuntu 18.04 and above
- RHEL 8.3 and above
- Oracle Enterprise Linux

Shared disks walkthrough

The following sections step you through the process of setting up an existing managed disk as a shared disk using the Azure portal, Azure PowerShell, and the Azure CLI.

IMPORTANT If you are following along, select resources and resource names based on your environment.

IMPORTANT **If you are following along, be sure to delete any unwanted resources after you have completed testing to reduce charges levied by Microsoft.**

USING AZURE PORTAL

To set up an existing managed disk as a shared disk using the Azure portal, follow these steps:

1. In the Overview page for the managed disk that you want to share, under **Settings**, click **Configuration**.
2. On the managed disk's Configuration page (see Figure 3-41), enter the following information and click **Save**:
   - **Enable Shared Disk** Select the **Yes** option button.
   - **Max Shares** Use this drop-down list to specify the number of VMs that will share the disk (in this case, select **2**).

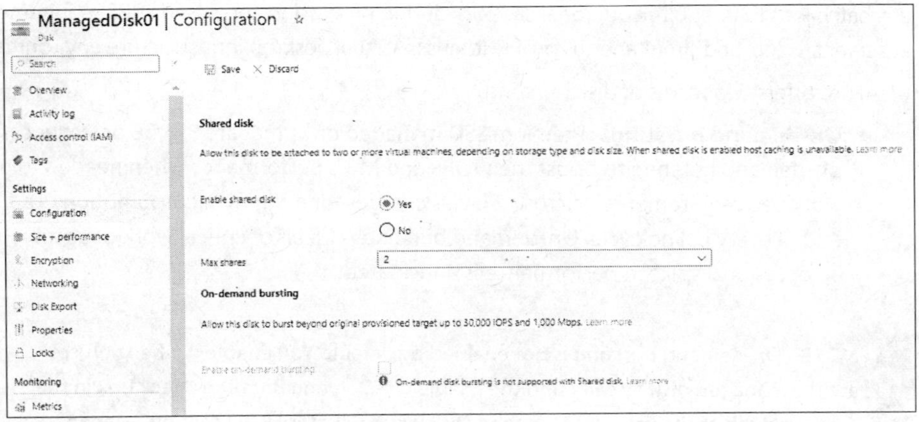

FIGURE 3-41 Sharing an existing managed disk.

USING AZURE POWERSHELL

Use the following Azure PowerShell code to convert an existing managed disk to a shared disk:

```
#Converting an existing managed disk to shared
#Define variables
$region = "EastUS"
$resourcegroup = "RG01"
$diskname = "ManagedDisk01"
#Define Shared disk config
$shareddiskconfig = Get-AzDisk -DiskName $Diskname
$shareddiskconfig.maxShares = 2
#Update disk config to shared
Update-AzDisk -ResourceGroupName $ResourceGroup -DiskName $Diskname -Disk
$shareddiskconfig
```

USING AZURE CLI

Use the following code to convert an existing managed disk to a shared disk in the Azure CLI:

```
#Converting an existing managed disk to shared
#Define variables
region="EastUS"
resourcegroup="RG01"
diskname="ManagedDisk01"
#Update disk config to shared
az disk update --name $diskname --max-shares 2 --resource-group $resourcegroup
```

Managed disk bursting

Premium and Standard SSDs managed disks support disk bursting. This important feature allows managed disks to handle additional IOPS and MB/s in bursts to boost their performance when faced with a sudden spike in resource requirements or a resource crunch. Disk bursting is great for tackling common problems like sudden unplanned traffic spikes on application and web servers, batch jobs that require additional capacity during processing, increased IOPS requirements at server startup, and simultaneous profile logins in virtual desktop infrastructure environments.

Azure offers two forms of disk bursting:

- **On-demand bursting** Premium SSD managed disks that are 512 GB or larger can use on-demand bursting to boost their IOPS and MB/s performance when needed to meet workload requirements. Microsoft levies charges for additional consumption used at the end of every billing cycle. On-demand bursting is ideal for critical workloads for which an occasional spike in performance is anticipated.

NOTE **On-demand bursting is not enabled by default. You enable it when you create the managed disk by selecting the Enable On-Demand Bursting check box in the Advanced tab of the Create a Managed Disk wizard. (Refer to the section "Managed disk creation walkthrough.") You can also enable it on an existing managed disk when the disk is detached from any VM or when the VM it is attached to is stopped. You can disable on-demand bursting 12 hours after it has been enabled.**

- **Credit-based bursting** By default, when a Standard or Premium SSD managed disk that is 512 GB or smaller consumes less IOPS and/or MB/s than its performance target, it accrues credits. The managed disk can then "spend" these credits on credit-based bursting to boost its IOPS and MB/s performance to meet higher workload requirements as needed, at no extra charge. Once the credits are consumed, the managed disk will be limited to the performance target defined for it.

NOTE **Credits are accrued independently for IOPS and MB/s, and are spent independently as well.**

Managed disk backup

Azure Backup provides a simple and cost-effective cloud-native backup solution for regular backups of managed disks. It provides snapshot lifecycle management of managed disks by performing incremental snapshots—as often as multiple times a day—which are retained for the period defined in the backup policy. It is an agent-less backup solution that does not interact with or affect the application performance.

You can use managed disk backup in conjunction with the once-a-day application-consistent VM-level backups via Azure Backup for a comprehensive backup solution. You can back up disks whether they are connected and actively in use by a VM or unattached to any workload. Because no backup agents, custom scripts, or service accounts are required to carry out these backups, they are considered to be highly secure.

> ***NOTE*** **If you require application-consistent backups, you will want to back up at the VM level instead.**

Backup walkthrough

The following sections step you through the process of creating a backup of a managed disk using the Azure portal.

> ***IMPORTANT*** **If you are following along, select resources and resource names based on your environment.**

> ***IMPORTANT*** **If you are following along, be sure to delete any unwanted resources after you have completed testing to reduce charges levied by Microsoft.**

USING AZURE PORTAL

To create a backup of a managed disk using the Azure portal, follow these steps:

1. Log into the Azure portal, type **backup center** in the search box, and select **Backup Center** from the list that appears. (See Figure 3-42.)

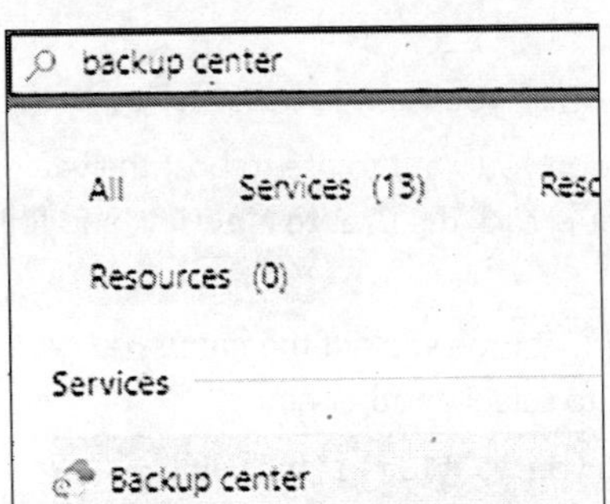

FIGURE 3-42 Searching for the Backup Center in the Azure portal.

2. On the Backup Center's Overview page (see Figure 3-43), click **Backup**.

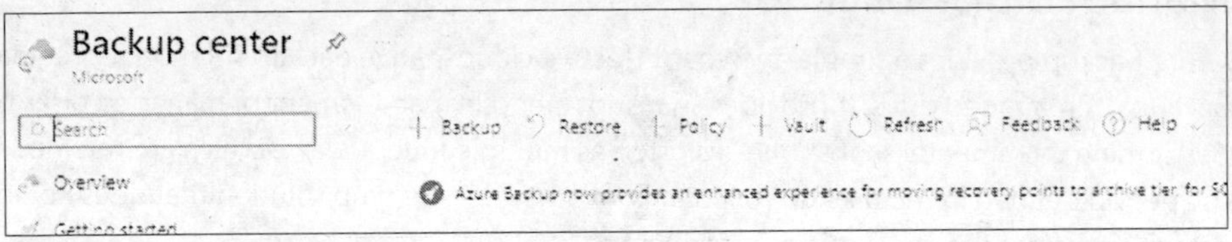

FIGURE 3-43 The Backup Center's Overview page.

3. In the **Basics** tab of the Configure Backup wizard (see Figure 3-44), enter the following information:
   - **Datasource Type** Select **Azure Disks**.
   - **Vault** You can select an existing backup vault or create a new one. In this example, click **Create Vault** to create a new one.

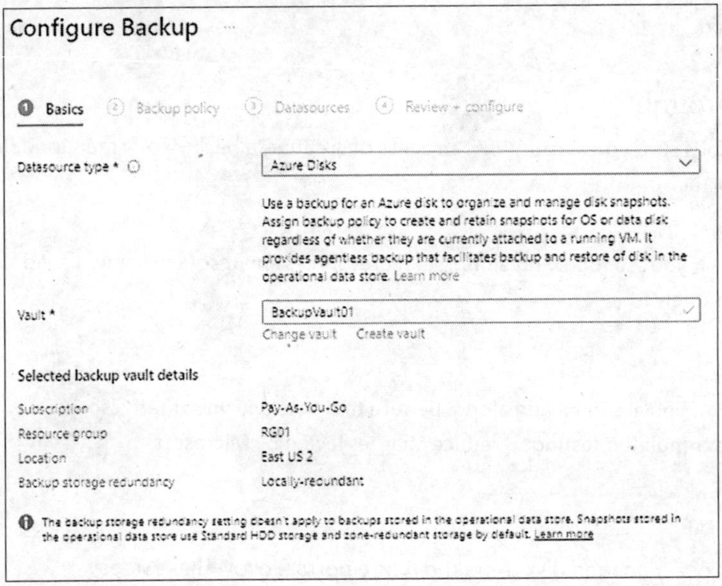

FIGURE 3-44 The Basics tab of the Configure Backup wizard.

4. In the **Basics** tab of the Create Backup Vault wizard (see Figure 3-45), enter the following information and click **Next**:
   - **Subscription** Select the subscription in which you want to host the vault.
   - **Resource Group** Select the resource group you want to use to host the vault. Alternatively, to create a new resource group, click the **Create New** link and follow the prompts.
   - **Backup Vault Name** Enter a unique name for the vault. If the name you type is already in use, the wizard will prompt you to select another name.
   - **Region** Select the Azure region in which you want to host the vault.
   - **Backup Storage Redundancy** Select the redundancy level for the backup storage.

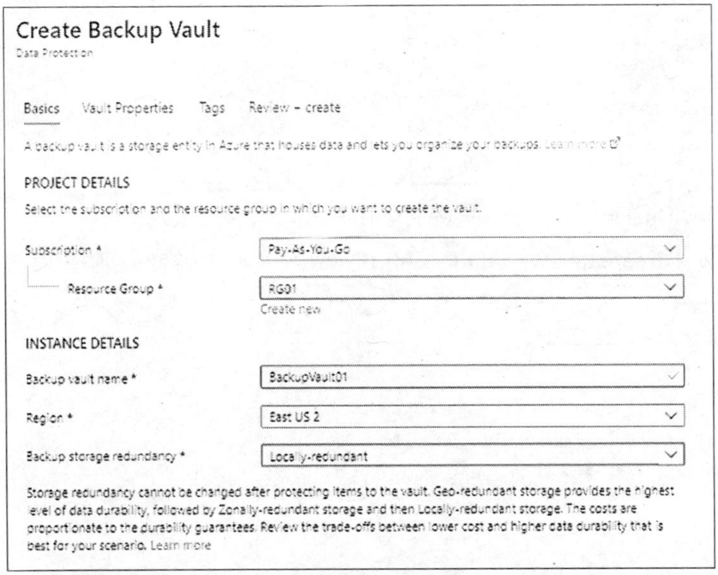

FIGURE 3-45 The Basics tab of the Create Backup Vault wizard.

5. In the **Vault Properties** tab (see Figure 3-46), enter the following information and click **Next**:
   - **Enable Soft Delete** Select this check box if you want to enable the soft delete feature (recommended).
   - **Retention Period** Specify how many days data should be retained before it is permanently deleted.

NOTE **Not all Azure regions support soft delete. If your region does not support this feature, you'll see text to that effect in the Vault Properties tab.**

6. In the **Tags** tab (see Figure 3-47), enter any tags you want to associate with the backup vault and click **Next**.

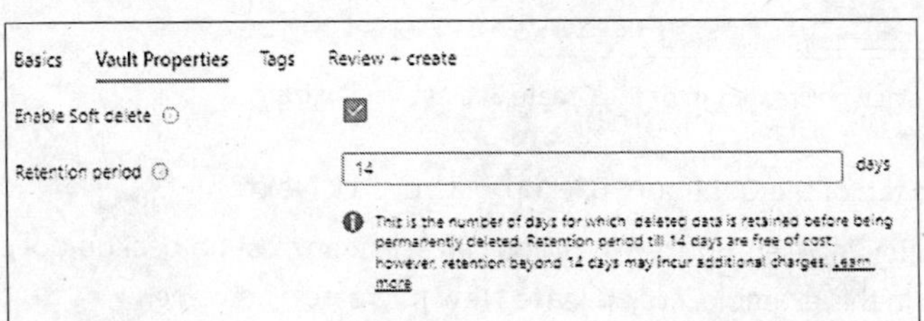

FIGURE 3-46 The Vault Properties tab of the Create Backup Vault wizard.

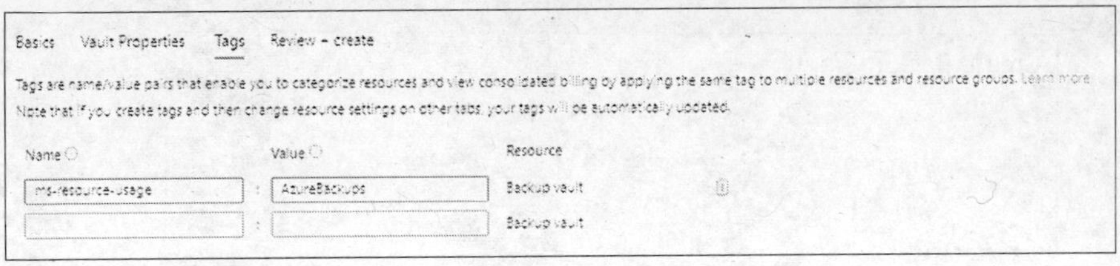

FIGURE 3-47 The Tags tab of the Create Backup Vault wizard.

7. In the **Review + Create** tab (see Figure 3-48), review your settings and click **Create**.

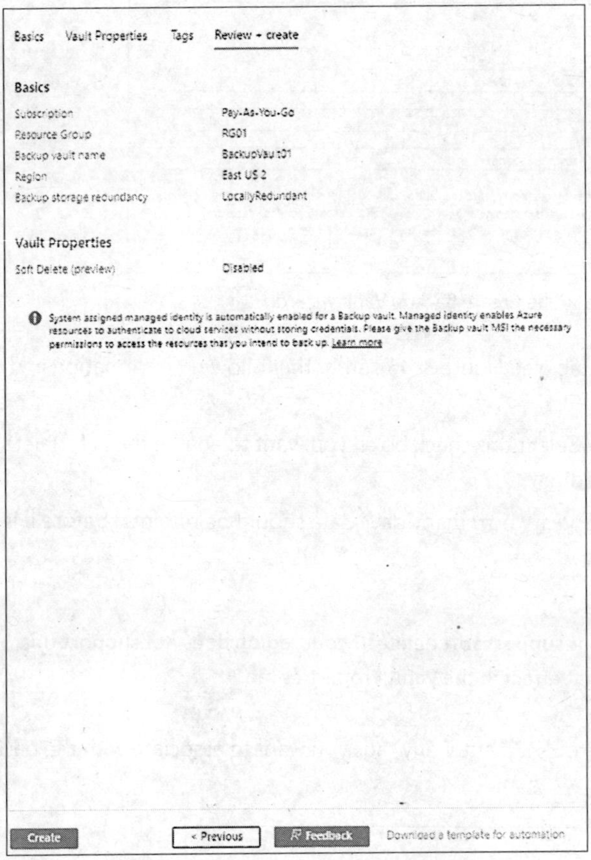

FIGURE 3-48 The Review + Create tab of the Create Backup Vault wizard.

8. Back in the **Basics** tab of the Configure Backup wizard, click **Next**.
9. In the **Backup Policy** tab (see Figure 3-49), you can select an existing backup policy or create a new one. In this example, click **Create New** to create a new one.

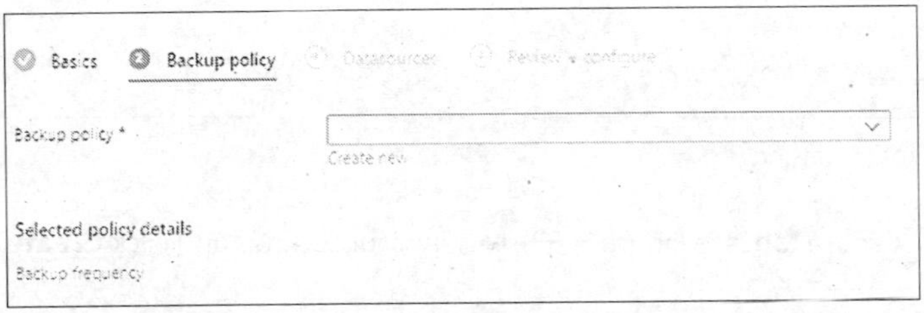

FIGURE 3-49 The Backup Policy tab of the Configure Backup wizard.

10. In the **Basics** tab of the Create a Backup Policy wizard (see Figure 3-50), in the **Policy Name** box, enter a unique name for the policy. Then click **Next**.

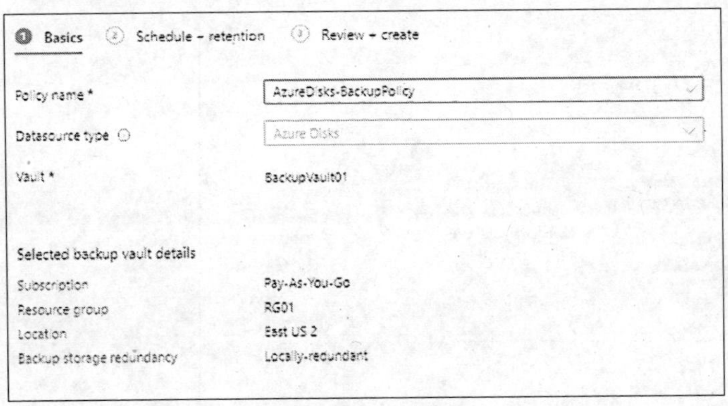

FIGURE 3-50 The Basics tab of the Create a Backup Policy wizard.

11. In the **Schedule + Retention** tab (see Figure 3-51), choose the **Hourly** or **Daily** option button next to **Backup Frequency** and choose the desired option from the **Time** drop-down list.

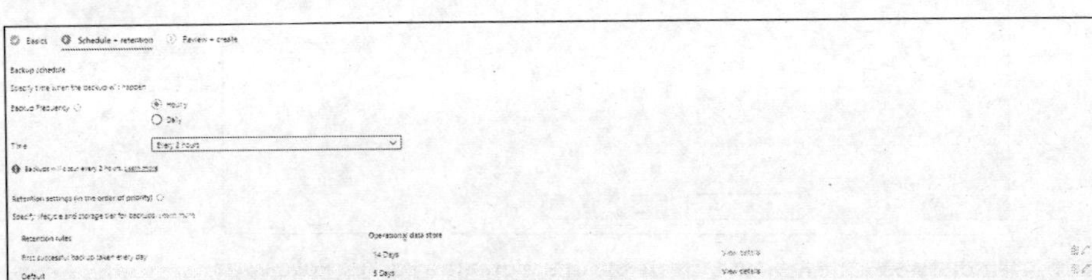

FIGURE 3-51 The Schedule + Retention tab of the Create a Backup Policy wizard.

12. Click the **Add Retention Rule** link (see Figure 3-52), set up a custom backup retention policy based on your retention requirements, and click **Next**.

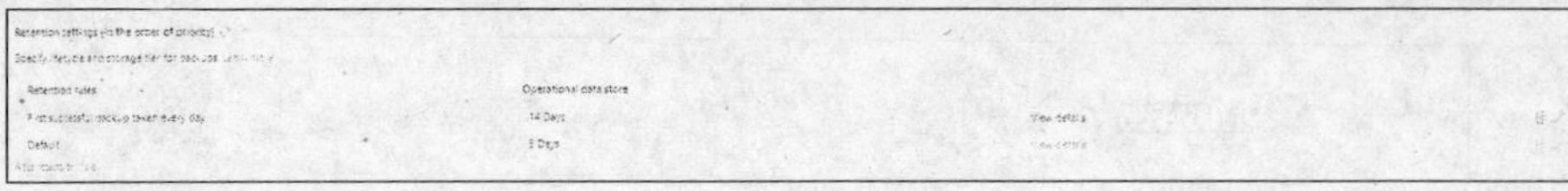

FIGURE 3-52 Retention settings.

13. In the **Review + Create** tab (see Figure 3-53), review your settings and click **Create**.

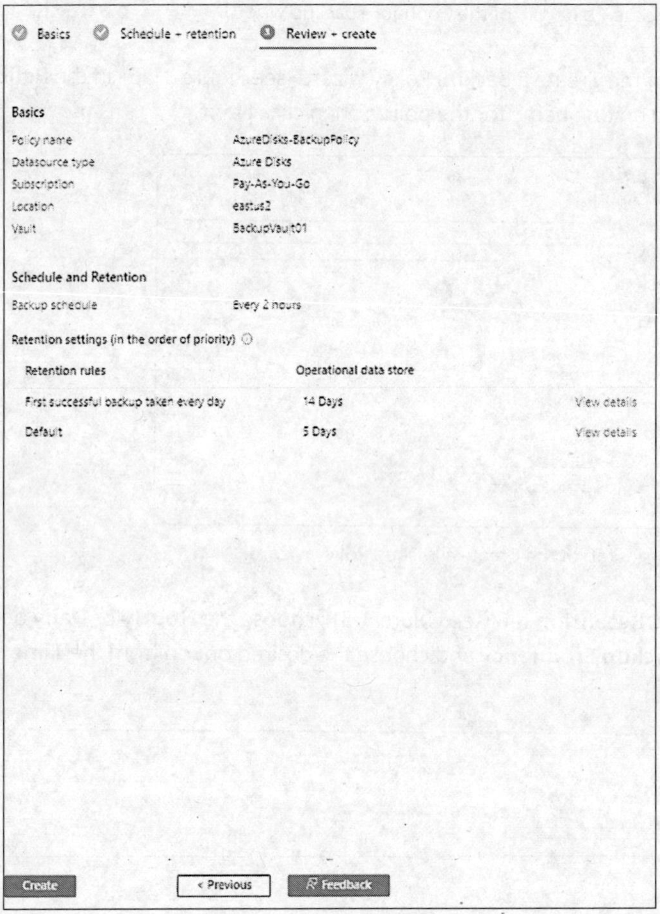

FIGURE 3-53 The Review + Create tab of the Create a Backup Policy wizard.

14. Back in the **Basics** tab of the Configure Backup wizard, click **Next**.

15. Back in the **Backup Policy** tab of the Configure Backup wizard (see Figure 3-54), click **Next**.

16. In the **Datasources** tab (see Figure 3-55), click **Add**.

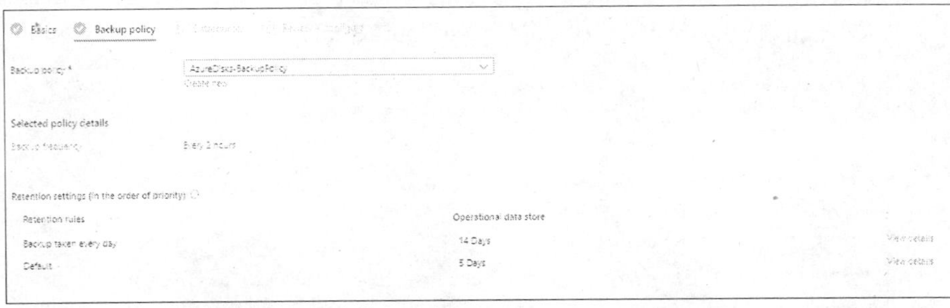

FIGURE 3-54 The Backup Policy tab of the Configure Backup wizard with the new backup policy selected.

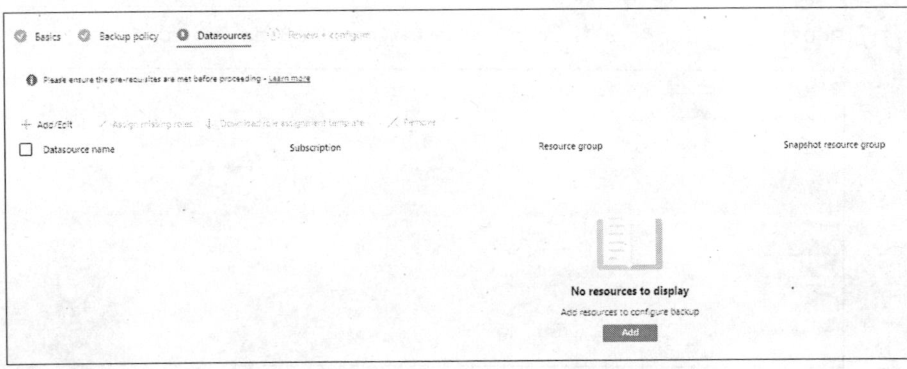

FIGURE 3-55 The Datasources tab of the Configure Backup wizard.

17. On the Select Resources to Backup page (see Figure 3-56), select the managed disks you want to back up and click **OK**.

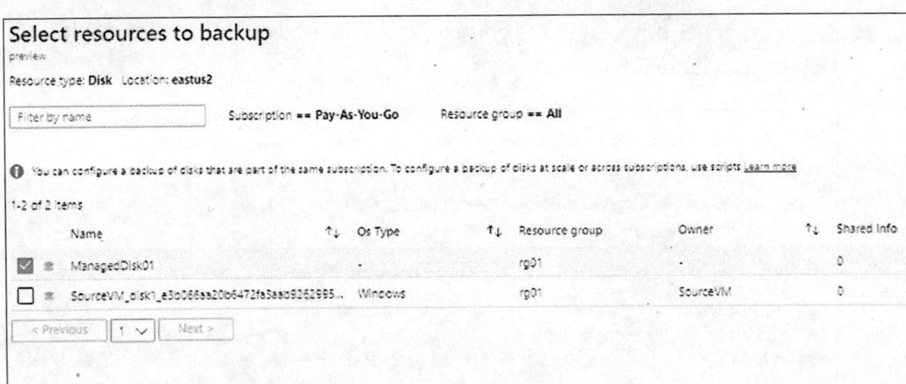

FIGURE 3-56 Select the managed disks you want to back up.

18. Back in the **Datasources** tab of the Configure Backup wizard (see Figure 3-57), open the **Snapshot Resource Group** drop-down list and select the resource group where the managed disk's snapshots are stored. Then click **Validate**.

    For the sake of example, let's step through what happens if the validation fails.

19. If the validation fails, click the **View Details** link on the right-most side of the managed disk's entry in the list of data sources. (See Figure 3-58.)

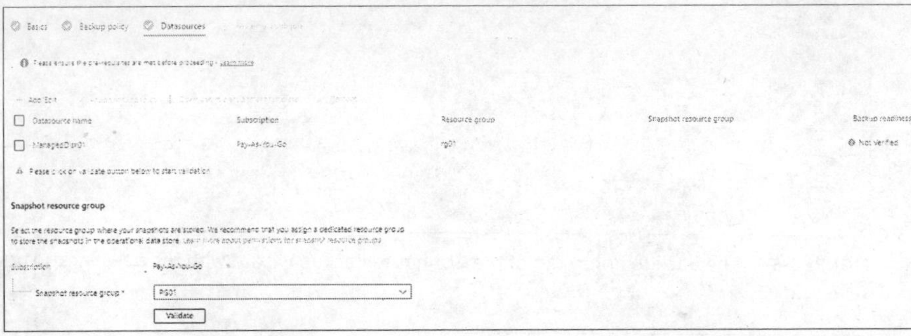

FIGURE 3-57 The updated Datasources tab of the Configure Backup wizard.

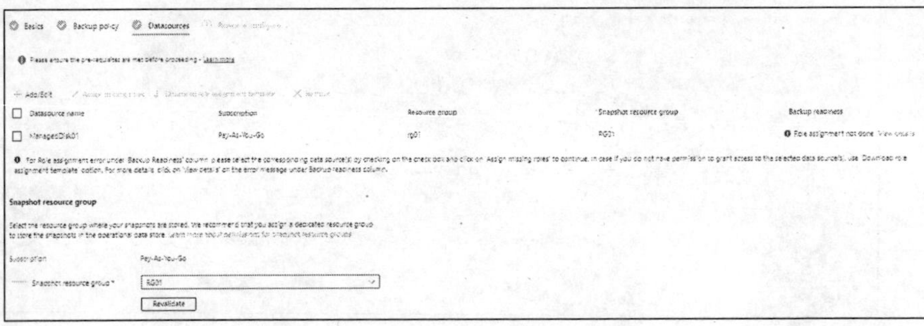

FIGURE 3-58 Viewing details about the data source.

As shown in Figure 3-58, the reason for the failure is a role assignment error. To fix this, you must assign the correct role.

20. Select the check box next to the entry for the managed disk. Then click **Assign Missing Roles**. (See Figure 3-59.)

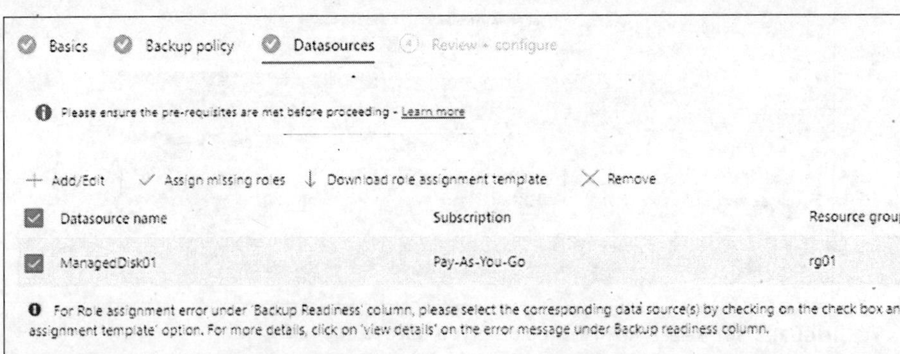

FIGURE 3-59 Correcting failures in the Datasources tab.

21. In the Grant Missing Permissions dialog box (see Figure 3-60), open the **Scope** drop-down list and select a scope for the role assignment—**Resource**, **Resource Group**, or **Subscription**. Then click **Confirm**.

22. Click the **Validate** button under **Snapshot Resource Group** a second time.
23. Assuming the validation is successful (see Figure 3-61), click **Next**.

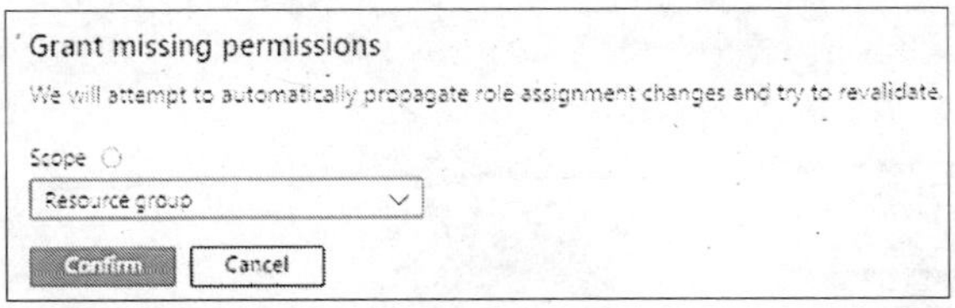

FIGURE 3-60 The Grant Missing Permissions dialog box.

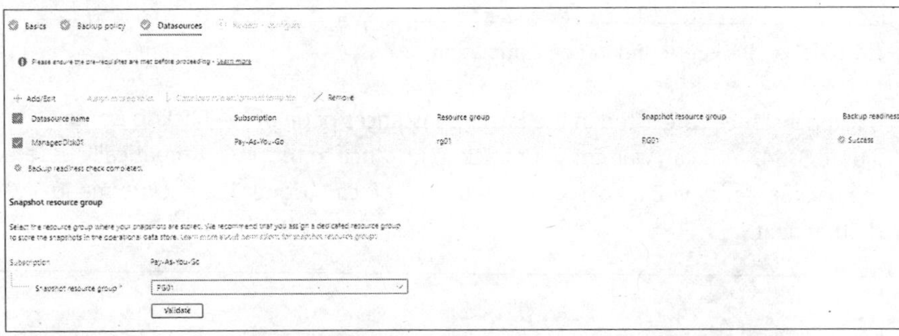

FIGURE 3-61 The corrected failure in the Datasources tab.

24. In the **Review + Configure** tab (see Figure 3-62), review your settings and click **Configure Backup** to configure the backup.

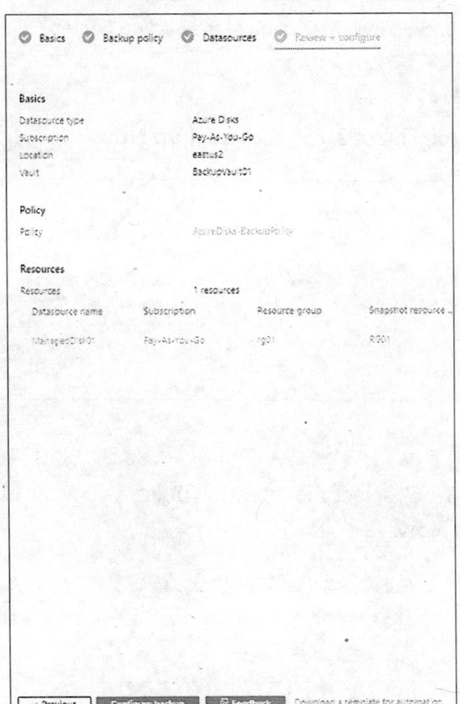

FIGURE 3-62 The Review + Configure tab of the Configure Backup wizard.

25. After the backup is configured, click **Go to Resource**. (See Figure 3-63.)

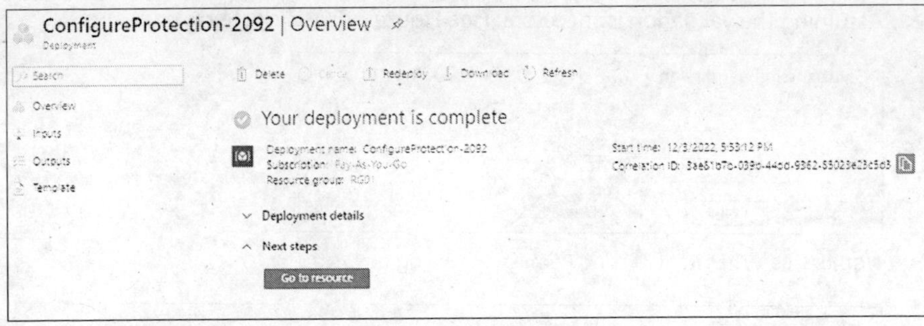

FIGURE 3-63 Backup configuration completion.

Backup instances are listed in the Backup Instances page of the Backup Center. (See Figure 3-64.) You can wait for your backup instance to trigger automatically based on the backup policy you created. Alternatively, you can trigger the backup manually. We'll do that next.

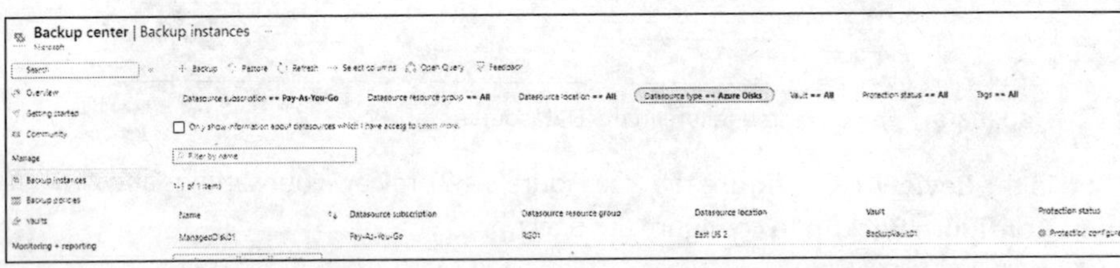

FIGURE 3-64 The backup is located in the Backup Instances page of the Backup Center.

26. Click the entry for the backup instance.
27. On the page for the backup instance (see Figure 3-65), click **Backup Now**.

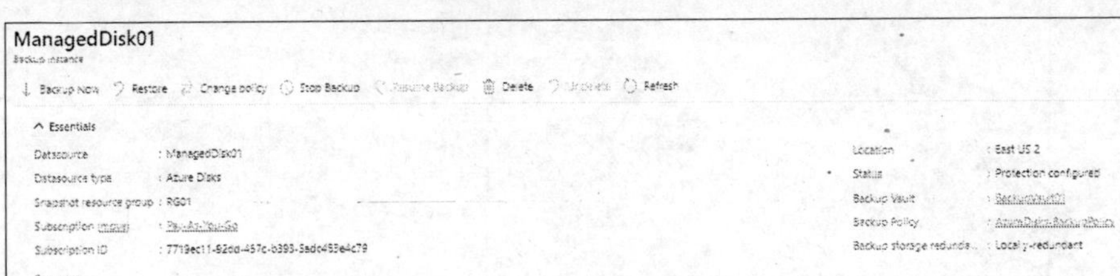

FIGURE 3-65 Click Backup Now.

28. On the Backup Now page (see Figure 3-66), select the retention policy you want to use for the backup job. Then click **Backup Now**.

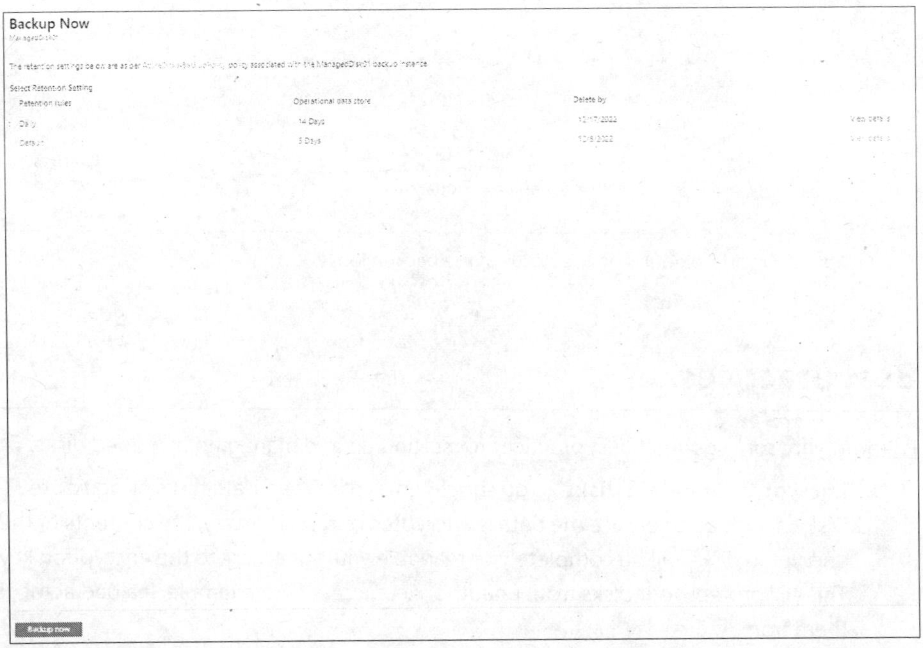

FIGURE 3-66 The Backup Now page.

29. Back on the page for the backup instance, you will see the on-demand backup job you just triggered is in progress. (See Figure 3-67.) Click the **In Progress** link.

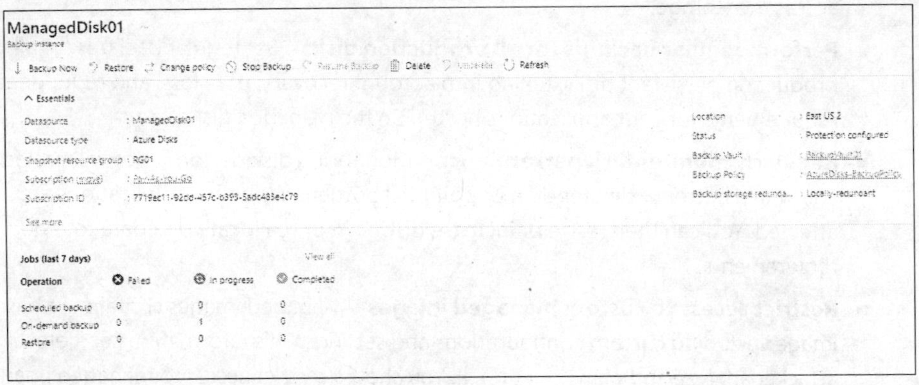

FIGURE 3-67 The on-demand backup job is in progress.

30. The Backup Jobs page shows more details on the status of the backup job. (See Figure 3-68.)

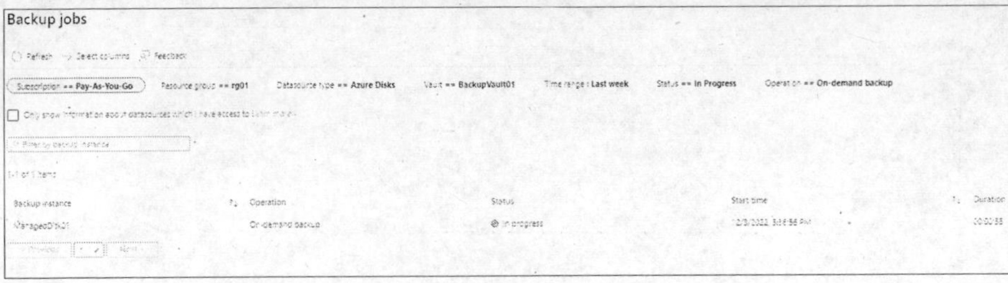

FIGURE 3-68 More details on the status of the backup job.

Best practices

Following are some general best practices for setting up and managing managed disks:

- **Encrypt OS and data disks** You should encrypt OS and data disks using Azure Disk Encryption to ensure the data is encrypted at rest. This way, the contents of the encrypted disks will be completely unreadable without access to the encryption keys. This will protect your disks from unauthorized access—for example, if a bad actor copies them from Azure.
- **Disable public access to managed disks** Limit access to managed disks to private networks over the private endpoint. You should disable public access as soon as possible unless you need it for some specific scenario. In such cases, limit access only to disks that require this capability, and monitor this access to detect brute-force attacks used to access the storage.
- **Perform regular backups for all production disks** Set regular backups for all production persistent disks, taking into account recovery, data loss, and redundancy requirements for your applications hosted on the managed disks.
- **Regularly monitor disk performance** Monitoring disk performance will provide you with a better understanding of potential bottlenecks before applications are affected. You can then resize or increase disk IOPS or reallocate disk data to reduce IOPS requirements.
- **Restrict access to custom managed images** Managed images contain the base image, including custom configurations and settings. This information can help an attacker analyze and plan their attack. You should restrict access to managed images to authorized personnel only. Do not share managed images with anyone else unless you have a good reason to. Review and ensure that access is in line with your security guidelines.

Chapter 4

Azure Queue Storage

Overview

A distributed application should not rely on data transfer using direct communication between components at all times. Network outages between components, bandwidth limitations due to changing demands, and other infrastructure issues could cause one or more of the components to go temporarily offline. When this happens, your application could lose data or break down completely.

A far better approach is to set up the application so that its various components post and consume messages based on resource and system availability. Azure Queue Storage supports such an approach. Azure Queue Storage stores and consumes a large number of messages over HTTP or HTTPS in a secure and resilient manner.

Azure Queue Storage consists of three main components:

- **Azure Storage account** To use Azure Queue Storage, you need a standard type v1 or type v2 general-purpose Azure Storage account. You cannot use a different type of account, such as an Azure Blob Storage account. This storage account provides a unique namespace that you can use to connect to the queue(s).
- **Queue** Queues facilitate the storing, retrieving, and deleting of messages. A queue can contain millions of messages and scale to 500 TB in size.
- **Message** A message, in any format, can be stored in the queue for between 1 second to 7 days. A message could be text, a variable, or some other type of message that requires processing. If the message is not retrieved before the end of its expiry period, it is deleted from the queue. You can also set a message to never expire until it is processed and deleted from the queue by the application. Messages must be smaller than 64 kilobytes (KB).

Each queue has a unique endpoint URL that is based on the storage account and queue name. For example, suppose you have a storage account, named *app01storageaccount*, and two queues, named *messages* and *images*. In that case, the URL for each queue would be as follows:

- Messages queue *https://app01storageaccount.queue.core.windows.net/messages*
- Images queue *https://app01storageaccount.queue.core.windows.net/images*

Once messages are in a queue, an application can use HTTP or HTTPS to connect to the queue and retrieve and process the messages asynchronously. The oldest messages are always retrieved first.

You can configure multiple queues per storage account to handle the needs of different applications or APIs. The maximum total number of messages across all the queues in a storage account is limited by a standard account's total capacity, which is currently 5 petabytes (PB).

Key features

Some key features and benefits of using Azure Queue Storage include the following:

- **Simple to use** Azure Queue Storage supports the use of multiple interfaces and methods to create and manage queues and messages, including the Azure portal, Azure PowerShell, Azure CLI, and REST APIs.
- **Support for multiple programming languages** Developers can integrate the Azure Queue Storage service using .NET, Java, Python, Node.js, C++, PHP, and Ruby-based applications. It is not limited to certain application builds, so it can be used extensively.
- **Scalability** Azure Queue Storage is extremely scalable. You can store millions of messages in a single queue and maintain multiple queues in a single storage account. Each storage account can be up to 5 PB and each queue can scale up to 500 TB.
- **Security** Azure Queue Storage is accessible using secure HTTPS endpoints. Each queue supports multiple methods to authorize access by applications or users before any messages are made visible.
- **Resiliency** Because Azure Queue Storage uses an Azure Storage account for message storage, the resiliency and redundancy options for Azure Storage accounts—geo-redundant storage (GRS), zone-redundant storage (ZRS), read-access GRS, geo-zone-redundant storage (GZRS), and read-access GZRS—are supported for Azure Queue Storage, too.
- **Reliability** Scalability, security, and resiliency, combined with the correct storage architecture, make Azure Queue Storage extremely reliable for use in application development. With Azure Queue Storage, messages can be safely stored and securely retrieved without data loss.
- **Cost-effective** With Azure Queue Storage, charges are levied based on actual storage consumption per month and on queue operations such as message creation, retrieval, reads, deletions, and so on. For example, 10,000 message read operations on queue storage hosted in the Azure West US region currently cost $0.0004. Microsoft's website includes detailed, up-to-date pricing options to help you estimate your monthly spending using Azure Queue Storage.

Key concepts

Following are some key concepts that explain in more detail how the components of Azure Queue Storage work.

Azure Storage account

As discussed in this book's introduction, Azure provides multiple types of storage services, such as standard general-purpose v1 and v2 Azure Storage accounts, Azure Blob Service, Azure Files, Azure Managed Disks, and so on. Each of these supports different types of storage, such as blob, file, queue, and table storage. Of these, only standard general-purpose v1 and v2 Azure Storage accounts support queue storage.

> ***NOTE*** **You cannot convert an existing storage account of another type into an Azure Storage account for use with Azure Queue Storage. Changing the storage type is not supported. Instead, you will need to create a new account of the correct type.**

Azure provides a set of unique service endpoints for each of its various storage offerings. The service endpoint enables you to access data in the storage using tools and APIs.

For Azure Queue Storage, the unique endpoint naming format is a combination of the storage account name and a static suffix (*queue.core.windows.net*). For example, a storage account named *myaccount* would have the following queue storage endpoint: *https://myaccount.queue.core.windows.net*.

You can create a maximum of 250 storage accounts in a single Azure region, with each storage account having its own corresponding blob, file, queue, and table endpoints.

> ***NOTE*** **Microsoft recommends that you use the HTTPS protocol for each endpoint to ensure a secure channel for data communications.**

Create Azure Storage account walkthrough

The following sections step you through the process of creating a standard general-purpose Azure Storage account for use with Azure Queue Storage using the Azure portal and the Azure CLI.

> ***IMPORTANT*** **If you are following along, select resources and resource names based on your environment, including unique storage account names for each of your deployments.**

IMPORTANT If you are following along, be sure to delete any unwanted resources after you have completed testing to reduce charges levied by Microsoft.

USING AZURE PORTAL

To create a standard general-purpose Azure Storage account using the Azure portal, follow these steps:

1. Log in to the Azure portal, type **storage accounts** in the search box, and select **Storage Accounts** from the list that appears. (See Figure 4-1.)

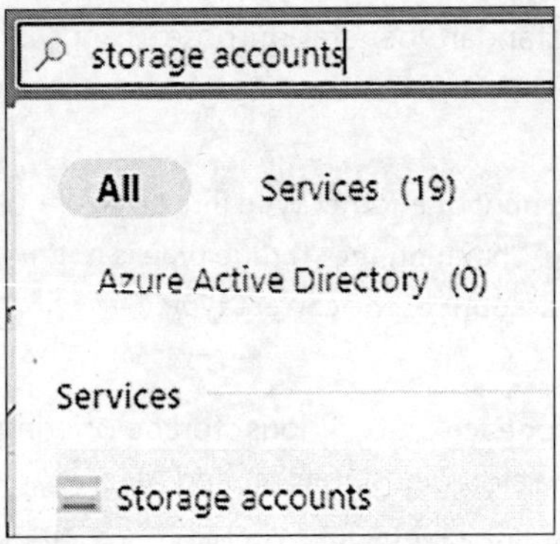

FIGURE 4-1 Storage accounts search.

2. On the Storage Accounts page, click **Create Storage Account**. (See Figure 4-2.)

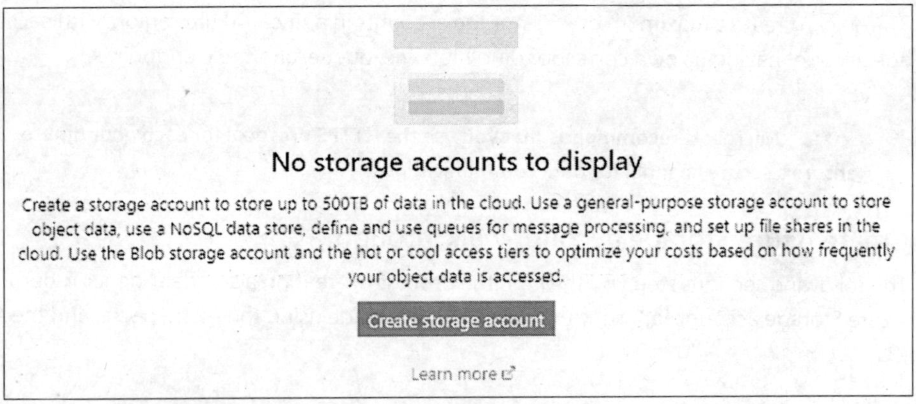

FIGURE 4-2 Click the Create Storage Account button.

NOTE If this is not the first storage account you've created using this subscription, you won't see the button shown in Figure 4-2. In that case, click the Create button near the top of the Storage Accounts page.

3. In the **Basics** tab of the Create a Storage Account wizard (see Figure 4-3), enter the following information and click **Next**:
   - **Subscription** Select the subscription in which you want to create the Azure Storage account.
   - **Resource Group** Select an existing resource group or create a new one in which to create the Azure Storage account.
   - **Storage Account Name** Enter a unique name for the storage account.
   - **Region** Select the Azure region in which you want to host the storage account.
   - **Performance** Select the **Standard** option button.
   - **Redundancy** Select the redundancy type you want to use for the storage. In this case, select the **Geo-Redundant Storage (GRS)** option.
   - **Make Read Access Data Available in the Event of Regional Unavailability** Select this check box.

NOTE **The Make Read Access Data Available in the Event of Regional Unavailability check box appears when you select the Geo-Redundant Storage (GRS) option for the Redundancy setting.**

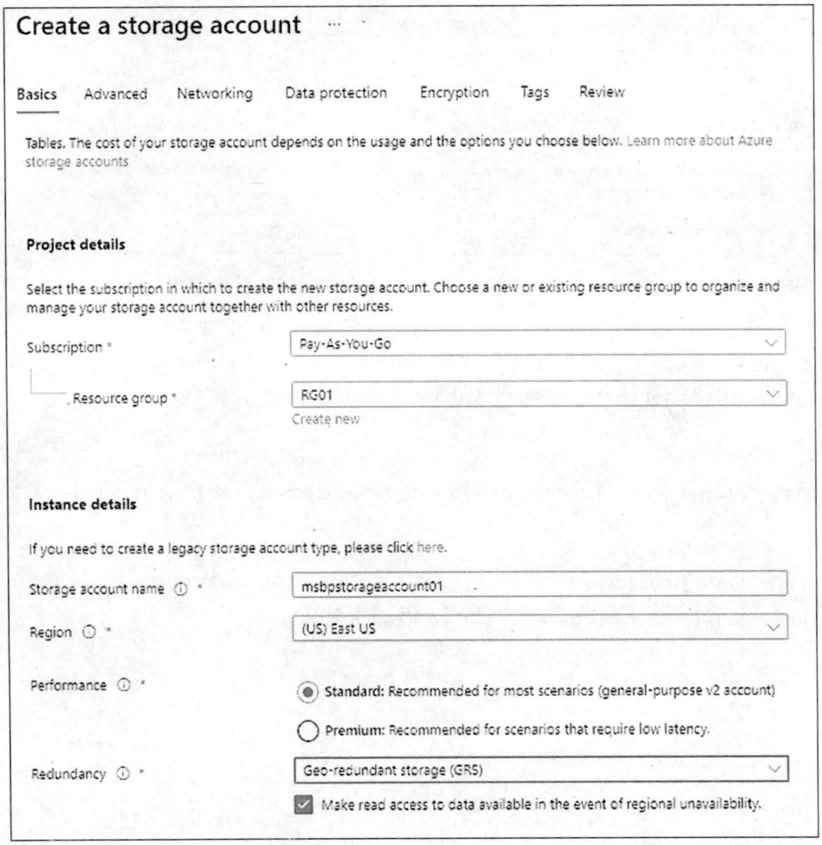

FIGURE 4-3 The Advanced tab of the Create a Storage Account wizard.

4. In the **Advanced** tab of the Create a Storage Account wizard (see Figure 4-4), optionally deselect the **Allow Enabling Public Access on Containers** check box (this account won't host containers) and select a higher setting for the **Minimum TLS Version** option, leave the other options set to their default values, and click **Next**.

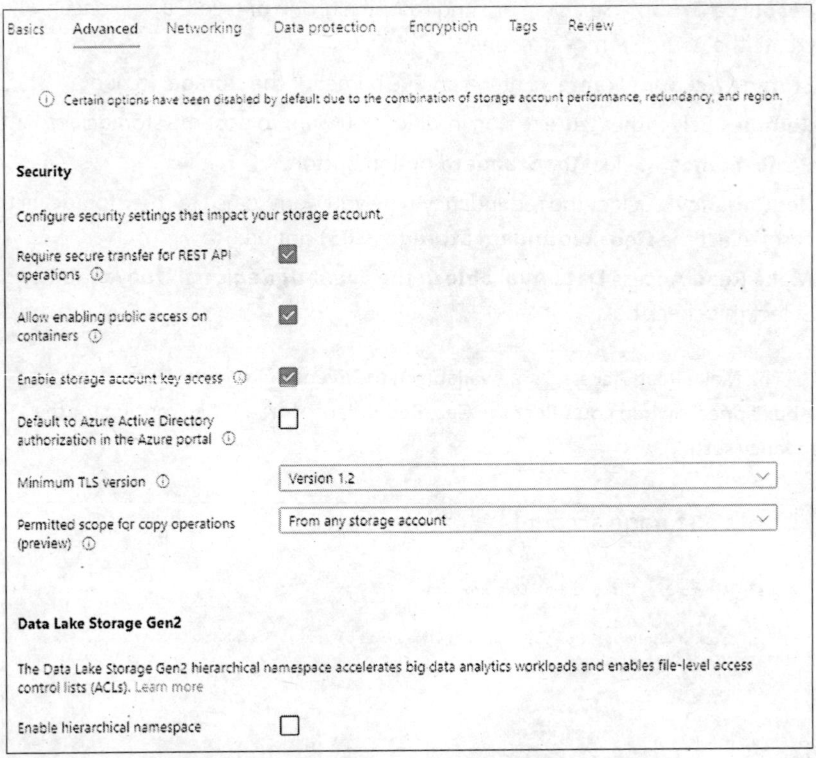

FIGURE 4-4 The Advanced tab of the Create a Storage Account wizard.

5. In the **Networking** tab of the Create a Storage Account wizard (see Figure 4-5), leave both options set to their default values and click **Next**.

NOTE **We talk more about the networking options on this tab later in this chapter.**

6. In the **Data protection** tab of the Create a Storage Account wizard (see Figure 4-6), leave all the check boxes unchecked and click **Next**.

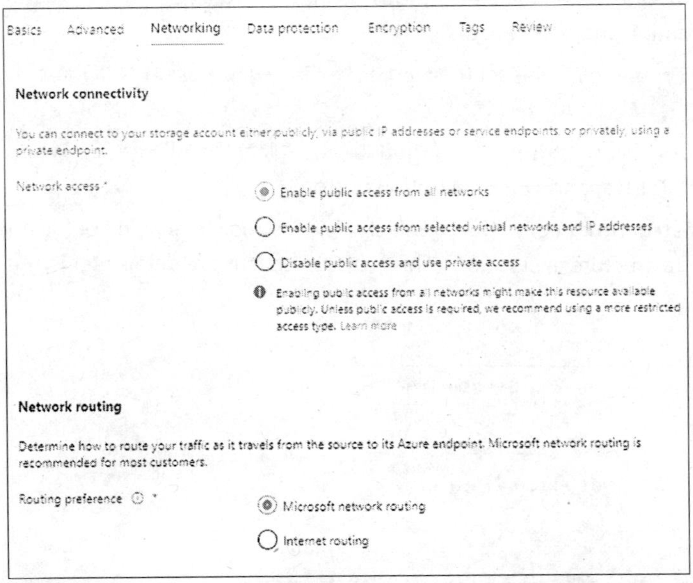

FIGURE 4-5 The Networking tab of the Create a Storage Account wizard.

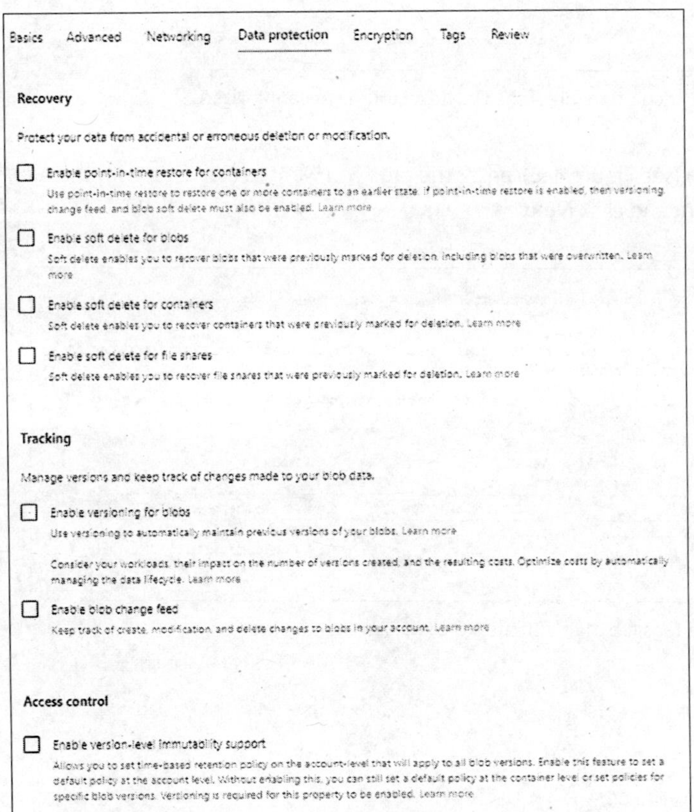

FIGURE 4-6 The Data Protection tab of the Create a Storage Account wizard.

7. In the **Encryption** tab of the Create a Storage Account wizard (see Figure 4-7), enter the following information and click **Next**:
   - **Encryption Type** Leave this set to **Microsoft-Managed Keys (MMK)** (the default).
   - **Enable Support for Customer-Managed Keys** Select the **All Service Types (Blobs, Files, Tables, and Queues)** option button.
   - **Enable Infrastructure Encryption** Select this check box to enable double encryption using infrastructure encryption. (This is discussed in more detail later in this chapter.)

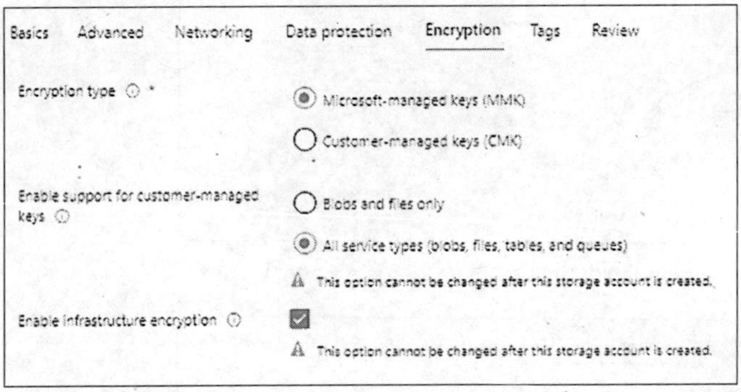

FIGURE 4-7 The Encryption tab of the Create a Storage Account wizard.

8. In the **Tags** tab (see Figure 4-8), enter the tags you want to associate with the Azure Storage account and click **Next**.

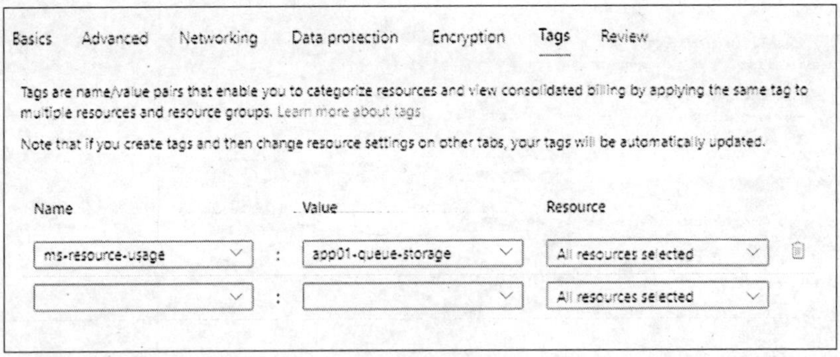

FIGURE 4-8 The Tags tab of the Create a Storage Account wizard.

9. In the **Review** tab (see Figure 4-9), review your settings. Then click **Create** to create the Azure Storage account.

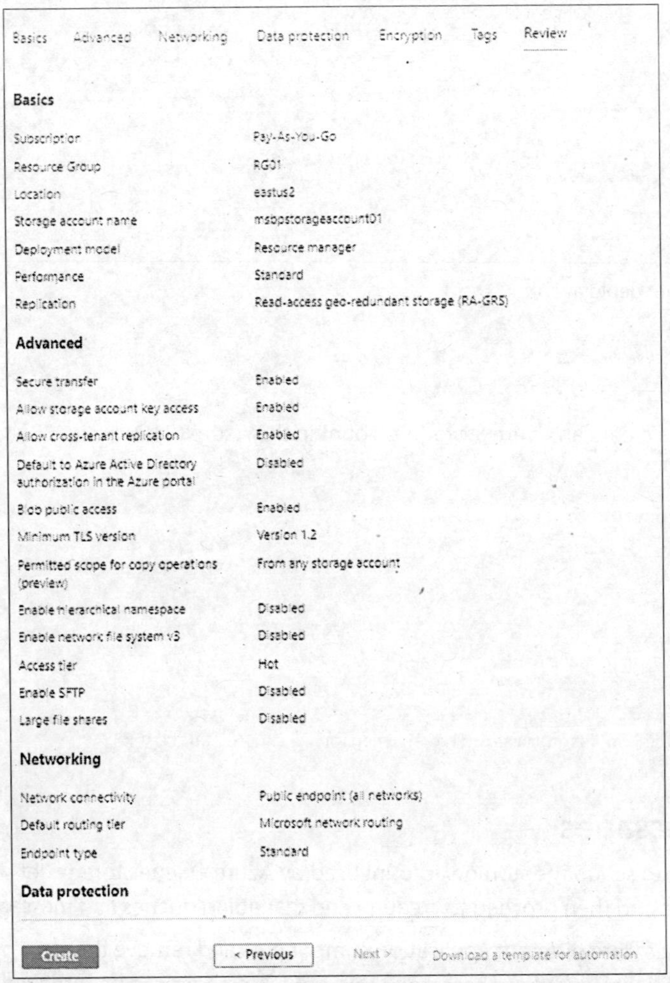

FIGURE 4-9 The Review tab of the Create a Storage Account wizard.

10. After the account is created, click **Go to Resource** to access the new account's page. (See Figure 4-10.)

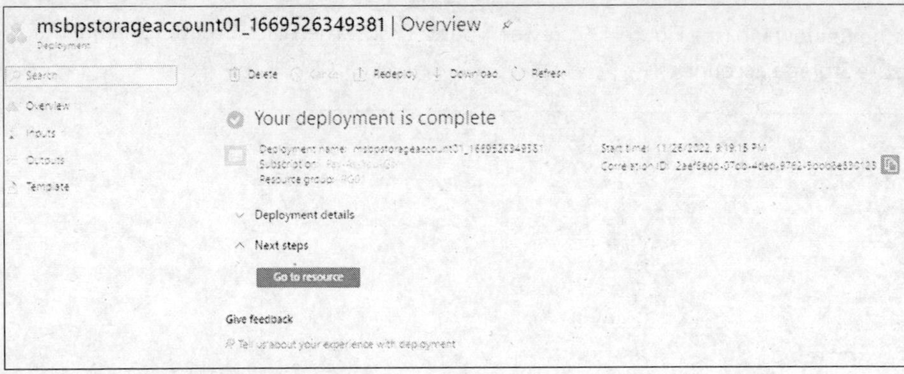

FIGURE 4-10 Storage account deployment.

USING THE AZURE CLI

Use the following code to create an Azure Storage account in the Azure CLI:

```
#Define variables
stgname="mbspstorageaccount01"
rg="RG01"
region="eastus2"
queuename="primaryqueue"
vnet="vnet-01"
subnet="default"
#Create storage account
az storage account create -n $stgname -g $rg -l $region --sku Standard_GRS
```

Queues and messages

Now that you know how to set up the storage account used by Azure Queue Storage, let's discuss in more detail are and then proceed to creating and managing queues and messages.

Queues store messages from different application components and retrieve them for processing or to trigger additional workflows based on their input. Messages can be retrieved in the order in which they arrived in the queue. When there are multiple application components retrieving messages from the same queue, a message being retrieved by an application component is made invisible to all other application components for a predefined period called the visibility timeout. After the visibility timeout expires, the message reappears in the queue for processing by other application components unless the component that retrieved it earlier deletes it from the queue after.

Queues are extremely scalable and reliable. You can access queues from any geography (unless restricted by you). This helps in designing distributed applications across multiple geographies to increase reliability and redundancy. In addition, Microsoft provides built-in fault tolerance and failover for the Azure Queue Storage service.

Manage queues and messages walkthrough

The following sections step you through the process of managing queues and messages using the Azure portal and the Azure CLI.

> ***IMPORTANT*** **If you are following along, select resources and resource names based on your environment, including unique resource names for each of your deployments.**

> ***IMPORTANT*** **If you are following along, be sure to delete any unwanted resources after you have completed testing to reduce charges levied by Microsoft.**

USING AZURE PORTAL

To manage queues and messages—including adding queues and messages, dequeuing messages, and clearing the queue—using the Azure portal, follow these steps:

1. In the left pane of the Azure Storage account page, under **Data Storage**, click **Queues**. Then click the Queue button along the top of the Queues page that opens on the right. (See Figure 4-11.)

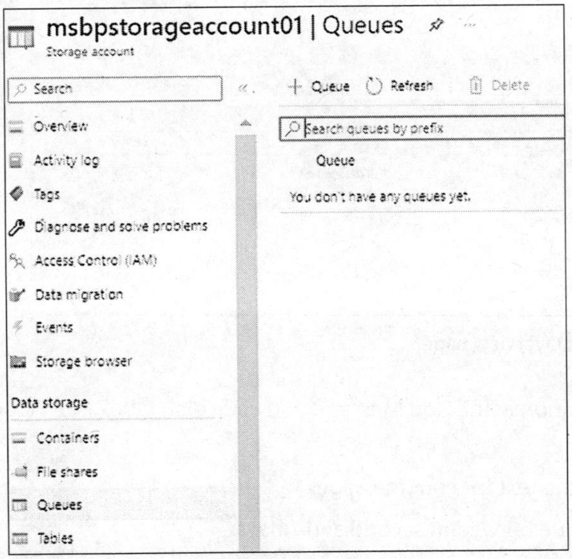

FIGURE 4-11 The Queues page.

2. In the Add Queue dialog box (see Figure 4-12), enter a unique name for the queue and click **OK**.

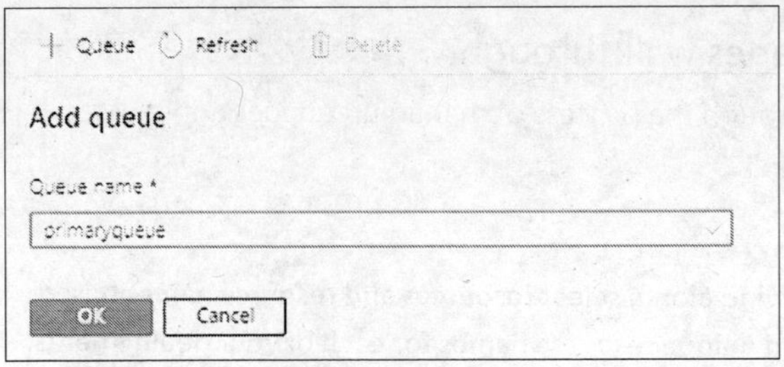

FIGURE 4-12 The Add Queue dialog box.

3. The new queue appears in the Queues page. (See Figure 4-13.) Click the queue to open it.

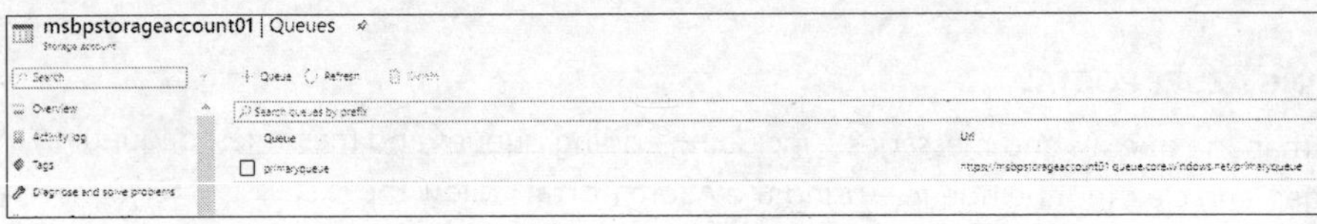

FIGURE 4-13 The queue is added to the Queues page.

4. On the queue's Overview page, click **Add Message**. (See Figure 4-14.)

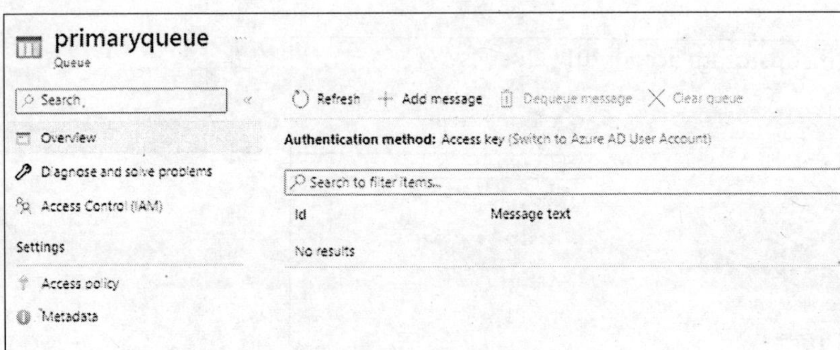

FIGURE 4-14 The new queue's Overview page.

5. Enter the following information in the Add Message to Queue dialog box (see Figure 4-15) and click **OK**.
   - **Message Text** Enter the text for your message.
   - **Expires In** Select a value between 1 second and 7 days.
   - **Message Never Expires** Select this check box if you don't want the message to ever expire.
   - **Encode the Message Body in Base64** Leave this check box checked (the default) to encrypt the message in the queue.

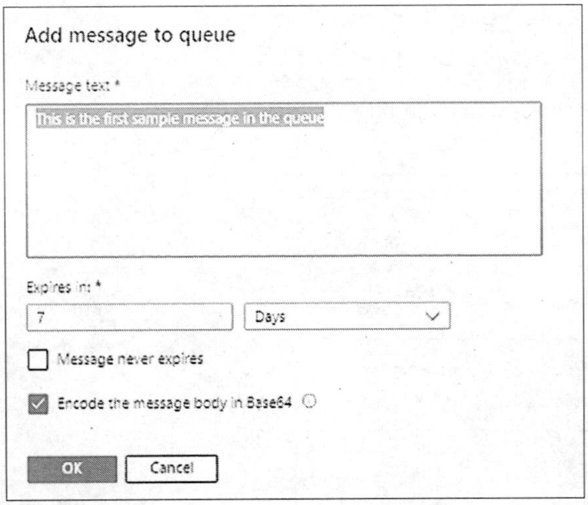

FIGURE 4-15 Add a message to the queue.

The new message appears in the queue's page, meaning that the message is in the queue. (See Figure 4-16.)

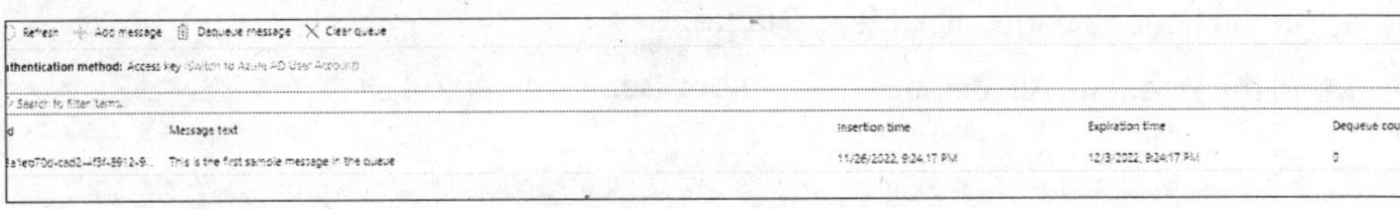

FIGURE 4-16 The message is in the queue.

6. Repeat steps 4 and 5 to add another message to the queue. (See Figure 4-17.)

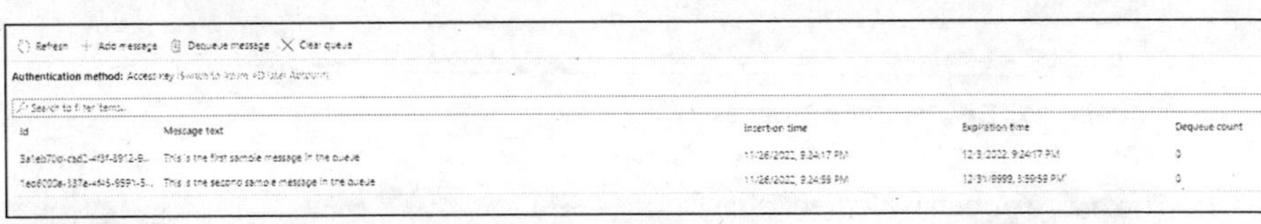

FIGURE 4-17 The queue now contains two messages.

Now let's dequeue one of the messages.

7. In the queue's page, select the check box next to the first message. Then click **Dequeue Message**.
8. In the Dequeue First Message dialog box (see Figure 4-18), click **Yes**.

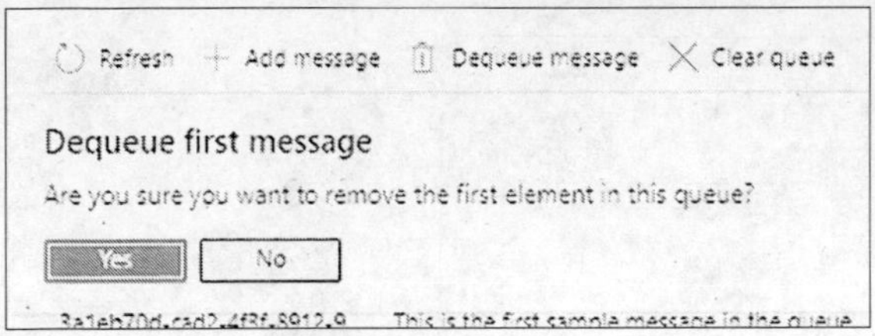

FIGURE 4-18 Dequeue the first message.

The first message in the queue is deleted. (See Figure 4-19.)

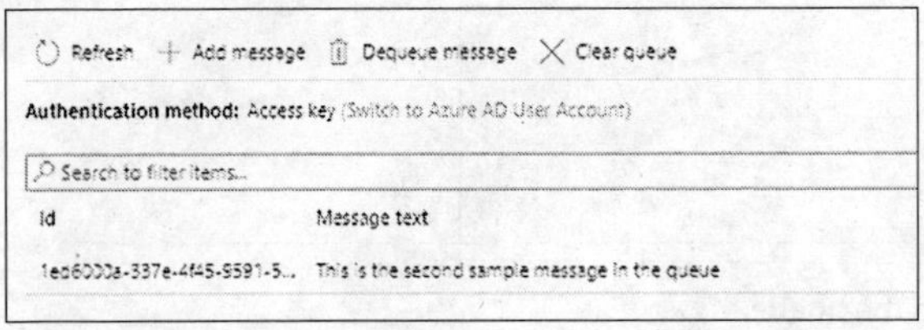

FIGURE 4-19 The message is deleted.

Next, let's clear the whole queue.

9. In the queue's page, click **Clear Queue**.
10. In the Dequeue All Messages dialog box (see Figure 4-20), click **Yes**.

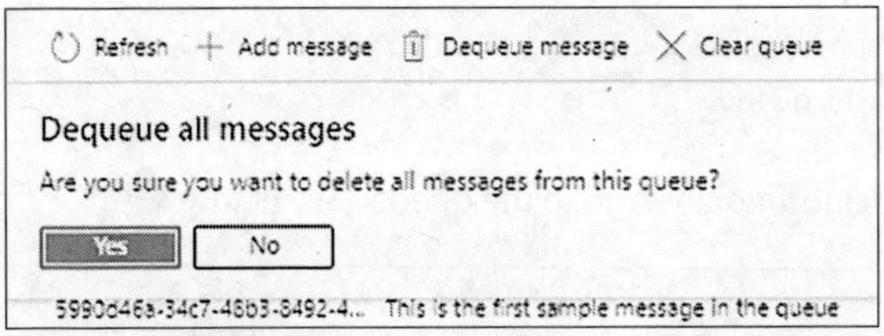

FIGURE 4-20 Dequeue all messages.

11. The entire queue is cleared. (See Figure 4-21.)

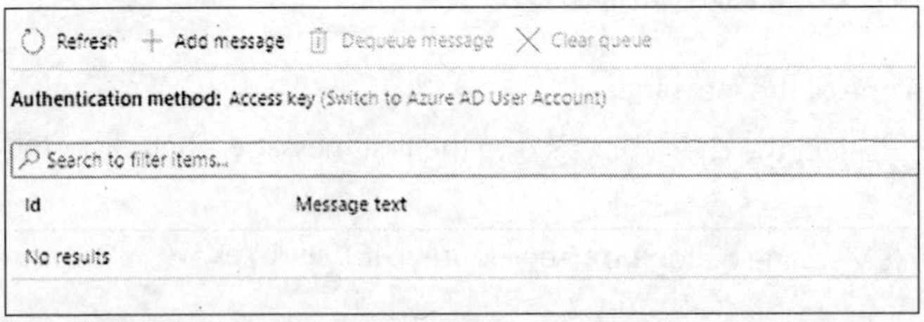

FIGURE 4-21 The queue is cleared.

The next steps show you how to create an access policy for the queue:

12. In the left pane of the queue's page, under **Settings**, click **Access Policy**.

13. On the Access Policy page (see Figure 4-22), click **Add Policy**.

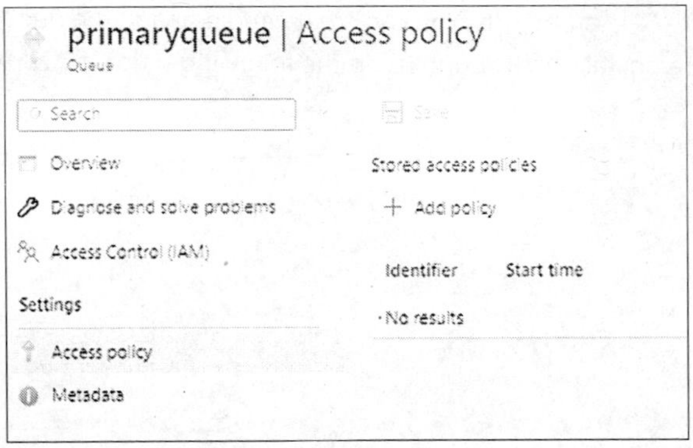

FIGURE 4-22 The queue's Access Policy page.

14. In the Add Policy dialog box (see Figure 4-23), enter the following information and click **OK**:

- **Identifier** Enter a unique name for the access policy.
- **Permissions** Select the permissions you want to apply to the access policy.
- **Start Time** Select a start date, time, and time zone for the policy.
- **Expiry Time** Select an expiry date, time, and time zone for the policy.

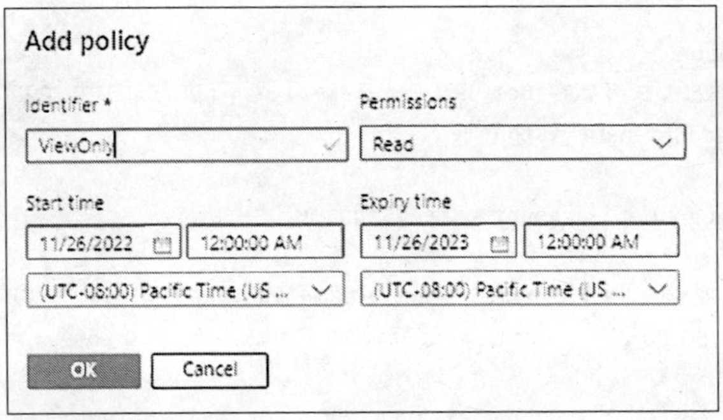

FIGURE 4-23 Add policy.

15. The policy is listed on the Access Policy page. (See Figure 4-24.) Click **Save**.

FIGURE 4-24 ViewOnly access policy.

USING THE AZURE CLI

Queues and messages can be created and managed using the `az storage queue create` and `az storage message` Azure CLI commands. You can create and manage the queues and messages discussed in the Azure portal walkthrough using the following script in Azure CLI:

```
#Define variables
stgname="mbspstorageaccount01"
rg="RG01"
region="eastus2"
queuename="primaryqueue"
vnet="vnet-01"
subnet="default"
policyname="ViewOnly"
#Create queue
az storage queue create -n $queuename --metadata key1=value1 key2=value2 --account-name
$stgname
#Create message
az storage message put -q $queuename --content "This is the first sample message in the
queue" --time-to-live 86400 --account-name $stgname
az storage message put -q $queuename --content "This is the second sample message in the
queue" --time-to-live 86400 --account-name $stgname
#get message ID
az storage message get -q $queuename --account-name $stgname
#Get message ID from the output of the above command and replace below BEFORE executing
the below command
#Delete specific message from queue
az storage message delete --id 84219a6c-f4a1-46c1-9975-1024e45418eb --pop-receipt popre-
ceiptreturned -q $queuename --account-name $stgname
#Delete all message in queue
az storage message clear -q $queuename --account-name $stgname
#Create storage access policy
az storage queue policy create --name $policyname --queue-name $queuename --account-name
$stgname --expiry 2023-11-26'T'00:00:00'Z' --permissions read
```

Networking considerations

Azure Queue Storage supports various types of network security configurations. These enable you to secure and restrict access to the associated Azure Storage account depending on your organizational and compliance needs. The options are as follows:

- Storage firewall and virtual networks
- Private endpoints
- Requiring secure transfers
- Enforcing TLS versions

Storage firewall and virtual networks

The storage firewall and virtual network restrictions are the same as the ones covered in Chapter 1 for Azure Blob Storage. To recap, the storage firewall offers four settings to restrict access to the queue storage account:

- **Enabled from All Networks** When you select this option, the storage account is accessible from any public network. This configuration is the least secure.
- **Enabled from Selected Virtual Networks and IP Addresses** With this option, you can configure the storage firewall to allow connections from selected Azure virtual networks or public IP addresses over the public internet. If you choose to permit connections from virtual networks, Azure prompts you to select the subnets you want to allow and creates service endpoints on each of those subnets. If you decide to allow connections from public IP addresses, you'll have to specify which addresses to allow.
- **Disabled** This disables access from all connections via the public internet. Only private endpoint connections are allowed. (More on private endpoints in a moment.)

> ***NOTE*** **You can configure certain Azure services, such as logging and monitoring, to connect to the storage account from any network, even if you disallow other connections.**

Storage firewall and virtual networks walkthrough

The following sections step you through the process of setting up a storage firewall that allows access to the Azure Storage account associated with Azure Queue Storage from a specific virtual network and IP address using the Azure portal and the Azure CLI.

> ***IMPORTANT*** **If you are following along, select resources and resource names based on your environment, including unique storage account names for each of your deployments.**

> ***IMPORTANT*** **If you are following along, be sure to delete any unwanted resources after you have completed testing to reduce charges levied by Microsoft.**

USING AZURE PORTAL

To set up a storage firewall that allows access to the Azure Storage account associated with Azure Queue Storage from a specific virtual network and IP address, follow these steps:

1. In the left pane of the Azure Storage account page, under **Security + Networking**, click **Networking**.
2. On the Networking page, under **Public Network Access**, select the **Enabled from Selected Virtual Networks and IP Addresses** option button.

The Networking page expands to display additional options. (See Figure 4-25.)

FIGURE 4-25 The Networking page expands to show additional options.

3. In the **Virtual Networks** section, click **Add Existing Virtual Network**.
4. In the Add Networks dialog box (see Figure 4-26), enter the following information and click **Enable**:
   - **Subscription** Select the subscription that contains the virtual network for which you want to allow access to the Azure Storage account.
   - **Virtual Networks** Select the virtual network for which you want to allow access.
   - **Subnets** Select the subnets for which you want to allow access.

FIGURE 4-26 Add existing virtual networks.

5. The virtual network is added to the Virtual Networks section of the Firewalls and Virtual Networks tab. (See Figure 4-27.)
6. Under **Firewall**, select the Add Your Client IP Address check box to allow your public IP address to access the storage.
7. Optionally, to allow additional public IP addresses or specific resource instances specify them in the **Address Range** box and **Resource Instances** settings.
8. Select all three check boxes in the **Exceptions** section. (See Figure 4-28.) Then click **Save**.

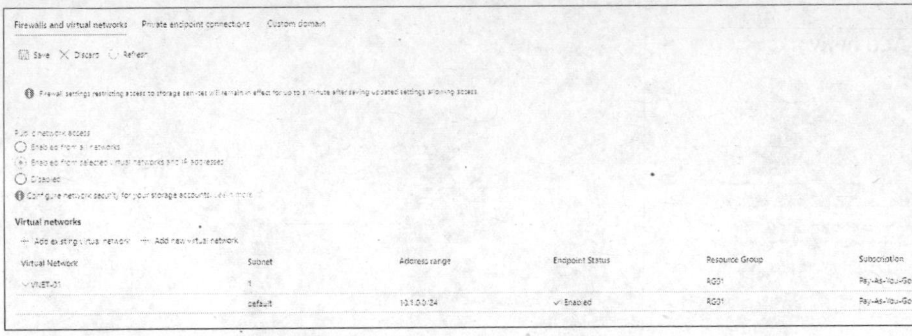

FIGURE 4-27 The virtual network is added.

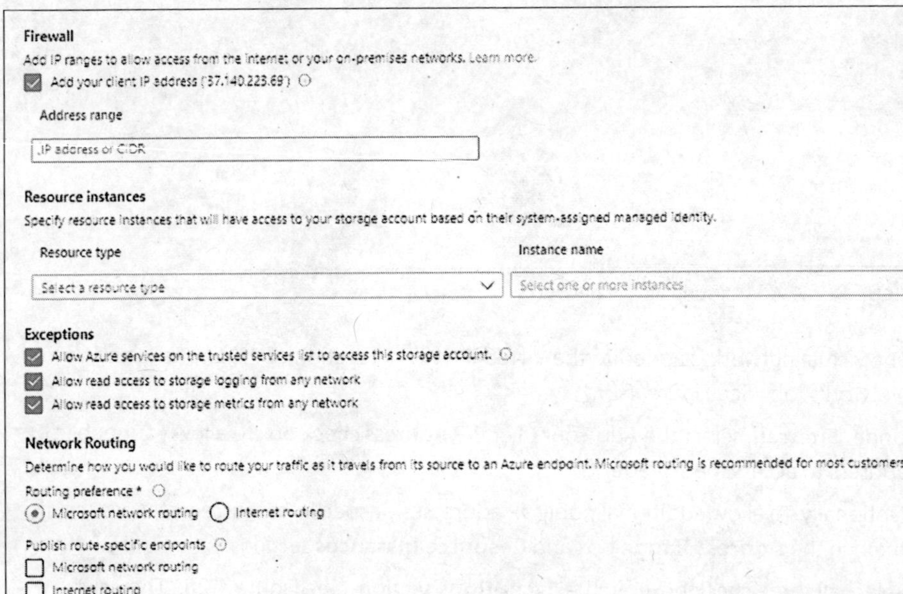

FIGURE 4-28 Finish configuring the storage firewall.

USING AZURE POWERSHELL

Use the following Azure PowerShell code to set up a storage account firewall:

```
#Define required variables
$resourceGroup = "RG01"
$region = "eastus"
$storageaccname = "mbspblobstorage01"
$container = "container"
$vnet = "vNET01"
$subnet = "default"
#Setting up Storage account firewall
```

```
#Setup access from Subnet
Update-AzStorageAccountNetworkRuleSet -ResourceGroupName $resourcegroup -Name $storage-
account -DefaultAction Deny
Get-AzVirtualNetwork -ResourceGroupName $resourcegroup -Name $vnet | Set-AzVirtualNet-
workSubnetConfig -Name $subnet -AddressPrefix "10.0.0.0/24" -ServiceEndpoint "Microsoft.
Storage" | Set-AzVirtualNetwork
$subnet = Get-AzVirtualNetwork -ResourceGroupName $resourcegroup -Name $vnet | Get-AzVir-
tualNetworkSubnetConfig -Name $subnet
Add-AzStorageAccountNetworkRule -ResourceGroupName $resourcegroup -Name $storageaccount
-VirtualNetworkResourceId $subnet.Id
```

USING THE AZURE CLI

You can manage the storage firewall and virtual networks using the `az storage account network-rule add` and `az network vnet subnet` CLI commands. You can make the storage firewall and virtual network changes discussed in the preceding walkthroughs using the following script in Azure CLI:

```
#Define variables
stgname="mbspstorageaccount01"
rg="RG01"
region="eastus2"
queuename="primaryqueue"
vnet="vnet-01"
subnet="default"#Set up Storage Firewall
az network vnet subnet update --resource-group $rg --vnet-name $vnet --name $subnet
--service-endpoints "Microsoft.Storage"
az storage account network-rule add -resource-group $rg --account-name $stgname --vnet-
name $vnet --subnet $subnet
```

Private endpoints

Azure Queue Storage supports the use of private endpoints to connect to the storage via Private Link. So, all traffic from a private endpoint to the storage account traverses the Microsoft backbone network rather than the public internet.

You create a private endpoint within a subnet. The private endpoint then uses an IP address from the subnet's IP range. You can set up a static IP address for the private endpoint or have Microsoft dynamically assign an unused one from the subnet range.

Private endpoint walkthrough

The following sections step you through the process of creating a private endpoint for use with Azure Queue Storage using the Azure portal.

> ***IMPORTANT*** **If you are following along, select resources and resource names based on your environment, including unique storage account names for each of your deployments.**

IMPORTANT If you are following along, be sure to delete any unwanted resources after you have completed testing to reduce charges levied by Microsoft.

USING AZURE PORTAL

To create a private endpoint using the Azure portal, follow these steps:

1. In the left pane of the Azure Storage account page, under **Security + Networking**, click **Networking**.
2. On the Networking page, click the **Private Endpoint Connections** tab.
3. Click **Private Endpoint** at the top of the tab. (See Figure 4-29.)

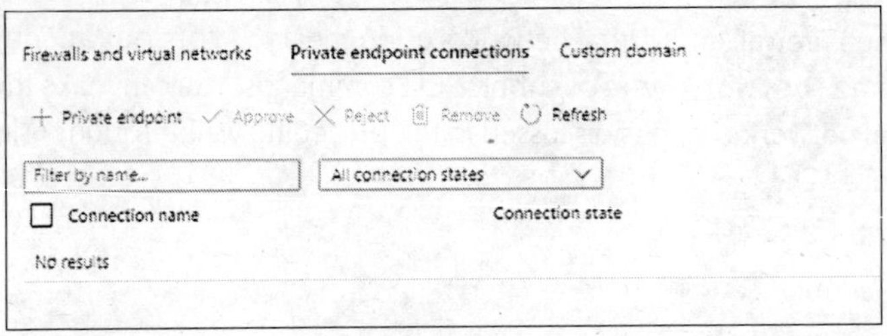

FIGURE 4-29 The Private Endpoint Connections tab.

4. In the **Basics** tab of the Create a Private Endpoint wizard (see Figure 4-30), enter the following information and click **Next**:
   - **Subscription** Select the subscription in which you want to create the private endpoint.
   - **Resource Group** Select an existing resource group or create a new one in which to create the private endpoint.
   - **Name** Enter a unique name for the private endpoint.
   - **Network Instance Name** Enter a unique name for the private endpoint network interface.
   - **Region** Select the Azure region in which you want to host the private endpoint.
5. On the **Resource** tab (see Figure 4-31), in the **Target Sub-Resource** drop-down list, select the **Queue**. Then click **Next**.

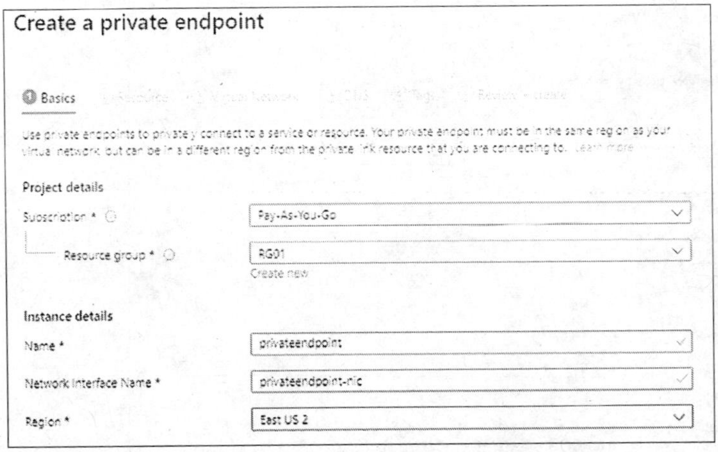

FIGURE 4-30 The Basics tab of the Create a Private Endpoint wizard.

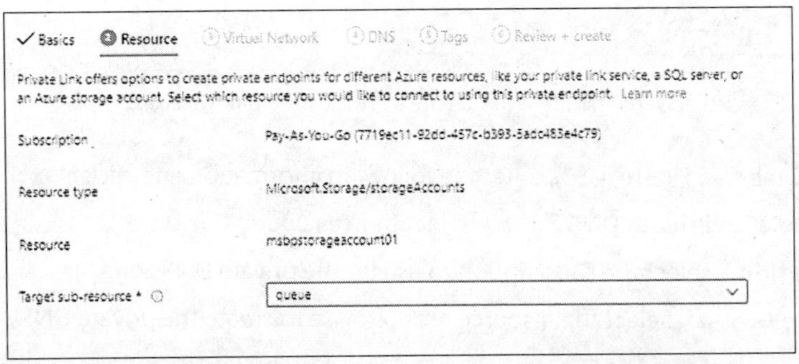

FIGURE 4-31 The Resource tab of the Create a Private Endpoint wizard.

6. On the **Virtual Network** tab (see Figure 4-32), enter the following information and click **Next**:
   - **Virtual Network** Select the virtual network in which you want to deploy the private endpoint.
   - **Subnet** Select the subnet on which you want to create the private endpoint.
   - **Private IP Configuration** Select the **Dynamically Allocate IP Address** or **Statically Allocate IP Address** option button, depending on your needs. If you select Static, define the private IP using the next two settings (`Name` and `Private IP`).
   - **Name** Enter a unique name for the private endpoint.
   - **Private IP** Enter an IP address for the private endpoint.
   - **Application Security Group** Leave this blank (the default) for this example.

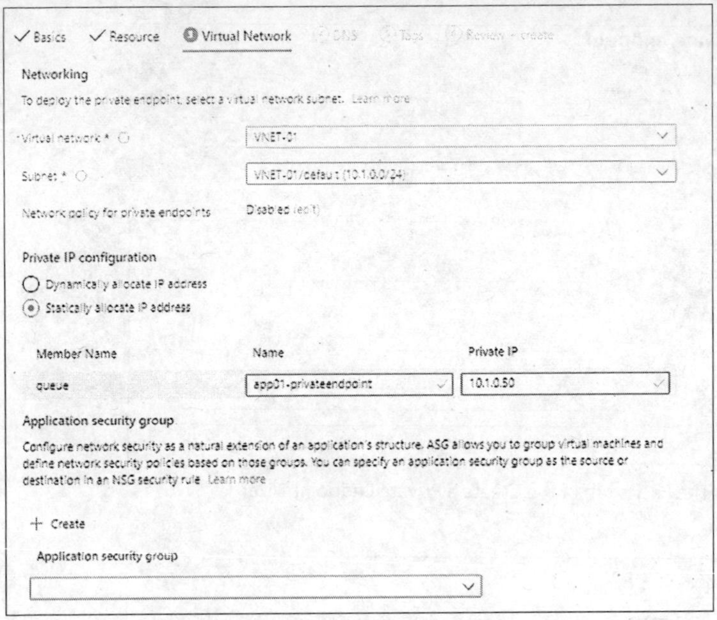

FIGURE 4-32 The Virtual Network tab of the Create a Private Endpoint wizard.

7. On the **DNS** tab (see Figure 4-33), enter the following information and click **Next**:
   - **Integrate with Private DNS Zone** Select the **Yes** option button.
   - **Subscription** Select the subscription to use for the private DNS zone.
   - **Resource Group** Select the resource group to use to create the private DNS zone.

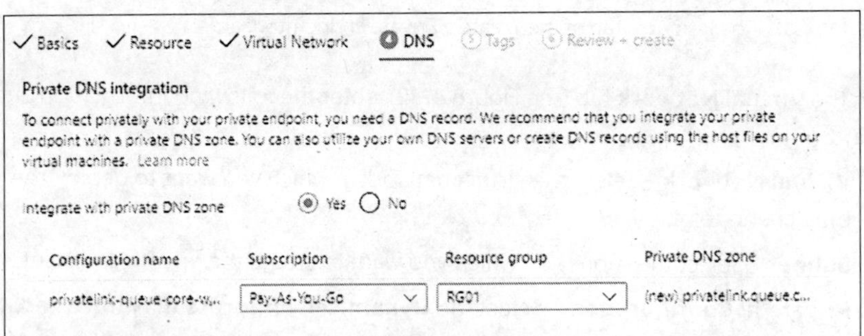

FIGURE 4-33 The DNS tab of the Create a Private Endpoint wizard.

8. On the **Tags** tab (see Figure 4-34), add any tags you want to associate with the private endpoint, and click **Next**.

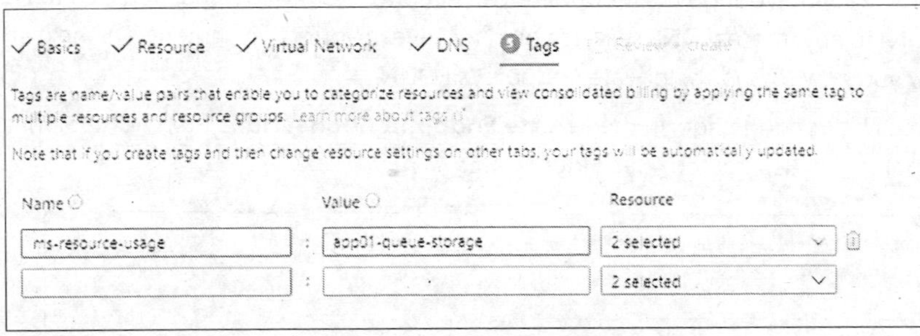

FIGURE 4-34 The Tags tab of the Create a Private Endpoint wizard.

9. On the **Review + Create** tab (see Figure 4-35), review your settings. Then click **Create** to create the private endpoint.

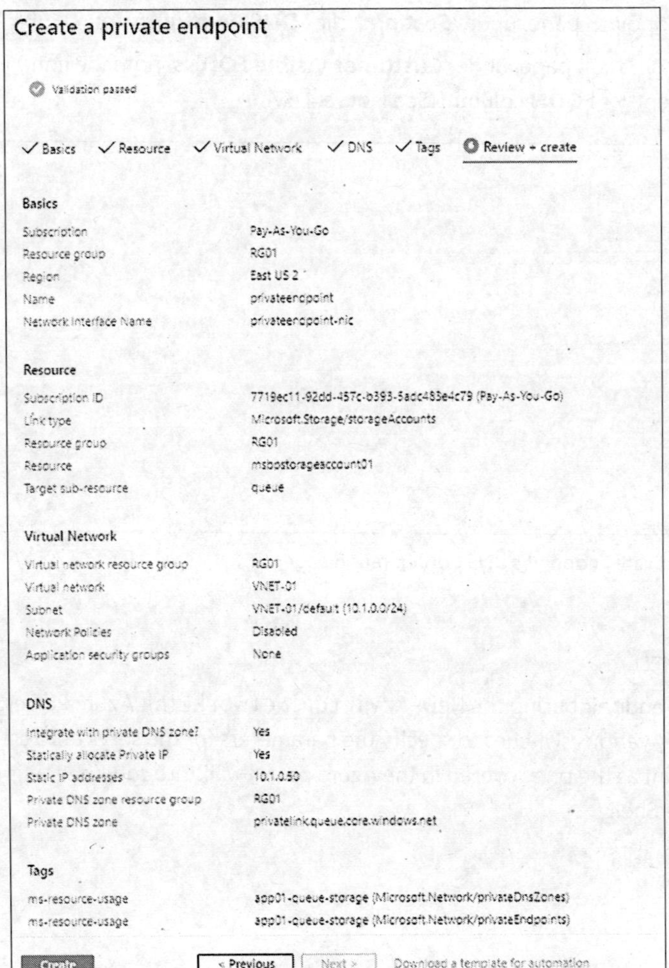

FIGURE 4-35 The Review + Create tab of the Create a Private Endpoint wizard.

10. After you set up your private endpoint, you need to add its fully qualified domain name (FQDN) to any internal DNS servers you may have in your environment. The next steps show you how to find the private endpoint's FQDN.

11. On the Networking page, in the **Private Endpoint Connections** tab, click the private endpoint you just created. (See Figure 4-36.)

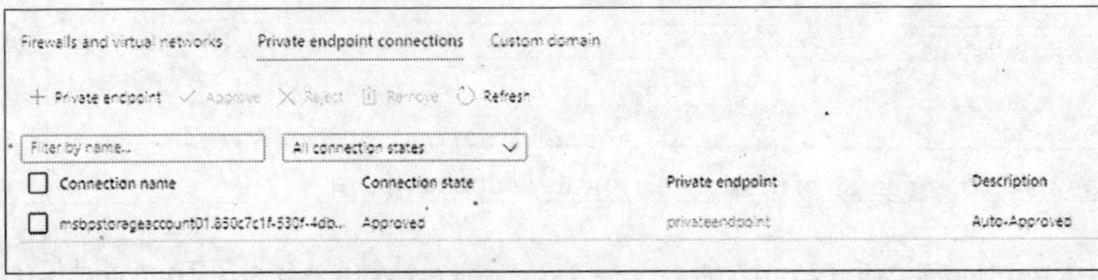

FIGURE 4-36 Private endpoint connections review.

12. On the private endpoint's page, under **Settings**, click **DNS Configuration**.

13. On the DNS Configuration page, under **Customer Visible FQDNs**, note the entry in the private endpoint entry's **FQDN** column. (See Figure 4-37.)

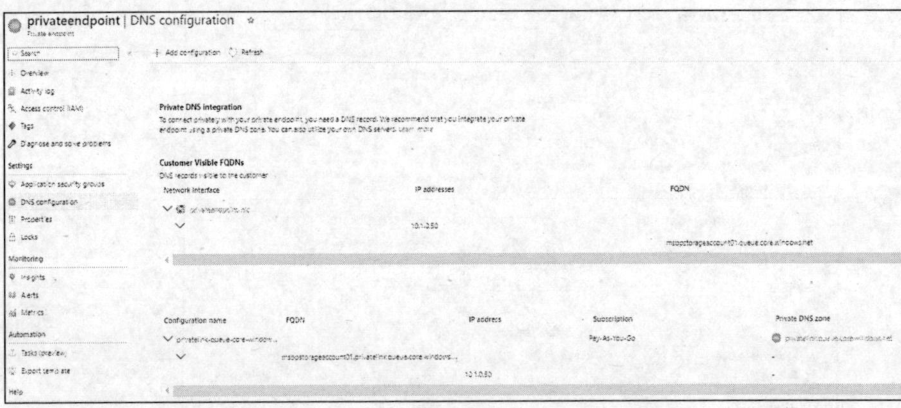

FIGURE 4-37 The private endpoint's DNS Configuration page.

USING AZURE POWERSHELL

You can create a private endpoint using the `New-AzVirtualNetworkLink` Azure PowerShell command. You can apply various switches to specify the parameters for the service. To create the same private endpoint as the one covered in the Azure portal walkthrough, use the following script in Azure PowerShell:

```
#Define required variables
$rg = "RG01"
$vnet = "vNET-01"
$subnetName = "default"
$endpointname = "PrivateEndpoint"
```

```
$privateendpointlink = "privateendpointlink"
$storagename = "msbpstorageaccount01"
$location = "East US 2"
# Create the Private Endpoint and Private link service connection
$storage = get-azstoragequeue -name $storagename
$PrivateLinkSvcConnection = New-AzPrivateLinkServiceConnection -Name $privateEndpointCon-
nectionName -PrivateLinkServiceId $storage.Id -GroupId "queue"
$privateEndpoint = New-AzPrivateEndpoint -Name "$endpointname" -ResourceGroup-
Name $rg -Location $location -SubnetName $subnet -PrivateLinkServiceConnection
$PrivateLinkSvcConnection
# Create the Private DNS zone
$PrivateDnsZone = New-AzPrivateDnsZone -Name "privatelink.queue.core.windows.net"
-ResourceGroupName $rg
# Create the Private DNS link
$PrivateDnsLink = New-AzPrivateDnsVirtualNetworkLink -Name $privateendpointlink `
-ResourceGroupName $rg `
-ZoneName "privatelink.queue.core.windows.net" `
-VirtualNetworkId $vnet.Id
# Create the Private DNS config
$PrivateDNSConfig = New-AzPrivateDnsZoneConfig -Name "privatelink.queue.core.windows.net" `
-PrivateDnsZoneId $PrivateDNSZone.ResourceId

$dnsZoneGroup = New-AzPrivateDnsZoneGroup -Name "PrivateDNSZoneGroup" `
-ResourceGroupName $rg `
-PrivateEndpointName $privateEndpoint.Name `
-PrivateDnsZoneConfig $PrivateDNSConfig
```

USING THE AZURE CLI

Private endpoint can be created using the `az network private-endpoint create` Azure CLI command. Different switches can specify the initial parameters for the service creation. The preceding private endpoint can be created using the following script in Azure CLI:

```
#Define required variables
rg="RG01"
vnet="vNET-01"
subnetName="Subnet01"
endpointname="PrivateEndpoint"
privateendpointlink="privateendpointlink"
storagename="msbpstorageaccount01"
location="East US 2"
# Create and configure the Private Endpoint
az network private-endpoint create \
    --name PrivateEndpoint \
    --resource-group $rg \
    --vnet-name $vnet --subnet $subnet \
```

```
    --private-connection-resource-id $storage.id \
    --group-id storage\
    --connection-name PrivEndpointConnection
# Create the Private DNS zone
az network private-dns zone create \
    --resource-group $rg \
    --name "privatelink.queue.core.windows.net"
# Create the Private DNS link
az network private-dns link vnet create \
    --resource-group $rg \
    --zone-name "privatelink.queue.core.windows.net" \
    --name privateendpointlink \
    --virtual-network $vnet \
    --registration-enabled false
# Create the Private DNS config
az network private-endpoint dns-zone-group create \
   --resource-group $rg \
   --endpoint-name PrivateEndpoint \
   --name PrivDNSZoneGroup \
   --private-dns-zone "privatelink.queue.core.windows.net" \
   --zone-name "privateendpointzone"
```

Requiring secure transfers

You can force Azure Queue Storage endpoints to work only over HTTPS by requiring secure transfers. When you require secure transfers, any client requests over HTTP (rather than HTTPS) are automatically rejected. You can use another Azure service called Azure Policy to enforce this requirement across all storage accounts in your organization. (Azure Policy is outside the scope of this book series. However, it will be covered in future editions.)

Enforcing TLS versions

By default, Azure storage accounts use Transport Layer Security (TLS) version 1.2. However, TLS 1.0 and TLS 1.1 can also be used. This is to support backward compatibility for client applications that use these versions of TLS. If this describes your client application, Microsoft highly recommends that you update it to use TLS 1.2 for all storage communications, and to enforce the use of that version on the storage account level to prevent future connections over those older protocols.

Identity and access considerations

When a user or a client application attempts to connect to Azure Queue Storage, the client request is authorized before the queue data is made available to the requester. This is done using Azure Active Directory (AD), storage account keys, or Shared Access Signature (SAS) tokens. The authorization process validates the client application's permissions for accessing the queue storage account.

Authentication comes into the picture when using Azure Active Directory (AD) for access. With Azure Active Directory, the identity of the user or application service principal used by the client application is authenticated by Azure AD, which issues an OAuth 2.0 token when authentication is successful. The OAuth 2.0 token can then be used to authorize a request against the Azure Queue Storage service.

> ***NOTE*** **The downside of using access keys and SAS tokens is that storage logs do not capture service principal details to identify who has used either method for data access. This can be limiting in environments where such level of logging is necessary. In such scenarios, the client application and all users must use Azure AD for authorization and authentication.**

Azure AD

Azure AD handles authorization using role-based access control (RBAC). You can use RBAC to assign access to users, groups, or managed identities. You can also limit access on the level of an individual queue, storage account, resource group, subscription, or management group. This makes it easy to delegate access based on your organizational needs.

RBAC grants access based on built-in pre-defined roles in Azure AD. Built-in Azure AD role groups for queue storage include Storage Queue Data Reader, Storage Queue Data Contributor, Storage Queue Data Message Processor, and Storage Queue Data Message Sender, among others. You can also create custom roles to meet your application requirements.

> ***NOTE*** **Storage accounts created using the Azure Resource Manager (ARM) deployment model support Azure AD authorization. Accounts deployed using the Classic deployment model, however, do not.**

Storage account access keys

By default, Microsoft generates two 512-bit access keys for every storage account when that account is created. You can use these keys to access all data in the storage account. This makes it extremely critical to secure and protect these keys.

You should not use access keys in client applications to access storage accounts. A breach in the application code could expose these keys to malicious third parties, who could gain full access to your storage account. You should also periodically rotate these keys manually or integrate them with Azure Key Vault so they are rotated automatically.

Shared Access Signature (SAS)

You can use a Shared Access Signature (SAS) token to provide delegated access to the queue storage account. The delegation provides granular control on what resources are accessible, what level of access is allowed, and for how long the access is available.

A SAS token is a more secure method for accessing queue storage using a client application because you control the token parameters. Any user, group, or service principal that has been assigned the permission Microsoft.Storage/storageAccounts/listKeys/action can generate a SAS URL using the account keys.

Shared Access Signature walkthrough

The following sections step you through the process of creating a SAS token for use with Azure Queue Storage using the Azure portal.

> ***IMPORTANT*** **If you are following along, select resources and resource names based on your environment, including unique storage account names for each of your deployments.**

> ***IMPORTANT*** **If you are following along, be sure to delete any unwanted resources after you have completed testing to reduce charges levied by Microsoft.**

USING AZURE PORTAL

To create a SAS token for use with Azure Queue Storage using the Azure portal, follow these steps:

1. In the left pane of the Azure Storage account page, under **Security + Networking**, click **Shared Access String**.
2. In the Shared Access Signature page (see Figure 4-38), enter the following information. Then click **Generate SAS and Connection String**:
   - **Allowed Services** Select the **Queue** check box.
   - **Allowed Resource Types** Select the **Service** and **Object** check boxes.
   - **Allowed Permissions** Select the check box next to each permission you want to allow.
   - **Blob Versioning Permissions** Leave this check box unchecked. (This setting pertains to blob storage, not queue storage.)
   - **Allowed Blob Index Permissions** Leave this check box unchecked. (This setting pertains to blob storage, not queue storage.)
   - **Start and Expiry Date/Time** Select the start and end date, time, and time zone for the SAS token.

- **Allowed IP Addresses** Enter any public IPs that should be allowed.
- **Allowed Protocols** Select the **HTTPS Only** (recommended, if your client application supports this) or **HTTPS and HTTP** option button.
- **Preferred Routing Tier** Leave this set to **Basic** (the default).
- **Signing Key** Select the signing key to use (**key1** or **key2**).

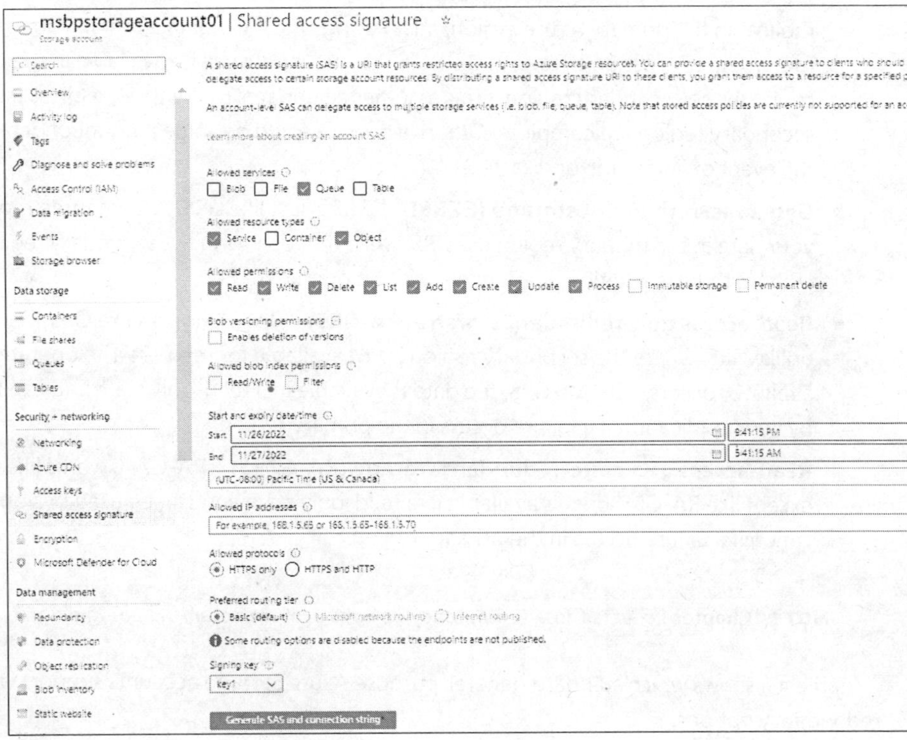

FIGURE 4-38 Creating a SAS token.

Data redundancy

Azure Storage accounts provide different levels of data redundancy and resiliency to enable you to access queue messages in the event of an outage. Chapter 1 covered these in detail, but let's do a quick recap here:

- **Locally redundant storage (LRS)** With LRS storage, Azure maintains three replicas of your data in a single datacenter within your primary Azure region to protect against local storage hardware, server rack, or network component failures. However, because all three replicas are stored in the same datacenter, if that datacenter experiences some type of disaster, all three copies of your data could be lost.

- **Zone-redundant storage (ZRS)** Like LRS, ZRS synchronously commits and maintains three replicas of your data in your primary Azure region, but instead of storing each replica in a single datacenter, they are spread across three availability zones. So, if a disaster occurs in one availability zone, your data will generally still be accessible.
- **Geo-redundant storage (GRS)** With GRS, Azure synchronously commits and maintains three replicas of your data in your primary Azure region in LRS. Then, three more replicas of your data in a secondary Azure region are updated to match the three replicas in the primary Azure region, again using LRS. If the datacenter in your primary region experiences an outage or disaster, then your data will be available in the datacenter in the secondary region. (This assumes all updates to the three replicas in the secondary region are complete. Otherwise, there could be some amount of data loss in the event of an outage or disaster.)
- **Geo-zone-redundant storage (GZRS)** GZRS is just like GRS, but the three replicas of your data in the primary region use ZRS, while the replicas in the secondary region use LRS. So, there is additional redundancy in the primary region.
- **Read-access geo-redundant storage (RA-GRS)** RA-GRS works like GRS. However, unlike GRS, where the secondary region is not available for read or write operations until a failover occurs, with RA-GRS, the data is available in a read-only state and can be used by your application if a failure occurs in the primary region.
- **Read-access geo-zone-redundant storage (RA-GZRS)** RA-GZRS works like GZRS except like RA-GRS, data is available in a read-only state and can be used by your application if a failure occurs in the primary region.

> ***NOTE*** **Chapter 1 covers these redundancy options in more detail, including diagrams.**

Table 4-1 shows which standard general-purpose Azure Storage accounts support which redundancy options.

TABLE 4-1 Standard general-purpose Azure Storage account support for data redundancy

Standard Azure Storage account type	Data redundancy options supported
Standard general-purpose v1	LRS GRS RA-GRS
Standard general-purpose v2	LRS GRS RA-GRS ZRS GZRS RA-GZRS

Depending on which data redundancy option you choose for your Azure Storage account, the associated queue storage will provide the same level of redundancy. Therefore, it is important to identify your queue storage redundancy requirements before setting up the

Azure Storage account. If you attempt to do so at a later stage, after you have started using the account, you will have to either migrate the data on your own or with Microsoft's support. Alternatively, if there is no data in the storage account as yet, you will need to delete and re-create the storage account to match the requirements.

> **NOTE** In some cases, you can change the redundancy level without a migration, and support for this continues to expand. Be sure to review the latest Microsoft guidance for your storage account to determine whether you can convert your data replication configuration without a migration.

Disaster recovery

Disaster recovery is a critical component of any application architecture. The higher the criticality of the application, the more redundancy is required to ensure minimal to no downtime or data loss.

Setting data redundancy options can enable you to recover queue messages in the event of an outage. However, you must take into account other application components in your disaster recovery planning, too. This ensures that in a disaster scenario, while the queue storage is online, all other related components are also online and can read the storage with minimal interruption.

Storage redundancy options such as GRS and GZRS can replicate your data asynchronously to another Azure region on an ongoing basis. When the secondary region is brought online and the corresponding DNS entries for the storage are up-to-date, your applications can start their read/write operations. You cannot perform read operations until the failover to the secondary region is complete.

You saw earlier that the primary queue storage endpoint points to *https://<storage-account-name>.queue.core.windows.net/<queue-name>*. Similarly, the secondary storage endpoint would be reachable at *https://<storage-account-name>-secondary.queue.core.windows.net/<queue-name>*. (The *-secondary* suffix is appended automatically by the secondary endpoint.) You can use this endpoint to connect to the secondary storage. The storage account access keys would remain the same in both the primary and secondary endpoints.

Storage account failover

There are two ways a GRS or GZRS storage account can be failed over to a secondary region:

- **Microsoft-managed failover** In the event of a region-wide outage, Microsoft performs a full region failover to the secondary region. In such cases, you need not perform manual failover operations on your storage accounts. You would only have to ensure that when the DNS entries for the storage are updated, your applications are ready to resume normal operations.

- **Customer-managed failover** When an outage occurs, Microsoft attempts to restore the data and operations in the primary region. If Microsoft is unable to do so, that region will be declared unrecoverable, and Microsoft will initiate the failover to the secondary region. If you cannot wait until such time, you can perform a manual failover from your storage account properties to bring your storage account online and make it accessible to your applications.

In either scenario, DNS entries must be updated automatically or manually before write operations to the storage can begin. Also take into account any private endpoints you may have created in the primary region; you need to make sure the same endpoints are set up in the secondary region, too.

Last Sync Time

Data synchronized using GRS is often behind data in the primary region. The data sync is asynchronous to avoid affecting write operations and storage performance in the primary region. This allows write operations to be committed on the primary storage without waiting for the same operations to be written and acknowledged by the secondary storage. However, at the time of a disaster, some data written and committed to the primary store might not yet have been committed to the secondary storage—in which case, that data would be lost.

You can determine whether this has happened by checking the Last Sync Time property for your storage account. This value is a GMT date/time value that you can query using Azure PowerShell, Azure CLI, or one of the Azure Storage client libraries. Any write operations performed after this Last Sync Time property value are most likely missing in the secondary region and might not be available for read operations. Incorporating this into your application logic can allow you to plan in advance how to handle such contingencies.

Last Sync Time walkthrough

The following sections step you through the process of checking the Last Sync Time property on a storage account using Azure PowerShell and Azure CLI.

USING AZURE POWERSHELL

Use the following Azure PowerShell code to retrieve the Last Sync Time property for a storage account:

```
#Define variables
$rg = "RG01"
$storageaccname = "mbspstorageaccount01"

#Retrieve the last sync time
$LastSyncTime = $(Get-AzStorageAccount -ResourceGroupName $rg `
    -Name $storageaccname `
    -IncludeGeoReplicationStats).GeoReplicationStats.LastSyncTime
```

USING THE AZURE CLI

Use the following Azure CLI code to retrieve the Last Sync Time on a storage account:

```
#Define required variables
rg="RG01"
storageaccname="mbspstorageaccount01"

#Retrieve the last sync time
$LastSyncTime=$(az storage account show \
    --name $storageaccname \
    --resource-group $rg \
    --expand geoReplicationStats \
    --query geoReplicationStats.lastSyncTime \
    --output tsv)
```

Data encryption

Azure Queue Storage supports multiple levels of data encryption for data that is persisted to the cloud to ensure customers can meet any regulatory or compliance requirements they may have. This includes infrastructure encryption, service-level encryption, and client-side encryption.

> ***NOTE*** **You can enable infrastructure and service-level encryption using the Azure portal, Azure PowerShell, Azure CLI, and ARM templates when setting up the storage account.**

Infrastructure encryption

Azure Queue Storage automatically encrypts all data in a storage account using 256-bit Advanced Encryption Standard (AES) encryption and supports the same level of encryption at the infrastructure level. This double encryption protects against scenarios in which one of the encryption algorithms or keys gets compromised.

In general, you can enable infrastructure encryption when you create the storage account or when you create the encryption scope. However, for storage accounts meant for use with Azure Queue Storage, you must enable infrastructure encryption at the storage account level when you create the account.

After you create a storage account, you cannot change the infrastructure encryption configuration. If you require infrastructure encryption at a later stage, you will have to create another storage account with infrastructure encryption enabled and migrate the data to that account.

> ***NOTE*** **Infrastructure encryption supports only Microsoft-managed encryption keys.**

Service-level encryption

You can set up service-level encryption using Microsoft-managed or customer-managed keys with Azure Key Vault or using the Key Vault Managed Hardware Security Model (HSM) service (currently in preview).

Although you can choose which key your storage account should use, you cannot disable service-level encryption. It is automatically enabled, and if you do not specify any custom configurations, it is protected by default using Microsoft-managed keys.

Even if you select Microsoft-managed encryption on both the infrastructure and service level, the keys used for the encryption are always different. This ensures that if one key is breached, the second key can continue to protect the resource.

Client-side encryption

You can set up client-side encryption for queue storage using Azure Queue Storage client libraries for .NET and Python. With client-side encryption, you set up the application to encrypt data within the application layer before uploading it to the queue storage and to decrypt data when a client downloads it. The Azure Queue Storage client libraries support integration with Azure Key Vault for encryption key management.

There are two versions of client-side encryption:

- **Version 1** This uses Cipher Block Chaining (CBC) mode with AES 256-bit encryption.
- **Version 2** This uses Galois/Counter Mode (GCM) mode with AES 256-bit encryption.

Due to security vulnerabilities with the client library's implementation of CBC mode, Microsoft recommends upgrading to version 2 as soon as possible.

Best practices

Following are some general best practices for setting up, securing, and managing the Azure Queue Storage service in your environment:

- **Monitor storage metrics using Azure Monitor** To get a better understanding of queue storage usage so you can determine whether your message volumes are too high for your applications to handle, use Azure Monitor to monitor storage metrics. This will enable you to plan any changes in application architecture or storage account parameters to optimize the storage performance and ensure messages are being handled in a timely manner.
- **Plan for data redundancy** Depending on your application requirements and budgetary constraints, choose the right data redundancy option so you can recover your queue storage data in case of a disaster. RA-GRS and RA-GZRS data redundancy have the added benefit of enabling you to spread the read-access loads to the secondary instance of the storage, thereby improving application performance. Take this into

consideration during the application design and architecture phase so you can incorporate it into your storage build planning. Although you can switch data-redundancy levels at a later stage, this might require a full migration of the data account and a complete reconfiguration of the application to work with it, depending on the type of storage and features involved. Review the redundancy conversion limitations in place at the time of your planning to identify the right options for your scenario.

- **Plan for disaster recovery** Depending on which data redundancy option you choose, your storage account data might already replicate to another Azure availability zone or Azure region. However, it is important to plan how you will handle a failover in case disaster strikes the primary Azure region where your queue storage is located. Familiarize yourself with the process of initiating a customer-driven failover in case the outage is limited to your storage account or availability group. (In the event of a disaster that affects an entire Azure region, Microsoft will perform failovers on its own.) Documenting the disaster-recovery plan enables you to identify any single points of failure in the application architecture and address them in advance.
- **Use customer-managed keys with Azure Key Vault** Microsoft-managed encryption keys use AES 256-bit encryption and are highly secure. However, some organizations require the use of their own custom-managed encryption keys for all their data. If your organization has such a requirement, use Azure Key Vault to store your personal encryption keys, and use those to encrypt your storage accounts. Using this in combination with Microsoft-managed infrastructure encryption offers the highest level of security for storage data.
- **Use private endpoints for secure application data exchange** Azure Queue Storage supports the use of private endpoints to access the storage for read and write operations. It is a good practice to use private endpoints for all your storage accounts that exchange application data within your environment, and to disable all public access to the storage. This reduces the attack surface area for your storage infrastructure because all traffic traverses a highly secure Microsoft backbone network.
- **Set up a storage network firewall** Allow access to the storage account only from known public IP addresses or virtual networks. This prevents the public endpoint from being accessible from unknown networks unless that is a core requirement. Review this access list on a scheduled basis and remove any unwanted access points. This ensures that public IPs no longer in your control can no longer access the storage account to initiate attacks.
- **Audit control and data plane operations** You can monitor and audit Azure Queue Storage account activity at the control plane and data plane levels. Control plane operations are those that pertain to creating, configuring, or modifying a storage account. Data plane operations relate to queue storage service endpoint requests, such as listing a queue message, deleting a queue message, and so on. You should monitor both types of operations and, depending on your regulatory requirements, store them in long-term storage accounts for audit or reporting purposes.

- **Use Azure AD when possible** Using Azure AD for storage authentication and authorization allows you to monitor and audit storage logs with the principal name of the user carrying out the operations. This can be critical in cases of investigation and compliance audits. Based on your application design and compliance requirements, you should consider transitioning to Azure AD authentication as soon as possible.
- **Use Log Analytics to store and query logs** Log Analytics natively provides rich log querying capabilities. You can export storage logs to a Log Analytics workspace and perform extensive querying against those logs for compliance, audit, and ongoing performance or security monitoring purposes.
- **Use Azure Synapse to optimize log querying costs** If your log querying requirements are minimal, you can leverage Azure Synapse instead of Log Analytics to run queries on an as-needed basis. Azure Synapse can use an Azure Storage account for log querying. This allows you to export storage logs to a diagnostic storage account. In combination with Azure Synapse, this can significantly reduce your overall costs compared to Log Analytics.

Chapter 5

Azure Data Box

Overview

The Azure Data Box family of appliances helps customers export and import large volumes of data to and from different Azure storage services. Microsoft introduced the Azure Data Box family of appliances in stages, starting with the Azure Data Box in September 2018, followed by the Azure Data Disk in January 2019, and finally the Azure Data Box Heavy in July 2019. Each appliance increased the data capacity that could be transferred offline to Azure:

- **Azure Data Box** 80 terabytes (TB) usable capacity.
- **Azure Data Box Disk** 35 TB usable capacity.
- **Azure Data Box Heavy** 800 TB usable capacity.

Which of these services for data ingestion to and from Azure is right for you will depend on your specific requirements.

Key features

- **Ability to transfer large amounts of data offline** You can use the Data Box appliances or disks to transfer large amounts of data offline to Azure Storage. You can transfer data on local devices over your local network or over USB, depending on the data box that you choose, and ship it to a Microsoft datacenter to have it uploaded directly into whichever Azure Storage account you choose.
- **Faster migration of data to Azure** Transferring up to 1 petabyte (PB) of data over the internet can be difficult, depending on where your data is stored and available internet capacity. If you must perform such a data transfer once, or more than once but on an irregular basis or with large gaps of time in between, it might not be financially viable to provision large internet lines for this purpose. Data Box appliances help overcome these challenges, as the transfer process is much shorter than transferring over the internet.
- **Secure and encrypted data transfer** The entire data-transfer process is secure and encrypted using keys that only the customer can access.

- **Support for various Azure storage services** You can use Data Box appliances to transfer data to and from different Azure services, such as Azure Blob Storage, Azure File Storage, Azure Managed Disks, and Azure Data Lake Storage (ADSL) Gen 2.
- **Flexibility to address changing needs** You can select the appliance option based on your data-transfer needs. For example, you can request an appliance on an ongoing basis or when needed. This can help in scenarios where large volumes of data are generated offshore or in remote areas where connectivity is an issue—for example, offshore oil or drilling rigs or windmill farms.

Key concepts

The following sections describe key concepts behind the Data Box appliances to help you identify which device is the right one for your needs.

Data Box components

Each of the Data Box products has different components:

- Azure Data Box
- Azure Data Box Disk
- Azure Data Box Heavy

Azure Data Box

This product consists of multiple components:

- **Data Box appliance** This appliance contains 100 TB of encrypted disks, with a usable capacity of 80 TB. Each device supports data transfer using network interfaces. There are four interfaces: one 1 gigabit ethernet (GbE) interface for management, one 1 GbE interface for data transfers, and two 10 GbE interfaces for data transfers. You can reconfigure both 1 GbE interfaces to function in 10 GbE mode, depending on your network setup requirements.
- **Azure Data Box service** You use this service, which you access from the Azure portal, to order and manage the data-transfer process to and from Azure.
- **Local web user interface (UI)** You use this local web UI to connect to the local device within your network to set up, configure, and manage the appliance.

Azure Data Box Disk

This product consists of two components:

- **Data Box Disk appliance** This appliance contains 40 TB of encrypted SSD disks with a usable capacity of 35 TB. Data transfer is supported using USB 3.0. Based on your data-transfer requirements, Microsoft will send you the appropriate number of 8 TB disks.

- **Azure Data Box service** You use this service, which you access from the Azure portal, to order and manage the data-transfer process to and from Azure.

Azure Data Box Heavy

Like the Azure Data Box product, this product contains multiple components:

- **Data Box appliance** This appliance contains 1 PB of encrypted disks with a usable capacity of 770 TB. Each device supports data transfer using network interfaces. There are four interfaces: one 1 GbE interface for management, one 1 GbE interface for data transfers, and two 40 GbE interfaces for data transfers.
- **Azure Data Box service** You use this service, which you access from the Azure portal, to order and manage the data-transfer process to and from Azure.
- **Local web UI** You use this local web UI to connect to the local device within your network to set up, configure, and manage the appliance.

Import/export workflow

Following is a standard workflow for importing data to Azure using the Data Box service:

1. Place the Data Box order. This involves the following steps:
   - Selecting which Data Box appliance you want to order.
   - Setting up the required encryption (Microsoft-managed or customer-managed).
   - Specifying where the data must be uploaded when Microsoft receives it.
   - Confirming the associated charges (if any).
2. After you receive the Data Box appliance, you must set it up using one of the following procedures (depending on which type of appliance it is):
   - **Data Box Disk** Connect the disks to the required client using USB 3.0 and unlock the disks using the key provided in your Data Box order in the Azure portal.
   - **Data Box or Data Box Heavy** Set up the appliance on your network for SMB or NFS transfer and unlock the disks using the key provided in your Data Box order in the Azure Portal.
3. Copy the required data to the appliance using one of the following procedures (depending on which type of appliance it is):
   - **Data Box Disk** Use robocopy to perform the data transfer to disk over SMB or supported Linux tools such as rsync, smbcacls, or cifsacl. (More on supported Linux tools in the section "Preserving ACLs, file attributes, and timestamps" later in this chapter.)
   - **Data Box or Data Box Heavy** After you set up and connect your appliance, you can select which protocol to use for data transfer, and the local web UI will guide you through the copy process. Use the supported client tools if you want to preserve ACLs, file attributes, and timestamps during the copy process. (For more on these, see the section "Preserving ACLs, file attributes, and timestamps" later in this

chapter.) Complete the copy process within the stipulated timeframe to avoid additional charges from Microsoft (as detailed with your order).

4. When the data copy operation is complete, return the appliance to Microsoft using the instructions provided with the appliance. Be sure to return the appliance in the same condition as received to avoid rejection or failure.
5. When Microsoft receives the appliance, the data is automatically uploaded to the service based on your order request.
6. After the import is successful, Microsoft erases all data on the appliance in line with NIST 800-88 Revision 1 standards.

Following is a standard workflow for exporting data from Azure using the Data Box service:

1. Place the Data Box order. This involves the following steps:
   - Selecting which Data Box appliance you want to order.
   - Providing details regarding the source data in Azure that you want to export.
   - Setting up the required encryption (Microsoft-managed or customer-managed).
   - Providing destination details.
   - Confirming the associated charges (if any).
2. Microsoft processes the order, transfers the required data to the Data Box appliance according to your order specifications, and ships the appliance to you.
3. When you receive the appliance from Microsoft, set up the appliance per the instructions provided in the entry for the order in the Azure Portal, unlock the disks, and copy the data on the appliance to your storage. Complete the copy process within the stipulated timeframe to avoid additional charges from Microsoft (as detailed with your order).
4. After the data export operation is complete, return the appliance to Microsoft using the instructions provided with the appliance. Be sure to return the appliance in the same condition as received to avoid charges for damage.
5. When Microsoft receives the appliance, it erases all data on the appliance in line with NIST 800-88 Revision 1 standards.

> ***NOTE*** **You will be notified by email during each step of the import or export process to inform you of its progress. This gives you the necessary time and clarity to prepare on your end to manage your activities in a timely manner.**

Data security

Each type of Data Box appliance is secured in different ways to protect both the appliance and customer data. Data Box appliances offer the following safety measures:

- **Azure Data Box** This appliance has a rugged casing with tamper-proof screws. In addition, stickers are placed at the bottom of the device to alert you and the Microsoft team of any physical tampering.

- **Azure Data Box Disk** The disks in this appliance are tamper-resistant and support secure update capabilities.
- **Azure Data Box Heavy** This appliance has a rugged casing protected with tamper-proof screws. In addition, stickers are placed at the bottom of the device to alert you and the Microsoft team of any physical tampering.

In addition, these appliances include various data-security measures:

- **Azure Data Box** This appliance comes with disks that are secured using BitLocker AES 256-bit encryption.
- **Azure Data Box Disk** This appliance has SSD disks that are secured using BitLocker AES 128-bit encryption.
- **Azure Data Box Heavy** This appliance comes with disks that are secured using BitLocker AES 256-bit encryption.

In each of these cases, the password to unlock the disks is available in the Azure portal. By default, the password is generated and managed by Microsoft. However, you can create your own customer-managed key by using the Azure Key Vault service when you order the Data Box appliance.

> ***IMPORTANT*** **Microsoft erases the disks on the Data Box appliance(s) after the completion of the import or export process in accordance with NIST 800-88 Revision 1 standards. For exports, this process is carried out after the appliance is received by Microsoft from the customer.**

Data-transfer speeds

Each type of appliance supports different data-transfer speeds:

- **Azure Data Box** This appliance supports a data-transfer rate of up to 80 TB per day over the 10 GbE network interface. If using the 1 GbE interface for data transfers, this would significantly slow down the transfer.
- **Azure Data Box Disk** This appliance supports a data-transfer rate of up to 430 megabytes per second (MBps).
- **Azure Data Box Heavy** This appliance supports data transfer using either the 40 GbE network interfaces or downgrading them to 10 GbE network interfaces. The exact data-transfer rates for this service have not been released at this time; however, depending on your interface, speeds would be close to or much higher than those of the Data Box appliance.

> ***NOTE*** **These are maximum transfer speeds in ideal scenarios. These speeds would differ based on actual file sizes.**

Supported Azure services

The Azure Data Box appliances support data import and export to various Azure storage services:

- Azure Blob Storage
- Azure File Storage
- Azure Managed Disks
- ADLS Gen 1 or Gen 2 (for imports only)

Depending on the type of data and its purpose, you can select the appropriate storage type in Azure. Different types of Data Box appliances may have limitations with regard to the various storage account types, such as support for hot/cool or standard/premium storage.

> ***NOTE*** **Microsoft regularly enhances each service's capabilities, so refer to the latest available guidance to identify whether your storage type is supported.**

Supported client operating systems

The data copy operation must be performed using one of the following operating systems supported by the Azure Data Box service:

- Windows Server 2016 RS1 and above
- Windows 7, 8, 10, and 11
- Linux OS Ubuntu, Debian, CentOS, and Red Hat Enterprise

> ***TIP*** **Use the latest version of these operating systems to avoid compatibility issues.**

Availability

Azure Data Box services are available in most Azure regions. However, not all Data Box appliances are available everywhere at this time. Use the following link to verify the availability of your required appliance before planning your next steps: *https://azure.microsoft.com/en-us/global-infrastructure/services/?products=databox&regions=all.*

Data resiliency

You can have only one instance of the Data Box service running in one geographical Azure region. All your requests within a region are tracked by the same service. However, a passive replica of the service also runs in the Azure region paired with your primary region. Microsoft maintains this replica in the paired region and activates it if your primary region goes offline.

The paired region may or may not be within the same country or commerce boundary. This can affect the steps required from your end after the replica is activated as follows:

- If the paired region is within the same country or commerce boundary (for example, the European Union), Microsoft is responsible for recovering the service within 72 hours, and no action is needed from the customer end.
- If the paired region is not within the same country or commerce boundary, Microsoft will contact you to ask you to create the Data Box order from an available region.

Partner integrations

The Azure Data Box service integrates with numerous partner solutions, and the list keeps growing. This integration helps you perform the initial data upload of large volumes of data to Azure for use by these partner solutions. There are different scenarios for which you would perform such transfers, including the following:

- Backup or archival data
- Disaster recovery data
- Big data
- Media or entertainment content (such as video and audio files)
- Data management services content for analytical or content-management purposes

> ***TIP*** **Verify whether your partner solution supports integration with the Data Box service for faster upload of your data to Azure.**

Preserving ACLs, file attributes, and timestamps

You can preserve all your access control lists (ACLs), file attributes, and timestamps during the data copy process, and the Azure Data Box service will retain these upon import into the Azure storage. However, to do so, you must use the correct tools and procedures for the copy process:

- **For Windows clients** Use robocopy to perform an SMB data transfer. Include the `/copyall` or `/dcopy:DAT` options in your `copy` command to ensure that all the required metadata is copied.
- **For Linux clients** The copy process for Linux clients involves two steps. First, you copy all the data, without metadata, to the Data Box appliance using a tool such as rsync. Then, using tools like smbcacls or cifsacl, you copy the metadata for the copied data.

Limitations

The Azure Data Box service and appliances have various limitations in terms of the following:

- Azure container and migrated data file and folder naming conventions
- Supported Azure storage types
- Total number of files
- Transfer speeds
- Supported protocols

There are many others, too.

Microsoft is working on addressing these limitations where possible. I expect that some or all of these limitations will either be resolved or reduced over time. After you identify the right Data Box appliance for your needs, review the list of limitations published online to ensure you do not run into issues during import or export operations.

Azure Data Box walkthrough

The following section steps you through the process of ordering, installing, and unlocking an Azure Data Box appliance; transferring data to the appliance; and scheduling a pickup using the Azure portal.

> ***IMPORTANT*** **If you are following along, select resources and resource names based on your environment, including unique storage account names for each of your deployments.**

> ***IMPORTANT*** **If you are following along, be sure to cancel your Data Box order before it is processed. Alternatively, read the steps, but don't perform them on your own systems unless you need to upload large volumes of data to Azure at this time. Otherwise, Microsoft will charge you for its use.**

> ***PREREQUISITES*** **Create a supported Azure Storage account that you can use during the ordering process.**

USING AZURE PORTAL

To order, install, and unlock an Azure Data Box appliance; transfer data to the appliance; and schedule a pickup using the Azure portal, follow these steps:

1. Log in to the Azure portal, type **data box** in the search box, and select **Azure Data Box** from the list that appears. (See Figure 5-1.)

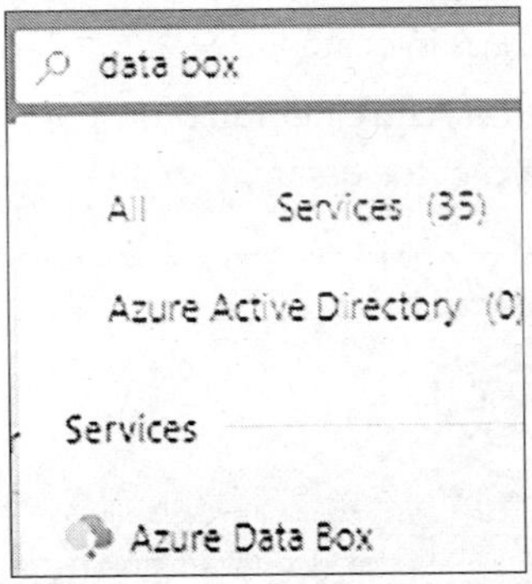

FIGURE 5-1 Search for the Data Box service.

2. On the Azure Data Box page, click **Create Azure Data Box.** (See Figure 5-2.)

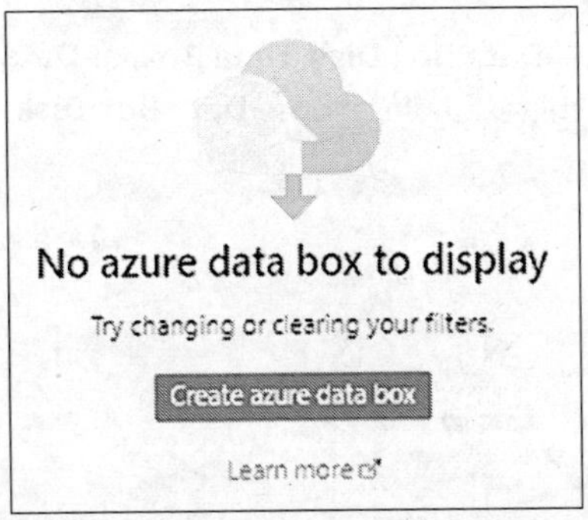

FIGURE 5-2 Create the Create Azure Data Box button.

> ***NOTE*** **If this is not the first Azure Data Box you've created using this subscription, you won't see the button shown in Figure 5-2. In that case, click the Create button near the top of the Azure Data Box page.**

3. On the Select Your Azure Data Box page (see Figure 5-3), enter the following information and click **Apply**:
   - **Transfer Type** Select the **Import to Azure** (to import data to Azure from an external environment, such as your company datacenter) or **Export from Azure** (to export data out of Azure to an external environment) option button. For this example, choose **Import to Azure**.
   - **Subscription** Open the **Subscription** drop-down list and choose the subscription you want to use to place the Data Box order.
   - **Resource Group** Select an existing resource group or create a new one in which to create the Data Box order.

- **Source Country/Region** Open the **Source Country/Region** drop-down list and specify where the source data to copy to the Data Box is located.
- **Destination Azure Region** Open the **Destination Azure Region** drop-down list to specify the Azure region where you want to transfer the data.

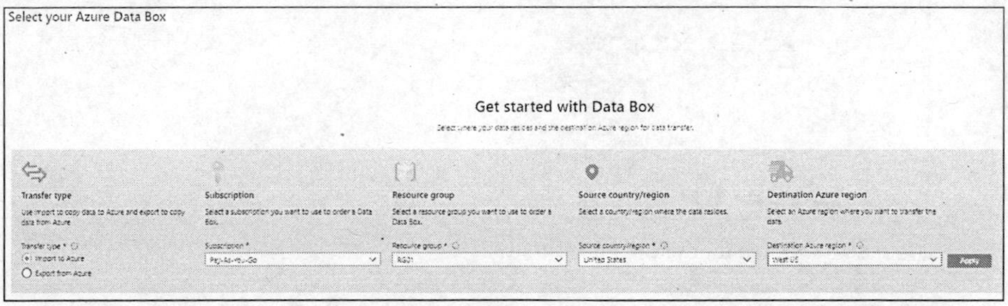

FIGURE 5-3 Starting your Data Box order.

4. Select the type of Data Box you want to order—**Data Box Disk**, **Data Box**, or **Data Box Heavy**—and click **Next**. (See Figure 5-4.) For this example, choose **Data Box Disk**.

FIGURE 5-4 Data Box types.

5. On the **Basics** tab of the Order Data Box Disk (Import to Azure) wizard (see Figure 5-5), enter the following information and click **Next**:
   - **Import Order Name** Enter a unique name for the order.
   - **Estimated Data Size in TB** Specify how much data (in TB) you expect to transfer to the Data Box.
   - **Use Custom Key Instead of Azure Generated Passkey** Specify whether you want to use a custom key to encrypt the data on the Data Box appliance. If you select the **Yes** option button, the tab expands to display additional fields to capture your custom key information. For this example, select the **No** option button (the default).

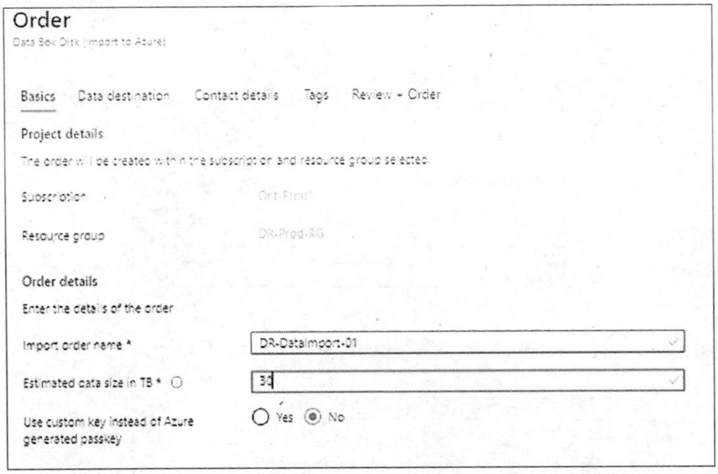

FIGURE 5-5 The Basics tab of the Order Data Box Disk (Import to Azure) wizard.

6. On the **Data Destination** tab (see Figure 5-6), enter the following information and click **Next**:
   - **Data Destination** Specify where the data from the Data Box will be stored. In this case, choose **Storage Account(s)**.
   - **Destination Azure Region** Select the Azure region where you want to send the data after it has been transferred to the Azure Data Box. Choose the one that is closest to your location—especially if you plan to test the service.
   - **Storage Account(s)** Select the storage account you want to use or click the Create a New Storage Account link to create a new one.

> ***NOTE*** **The storage accounts shown in this drop-down list will change depending on which Azure region you selected from the Destination Azure Region drop-down list.**

7. On the **Contact Details** tab (see Figure 5-7), enter the following information and click **Next**:
   - **Address** Click the **Modify Address** link and enter the address where the Data Box appliance should be delivered.
   - **Email** Enter one or more email addresses to receive notifications regarding the Data Box order, delivery, and pickup.

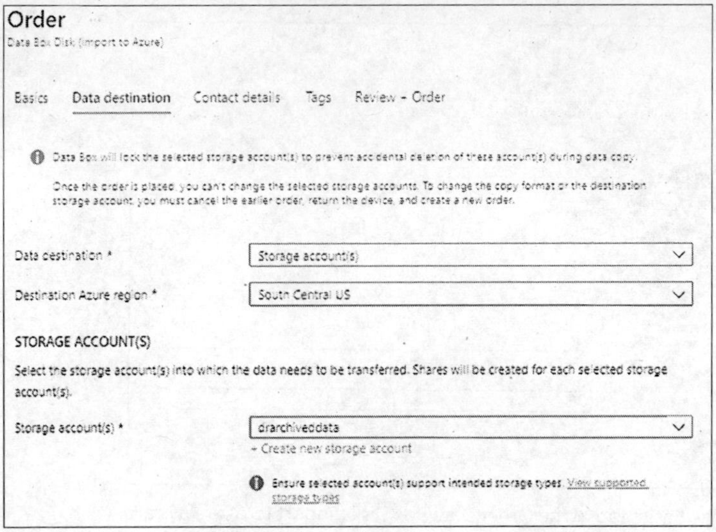

FIGURE 5-6 The Data Destination tab of the Order Data Box Disk (Import to Azure) wizard.

NOTE You can enter as many as 10 email addresses, separated by semicolons.

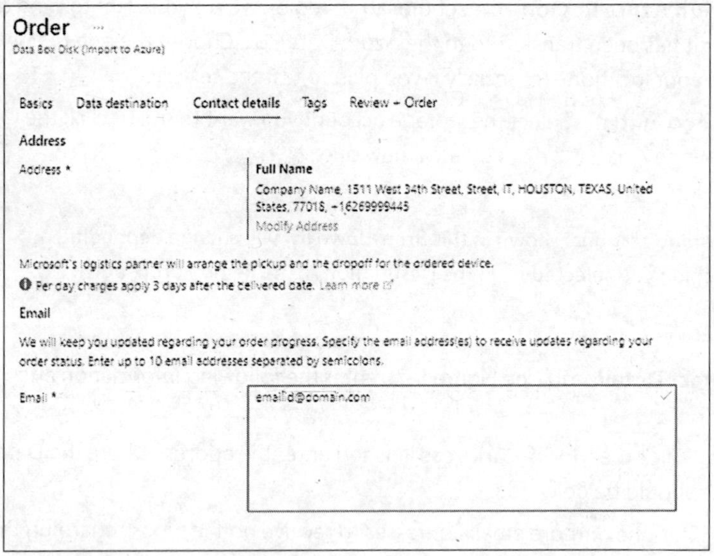

FIGURE 5-7 The Contact Details tab of the Order Data Box Disk (Import to Azure) wizard.

8. In the **Tags** tab (see Figure 5-8), enter the tags you want to associate with the Azure Data Box order and click **Next**.

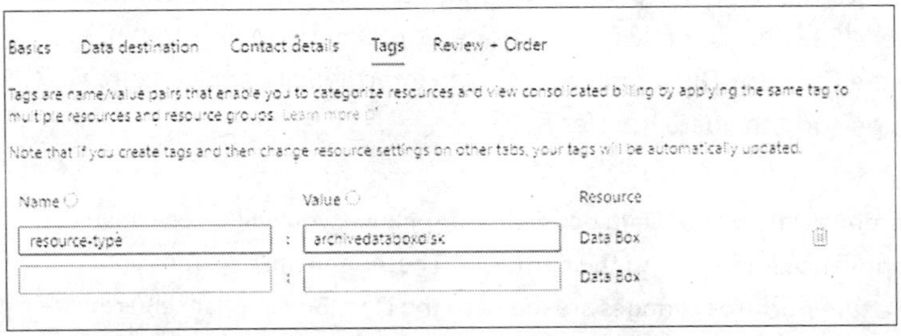

FIGURE 5-8 The Tags tab of the Order Data Box Disk (Import to Azure) wizard.

9. On the **Review + Order** tab (see Figure 5-9), review your settings. Then click **Submit** to submit the order request.

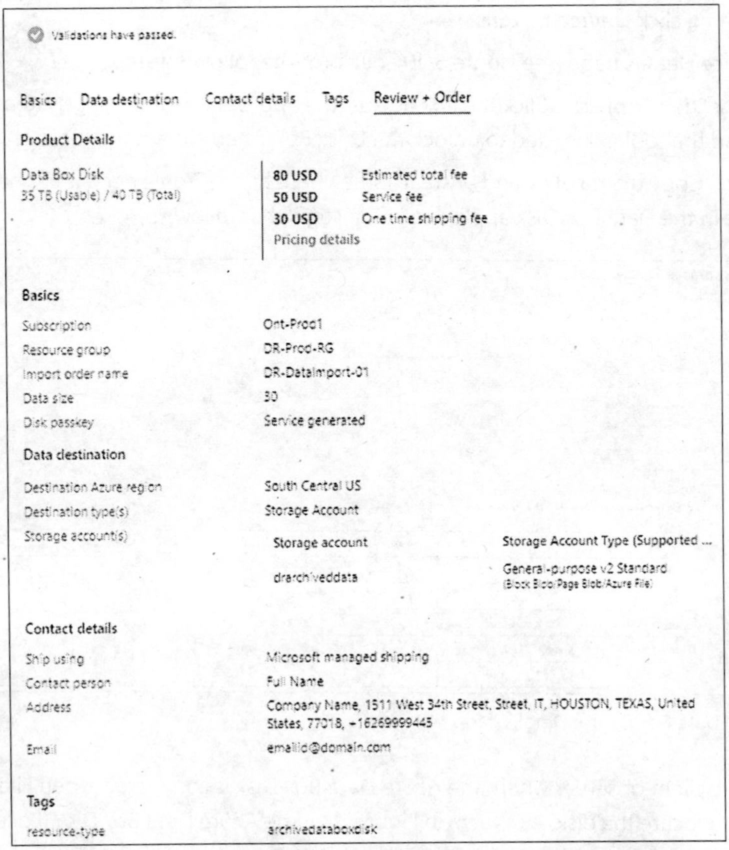

FIGURE 5-9 The Review + Order tab of the Order Data Box Disk (Import to Azure) wizard.

After you place the order, you must wait to receive the Data Box Disk appliance from Microsoft. You can open the order details, monitor the status of the order, and track delivery timelines from the Azure portal.

10. When you receive the Azure Data Box Disk appliance from Microsoft, connect the appliance over USB either directly to the storage containing the data that needs to be copied to the Data Box Disk appliance or to an intermediary appliance/device that allows you to perform the data transfer.

> ***NOTE*** **If you order a Data Box or Data Box Heavy appliance, you will receive instructions with the appliance for installing the hardware. These same instructions are updated in the Azure portal as changes are made to the Data Box appliance hardware. Refer to the latest guidance before your installation for details.**

Next, you must unlock each of the disks in the Data Box Disk appliance.

11. In the Azure portal, browse to the page for the Data Box order. Then, in the left pane, under **General**, click **Device Details**.
12. On the Device Details page (see Figure 5-10), perform the following steps:
    - **Data Box Disk Toolset** Click the link next to the appropriate operating system to download the toolset needed to unlock the Data Box. Then extract the toolset.
    - **Passkey** Copy the passkey and paste it somewhere handy. You'll need it to unlock the disks in the Data Box Disk appliance in the steps that follow.

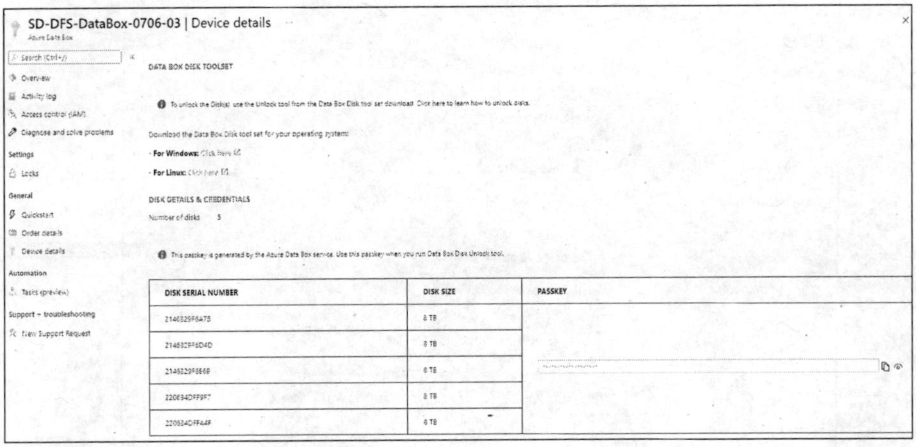

FIGURE 5-10 Data Box Device Details page.

13. Switch to the client or server where the Azure Data Box Disk is connected, open File Explorer, and locate the disk. As shown in Figure 5-11, the Azure Data Box Disk (Local Disk D:) is locked.

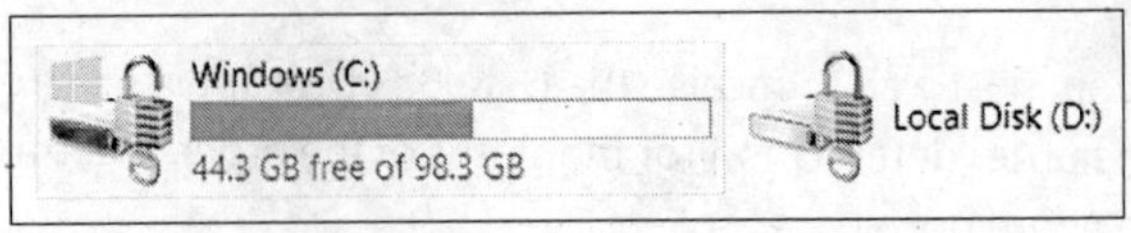

FIGURE 5-11 Local Windows disks.

14. Locate the folder where you extracted the Data Box Disk toolset and double-click the DataBoxDiskUnlock application to run it. (See Figure 5-12.)

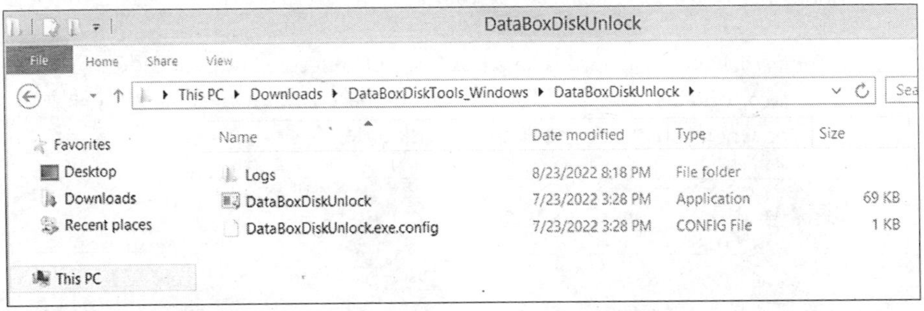

FIGURE 5-12 DataBoxDiskUnlock tool.

15. In the command prompt window that opens (see Figure 5-13), paste the passkey you copied earlier.

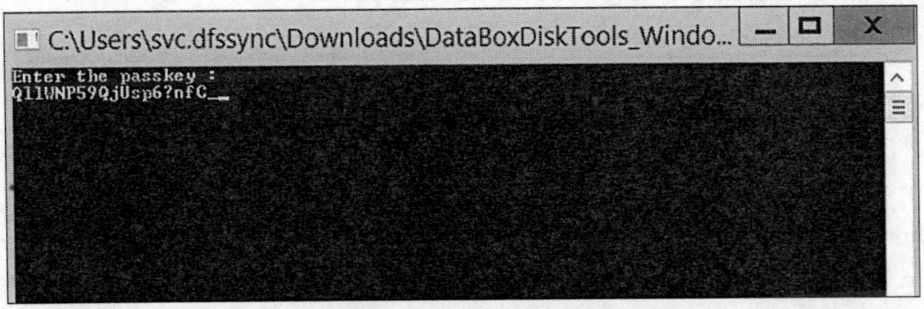

FIGURE 5-13 Copy the passkey to unlock the Data Box Disk appliance.

Microsoft verifies the key, unlocks the Data Box Disk appliance, and notifies you that the appliance's disks are ready to use. (See Figure 5-14.)

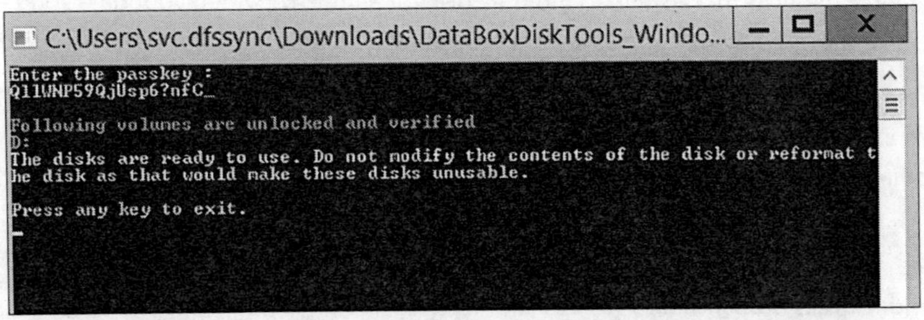

FIGURE 5-14 The Data Box is unlocked.

16. Switch back to File Explorer. As shown in Figure 5-15, the Azure Data Box Disk appliance is unlocked.

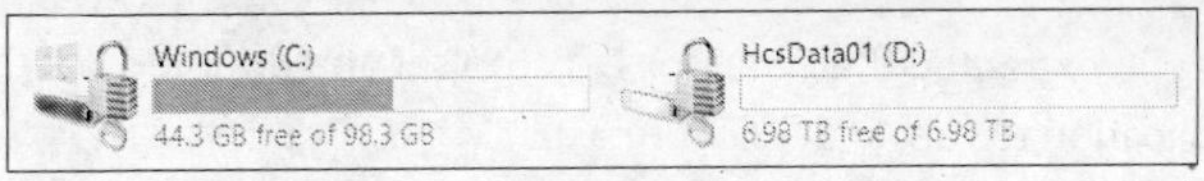

FIGURE 5-15 The unlocked Data Box Disk appliance in File Explorer.

17. Double-click the drive for the Data Box Disk appliance. As shown in Figure 5-16, the appliance contains a pre-built folder structure based on the destination type you selected when you placed the Data Box Disk order.

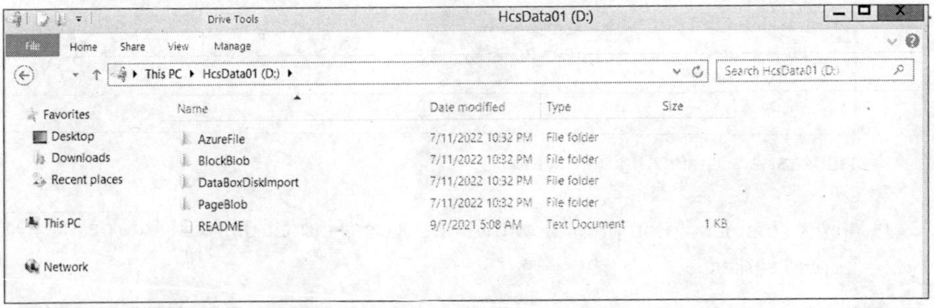

FIGURE 5-16 Data Box Disk appliance: default folder structure.

18. After you unlock the Data Box Disk appliance, transfer your data using any data-transfer tool (such as robocopy) or by copying and pasting the required data to the Data Box Disk appliance's folders.

    When you transfer data, keep these points in mind:

    - Because you selected to copy data to a storage account during the order process, you must copy the data to the AzureFile, BlockBlob, or PageBlob folder, depending on the storage container created in the destination Azure storage account.
    - Because each disk has limited storage, you must plan the data transfer to ensure you transfer unique data to each disk.
    - You can perform transfers to multiple disks at a time, provided your data source and any intermediary used for the data transfer can handle the read-and-write IO loads.

    After all the data has been transferred, you schedule a pickup to ship the Azure Data Box Disk appliance back to the Azure region you selected during the order process. Do not initiate this process until after *all* the data is transferred.

> ***NOTE*** **You must return the entire set of disks all at one time. You cannot ship back individual disks in an order.**

19. To schedule a pickup, browse to the page for the Data Box order in the Azure portal. Then, near the top of the Overview page, click **Schedule Pickup**. (See Figure 5-17.)

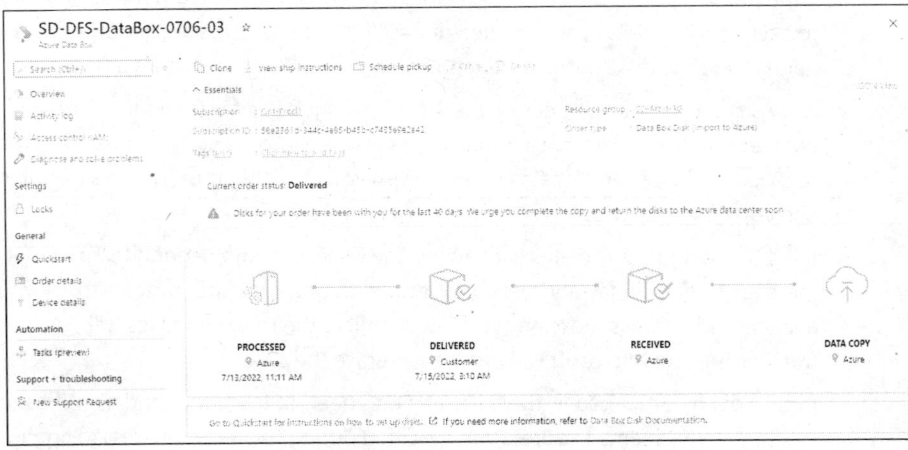

FIGURE 5-17 The Overview page for the Azure Data Box order.

A Schedule Pickup pane opens. (See Figure 5-18.) It details how you should prepare the package and request a pickup.

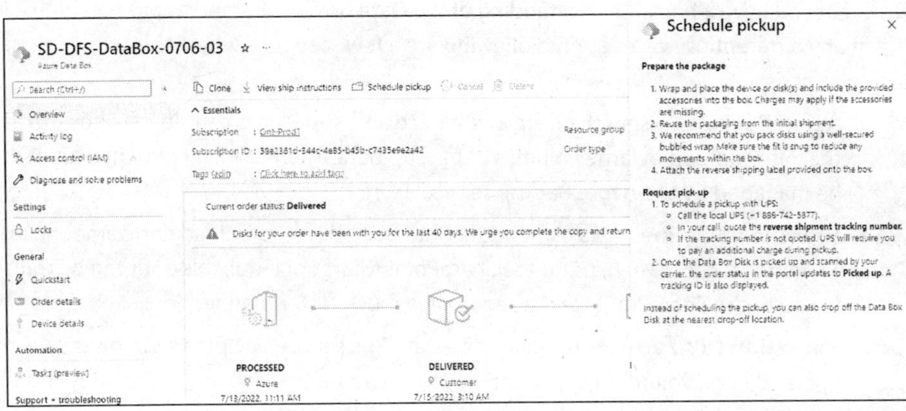

FIGURE 5-18 Azure Data Box - Schedule Pickup information

20. Follow the directions in the Schedule Pickup pane to prepare the Data Box for shipment.
21. In the Data Box order's Overview pane, near the top, click **View Ship Instructions** to download a PDF file to your PC containing the shipping label and detailed instructions on how to print and apply it to the package. The PDF file also outlines the steps to ship the disks back to Microsoft.
22. After the package arrives at the Azure region datacenter you specified, the Microsoft team connects the disks in the Azure Data Box Disk appliance to the Azure datacenter network. The data on the disks is then automatically uploaded to the storage account you specified during the order process. Depending on the outcome of the transfer job, you might experience the following:

- If the job completes successfully, the Microsoft engineering team will send a message to each email address you specified during the order process. Microsoft will permanently wipe the disks in the order and confirm when this is done via email.
- If the storage account is unavailable, the transfer job will fail, and the Microsoft engineering team will send a notification message to each email address you specified during the order process and work with you to rectify the storage account issue and copy the data over.
- If the transfer job completes with errors, the Microsoft engineering team will send a message to each email address you specified during the order process to ask you to analyze and address those errors. Once rectified, the remaining files will be transferred, and Microsoft will proceed to erase the disks.
- In case of any other issues, the Microsoft engineering team will send a notification message to each email address you specified during the order process to engage with you to resolve them.

Data Box use cases

Now that you have a better understanding of the Data Box service and appliances, you can see that many different use cases apply. Following are a few scenarios where this service is used on a regular basis:

- **Azure Backup** Using the Data Box service and appliances can significantly increase the initial upload of large volumes of backup data. Thereafter, incremental uploads can be managed by the Azure Backup service itself.
- **SharePoint Online** You can use the Data Box service to upload large amounts of data to Azure Storage. Then, using the SharePoint Migration Tool, this data can be transferred to the SharePoint Online service in a much faster manner.
- **Migration to Azure** You can use the Data Box service to upload VM disks, SQL backups, and large volumes of application data to Azure to perform faster builds and the migration of your on-premises datacenter.
- **Migration from Azure** You can use the Data Box service to export your Azure data for migration back to on-premises datacenters or other cloud service providers.
- **HDInsight Data Upload** You can upload large volumes of historical data for analysis using HDInsight.
- **Migrate Hadoop Data to Azure Blob or Data Lake Storage** You can migrate data from your on-premises Hadoop cluster to Azure Blob or Data Lake Gen 2 storage using the Data Box or Data Box Heavy appliance.
- **Seeding File Server Data for Use with Azure File Sync** You can perform initial seeding of your on-premises file server to Azure File Storage using the Data Box service, and set up Azure File Sync to perform incremental syncs thereafter.

This list should give you a good idea of the various possibilities for leveraging this service. It is not an exhaustive list, but it does give you an indication of what is possible.

Best practices

Following are some general best practices related to the Azure Data Box service:

- **Review limitations carefully** Azure Data Box has numerous limitations related to naming conventions, data sources, and supported destinations for each of the different Data Box appliances. Be sure you review these carefully before placing your order.
- **Prepare your environment before placing your order** When you receive the Data Box device, you must perform the copy operation and ship the device back to Microsoft within a limited timeframe or incur additional costs. It is a good practice to review the documentation related to the Data Box appliance that you are planning to order and to complete all the prerequisites for your network, client OS, Azure services, etc. before you place the order. This way, you can initiate the data copy soon after you receive the Data Box device and avoid charges for delayed returns.
- **Use customer-managed keys when possible** You have two options for encrypting the Data Box device: a Microsoft-managed encryption key or a customer-managed encryption key. While the key generated by Microsoft is automatic and only available in your Azure subscription, if security is of paramount importance in your environment, it is a good practice to use customer-managed keys instead. That way, you can define your own key for the encryption.

Chapter 6

Azure Data Share

Overview

Azure Data Share helps companies set up secure, automated, and easy-to-manage data-sharing services for global use with customers and partners. You can use this service to share multiple Azure data stores to schedule automatic data updates. With Azure Data Share, you can easily identify who shared the data, track when it was shared, and access detailed update and audit logs, making the service highly reliable.

Azure Data Share could be used in virtually any organization to securely share data for collaboration purposes, to improve efficiency, and to consolidate data sharing. For example:

- A company could share up-to-date point-of-sales data with its suppliers on an hourly or daily basis to improve efficiency in the supply chain and to facilitate the planning of resources on the supplier end.
- A government institution could share raw population-related data sourced from various agencies with a third party for research or data analytics. Analyzed data could then be shared with other parties or government institutions for better planning, modeling, and forecasting.

Key features

Key features of this service are as follows:

- **Ease of sharing, monitoring, and management** Azure Data Share is extremely easy to set up, monitor, and manage. You can get the service online and ready to use in minutes, making it a great solution to address urgent and long-term sharing scenarios.
- **Secure data sharing** Azure Data Share stores and shares all data securely. Stored data is encrypted at rest, data in transit is secured using TLS 1.2, and metadata is stored in encrypted storage.
- **Authentication using managed identities** Azure managed identities manage access to source data. Managed identities ensure that no credentials are exchanged in the process, making it less susceptible to credential attacks.

- **Multiple sharing options** Azure Data Share supports multiple sharing options, such as snapshot-based or in-place sharing. So, you can share or receive data based on your compliance or data-sharing requirements.
- **Supports both sending and receiving of data** Azure Data Share supports sending and receiving data using various sharing options. This supports two-way data-sharing requirements—for example, in scenarios where you send raw data to a partner, who processes the data and sends it back to you.
- **Terms of use** With Azure Data Share, you can specify your terms of usage and ensure that the receiving party accepts them before they receive data.
- **Scheduled snapshots** With Azure Data Share, you can specify the frequency of snapshots that help update and share new data automatically.
- **Support for multiple Azure storage services** Azure Data Share supports Azure data stores such as Azure Blob Storage, Azure Data Lake Storage (ADLS) Gen 1 and 2, Azure SQL Database, Azure Synapse Analytics, and Azure Data Explorer.
- **Azure subscription required** Azure Data Store requires both parties—the sharer of the data and the consumer of the data—to have an Azure subscription. This ensures the security of the end-to-end data-sharing process.
- **Compatibility with the Azure portal and REST APIs** All these capabilities are supported using the Azure portal or REST APIs.

Key concepts

Now that you have a basic overview of Azure Data Store and its key features, let's discuss the key concepts underlying this service.

Data types

There are various types of data. Broadly speaking, there is raw data, which requires processing or analytics, and processed data, which is ready for consumption.

Data provider

At a minimum, data sharing involves two parties: the data provider and the data consumer. The data provider is the entity that shares the data. The data provider decides what data will be shared, with whom, and the sharing model used (discussed in a moment).

Data consumer

The data consumer is the party that receives data from the data provider. Based on the type of data received, the data consumer can either consume the data as is, or process and analyze it in some way before consuming or sharing it.

Sharing models

Azure Data Share supports two types of sharing models (see Figure 6-1):

- **In-place sharing** With this model, the data provider shares data directly from the location where it is stored rather than sending a copy of the data to the data consumer. So, the data, and any changes made to that data, are available to the data consumer in real-time. This helps in scenarios in which a partner organization must process or analyze the source data in real time.

> ***NOTE*** **The in-place sharing model is currently supported only by the Azure Data Explorer service. This service provides the ability to perform real-time data analytics on large data streams.**

- **Snapshot-based sharing** With this model, a snapshot of data captured at a specific moment is copied from the data provider's Azure subscription to the data consumer's Azure subscription. The data—which can arrive in CSV or Parquet form—is stored in the location of the data consumer's choice: Azure Blob Storage, ADLS Gen 1 and ADLS Gen 2, Azure SQL Database, or Azure Synapse Analytics. In this scenario, the data provider can supply the data consumer with incremental updates on an hourly or daily basis, in an automated or manual manner. If this process is performed manually, then the data consumer must set up their Azure subscription to receive the incremental data.

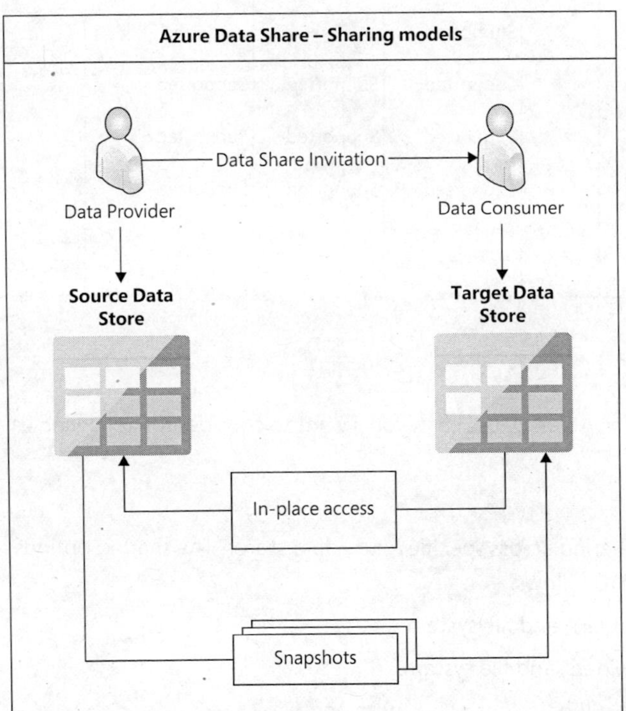

FIGURE 6-1 Azure Data Share sharing models.

Data stores

Azure Data Share supports the use of various Azure data stores to share and receive data. The source and destination data stores can be different, making the service extremely flexible to address different scenarios. Table 6-1 shows the various data stores supported by Azure Data Share for both the in-place and snapshot-based sharing models.

TABLE 6-1 List of available data stores

Azure data store	In-place sharing model	Snapshot-based sharing model
Azure Blob Storage		Supported
ADLS Gen 1 and Gen 2		Supported
Azure SQL Database		Supported
Azure Synapse Analytics		Supported
Azure Data Explorer	Supported	

Table 6-2 lists the various supported Azure data stores for receiving data based on the source data store.

TABLE 6-2 List of data stores for receiving data based on the source data store

Azure data store	Azure Blob Storage	ADLS Gen 1	ADLS Gen 2	Azure SQL Database	Azure Synapse Analytics (Workspace)	Azure Data Explorer
Azure Blob Storage	Supported		Supported			
ADLS Gen 1 and Gen 2	Supported		Supported			
Azure SQL Database	Supported		Supported	Supported	Supported	
Azure Synapse Analytics	Supported		Supported	Supported	Supported	
Azure Synapse Analytics (workspace)	Supported		Supported	Supported	Supported	
Azure Data Explorer						Supported

Sharing caveats

When deciding whether to use Azure Data Share, you'll want to consider the following caveats.

Storage services

Azure Data Share supports sharing across specific Azure data stores. The sharing options available for each service are as follows:

- **ADLS Gen 1** Files, folders, and file systems.
- **ADLS Gen 2** Files, folders, and file systems.
- **Azure Blob Storage** Blobs, folders, and containers.

Snapshot-based sharing

When you use snapshot-based sharing to share containers, file systems, or folders, keep these points in mind:

- The data consumer can choose to use incremental snapshots instead of ingesting a full copy of the shared data for each share operation, copying over only those files that are new or have been updated since the last snapshot.
- The snapshot-based sharing model does not cause files deleted in the source location (data provider) to be deleted in the target location (data consumer).
- Snapshots that fail or are interrupted for any reason—such as the cancellation of the snapshot operation, Azure back-end issues, or networking issues—will not be resumed. The next snapshot will ignore the failed snapshot and create an incremental snapshot from the last successful snapshot.

SQL-based source

The data provider can use Azure Data Share to share tables and views stored in Azure SQL Database and in a dedicated Azure Synapse Analytics SQL pool.

> ***NOTE*** **At the time of this writing, sharing using an Azure Synapse Analytics (workspace) serverless SQL pool is not supported. This might change by the time you read this. Check the latest guidance on this from Microsoft.**

The data consumer, on the other hand, can accept and store data in tables, CSV files, or Parquet files, using any of the following services:

- **Tables** Azure Synapse Analytics or Azure SQL Database.
- **CSV file** Azure Blob Storage or ADLS Gen 2 storage.
- **Parquet file** Azure Blob Storage or ADLS Gen 2 storage.

Each of these methods introduces some caveats of their own, however:

- **Tables** If data is accepted and stored in a table in Azure Synapse Analytics or Azure SQL Database, any existing tables of the same name will be overwritten completely. In addition, if the snapshot fails at the source or if its transfer to the target location is interrupted, the subsequent snapshot will attempt a full copy of the entire table or view.
- **CSV or Parquet files** If data is accepted and stored in Azure Blob Storage or ADLS Gen 2 storage, full snapshots overwrite all existing contents at the target location.

Azure Data Explorer

Azure Data Explorer supports sharing at a cluster, database, and table level using Azure Data Share. You can set this up using either the Azure portal or the Azure Data Share API. Depending on which option you choose, you can configure different levels of sharing. For example:

- **Azure portal** In the Azure portal, you can set up sharing on two levels:
  - **Cluster** This establishes access for all current and future databases in the cluster.

- **Database** This sets up access only for the databases you specify. If you want to share any additional new or existing databases, you must set those up as needed.

- **Azure Data Share API** With the Azure Data Share API, you can set up sharing on the database-table level, only for the database tables you specify. If you want to share, any additional new or existing tables, you must set those up as needed.

NOTE **To consume the shared database data, the data consumer must set up an Azure Data Explorer cluster of their own, in the same Azure datacenter as the data provider.**

Managed identities

You can create and use managed identities to exchange data using Azure Data Share. With managed identities, the data provider can share data without setting up and sharing any credentials with the data consumer. This reduces the risk of credential leaks that can expose sensitive data to third parties. To use managed identities, both the data provider and data consumer must configure their Azure subscriptions to ensure that Azure Data Share's managed identity has access to read from the data source and write to the data target as needed.

Data provider

The data provider must configure the Azure Data Share data source to use managed identities. If your data source is Azure Blob Storage or ADLS Gen 2, you can do this in one of two ways:

- **Automatically** If the user setting up the data share has owner or write access to the data source, the read permissions for the managed identity are added automatically.
- **Manually** If the user setting up the data share does not have the requisite permissions on the data source, then a user with the appropriate permissions must set up the Storage Blob Data Reader Role for the Azure Data Share resource's managed identity.

If your data source is Azure SQL Database or Azure Synapse Analytics, then this must be configured manually. This requires the user who sets up the data share to first create a SQL user with at least db_datareader permissions on the SQL database. This SQL username must match the Azure Data Share resource name in the source subscription.

Data consumer

Like the data provider, the data consumer must set up access to the target data storage for the Azure Data Share resource's managed identity. The difference is, the service must have write access to ensure that the accepted data can be stored in the target destination. This can be achieved in much the same way as the data provider methods, with slight variations:

- **Azure Blob Storage or ADLS Gen 2 automatic provisioning** If the user setting up the data share has owner or write access to the data source, the write permissions for the managed identity are added automatically.
- **Azure Blob Storage or ADLS Gen 2 manual provisioning** If the user setting up the data share does not have the requisite permissions on the data source, then a user with

the appropriate permissions must set up the Storage Blob Data Contributor Role for the Azure Data Share resource's managed identity.

- **Azure SQL Database or Azure Synapse Analytics manual provisioning** The user setting up the data share must first create a SQL user with db_datareader, db_datawriter, and db_ddladmin permissions on the SQL database. The SQL username must match the Azure Data Share resource name in the destination subscription.

Share and receive data with Azure Data Share

In this section, you will learn how to set up an Azure Data Share resource as a data source to share data. You'll also discover how to set up an Azure Data Share resource to receive data.

In the case of the data provider, before you can set up an Azure Data Share data source, you must know what data you want to share and in what storage account that data is located. This might mean provisioning a new storage account before you begin. (In this example, we use data stored in an Azure Blob Storage account.)

You will also need to know where you plan to create the Azure Data Share for the data consumer to receive and store data shared by the data provider. As with the data provider, this might mean provisioning a new storage account before you begin. (Again, we use an Azure Blob Storage account in this example.)

> ***TIP*** **Use an account with Owner or Write permissions. That way, permissions for the data share's managed identity are set up automatically.**

Set up an Azure Data Share resource to share data walkthrough

The following section walks you through the process of setting up an Azure Data Share resource as a data source.

> ***IMPORTANT*** **If you are following along, you'll want to select resources and unique resource names based on your environment for each of your deployments.**

> ***IMPORTANT*** **If you are following along, delete any unwanted resources after you have completed testing to reduce charges levied by Microsoft for these resources.**

Using the Azure portal

To set up an Azure Data Share resource using the Azure portal, follow these steps:

1. Log in to the Azure portal, type **data shares** in the search box, and select the **Data Shares** option from the list that appears. (See Figure 6-2.)

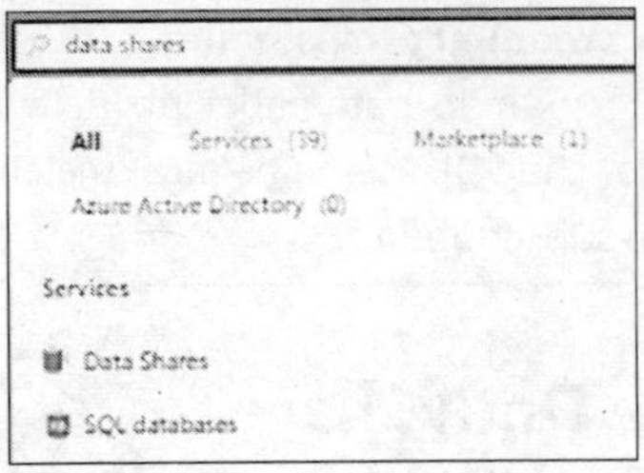

FIGURE 6-2 Type data shares in the search box.

2. On the **Azure Data Shares** page, click the **Create Data Share** button. (See Figure 6-3.)

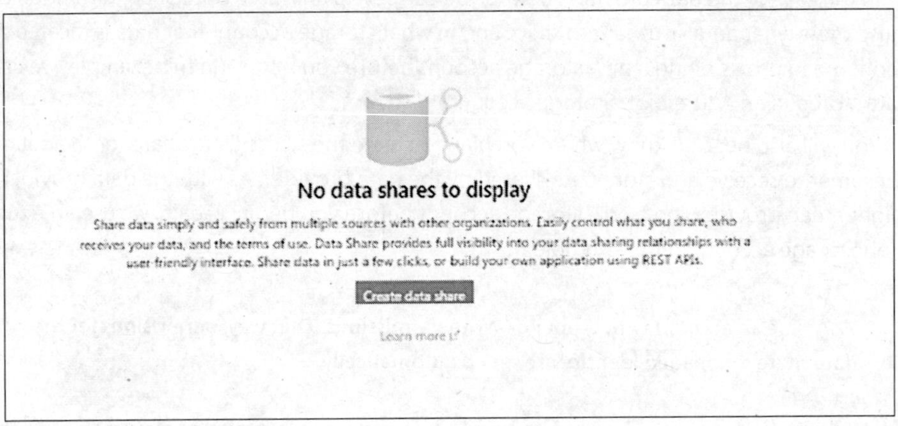

FIGURE 6-3 Create a data share.

3. In the **Basics** tab of the Create Data Share wizard (see Figure 6-4), enter the following information and click **Next**:
   - **Subscription** Select the subscription you want to use.
   - **Resource Group** Select the resource group you want to use to host the data share. Alternatively, click the **Create New** link and follow the prompts.
   - **Location** Select the Azure region you want to host the data share.
   - **Name** Choose a unique name for the data share resource.
4. In the **Tags** tab (see Figure 6-5), enter a name and value for any tags you want to associate with the data share, and click **Next**.

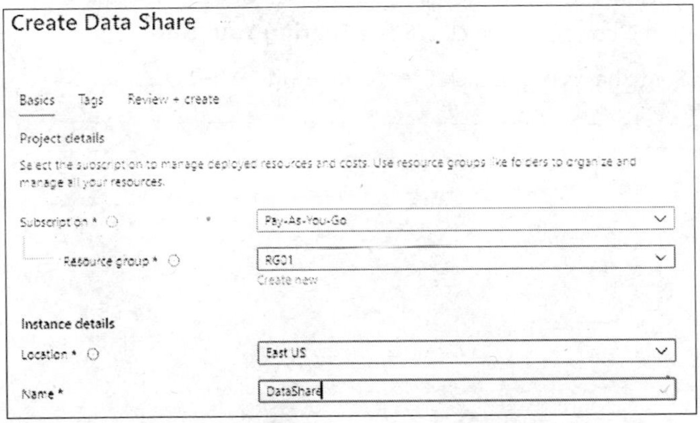

FIGURE 6-4 The Basics tab in the Create Data Share wizard.

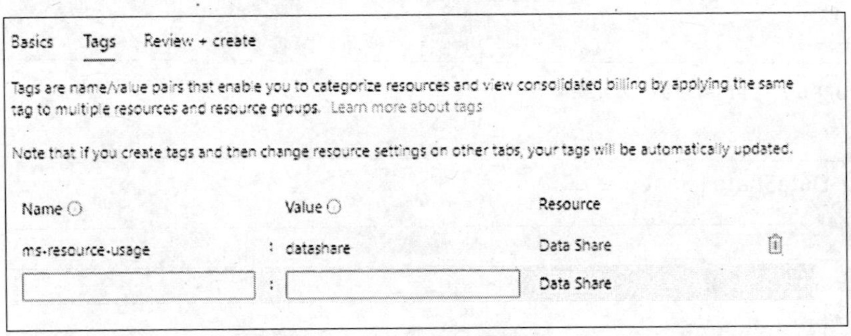

FIGURE 6-5 The Tags tab in the Create Data Share wizard.

5. In the **Review + Create** tab (see Figure 6-6), review your settings, and click **Review + Create** to create the data share.

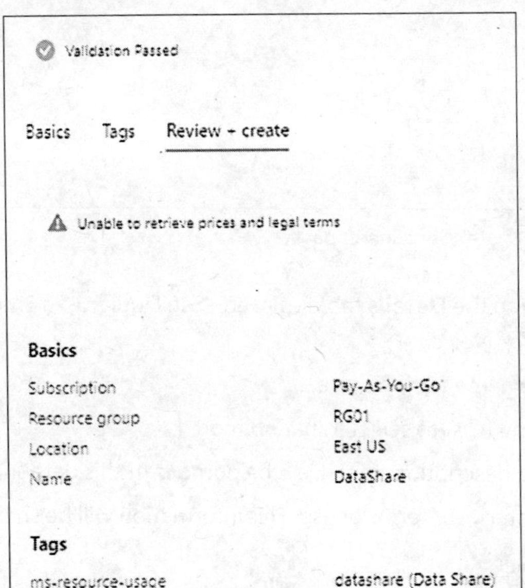

FIGURE 6-6 The Review + Create tab of the Create Data Share wizard.

6. In the Azure portal, navigate to the data share you just created (see Figure 6-7) and ensure its configuration is correct. Then click **Start Sharing Your Data**.

7. On the data share's Sent Shares page, click **Create**. (See Figure 6-8.)

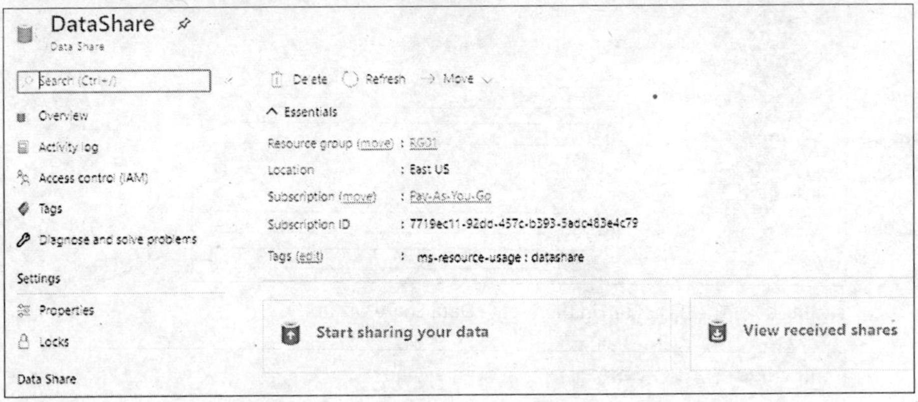

FIGURE 6-7 Data share overview.

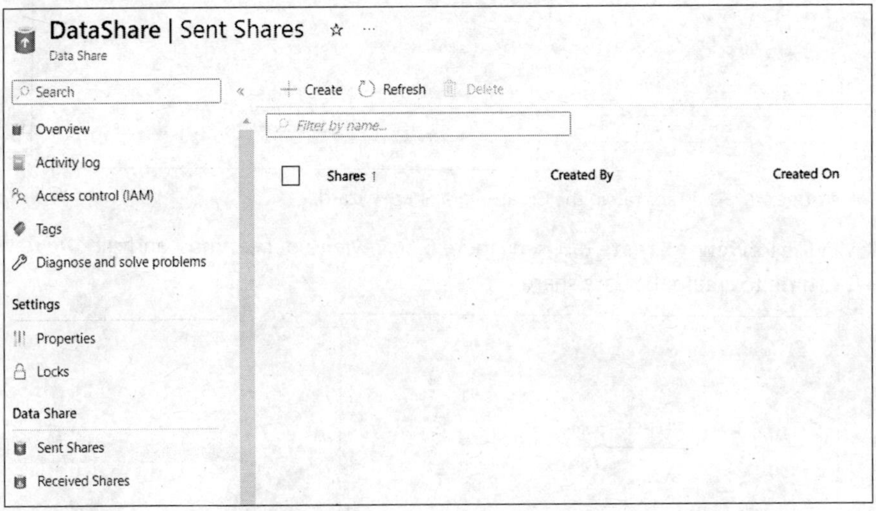

FIGURE 6-8 Click Create on the data share's Sent Shares page.

8. The **Sent Shares** wizard opens with the **Details** tab displayed. (See Figure 6-9.) Enter the following information and click **Next**:

   - **Share Name** Enter a unique name for the share.
   - **Share Type** Use the drop-down list to select a sharing model.
   - **Description** Type a detailed description to convey the purpose of this data share.
   - **Terms of Use** Optionally, enter your terms of use. This information will be shown to the data consumer.

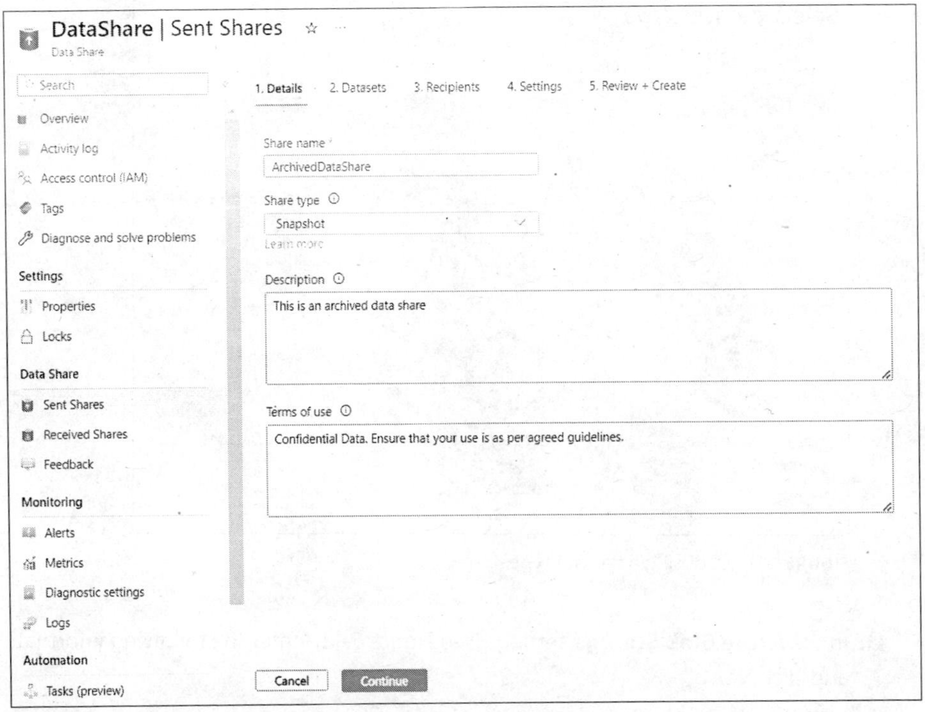

FIGURE 6-9 The Details tab of the Data Sharing wizard.

9. In the **Datasets** tab, click the **Add Datasets** button. (See Figure 6-10.)

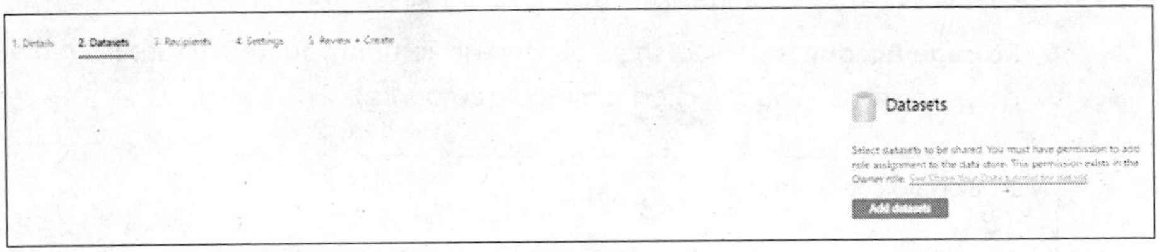

FIGURE 6-10 The Datasets tab of the Data Sharing wizard.

10. In the **Select Dataset Type** settings (see Figure 6-11), select the dataset type for the data you'll place in this data share based on your needs. For this example, I'll select **Azure Blob Storage**.

> ***NOTE*** **You will see different options in this list depending on what share type you selected in step 8.**

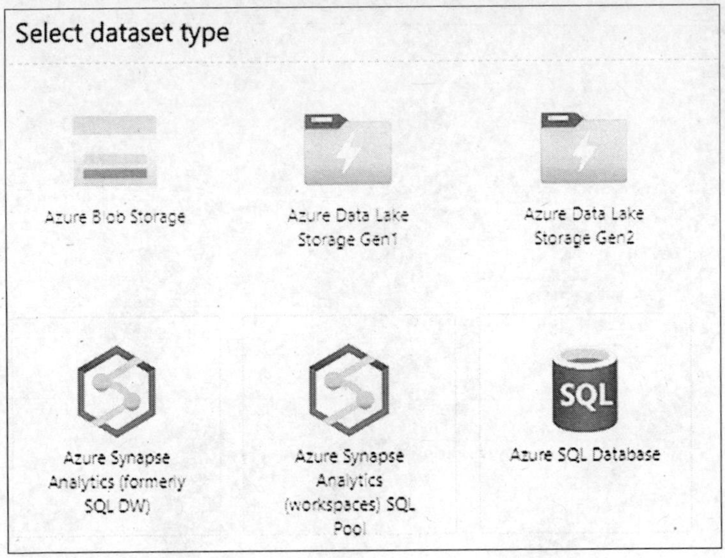

FIGURE 6-11 Choosing a dataset type.

11. In the **Azure Blob Storage** settings (see Figure 6-12), enter the following information and click **Next**:
    - **Subscriptions** Choose the subscription that contains the blob storage account you want to use.
    - **Resource Groups** Leave this set to **All** or choose the specific resource group that contains the blob storage account you want to use.
    - **Storage Accounts** Select the blob storage account you want to use from the drop-down list. (You can choose multiple accounts.)

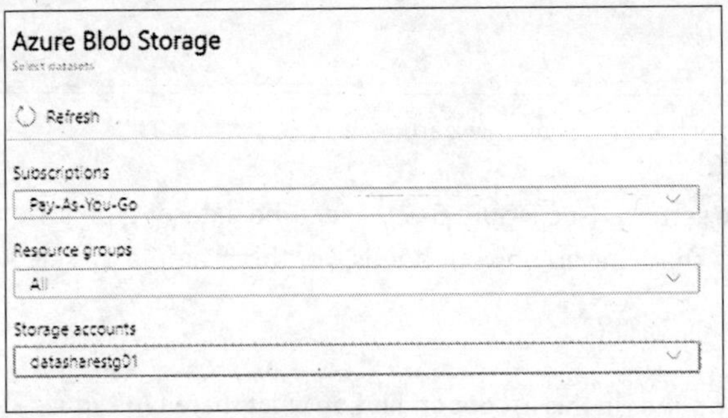

FIGURE 6-12 Identify where the datasets you want to share are located.

12. In the **Azure Blob Storage** section of the **Datasets** tab (see Figure 6-13), select the check box next to the dataset that contains the data you want to share. (You can choose more than one dataset.)

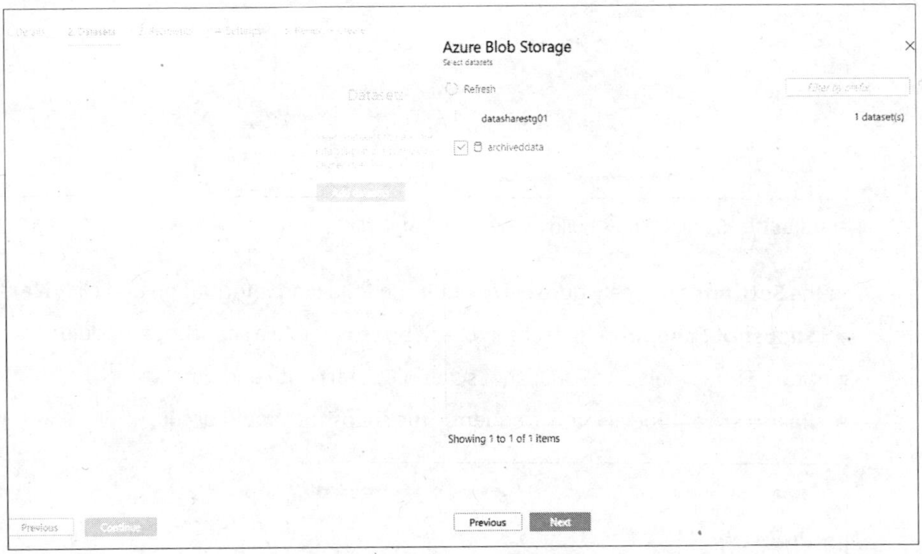

FIGURE 6-13 Choose the dataset you want to share.

13. Type a unique name for your dataset in the **Dataset Name** box. (See Figure 6-14.)

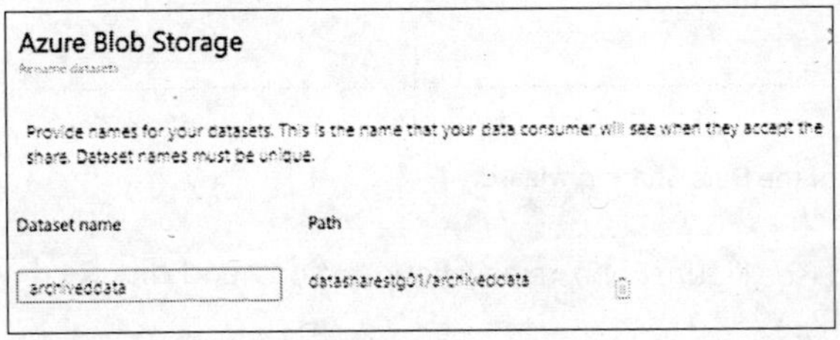

FIGURE 6-14 Rename the dataset.

14. Confirm that you've shared the correct dataset (see Figure 6-15) and click **Next**.

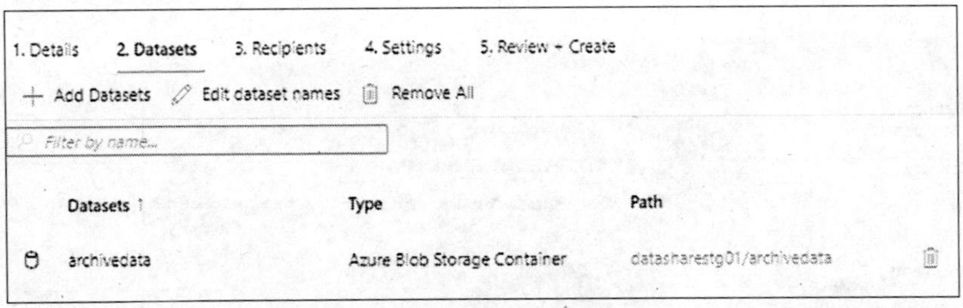

FIGURE 6-15 Confirm that you're sharing the correct dataset.

15. In the **Recipients** tab (see Figure 6-16), in the **Email** box, type the email for the recipient(s) of the data in the share.
16. Optionally, if you want to share the data for only a limited time, select the **Share Expiration** check box and use the calendar and clock settings to indicate the day and time the share should expire. Then click **Next**.

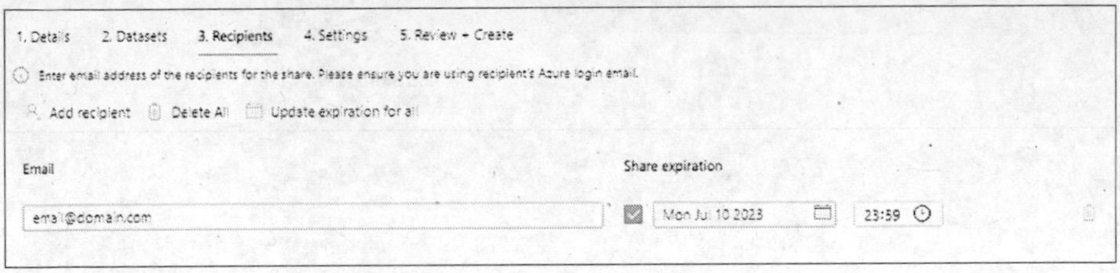

FIGURE 6-16 Specify who should receive the shared data.

17. In the **Settings** tab (see Figure 6-17), enter the following information and click **Next**:
    - **Snapshot Schedule** Select this check box to enable a snapshot schedule.
    - **Start Time** Select the snapshot schedule's start date and time.
    - **Recurrence** Specify how frequently the snapshot should occur.

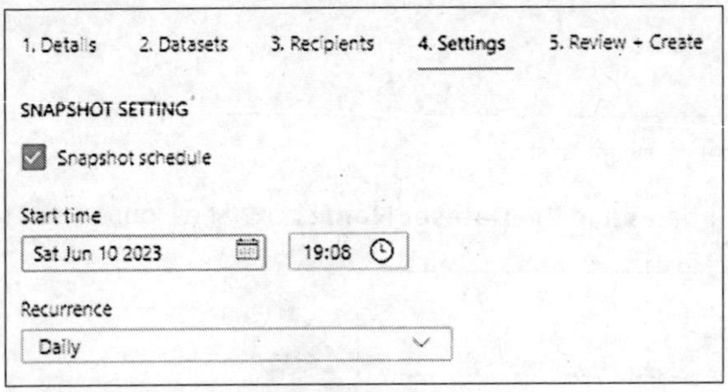

FIGURE 6-17 The Settings tab of the Data Sharing wizard.

18. In the **Review + Create** tab (see Figure 6-18), review your settings, and click **Review + Create** to create the data share.

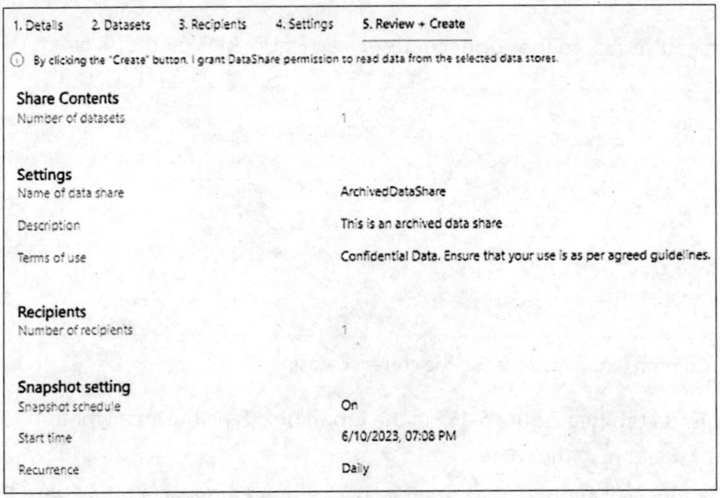

FIGURE 6-18 The Review + Create tab of the Data Sharing wizard.

19. Verify the creation of the data share. (See Figure 6-19.)

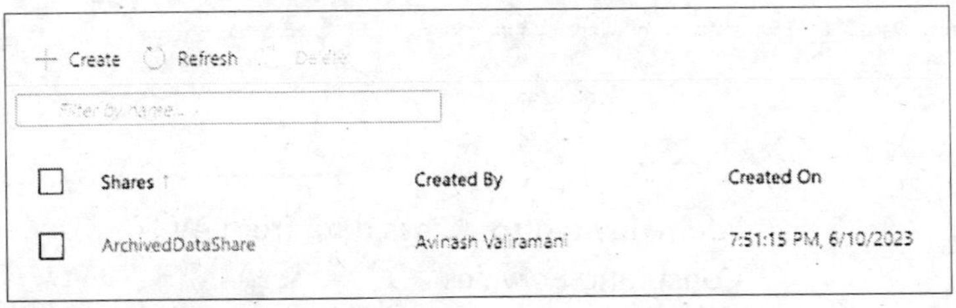

FIGURE 6-19 The data share is created.

> ***IMPORTANT*** **After you create the data share, the recipient you specified in step 14 will receive an email message inviting them to access the share.**

Set up an Azure Data Share resource to receive data walkthrough

The following section walks you through the process of setting up an Azure Data Share resource to receive and store data from a data share to which you have been granted access.

> ***IMPORTANT*** **If you are following along, you'll want to select resources and unique resource names based on your environment for each of your deployments.**

> ***IMPORTANT*** **If you are following along, delete any unwanted resources after you have completed testing to reduce charges levied by Microsoft for these resources.**

> ***TIP*** **For testing purposes, you can use the same subscription and set up a different Azure Data Share resource and target storage account.**

Using the Azure portal

To set up an Azure Data Share resource to receive and store data using the Azure portal, follow these steps:

> ***IMPORTANT*** **To perform these steps, you must have received an email from the data provider inviting you to access the data share.**

1. In the email you received inviting you to access a data share, click the **View Invitation** button. (See Figure 6-20.)

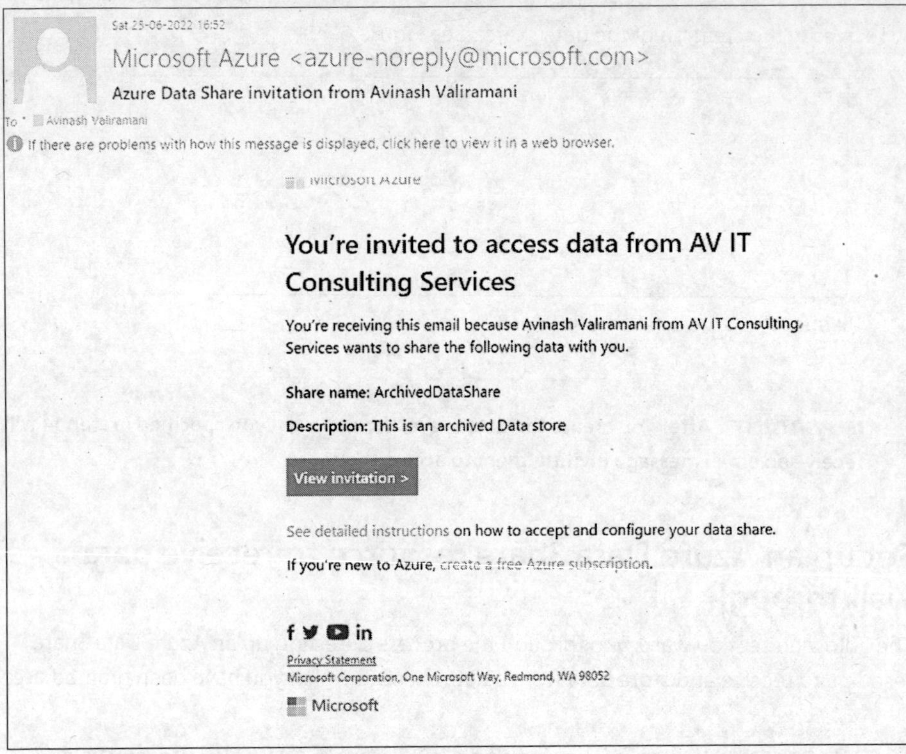

FIGURE 6-20 Click View Invitation in the email invite.

2. The Data Share Invitations page in the Azure portal opens, showing the pending invitation. (See Figure 6-21.)

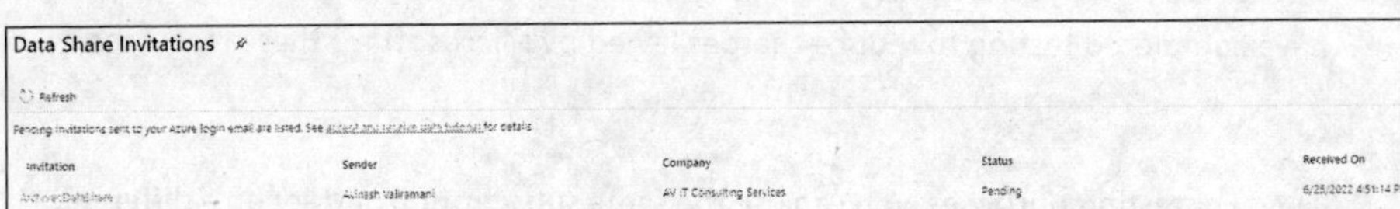

FIGURE 6-21 The Data Share Invitations page.

3. Click the link for the share (in this example, **ArchivedDataShare**).
4. In the Data Share Invitations page (see Figure 6-22), enter the following information:
   - **Terms of Use** Select this check box to accept the terms of use.
   - **Subscription** Select the subscription you want to use.
   - **Resource Group** Choose the resource group you want to use to store data from the data share. Alternatively, click the **Create New** link and follow the prompts.
   - **Data Share Account** Select an existing storage account to receive the incoming data or click **Create New** to create a new one. For this example, click **Create New**.

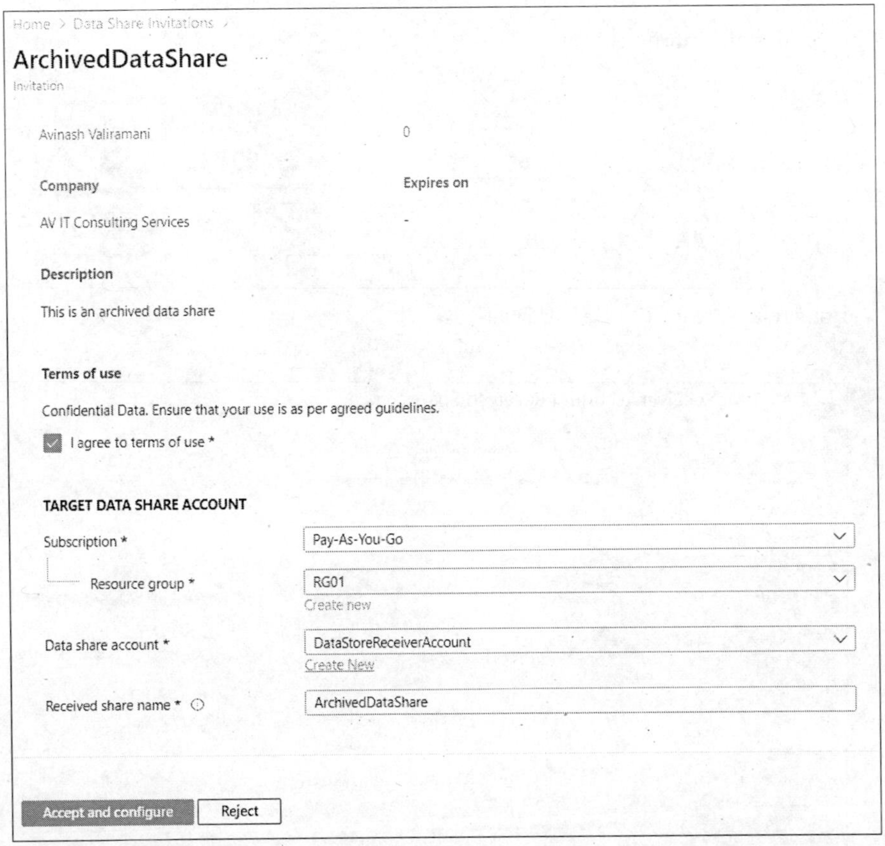

FIGURE 6-22 Accepting a data share invitation.

5. In the Create Data Share Account dialog box (see Figure 6-23), enter the following information and click **Create**:
   - **Data Share Account Name** Enter a unique name for the data share account you want to create.
   - **Subscription** This should be set automatically based on the information you provided in step 3.
   - **Resource Group** This should be set automatically based on the information you provided in step 3.
   - **Location** Select the Azure region you want to host the data share account.
6. Back in the Data Share Invitations page (refer to Figure 6-22), in the **Received Share Name** box, type a unique name for the data share from which you will receive data.
7. Click **Accept and Configure**.

   A confirmation screen appears when the request is accepted. (See Figure 6-24.)

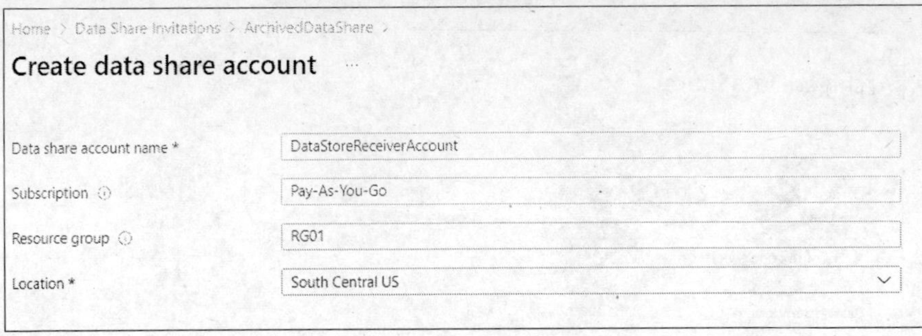

FIGURE 6-23 Create data share account.

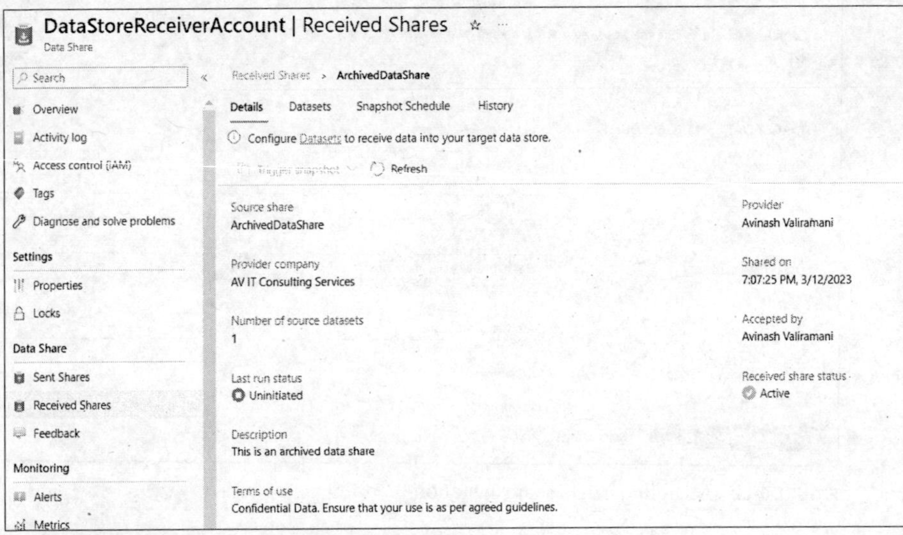

FIGURE 6-24 View details about the received share.

Next, you need to map the datasets on the data consumer subscription.

8. Click the **Datasets** tab (see Figure 6-25). Then click **Map to Target**.

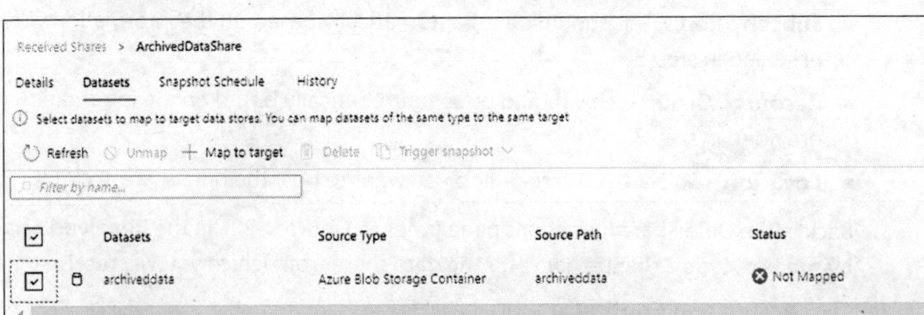

FIGURE 6-25 Click Map to Target in the Datasets tab.

9. On the **Map Datasets to Target** page (see Figure 6-26), enter the following information and click **Map to Target**:

- **Target Data Type** Choose the type of storage you plan to use to store the shared data (in this case, **Azure Blob Storage**).
- **Subscriptions** This should be set automatically based on the information you provided in step 3.
- **Resource Groups** This should be set automatically based on the information you provided in step 3.
- **Storage Accounts** Select the storage account to host the data.
- **Path** Select or enter the path to the location where the data should be stored.

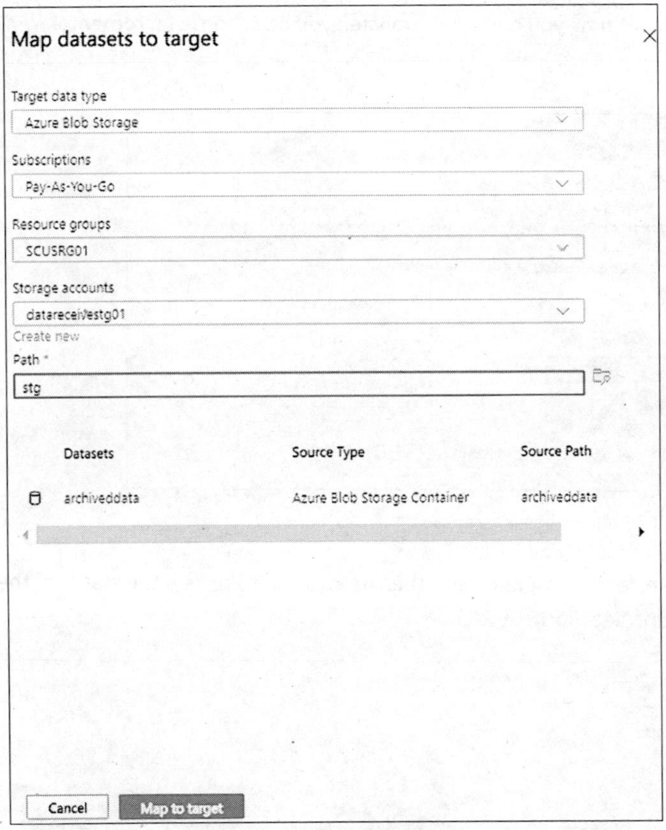

FIGURE 6-26 The Map Datasets to Target page.

10. When the mapping is complete, click the **Datasets** tab. You should see the mapped dataset listed there. (See Figure 6-27.)

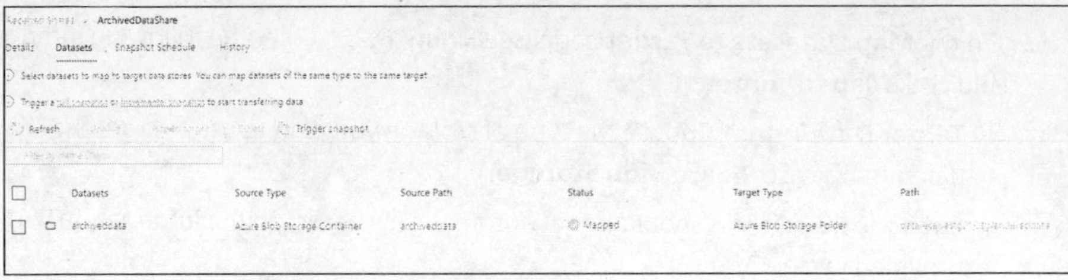

FIGURE 6-27 Mapped datasets.

11. To receive a snapshot from the data provider's data share, click the **Trigger Snapshot** button and, because this is the first time you're receiving a snapshot, choose **Full Copy**. (See Figure 6-28.)

NOTE **Each subsequent time you perform a transfer, you can choose Incremental.**

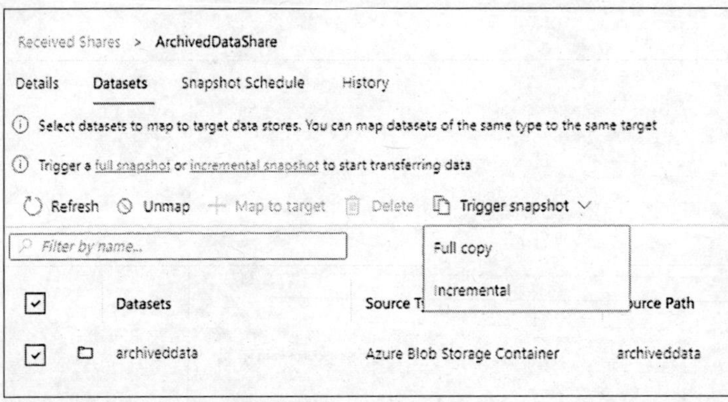

FIGURE 6-28 Trigger a snapshot.

12. When the data transfer is complete, click the **History** tab to review the status of the snapshot operation. (See Figure 6-29.)

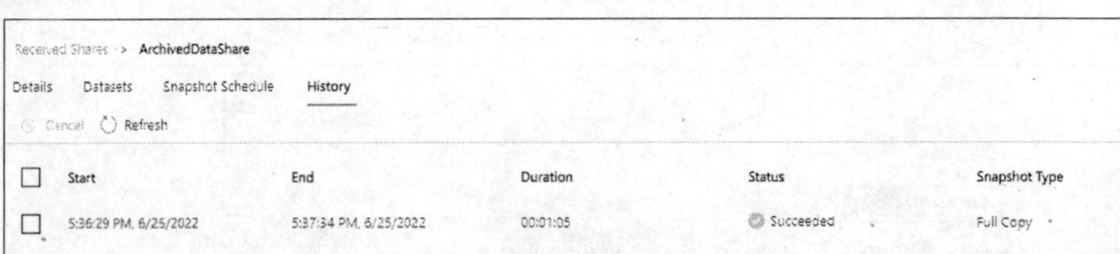

FIGURE 6-29 Click the History tab to view the status of the snapshot operation.

13. Navigate to your Azure Blob Storage page to verify that the snapshot has been transferred from the data provider's data share. (See Figure 6-30.)

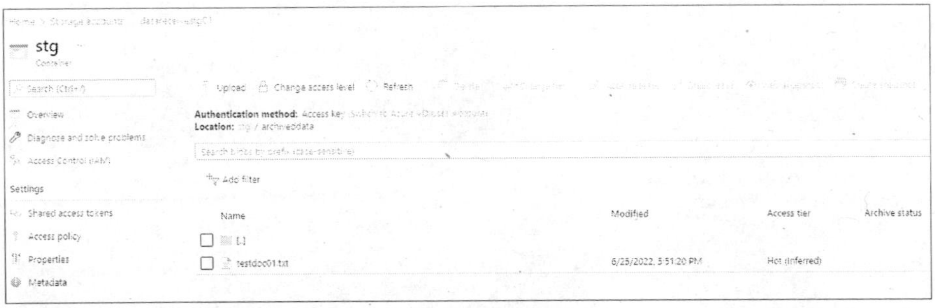

FIGURE 6-30 Verify that the snapshot appears in your Azure Blob Storage.

Best practices

Following are some general best practices regarding the Azure Data Share service:

- **Monitor invitations** Monitoring invitations enables you to identify and act on invitations that haven't been accepted for a period of time. Unaccepted invitations can indicate accidental sharing, unwanted access, or incorrect data consumer details.
- **Conduct regular audits of shared data** It is highly recommended that you conduct regular audits of data shared using the Azure Data Share service. You can use these audits to identify and remove unwanted permissions or unused data shares.

> ***TIP*** **One way to identify unused accounts is to inspect Azure AD identity logs.**

- **Set up storage accounts with firewalls enabled** This enables you to control access from known networks and services. Be sure to allow access to trusted Microsoft services in the storage account settings so the Azure Data Share service will function correctly.
- **Plan for disaster recovery** Depending on the criticality of your data share, you should plan for disaster recovery (DR) to ensure continuity in services. The current strategy to achieve this is to set up a secondary data consumer share in a secondary DR region, and share data with that share before or at the time of a manual DR failover. (Be sure to inform data consumers which share is the primary share and when to use the secondary share.)
- **Store and analyze logs** You can connect Azure Data Share logs with Log Analytics workspace to store logs for a longer time. It is a good practice to inspect these logs on a regular basis for anomalous logins and suspicious user behavior that can indicate compromised data consumer accounts. You can perform queries on log data to analyze the logs in an automated manner.

Index

A

B

C

D

E

F

G

H

I

L

M

Q

R

S

T

U

V

W

X - Y- Z